Instructor's Manua

D1281649

to accompany

The Longman Anthology
of World Literature

SECOND EDITION

VOLUME I
VOLUME A: THE ANCIENT WORLD
VOLUME B: THE MEDIEVAL ERA
VOLUME C: THE EARLY MODERN PERIOD

David Damrosch
David L. Pike
General Editors

April Alliston
Marshall Brown
Page duBois
Sabry Hafez
Ursula Heise
Djelal Kadir
Sheldon Pollock
Bruce Robbins
Haruo Shirane
Jane Tylus
Pauline Yu

Longman

New York   San Francisco   Boston
London   Toronto   Sydney   Tokyo   Singapore   Madrid
Mexico City   Munich   Paris   Cape Town   Hong Kong   Montreal

⚠ This work is protected by United States copyright laws and is provided solely for the use of instructors in teaching their courses and assessing student learning. Dissemination or sale of any part of this work (including on the WorldWideWeb) will destroy the integrity of the work and is not permitted. The work and materials from it should never be made available to students except by instructors using the accompanying text in their classes. All recipients of this work are expected to abide by these restrictions and to honor the intended pedagogical purposes and the needs of other instructors who rely on these materials.

Vice President and Editor-in-Chief: Joseph Terry
Senior Supplements Editor: Donna Campion
Text Design, Project Manager, and Electronic Page Makeup: Grapevine Publishing
Services, Inc.

Instructor's Manual to accompany The Longman Anthology of World Literature, Second Edition, Volume I, by David Damrosch et al.

Copyright © 2009 Pearson Education, Inc.

All rights reserved. Printed in the United States of America. Instructors may reproduce portions of this book for classroom use only. All other reproductions are strictly prohibited without prior permission of the publisher, except in the case of brief quotations embodied in critical articles and reviews.

1 2 3 4 5 6 7 8 9 10–OPM–11 10 09 08

Longman
is an imprint of

www.pearsonhighered.com

ISBN 10: 0-205-64605-0
ISBN 13: 978-0-205-64605-0

CONTENTS

Copyright © 2009 Pearson Education, Inc. Publishing as Longman.

Early South Asia

Copyright © 2009 Pearson Education, Inc. Publishing as Longman.

China: The Classical Tradition

Rome and the Roman Empire

Copyright © 2009 Pearson Education, Inc. Publishing as Longman.

VOLUME B: The Medieval Era

Medieval China

Japan

Copyright © 2009 Pearson Education, Inc. Publishing as Longman.

Classical Arabic and Islamic Literatures

Medieval Europe

Copyright © 2009 Pearson Education, Inc. Publishing as Longman.

VOLUME C: The Early Modern Period

The Vernacular Revolution

Early Modern Europe

Copyright © 2009 Pearson Education, Inc. Publishing as Longman.

Copyright © 2009 Pearson Education, Inc. Publishing as Longman.

General Editors' Preface

The tremendous wealth of world literature available today is also a kind of embarrassment of riches: How can we best present this great range of works in class? We've designed the second edition of *The Longman Anthology of World Literature* with this issue constantly in mind, giving teachable groupings and illuminating juxtapositions throughout the *Anthology* and framing compelling texts with introductions and notes that give the context needed for an informed and pleasurable reading. Yet finally it comes down to individual class sessions and the detailed discussion of particular works, and here is where this teaching companion comes in. In this book we suggest fruitful modes of approach, presenting ways to engage students, to foster understanding, and to stimulate lively discussion of all our major texts and groupings of works.

We have set three ambitious goals for ourselves in creating this teaching companion. First, it has been written directly by the editors responsible for each section of the *Anthology*—the use of the *Anthology* in class isn't some afterthought; it's an integral part of our own work on the project. In seeking people to join us on the editorial board, we looked for coeditors who are dynamic and experienced teachers as well as deeply knowledgeable scholars and clear, lively writers. We've seen this teaching companion as the opportunity to share directly with you our best ideas on how to bring these texts alive in class.

To this end, our second goal has been to discuss every major author or combination of authors in the *Anthology*, opening up possible lines of approach, indicating good connections that can be made, and sketching important trends in scholarly debate. Third, we've tried to be suggestive rather than prescriptive, and we hope to inform instructors who are new to some of this material while also intriguing people interested in a fresh take on familiar works. This volume gives us a chance to expand on the reasons behind our choices and to indicate ways that we have found these materials to work best during many years of teaching them.

Teaching with and across Groupings

A distinctive feature of our *Anthology* is the grouping of works in Perspectives section, and as Resonances between texts. Together, these groupings are intended both to set works in cultural context and to link them across time and space. These groupings have a strategic pedagogical function as well. We have observed that in other anthologies, brief author listings rarely seem to get taught. Added with the laudable goal of increasing an anthology's range and inclusiveness, the new materials too often get lost in the shuffle. Our groupings of works cluster shorter

Copyright © 2009 Pearson Education, Inc. Publishing as Longman.

selections in ways that make them more likely to be taught, creating a critical mass of readings around a compelling literary or social issue and economically providing cultural context for the major works around them.

We expect that our contextual groupings will be used variously by different people. A Perspectives section can be taught entirely as a freestanding unit, or it can share a week with an important work or major author. "Perspectives: Strangers in a Strange Land" in Volume A, for example, works well as a freestanding assignment. It contains a major unit of biblical narrative, the Joseph Story, together with the Book of Ruth, each of which gains by being taught with the other. Leading into the Joseph Story are a pair of Egyptian narratives: "The Story of Sinuhe," an evidently real-life autobiography of migration between Egypt and Palestine, and a mythological tale, "The Two Brothers," which presents an early Egyptian version of the young man resisting seduction by his superior's wife. So this Perspectives section in itself links well-known biblical works to the existing Near Eastern literary context, both in terms of theme and of genre. At the same time, it directly follows our selections from the Book of Job, whose hero—interestingly, not an Israelite himself—finds himself suddenly a stranger in his own land. A little further afield, "Perspectives: Strangers in a Strange Land" can also be taught in conjunction with other narratives of foreign travel and estrangement, such as the *Epic of Gilgamesh* earlier in the "Ancient Near East" section and the *Odyssey* in the ensuing section of the volume.

While entire Perspectives sections can be assigned, individual works within them can also be paired with works elsewhere. For example, in "Classical Arabic and Islamic Literatures" (Volume B), the poems of Abu-Nuwas in "Perspectives: Poetry, Wine, and Love" can be taught alongside the tale of Abu-Nuwas that appears in *The Thousand and One Nights*. In Volume E, Walt Whitman can either be taught with the other writers next to him in "Perspectives: The National Poet" or he can be assigned instead with Emily Dickinson and Rubén Darío later in the volume. Darío's poem, "Walt Whitman," indeed, makes a direct link to work from, whether the two poets are assigned together or in different weeks.

Particularly in the case of our fuller Perspectives sections, like the Enlightenment-era section on "Liberty and Libertines" (Volume D), it can be productive to assign different readings to different members of the class, with students working in teams to explore contrasting viewpoints; these can then be debated in class or presented as written projects. Students interested in exploring Perspectives section issues in greater depth should be alerted to the extensive bibliographies at the end of each volume; Perspectives sections, as well as individual author listings, have bibliographies that can lead students further into the primary sources.

Obviously, the various Perspectives sections and the juxtapositions of works and Resonances are only a few of the many groupings that could be created. We wouldn't want any student to come away from the course with the misconception that these were the only issues that mattered in the period or culture in question. Rather, these groupings should be seen as exemplary of the *sorts* of literary and cultural debate that were current in a region or an era. Students can be encouraged—

Copyright © 2009 Pearson Education, Inc. Publishing as Longman.

individually or in small groups—to research and develop their own perspectival clusters of materials, using as a point of departure some text or some issue that has particularly intrigued them. They could then present their own Perspectives section to the class as a whole or write it up and analyze it as a term project.

On a larger scale, we have followed custom in dividing the *Anthology* according to the broad period divisions that have become ubiquitous in modern literary study, with further division by region in the first three volumes, but there is no reason that a survey course should treat these divisions as sacrosanct. Even within a generally chronological presentation, it can be interesting to have some cross-cutting sessions or weeks, such as an overview of the sonnet, or a section on travel writing, or one on short prose narratives. Such groupings can bring together material from two, three, or more sections and even volumes of the *Anthology*. Courses organized by genre or by theme will mine the *Anthology* for entirely different groupings suited to individual needs. We hope and expect that teachers and students alike will use our tables of contents as a starting point for ongoing explorations and reconfigurations of their own.

Reading the Illustrations

Our hundred black-and-white illustrations and fifty color images are very much conceived as part of the *Anthology*'s teachable material, and the extensive captions for the color images and for many of the black-and-white ones are intended to signal effective avenues of approach to them. Many of the images work directly with particular authors or works, but valuable points can be made with images of more general import, including our six cover illustrations. These are teachable images, not mere window dressing, and a detailed caption for each appears at the end of the list of illustrations that follows each volume's table of contents.

Inter-arts comparisons have to be made with care, respecting the differences embodied in different media—differences often of patronage and audience as well as of materials and method. We wouldn't want such comparisons to create simplistic images of "The Medieval Mind" or "Oriental Art." Yet to speak of a culture at all is to recognize that its participants share (and may struggle against) commonalities of history and of worldview, and the varied artistic productions of a given region or era will often show certain family resemblances. Visual art, architecture, and music can be particularly useful in a world literature classroom because they don't have to be experienced in translation (except in the significant but more limited translation of reproduction). Important aesthetic values have often been shared by poets and painters (who at times have even been one and the same person), and these values and strategies can often be seen most directly and vividly in visual arts, while they may be somewhat muted in translation. As we know, too, our students are growing up in a culture that is more visual than verbal, and seeing can help them to then read. For both these reasons, starting from visual art can help sensitize students to what to look for in the literary works of the region and period.

Copyright © 2009 Pearson Education, Inc. Publishing as Longman.

Reading and Listening

An important addition to our *Anthology*'s resources is our pair of audio CDs, which can show students how literature has played out in the larger aural culture of its times. As with painting, music can illustrate aspects of a culture's aesthetics, from reconstructed ancient Egyptian and Greek music, to medieval Japanese court music, to Bach and Handel in the Enlightenment and Jelly Roll Morton and Igor Stravinsky in the twentieth century. Equally, our CDs allow students to hear poetry read—or sung—aloud, in the original and in translation, giving direct access to the sounds of a variety of the languages included in the *Anthology* and restoring the aural dimension that great poetry has always had. Our twentieth-century selections include several major poets reading their own work, including T. S. Eliot, Anna Akhmatova, and Pablo Neruda, as well as noted performers and poets reading earlier poetry: Dylan Thomas declaiming a speech by Milton's Satan with evident relish, Adrienne Rich reading a haunting poem by the great Urdu poet Ghalib. A number of our selections also show the kinds of cross-cultural connections found in many of our *Anthology* texts, as with a gorgeous early Arab Christian hymn of the Byzantine era on the first CD and a Spanish Jewish lullaby recorded in Eastern Europe on the second CD.

Teaching with the Web

Our course Website is designed to enhance teaching in a variety of ways. It provides an interactive timeline, practice quizzes for major authors and periods, and annotated links for our major authors and groupings, giving students guidance in further exploration and research for projects and term papers. We include a glossary of literary and cultural terms and also an innovative audio glossary. This allows students to click on each author's name, and each name or term included in the pronunciation guides at the end of many of our introductions, so as to hear directly how each should be pronounced. Finally, we have a section of original texts and variant translations for each of the *Anthology*'s six volumes. Each section includes several poems printed in the original and in two or three translations, giving an opportunity to explore the ways meaning shifts in translation. Finally, we have a supplementary component to the new Translations feature in the second edition. Each original text in these sections is also read aloud in a connected audio file, so that students can hear the original as they look at it in print and in translation. These selections can be downloaded for use in class or given as assignments for students to experience on their own.

Typo Alert!

As you and your students read the *Anthology*, we would be very grateful if you let us know of any typos you find in the *Anthology* (or indeed, in this volume too). Every page has been proofread with care, and we've fixed all the typos we've found, even

Copyright © 2009 Pearson Education, Inc. Publishing as Longman.

though a few of them had a weird logic of their own. The enraged Achilles, for example, disputing Agamemnon's claim on his prize at the start of the *Iliad*, swears "a great oath," which in our page proofs became "a great bath"—an oddly appropriate highlighting of the childishness within his heroism, which we corrected with some regret. Some typos are no doubt still hiding in the 6,500 pages of the *Anthology* and in this companion volume as well. So please let us know of any lingering errors you encounter and also send us broader ideas and suggestions of all sorts.

An Evolving Collaboration

The scope and definition of world literature has been changing rapidly in recent years, and the second edition of *The Longman Anthology* has provided us with an opportunity to keep pace with these changes. We've designed the *Anthology* to be open and flexible in form, and it is sure to be used in a variety of ways: in courses with a historical, or a generic, or a thematic basis; in survey courses using the full *Anthology* and in upper-level courses using only one of its volumes; in quarter-system as well as semester-based schools; in community colleges, in liberal arts colleges, and in universities. We have posted onto our course Website selected syllabi and other teaching materials reflecting actual practice as the *Anthology* is used in class. We invite contributions for this purpose. The print *Anthology* itself reflects a collaboration between the editorial board and the many reviewers we thank in our Acknowledgments; our reviewers often went far beyond the call of duty in helping us select texts and find the best ways to present them. The publication of the second edition of the *Anthology* is only the next stage in this ongoing collaboration with everyone who is using it in class and sharing their experiences with the rest of us who are working on and with the book.

Finally, we also welcome suggestions for continuing improvements to the *Anthology* itself. Our *Anthology* is meant as a resource for teachers in an evolving and growing field, and with your help future editions will allow the *Anthology* to continue to reflect these changes. So we would be delighted to hear what things you would most like to see added in the future and to learn what existing conjunctions and combinations work best for you, what others might better be rethought. We can be reached by e-mail at the addresses below or by letter at the Department of English and Comparative Literature, 602 Philosophy Hall, Columbia University, New York, NY 10027 (David Damrosch) and the Department of Literature, American University, 4400 Massachusetts Ave. NW, Washington, DC 20016-8047 (David L. Pike).

Our coeditors and we hope that the entries in this teaching companion will assist you in teaching our *Anthology*. We hope too that you'll find *The Longman Anthology of World Literature* as enjoyable to use as it has been to create, and we look forward to hearing from you as you work with it in the coming years.

    —*David Damrosch*, dnd2@columbia.edu

    —*David L. Pike*, dpike18@gmail.com

Copyright © 2009 Pearson Education, Inc. Publishing as Longman.

Guide to

myliteraturelab™

*W*here literature comes to life!

http://www.myliteraturelab.com

You may check the Instructor Resources section of
MyLiteratureLab for a more extensive Faculty Teaching Guide.

MyLiteratureLab offers the best multimedia resources for literature. The
site includes detailed online lectures, interactive readings, a glossary of literary and critical terms, extensive help with the writing and research
processes, avoiding plagiarism tutorials, and Exchange (Longman's online
peer and instructor review program).

Every Longman Lecture in MyLiteratureLab includes thoughtful questions to prompt discussion and/or to become a topic for an essay. As you
have probably already found, the *Guide to MyLiterature Lab* is in the front
of this supplement for your convenience.

MyLiteratureLab Browser Tune-up

To use all of the features of MyLiteratureLab, you will need to install the
following plug-ins: **Shockwave and Adobe Acrobat Reader.** Use the
Browser Tune-up to check if you have all of these plug-ins installed and to
install them if you do not.

Register to use MyLiteratureLab Resources in your WebCT Course

You will need the access code that is beneath the pull tab of your access code
card that either came with your purchase of a new textbook or that you purchased separately. **(If you do not have an access code you can purchase access online through the MyLiteratureLab site in your WebCT link.) You
only have to register once.** Once you have created your own, unique log-in
name and password, you will use them each time you link to
MyLiteratureLab resources from your course. Whenever you link to the

Copyright © 2009 Pearson Education, Inc. Publishing as Longman.

MyLiteratureLab resources from your course for the first time during an on-line session, you will be asked for your log in name and password. Type the name and password that you created during registration. You will not be asked again for your log-in name and password to access other MyLiteratureLab resources. If you close your Internet browser, end your on-line session, or turn off your computer, you may have to enter them again.

Longman Lectures

Experience how listening to literature being read can bring it to life! Listen to these richly illustrated concise ten-minute audio "lectures" narrated by Longman's textbook authors to help you connect with authors and works. Each lecture is divided into three segments, and each segment concludes with Questions for Thinking and Writing to help you analyze and reflect on what you have heard.

Interactive Readings

Read and explicate stories, poems, and scenes from plays through a series of interactive questions that guide you in the study of the literary elements. Select a Literary Element to view its Interactive Reading and Questions for Thinking and Writing.

Introduction

Welcome, instructors, to *MyLiteratureLab*. This brief guide highlights the main benefits and features of *MyLiteratureLab*. In this guide you will find an overview of the three main sections.

1. The Literary Elements: Testing Your Knowledge
2. Where Literature Comes to Life: The Longman Lectures
3. Writing and Research: Tools and Techniques

For more extensive information on these portions of *MyLiteratureLab*, including detailed descriptions of each of the Longman Lectures and teaching tips for using it in your classroom, please see the Instructor Resources section.

The Literary Elements: Testing Your Knowledge

This section of the site features *Diagnostics* (linked to the Glossary of Literary and Critical Terms) and *Interactive Readings*.

Copyright © 2009 Pearson Education, Inc. Publishing as Longman.

Diagnostics

The *Diagnostics*, including multiple-choice and fill-in-the-blank questions, enable students to assess their understanding of literary theory and criticism by quizzing them on terms such as imagery, archetype, point of view, and soliloquy. Upon completing each diagnostic, students are forwarded to the *Glossary of Literary and Critical Terms* to fill any gaps in their knowledge.

Interactive Readings

The *Interactive Readings* section is designed to help students understand how to use literary elements to interpret works of literature. Each reading focuses on a particular literary element, such as word choice, tone and style, and character analysis. As students read a particular selection, key passages are highlighted. When students click on the highlighted text, a box appears that contains explanations, analysis, and/or questions highlighting how the passage can be interpreted using the literary elements. These readings can be assigned as homework, and students may be required to submit their written responses to the questions.

Where Literature Comes to Life: The Longman Lectures

This section of *MyLiteratureLab* features a menu of nine-minute lectures. All of the *Longman Lectures* are given by Longman's authors—critically acclaimed writers, award-winning teachers, and performance poets. Longman's "guest lecturers" discuss some of the most commonly taught literary works and authors in depth. In the process, they encourage students to analyze stories, poems, and plays, and develop thoughtful essay ideas.

The lectures are richly illustrated with words and images to contextualize and enrich the content of each lecture. As you will hear, each lecture is divided into three parts—Reading, Interpreting, and Writing. Each part of each lecture is accompanied by a diverse selection of Critical Thinking and Writing Questions. Some questions provide feedback and suggestions for online research and essay development. Students' answers to the questions can be e-mailed to you or used to spark class discussion.

As a whole, the lectures are designed to complement in-class discussion of particular works and augment related assignments in your syllabus. Available to students around the clock, the three-part structure of the lectures encourages students to read and interpret works more thoughtfully and spark ideas for research and writing. The lectures may also be assigned as extra-credit work or be used as an emergency substitute instructor.

Below we discuss the primary purpose of each part of the lectures and provide examples.

Copyright © 2009 Pearson Education, Inc. Publishing as Longman.

Part 1: Reading

Students often are reluctant readers. The first part of each lecture, Reading, sparks student interest through the lecturer's interpretative reading. The reading of a key passage places the work within a context that appeals to students. Some readings are dramatic and performative; others provide analysis about how a work is structured. The lecturers' varying approaches to their subject matter help reach students with different learning styles. At the same time, related visuals help students *see* the work while reading it. Here are a few examples of opening statements in Part 1 of the lectures.

- From Shakespeare's sonnets lecture: *In Shakespeare's Sonnets (published in 1609 but probably written in the middle 1590s), love—whether for the fair youth or the dark lady—is only one of several themes. Some of these themes—for instance beauty and the tragic effect of time on beauty—are easily connected with love. Let's glimpse a few of the themes by looking at the opening line of some of the sonnets.*

- From the Flannery O'Connor "A Good Man Is Hard to Find" lecture: *What if I told you about a writer who included in her works a youth who, in baptizing his mentally defective nephew, manages to drown him, or a woman with a wooden leg and a Ph.D. in philosophy who . . . is robbed of her wooden leg and stripped of her self-confident belief in nothing . . . ? If I then told you that this author is a devout Catholic, would you be astonished? If so, you are not yet familiar with the works of Flannery O'Connor.*

- From the James Baldwin "Sonny's Blues" lecture: *From the opening scene . . . until the final scene in a darkened nightclub when Sonny, bathed in blue light, performs the magic of improvisational jazz on his piano, these two brothers move in and out of each others' lives, attempting to communicate but most often failing.*

Part 2: Interpreting

Many students lack confidence in their ability to analyze and interpret works of literature. Some students are impatient to find the "right" answer. Part 2 of each lecture provides provocative "keys" for understanding. The lecturers' comments humanize both the work and its author. For example:

- From the Seamus Heaney "Digging" lecture: *Not only is he [Heaney] honoring the work of his father and grandfather, he is using his own kind of digging—that is, writing poetry—to show us the worth of the work they did. And in this respect, he honors and carries on their tradition—but with a different tool. As such, it's a poem about writing poetry—with digging as its metaphor.*

- From the James Joyce "Araby" lecture: *Notice how the bright images of his love, Mangan's sister, always appear out of the dreary background that sur-*

Copyright © 2009 Pearson Education, Inc. Publishing as Longman.

rounds them. *Compare the words and phrases that are used to describe Mangan's sister and the boy's feelings about her with the language that describes his neighborhood or his everyday activities. Let the words open your senses—visualize and feel the bright, warm image of Mangan's sister as her dress swings and the soft rope of her hair tosses from side to side and contrast it with the dark, cold image of the short days of winter and the acrid smell of ashpits and horse stables in the surrounding neighborhood.*

- From the Billy Collins "The Names" lecture: *A typical Collins poem begins in the morning. The poet walks around his empty house, thinks about last night's supper or tonight's bottle of wine, puts on some jazz, goes out and runs a few errands or takes a train into the city, comes home, looks out the window, and makes a poem. To say that Collins writes a low-pressure kind of poetry is like observing that a flat tire could stand a little air. It's the poetic equivalent of an episode of* Seinfeld, *"the show about nothing." But . . . I sympathize. Indeed, I'm a little envious. Collins's saving grace is the wit that laces his observations of everyday matters. Poets, he says, "have enough to do / complaining about the price of tobacco, // passing the dripping ladle, / and singing songs to a bird in a cage. // We are busy doing nothing. . . ."*

- From the Hawthorne "Young Goodman Brown" lecture: *Let's consider two specific ways to better understand and enjoy this famous story. First, can you sum up its theme—what's its central message? In some stories, the theme is easy to find. You can just underline its general statements, those that appear to sum up some large truth. In a fable, the theme is often stated in a moral at the end, such as: "Be careful in choosing your friends." In Stephen Crane's story of a shipwreck, "The Open Boat," Crane tells us, among other things, that "it occurs to a man that Nature does not regard him as important." But Hawthorne's story is trickier. If you underline its general statements and expect one of them to be its theme, you'll miss the whole point of the story. See paragraph 65: "Evil is the nature of mankind." Does Hawthorne believe that? Do you? Those are the words of the Devil, always a bad guy to believe. No, after you finish reading the story, especially pondering its closing paragraph, you can sum its theme much better in your own words.*

Part 3: Writing

In Part 3, Writing, the lectures further the discussions in Part 2 and help students form their own interpretations. The historical and cultural backdrop of the times, the writer's life experiences, and a close reading of the text all help students make connections. The lectures are peppered with ideas that students might pursue to write a critical essay or even a research paper. Here are a few examples:

- From the Seamus Heaney "Digging" lecture: *While both use natural imagery, Yeats writes of nature in idealized terms that seem to transcend everyday*

Copyright © 2009 Pearson Education, Inc. Publishing as Longman.

life. Images like "Dropping the veils of morning to where the cricket sings" and "midnight's all a glimmer, and noon a purple glow" remove us from the gritty world of toil. For Heaney, nature is anything but an escape. It is the here and now substance of everyday living—the harsh "rasping" of the spade—the "straining rump"—and the "heaving of sods." No pun intended on the title "Digging," but Heaney's poetry is much earthier and grounded than that of Yeats. And much of this attitude toward nature can be attributed to his own background.

- From the Baldwin "Sonny's Blues" lecture: *Though the setting in Harlem in the mid twentieth century is in many ways crucial to an understanding of the problems faced by these two African American brothers, their story is universal. Therefore, an essay on the theme or themes in "Sonny's Blues" can be especially informative. Ask yourself what major ideas Baldwin is suggesting in the story. One theme, the theme of learning wisdom through suffering, is as old as literature, and Baldwin shows us through the searching and suffering of the two brothers that literature can share with us the wisdom of the ages, that we can learn about the agony and the beauty and the creativity within ourselves by vicariously sharing theirs.*

- From the Kate Chopin "The Story of an Hour" lecture: *Kate Chopin published several of her stories in the magazines of her time. However,* Vogue *and* The Century *initially refused to publish "The Story of an Hour." The* Century *regarded the story as "immoral" and* Vogue *only published it after Chopin's* Bayou Folk *became a success. Discuss "The Story of an Hour" in terms of the artistic, moral, and intellectual sensibilities of Chopin's time. Consider why Chopin's story was branded as "immoral" and why literary perceptions have changed over the years.*

- From the Sophocles *Oedipus the King* lecture: *Over time, this play has drawn many conflicting interpretations. Here are a few long-debated questions for you to think about. Is Oedipus a helpless, passive tool of the gods? Who is responsible for his terrible downfall? Does he himself bring about his own misfortune? Is he an innocent victim? If the downfall of a person of high estate (as Aristotle thought tragedies generally show) is due to a tragic flaw or weakness in the person's character, does Oedipus have any tragic flaw? If he does, how would you define it? Consider his speeches, his acts, his treatment of others. Does Oedipus seem justified in afflicting himself with blindness? Does his punishment fit, or fail to fit, his supposed crime?*

Critical Thinking and Writing by Lecture

Each part of the three-part lectures is accompanied by Questions for Thinking and Writing. These questions help reinforce the content given in the lecture and provide helpful suggestions for research and writing. Students can respond to the questions directly on screen and have their responses e-mailed to you.

Copyright © 2009 Pearson Education, Inc. Publishing as Longman.

Writing and Research: Tools and Techniques

From formulating an original idea to citing sources, this section of *MyLiteratureLab* offers students step-by-step guidance for writing powerful critical essays and research papers. This section of the site can reinforce and augment the writing coverage in your text. Below is a brief description of what each section covers.

Overview

Writing and Research contains seven main sections. Five are discussed here, while we cover **Exchange** and **Avoiding Plagiarism** in more detail below. **Writing About Literature** facilitates effective writing by providing useful information on both the writing process and writing about literature, including such key topics as invention, planning, and strategies for organizing, drafting, and revising. **Writing the Research Paper** offers comprehensive instruction for writing research papers, including finding a topic, evaluating sources, taking notes, tips for summarizing, developing a thesis, suggestions for organizing the paper, choosing a pattern of development, guidance for writing introductions and conclusions, and comprehensive MLA documentation. A dozen **Student Papers** are integrated throughout, providing helpful models of a variety of critical essays and the research paper. Comprehensive coverage of **MLA Documentation** provides numerous models of all types for citing a range of sources, from interviews to periodicals to electronic sources. Access to our **Tutor Center** is provided free of charge with your subscription to *MyLiteratureLab*. The Tutor Center gives your students help with reviewing papers for organization, flow, argument, and consistent grammar errors. Students can contact tutors toll-free via phone, e-mail, Web access, or fax, often at times when your campus writing center is not available.

Using *Exchange*

Exchange, Pearson's powerful interactive tool, allows students to comment on each other's drafts and instructors to review and grade papers—all online. More information about *Exchange* can be found in the Instructor Resources section of *MyLiteratureLab*. Please visit the Instructor Resources area to learn about creating and administering *Exchange* as part of your teaching apparatus. Highlights of *Exchange* include the ability to:

- Quickly and easily add comments at the word, sentence, paragraph, or paper level.
- Save and re-use your favorite comments.

Copyright © 2009 Pearson Education, Inc. Publishing as Longman.

- Help students identify and overcome common grammar errors through links to practice exercises and an online handbook.
- Decide how many students are in each group.
- Assign students by name, or create random groups.
- Let all students see comments, or only the author and instructor.
- Allow students to post comments anonymously.
- And more!

Avoiding Plagiarism

Avoiding Plagiarism allows students to work through interactive tutorials to learn how to cite and document sources responsibly in MLA format. This section guides students through a step-by-step tutorial, complete with self-tests and items for extended analysis. The steps include:

- What is Plagiarism?
- When to Document
- Using Print & Electronic Sources
- Avoiding Plagiarism
    - ✧ Attribution
    - ✧ Quotation Marks
    - ✧ Citation
    - ✧ Paraphrase
    - ✧ Loyalty to Source
    - ✧ Works Cited
    - ✧ Citation for Images
- Extended Analysis
- Wrap-Up

Each step in the MLA tutorial guides students to read and click to navigate to the next step. Students do not need to complete the tutorial on one visit to the site; they can jump ahead to continue their work or return to previous steps to review an earlier discussion. The *Avoiding Plagiarism* tutorial contains many practice sets for students.

Extended Analysis

The extended analysis section allows students to apply what they have learned from the *Avoiding Plagiarism* tutorials. Here students can test how well they recognize plagiarism as they read a student research paper. Students must pay careful attention to the sources that are being quoted, paraphrased, or summarized in consideration of the seven rules of avoiding plagiarism discussed during the tutorial.

Copyright © 2009 Pearson Education, Inc. Publishing as Longman.

Tips for Instructors and Suggestions for Use

Student writers can benefit from their work in *Avoiding Plagiarism* throughout a composition course and at different stages in the research writing process. *Avoiding Plagiarism* helps students to correctly paraphrase, summarize, and quote source material, as well as cite and document sources in both MLA and APA style. Students can use the *Avoiding Plagiarism* tutorials on their own, working through the tutorials at their own pace and returning to them as needed throughout their research projects. Most pages or "steps" in each tutorial can also be printed for quick student reference.

We encourage you to explore the tutorial yourself so that you understand the tutorial's content and can make connections to your own course, your students and their research projects, and to other areas of *MyLiteratureLab*. We encourage you to identify teaching opportunities, learn to navigate *MyLiteratureLab*, and view the additional resources and links.

Students should also be encouraged to review *Avoiding Plagiarism* before they submit both drafts and final versions of their research projects for review. With peer review of drafts, for example, students who have reviewed the appropriate tutorial will be better prepared to give informed feedback about documentation of sources in other student papers. And students who review the tutorial before submitting papers to instructors are more likely to correct their in-text and end-of-text citations during the final editing stage.

Copyright © 2009 Pearson Education, Inc. Publishing as Longman.

Volume A
The Ancient World

The Ancient Near East

A Babylonian Theogony

This short text reveals an ancient world very different from our own—the early generations of gods and goddesses indulge in incest and murder as the world begins in a chaos of violence and desire. The antiquity of this text is suggested on the page by its sheer fragmentation. We see the earliest writing emerging from the wreckage of early history, in a fitting embodiment of the poem's own themes. Cosmic though these themes are, they are grounded in realistic details: the first gods dig into the primordial mass of earth with a plough, just as if they were human farmers, evidently digging down to release groundwater that forms the sea. One of the early divinities' first acts is to build a city, "Dunnu, the twin towers" (line 6), as the seat of their earthly rule, as Babylon and other cities would also portray themselves. Already here, as in *The Epic of Gilgamesh* (p. 56), we see the importance of settled farming culture and the great cities it supported, in contrast to the nomadic shepherds' culture of the Hebrews and their suspicion of cities (see the discussion of Genesis 1–11, below).

Students will be struck by the frank immorality of the Babylonian gods, a theme that will resonate on through Homer and beyond. Students raised in one of the monotheistic traditions are accustomed to an all-wise and entirely good God, not to a pantheon of violent, lustful, and duplicitous divinities. The Near Eastern gods and goddesses can be seen as personifications of powerful, arbitrary natural forces, but they can also be seen as embodying very human motives of desire, jealousy, and the will to power. Chaotic and unbridled though the action seems at first sight, on closer examination it can be shown to display elements of incipient order: the bases of modern political and social life are here being worked out in their first forms. Note how Earth doesn't simply force herself on her son: "Come, let me make love to you," she entreats (line 9). Having married his mother and killed his father—the crucial pair of crimes underlying Sophocles' *Oedipus the King* (p. 618)—the young Amakandu treats his father's corpse with reverence, laying him "to rest in the city of Dunnu, which he loved" (line 12). Amakandu in turn is treated the same way, murdered but then laid to rest with his father. Patterns begin to emerge, showing the repetitious violence of desire (both sexual lust and the desire for power) and also inaugurating the ritual order and the dynastic order that will channel these desires and lead to the building of society.

Copyright © 2009 Pearson Education, Inc. Publishing as Longman.

The "Babylonian Theogony" makes a good beginning, not only for its themes but also for the sense it gives of the first emergence of a minimal literariness out of the pure sequence of events: the verbal repetitions from one set of events to the next create order out of chaos. The single line of direct speech and the very brief characterization of Dunnu as the city that Amakandu's father loved set the stage for the far more elaborate dialogues and characterizations that are found in Genesis.

✦✦✦

The Memphite Theology

This text pairs well with the "Babylonian Theogony," showing how the early gods' struggle for mastery became more fully presented over time, both in terms of theme and of literary method. Dialogue begins to be used more extensively, and a hymn to Ptah is inserted at the point he takes control (p. 27). This text also hints at a complex theological understanding that gives the creator god Ptah a kind of primacy over most of the other gods, and it combines physicality with a more verbal, "spiritual" understanding. The god Atum's court of nine gods (the Ennead) is described as created by his semen and fingers, and yet these physical details are reframed as essentially verbal events: Ptah "is in every mouth of all gods, all men, all cattle, all creeping things, whatever lives, thinking whatever he wishes and commanding whatever he wishes. . . . the Ennead is the teeth and lips in this mouth which pronounced the name of every thing" (p. 26-27). This story thus combines two very different modes of creation, physical and verbal. The world is created from divine semen, yet this sexual creation is doubled with a purely verbal creation, comparable to God's verbal commands that create the world and its features in Genesis 1 (p. 29).

The "Memphite Theology" also takes further the political aspect of the "Babylonian Theogony": the battling brothers Horus and Seth reflect ongoing divisions between northern and southern Egypt, "the Two Lands" uneasily joined to create Egypt. Like Dunnu in the Babylonian text, here Memphis, Ptah's city and the place of the text's composition, is the central earthly city, and the Egyptian pharaoh identifies himself as Ptah's agent on earth or even his literal embodiment. Interestingly, this divine king is also an early archaeologist. The text's preface tells us that the king had it recopied, "for his majesty found it to be a work of the ancestors which was worm-eaten, so that it could not be understood from beginning to end. His majesty copied it anew so that it became better than it had been before" (p. 26)—a result that not only emphasizes the king's loyal connection with the past but also gives the modern world pride of place over the very antiquity it celebrates.

✦✦✦

Genesis 1–11

However we and our students assess the Bible's claims of truth and its status as revelation, it should be evident that the old traditions presented in Genesis 1–11 re-

Copyright © 2009 Pearson Education, Inc. Publishing as Longman.

work elements seen in the earlier creation stories. One advantage of Robert Alter's vivid new translation, used in the *Anthology*, is that it allows us to read these chapters freshly. Alter's translation stays very close to the oral quality of the original and respects the rhythms and the patterns of phrase used in the Hebrew text (the sort of patterning he has so effectively unfolded in his book *The Art of Biblical Narrative*, 1981). Comparisons can be made most directly to the Flood story in the *Epic of Gilgamesh* (pp. 91–95). You can ask students to make lists of the points of similarity and the major differences they can find. These lists can become a kind of scavenger hunt and will help train them in looking for details as well as providing a ready basis for class discussion. The biblical Flood story also ends with a divine bow (the rainbow) set in the sky as a sign of peace, and there are manifold parallels between Utanapishtim's story of his survival of the Flood and Noah's in Genesis 6–9.

Once students have seen these parallels, the Bible's distinctive approach to these old materials becomes all the clearer. The world's creation doesn't require a titanic struggle, or any struggle at all: God simply creates everything (like Ptah in the "Memphite Theology") by verbal command, not by subduing any monstrous forces of chaos. Hints of alternative traditions of heavenly struggle are, in fact, preserved elsewhere in the Bible itself, particularly in several of the psalms and in passages in the Book of Job, in which God has to subdue unruly forces as he creates the world. One such passage can be found in Job 38 (Vol. A, p. 135), when God declares that he "shut in the sea with doors, / when it burst forth from the womb; / . . . and said, 'Thus far shall you come, and no farther, / and here shall your proud waves be stayed'" (lines 13–20). The proud waves bursting forth from the womb of the sea sound much like Tiamat and the roiling gods in her belly, and the watery deep at the start of Genesis, *tehom* in Hebrew, is actually cognate with "Tiamat." Genesis 1, however, doesn't show any such conflict openly: the Priestly writers who are thought to have composed the opening chapter give no space to any defeat of rival forces in heaven.

As the *Anthology*'s introduction to Genesis 1–11 notes, the absence of rivals to an omnipotent and just God led the biblical writers to a searching exploration of the problem of the origins of evil, which could not be portrayed (as in polytheistic works) as rooted in struggles between rival gods. What Genesis 1–11 shows is a gradual, tragic process of separation of humanity from God. Students can trace this growing separation across these chapters, beginning as early as Chapter 2, before the famous prohibition against eating the fruit of the tree of the knowledge of good and evil has been breached, and indeed before Eve has been created. God realizes that his new human being needs company, but God himself seems unsure just what companion to offer, and he creates a whole series of animals and birds, bringing each in turn to his new, still nameless human being, "to see what he would call it. . . . but for the human no sustainer beside him was found" (p. 30). This terse passage is a classic "Jahwistic" composition, an old, enigmatic account that doesn't try to solve the mystery it presents: How is it that God doesn't know what his human needs? In making the human in his own image, it seems that God

Copyright © 2009 Pearson Education, Inc. Publishing as Longman.

has created a being who shares something of his own mysterious unknowability, and there even seems to be a note of impatient relief in the hymn the man offers once he is finally presented with the woman made from his rib: "This one *at last*, bone of my bones / and flesh of my flesh, / This one shall be called Woman" (p. 30, emphasis added).

In the next chapter, the serpent is not yet the evil Satan of later biblical tradition; newly created by God, he is not evil but simply "cunning," and he tempts Eve by exploiting her genuine confusion as to what God had prohibited Adam. As early rabbinic commentators already noted two thousand years ago, Eve doesn't manage to get the prohibition right: in Chapter 2, God had commanded Adam not to eat of the fruit, but in her telling, she adds a new clause: "God has said, 'You shall not eat from it and you shall not touch it, lest you die'" (p. 31). Long passages of dialogue are repeated word for word in ancient texts as a matter of course; but here, Eve has misremembered the short and simple command given to her husband just a page earlier. The serpent has reason enough to question whether God really said what Eve thinks he said, and it can be imagined that when she touches the fruit and suffers no harm, the seriousness of the whole prohibition could be called into question. The separation from God is growing wider even before she touches the fruit, which tempts her for its goodness and beauty—she responds, in other words, as God himself has done to his creation: as we're told in Chapter 1, at each stage of creation, "God saw that it was good" (p. 29).

Early Christian theologians (and later poets like Milton) saw the serpent as a figure of pure evil, a fallen, rebellious angel, and Adam and Eve embodied the Catholic sin of pride. Genesis itself never uses any such term, however, but seems instead to see Eve as thoughtless, not fully in control of her divinely given senses (the tree "was good for eating and . . . it was lust to the eyes," as Alter's translation puts it). The degree to which our understanding of these chapters has been shaped by centuries of much later commentary can be illustrated for students by the fact that everyone "knows" that the forbidden fruit was an apple—portrayed as such in countless Renaissance paintings and still stuck in our throats in the form of our "Adam's apple." Yet the forbidden fruit can't be an apple, as apple trees aren't prohibited, just the sole "tree of knowledge." How then did this singular fruit come to be thought of as an apple? Thanks to a pun in Latin, exploited by early Church fathers, which then passed into common consciousness: "apple" in Latin is *malus*, which makes a useful play on words with the adjective "evil," *malum*. So we still refer today to our "Adam's apple" as a result of a pun in Latin, which wasn't yet a written language when the Genesis story was composed and which has ceased to be spoken or written outside the Vatican for centuries now. Reading Genesis 1–11 closely, we can help our students discover anew a text they probably don't know well even if they think they do.

The devolution of humanity away from God continues through the balance of Genesis 1–11, with Cain's murder of Abel (the settled farmer resenting God's unexplained preference for Hebrew-style sheep herding), the improper sexual mingling of human women with "the sons of God" (apparently semidivine members

Copyright © 2009 Pearson Education, Inc. Publishing as Longman.

of God's heavenly court) and the punishment of shortened lives, and then the disaster of the Flood and humanity's tenuous redemption in Noah and his immediate family. Even this redemption is immediately called into question by Noah's drunkenness in Chapter 9, leading to a murky scene of sexual exposure and possible incest, which leads in turn to Noah's curse on his youngest son, ancestor of the Hebrews' Canaanite rivals. The primeval history ends with the establishment of Babylon or Babel (Chapter 11), but here the earthly city is an embodiment of arrogance, and the Hebrew writers satirically derive "Babylon" from the Hebrew verb *balal*, "to babble" (p. 38), pretending not to know its quite obvious, glorious meaning in Akkadian, "Gate of God."

It's important for students to keep in mind that the disaster of the Tower of Babel and the splitting up of human languages and societies are not the end of the story: this is only the end of the prologue to Genesis, which turns to God's new covenant with Abram/Abraham and his wife Sarai/Sarah, who appear at the very end of Chapter 11 and will be the founders of the Hebrew people. A disaster in remote antiquity, the splitting apart of languages is not necessarily a bad thing from the perspective of the biblical writers themselves: the result is that they can speak—and write—Hebrew, the language of their own small people, feigning ignorance of Akkadian, the language of the dominant imperial powers to the east, the language spoken around them during their long exile in Babylon in the sixth century B.C.E., the time when the Hebrew Bible began to take its final shape. The old stories of Genesis 1–11 continued to serve present needs throughout antiquity as they have in the two millennia since then.

Poetry of Love and Devotion

These delightful and highly accessible poems have been selected to work effectively with the Song of Songs, which follows in the *Anthology* (p. 46); they can also be assigned in combination with the Psalms given as Resonances to the Book of Job (pp. 142–144), showing a range of sacred and secular poetry from the Near East. The Sumerian poem "Last night, as I, the queen, was shining bright" shows the love of repetition that gives Sumerian poetry a stately, chant-like quality, while at the same time it portrays Inanna, goddess of love, in charming terms drawn from "secular" love poetry. The poem illustrates the fluidity of the boundaries between "sacred" and "secular" in the ancient Near East, and even the tendency for the two realms to be overlaid directly. Inanna is shown as a girl wondering what she'll say to her mother to explain her dalliance with her lover, yet at the same time she is seen in the heavens as the twinkling planet Venus, "shining bright . . . dancing about" (line 3).

The Egyptian poems that follow are clearly earthly in setting and their lovers are human men and women, yet the gods and goddesses are everywhere present, upholding and furthering the speakers' love affairs. The poem "I sail downstream

Copyright © 2009 Pearson Education, Inc. Publishing as Longman.

in the ferry by the pull of the current" shows the entire Nile Valley coming alive with divinity under the force of the speaker's passion. As the speaker sails downstream to Memphis, he invokes its patron god, Ptah, shown in the "Memphite Theology" (p. 25) as the august creator of the world. In the poem, Ptah is charged with a very specific task: "give me my girl tonight" (line 5).

This is the oldest body of love poetry to have survived anywhere in the world, and these poems already show many features that will appear regularly in later love poetry: the anatomy of the beloved's body from head to foot ("One, the lady love without a duplicate"), the "aubade," in which lovers complain at being awoken by a bird at dawn, signaling their need to part ("The voice of the turtledove speaks out"), and themes of love as a hunt and as a delicious trap. Particularly close relations can be seen between these poems' images and those of the Song of Songs, which follows.

The Song of Songs

The title, *shir ha-shirim* or "song of songs," is a superlative meaning "best of all songs," but the plural term is also appropriate in that this text seems to be a collection of loosely linked short lyrics rather than a single narrative poem. Several ancient Egyptian collections survive, with titles like "The Songs of Excellent Enjoyment" and "The Songs of Extreme Happiness," and the Song of Songs can be seen as a collection put together to be sung as an evening's entertainment at a banquet by two singers, male and female, and a chorus. Like the Egyptian poems in the preceding section, the Song of Songs gives a sense of freshness and spontaneity through what is in fact a highly artistic refinement of popular or folk materials. There is no way to know who composed these songs (the attribution to Solomon, like the attribution of the Psalms to his father David, is unlikely to be factual), but as in the Egyptian poems the speakers alternate freely between men and women. Particularly in the context of the largely patriarchal societies of the ancient world, it is striking to see how freely the female speaker voices her passion and her desires, freely praising her lover's body as he will praise hers in turn.

Few modern readers see the Song of Songs as an allegory of the love of God and Israel, as did the rabbis who grudgingly allowed it into the canon of Scripture on that basis (and thanks to its attribution to Solomon), yet these poems were composed in a milieu in which "sacred" and "secular" poetry fed into each other, as they did in Mesopotamia and Egypt. The Song of Songs appears in the Bible directly before the book of Isaiah, which directly includes a love song as an allegory for God and an unfaithful Israel:

Let me sing for my beloved
A love song concerning his vineyard:
My beloved had a vineyard on a very fertile hill.

Copyright © 2009 Pearson Education, Inc. Publishing as Longman.

He dug it and cleared it of stones,
And planted it with choice vines;
He built a watchtower in the midst of it,
And hewed out a wine vat in it;
And he looked for grapes, but it yielded wild grapes.
And now, O inhabitants of Jerusalem and men of Judah,
Judge, I pray you, between me and my vineyard.
What more was there to do for my vineyard
That I have not done in it?
When I looked for it to yield grapes,
Why did it yield wild grapes?

(Isaiah 5:1–4)

The prophet's "love song" uses imagery and scenes from the love poetry tradition, as seen in the opening chapter of the Song of Songs itself, in which the woman laments that her angry brothers (perhaps angry at her love affair) have set her to tending their vineyards, to the neglect of her own, evidently hoping both to punish her and to leave her worn down and unattractive. She has become sunburnt—but still, she insists, lovely.

As captivated as students will be by the poem's erotic charm, they are also likely to be intrigued by the lover's mysterious disappearance in Chapter 3 and then again in Chapter 5, even as he has knocked on his beloved's door. (Students can debate whether the scene of knocking is to be seen purely literally or also involves a thinly veiled representation of a sexual act, as the lover thrusts his hand through the hole in the door, causing the woman to tremble to the core of her being.) The drama of seduction and withdrawal at the woman's door can be compared to the very similar scene in the Egyptian poem "I passed by her house in the dark" (p. 45), which begins with the lover knocking on his beloved's door but finding no response. In the Egyptian poem, though, instead of departing, the lover invokes the magical power of spells to induce the door bolts to open of their own accord, planning further to bribe the carpenter's assistant to make a door of grass and reeds, seemingly solid but easily penetrated at any time. The Egyptian gods are everywhere present and constantly available to help the lovers, while in the Song of Songs human love itself takes on qualities of Yahweh's mystery and his passionate, exacting love. The Song of Songs ends by asserting that "love is strong as Death, / jealousy relentless as Sheol," the underworld (lines 383–384). "Death," *Maweth*, was originally not a mere physical fact but a grim personality, the lord (formerly the god) of the underworld. The word "jealousy," *kinah*, is the very same word that God uses to describe himself in the Ten Commandments: "I the Lord your God am a jealous God" (Exodus 20:4). If Isaiah uses a human love song as a metaphor for divine love, the Song of Songs does the reverse: God's intense, all-encompassing, even violent love becomes a resonant metaphor for the love of men and women.

Copyright © 2009 Pearson Education, Inc. Publishing as Longman.

The Epic of Gilgamesh

This great poem is a teacher's dream: it is both gripping and mysterious, vivid and puzzling, fascinating to work through in itself and also a treasure-house of issues and themes that can resonate throughout the year under almost any configuration of a world literature course. All this in only forty pages—which means that it can readily be contextualized by assigning it together with the Perspectives section that follows it, on death and immortality. Broader connections can be drawn to Genesis 1–11, to the Joseph Story and the other texts in "Perspectives: Strangers in a Strange Land," and Gilgamesh's diatribe against the fickle goddess Ishtar can be compared to Job's complaints against God in the Book of Job. Further connections can later be drawn to the Homeric and Sanskrit epics and on to Virgil and Ovid in the Roman section at the end of Volume A.

As the introduction to *Gilgamesh* notes, in some ways the epic is closer to a late work like the *Aeneid* than to Homer's early Greek epics, as it is a literary reworking of older materials rather than a "primary" oral epic itself. A good way to orient students toward the sophistication of this ancient text is to draw their attention to the theme of reading that Sîn-liqe-unninni, reputed creator of the standard form of the epic, emphasizes in the prologue:

> Find the copper tablet box,
> open the hasp of its lock of bronze,
> undo the fastening of its secret opening.
> Take and read out from the lapis lazuli tablet
> how Gilgamesh went through every hardship. (p. 60, lines 22–26)

According to the prologue, Gilgamesh not only experienced these hardships but wrote them down himself, bringing back information "of the time before the Flood" (p. 59, line 5). This ancient epic, then, is also an epic *about* antiquity: its recovery, its study, and its lessons for us today.

Building on this indication of the poem's self-conscious, writerly stance, one way to enter the poem is by exploring its use of narrative and stylistic patterns derived from earlier oral tradition. Memorized oral texts, for example, often repeat phrases and whole speeches word for word. *Gilgamesh* is a written text based on older written versions, and yet repetitions are prominent, as can first be seen with the speeches discussing Enkidu, after the gods create him and set him down in the wilderness: the trapper and his father discuss his alarming appearance and the plan to have Gilgamesh send the harlot Shamhat to him (pp. 61–62), and then these speeches are repeated almost word for word in Uruk, with Gilgamesh saying exactly what the trapper's father had predicted he would say (p. 62). Why does the poet do this? Partly, these repetitions are valued in themselves as signifying a formal "literary" work; more particularly, they show Gilgamesh as someone who is much less the master of his fate than he supposes, even though he is king of a major city and seemingly able to work his will even at the expense of his own subjects.

Copyright © 2009 Pearson Education, Inc. Publishing as Longman.

As the epic proceeds, repetitions occur, particularly in the repeated and variant dreams that pepper the narrative. You can ask students to look at each set of
dreams. Not all are complete in the surviving versions of the poem, but three sets
are especially good to examine: Gilgamesh's two dreams of the meteorite and the
axe that foreshadow Enkidu's arrival (pp. 64–65); Gilgamesh's dreams of a falling
mountain, a wild bull, and a thunderstorm as he and Enkidu approach the monster Humbaba's lair (pp. 70–72); and Enkidu's dreams of death and the House of
Dust (pp. 78–82). Dreams were commonly understood throughout the ancient
world to be a prime means by which the gods communicated with mortals, to foreshadow future events and give warnings or make promises. Gilgamesh's first
dreams work in this traditional manner: his mother correctly interprets them as
foreshadowing Enkidu's arrival, and at the close of their long association
Gilgamesh will in fact call Enkidu the trusted axe at his side (p. 83, line 31).

The second set of dreams disrupts this expected sequence of promise, or warning and fulfillment: Gilgamesh has four troubling dreams as he and Enkidu approach Humbaba, but Enkidu assures him they are really all positive. Students
should discuss this discrepancy between the feel of the dream and its meaning: Are
the dreams not the clear messages they first seemed to be, or is Enkidu foolishly or
willfully misinterpreting them? This ambiguity carries on in the action: Were they
right to slay Humbaba, or are they ruthlessly killing a helpless prisoner who should
be spared? Does Enkidu's advice to kill Humbaba reflect pragmatism in the face of
an untrustworthy enemy, or is this an unjust over-reaching that rightly brings down
a curse on his head?

The third set of dreams, of the House of Dust, serves a rather different pur-
pose. The poet has lifted Enkidu's vision from an earlier text, *The Descent of
Ishtar to the Underworld*, which can be found on p. 98 in "Perspectives: Death and
Immortality." Students can compare these two versions and ask how the
Gilgamesh poet has adapted the description and how it works in its new setting.
It is particularly noteworthy that Enkidu sees Etana in the House of Dust (p. 82).
Etana was a Sumerian king who had become, like Gilgamesh, the hero of a popular narrative poem. His poem also concerns a quest for immortality, not in literal form but in the form of an heir. Childless, Etana befriends an eagle and flies
up to heaven to receive a plant that will grant fertility to him and his queen. (A
translation of *Etana* can be found in Stephanie Dalley, *Myths from Mesopotamia*,
1989, pp. 189–202.) Enkidu's dream-voyage vision of Etana is the earliest known
example of an epic hero encountering an earlier hero in the underworld, a motif
famously found both in Book 11 of the *Odyssey* (Vol. A, p. 384) and in Book 6
of the *Aeneid* (p. 1166). Already here the encounter underscores the vanity of
earthly fame.

Gilgamesh's sophisticated use of dreams can be compared to the dreams at the
start of the biblical Joseph Story, given a double valence since they are true prophecies of Joseph's coming ascendancy over his brothers yet also the direct cause of his
misfortunes, when he rashly boasts of his dreams to his family. Enkidu and
Gilgamesh similarly are characters whose boldness all too readily shades over into

Copyright © 2009 Pearson Education, Inc. Publishing as Longman.

high-handedness and outright foolhardiness, most notably seen when Gilgamesh insults Ishtar in great detail in spurning her advances (p. 76) and Enkidu taunts her as he hurls the bull of heaven's haunch at her (p. 78).

One question to pursue with students as they examine such sequences is whether the epic shows anything like novelistic character development. Some commentators have seen the epic as a kind of early *Bildungsroman*. The Sumerologist Thorkild Jacobsen described it as a story "of learning to face reality, a story of 'growing up'" ("The Gilgamesh Epic: Romantic and Tragic Vision," in *Lingering Over Words*, eds. Tzvi Abusch et al., 1990, pp. 231–249). Yet the poem makes little effort to individualize Gilgamesh in any personal way; rather, he exemplifies general features of a powerful, willful ruler who must be taught restraint and who comes to an acceptance of his situation, but this is something different from a shift in his emotional makeup.

Gilgamesh has the forcefulness of Agamemnon in Homer's *Iliad* or of Creon in Sophocles' *Antigone*, but the poem spends little time on probing his motives or exploring his personality. Instead, the epic's characters represent broad types or even, more generally, universals of the human condition. Enkidu provides a good example of this: the poem presents an almost Darwinian theory of human evolution through his story, as he begins life as a hairy wild man, then acquires culture as he moves into the city once his sexual awakening separates him from his beloved animals—a theme of separation that can be compared to Adam and Eve's experience in Eden, though notably without any ethical issues associated with Enkidu's loss of innocence. When the harlot (likely a temple prostitute) Shamhat exclaims to him that "you are become like a god" after sex with her (p. 63, line 180), this isn't blasphemy on her part or fatal pride on his but pure praise. Similarly, the city of Uruk is a center for all that's fine and beautiful, a place of abundance and sexual enjoyment.

One significant personal dichotomy the epic plays with is the distinction between men and women. Students can look at the series of women who appear in the epic, from the seductive, civilized Shamhat to the imperious, fickle Ishtar, to the mysterious tavern-keeper Siduri (p. 86), who first bars her door against Gilgamesh as he seeks the path to Utanapishtim, then reveals the way to him. As Stephanie Dalley has noted in her introduction to her translation of the epic:

> The story of Odysseus and Calypso in *Odyssey*, V is recognized to have some close resemblances to the episode of Gilgamesh and Siduri: the lone female plies the inconsolable hero-wanderer with drink and sends him off to a place beyond the sea reserved for a special class of honored people. To prepare for the voyage he has to cut down and trim timbers. Atrahasis [Utanapishtim] at the mouth of the rivers is replaced by Alkinoos and the blessed isle of the Phaeacians, kinsmen of the gods. (*Myths from Mesopotamia*, 1989, p. 48)

Though the epic's men are often contrasted to the women, both Gilgamesh and especially Enkidu take on feminine qualities at significant moments. The primi-

Copyright © 2009 Pearson Education, Inc. Publishing as Longman.

tive, hairy Enkidu is explicitly feminized, with his "full head of hair like a woman" (line 79) and his resemblance to the goddess of grain and the goddess of cattle (p. 61). When he dies, Gilgamesh mourns him like a lost lover, covering his face "like a bride" (p. 83, line 44). The hero's love for his quasi-feminine companion can be compared with that between Achilles and Patroklos (where a direct sexual relationship may exist, not implied in *Gilgamesh*) and with such other early pairings as David and Jonathan. Much like Gilgamesh, in fact, David mourns his slain friend with a lament that speaks of him almost as a bride:

> I am distressed for you, my brother Jonathan;
> very pleasant have you been to me;
> your love to me was wonderful,
> passing the love of women.
>   (2 Samuel 1:28)

Gilgamesh himself starts to "shriek in anguish like a mourner" at Enkidu's death (p. 83, line 30)—that is, like a professional funeral mourner, a women's occupation. He then paces over Enkidu's body "like a lioness deprived of her cubs" (line 46), shearing off his own luxuriant curls and ripping off his fine clothing. The hero who began the epic violating brides on their wedding night experiences a certain reversing of roles, heightened when he abandons his city in search of immortality, looking more and more like the wild Enkidu as a mat of hair grows on his body and he replaces his clothing with a lion's skin (p. 84), rather as the Greek hero Hercules does during his labors (see Color Plate 4 in Vol. A).

His voyage to Utanapishtim in search of immortality becomes the occasion for the poet to insert a long account of the Flood. You can ask students why the action suddenly stops for Utanapishtim's detailed account of these old events. Clearly, the epic shows a different sense of pacing than a modern narrative. Sîn-liqe-unninni was also comfortable giving his story a fairly loose construction, as can also be seen in the doubled curses pronounced by Humbaba and Ishtar: only one is really needed for plot purposes, but the poet was bringing together older, separate stories and clearly didn't want to give either of them up. It is particularly interesting to compare *Gilgamesh*'s version of the Flood story with the Bible's version, with such close similarities as the sending out of birds to test the drying up of the land after the Flood and such interesting differences as the realistic, boat-like dimensions of Noah's Ark versus Utanapishtim's much more symbolic boat, cubical in form, a kind of floating temple pyramid. (For a detailed discussion of these parallels and differences, see "Gilgamesh and Genesis," in David Damrosch, *The Narrative Covenant: Transformations of Genre in the Growth of Biblical Literature*, 1987, pp. 88–143.) It is likely that both versions developed from a common literary source, an Old Babylonian narrative poem known as the *Atrahasis Epic*, in which Atrahasis ("Exceedingly Wise") is the name given there to the Noah/Utanapishtim figure. At one point in the *Gilgamesh* epic, Utanapishtim is actually called Atrahasis (p. 95), either in a slip by the poet or

Copyright © 2009 Pearson Education, Inc. Publishing as Longman.

in deliberate reference to the earlier source. In *Gilgamesh*, no human misbehavior is mentioned as a cause for the Flood, though in the underlying source the cause is given as the noisiness of the rapidly growing human race, which disturbs the gods in heaven and leads them to decree the Flood in hopes of getting some peace and quiet. *The Epic of Gilgamesh* may assume the reader knows this, though the lack of any mention of causes is in keeping with the poem's relative lack of interest in issues of motive.

Where there is a clear ethical debate, it is located in the gods' arguments with one another over the justice and wisdom of their actions: "How, how could you bring about a Flood without consideration?" the wise god Ea asks the enraged Enlil (p. 94), and Ishtar openly repents her role: "How could I say evil things in the Assembly of the Gods, / ordering a catastrophe to destroy my people?" (p. 93, lines 118-119). This is the same Ishtar who was perfectly willing to cause seven years of famine in order to get her revenge on Gilgamesh and Enkidu (p. 77); her passionate, violent character is not about to change, but at least she is learning to restrain herself. In the climactic eleventh tablet, Gilgamesh goes to visit his now immortal ancestor Utanapishtim and hears the story of the Flood, but the moral of the story is that it won't apply to Gilgamesh, for all his eagerness to avoid death. Gilgamesh is denied his wish not for any sins or moral failings; the human condition, embodied in his need for sleep, simply doesn't allow for immortality. Utanapishtim achieved his special status not through any greater virtue or strength than Gilgamesh possesses. Indeed, Gilgamesh closely resembles his ancestor, as he realizes when they meet ("your appearance is not strange—you are like me!" he exclaims, p. 91, line 3). The difference between them is simply, and tragically, that times have changed. As Utanapishtim remarks as he concludes his tale, "Now then, Gilgamesh, who will convene the gods on your behalf, / that you may find the life that you are seeking?" (p. 95, lines 202-203).

The epic began by describing its hero's journey to recover lost knowledge and record it for us to read. At the end, when Gilgamesh visits Utanapishtim, the modern world of history visits the archaic world of myth, both to learn from it and to measure our distance from "Utanapishtim whom they call 'The Faraway'" (p. 90, line 165).

PERSPECTIVES

Death and Immortality

This Perspectives section can readily be taught together with *Gilgamesh* or with the Book of Job that follows it, as it gives context for both works' explorations of mortality, evil, and salvation. Most directly, *The Descent of Ishtar to the Underworld* is a source text for Enkidu's nightmares of the underworld and its House of Dust. Students can trace the ways the epic takes up its themes of underworld descent and sibling rivalry; apart from Enkidu's direct dream (p. 81), the earthly sterility

Copyright © 2009 Pearson Education, Inc. Publishing as Longman.

that follows Ishtar's descent is echoed in *Gilgamesh* when Ishtar sends down the Bull of Heaven (p. 77), and the descent of Ishtar to the perilous underworld can be compared to Gilgamesh's own climactic journey to Utanapishtim.

Our selections from *The Book of the Dead* illustrate the magical power that language could take on, helping the soul navigate the perils of the underworld and achieve union with Osiris and eternal life. The soul's "negative confession" or declaration of innocence (pp. 105–106) can be directly compared to Job's assertions of innocence in Chapter 31, which even includes the image of Job being weighed in a balance scale (p. 133), like the heart in the Egyptian underworld (as in the illustration on p. 103). The common modern title for this collection of spells, *The Book of the Dead*, is unfortunate, as it suggests a work of gloom and doom; what students should see is that the book really is a magnificent insurance policy, "effective a million times," intended to assure eternal joy and prosperity, starting with a hearty meal of "bread, beer, and a big chunk of meat from the altar of the great god" (p. 108). Here the cover of Volume A is relevant as well, as the deceased man steps forward into death carrying the scroll that will ensure his safe passage. As that image suggests, it is artfully phrased, magically powerful language that will bring all these benefits to the fortunate soul who has commissioned a book of these spells.

The Egyptian *Letters to the Dead* show the degree to which their writers expected language to work on their behalf, even across the divide between the living and the dead. Particularly striking is the first writer's assertion that his letter will itself serve as his brief before the nine judges of the underworld in the lawsuit he intends to bring against his deceased wife (p. 109). The writers' trust in writing is comparable to that of Job, who wishes that "my words were written . . . inscribed in a book" (Job 19:23) and who longs to have "the indictment written by my adversary" (p. 134, line 73) to which he could respond.

If earthly life was often seen as extending almost seamlessly into the afterlife, the opposite could occur as well, and the narrative poem *Erra and Ishum* gives a complex, intense account of the god of death's depredations when he takes power in Babylon. A good way to approach this poem is to have students examine the motives for the attack on Babylon. The seven disease demons use a remarkably modern series of military and political arguments to foment the war (pp. 112–113): Erra's approval ratings will go up if he fights a spectacular little war; his power will increase among his fellow gods; the heavenly gods will be relieved by the peace and quiet brought about by slaughtering and subduing the Babylonians (an argument that echoes old accounts of the reasons for the Flood); and, finally, the military leaders themselves will welcome the war in order to hone their battle tactics and keep their weapons in good working order.

Having seen all this, students will be ready to track Erra's actions in terms of power politics and to see the important, but importantly constrained, role of his herald and counselor, Ishum. Ishum illustrates the limits of wise counsel in guiding the violence of an out-of-control leader and may stand in for the poet Kabti-ilani-Marduk himself and his fellow priests.

Copyright © 2009 Pearson Education, Inc. Publishing as Longman.

Erra and Ishum is remarkable for its poetic power as well as the complexity of its themes. Like the Book of Job and like the Homeric epics, it can be seen as a protodramatic work, with the extended dialogues between Erra and Ishum foreshadowing the development of formally staged drama. The poem works through a steady building of tension and horror, climaxing in Erra's raging call for universal destruction, in a speech whose very language collapses on itself: "The sea-folk, the sea-folk; the Subartean, the Subartean; the Assyrian, the Assyrian / . . . one man, another man; one brother, his brother, without mercy: / May they all kill each other!" (lines 569–574). The poem's ending may surprise students: even as Ishum is praised for calming Erra before the whole world is laid waste, Erra is confirmed in his power. An ancient realism is shown here; the God of Death is not about to go away. The closing section of the poem reveals that Ishum has sent the poem to Kabti-ilani-Marduk in a dream (lines 630–632), and, remarkably, Erra himself becomes its first and most enthusiastic reader, proclaiming that it will protect its listeners from his own violence in the future. Erra here makes a very interesting comparison to God in the closing chapters of the Book of Job: violent, unpredictable, yet powerful beyond human conceptions of good and evil.

The Book of Job

The Book of Job follows well from "Perspectives: Death and Immortality," but it can also be introduced through its Resonances. With its sufferer who questions the gods' ways and his friend who tries to comfort him, "The Babylonian Theodicy" (Vol. A, p. 140) is likely a direct predecessor of the biblical account. The sufferer voices a central question of theological inquiry: If the world is controlled by a just and beneficent deity or pantheon, how can evil flourish unpunished on earth? "A cripple does better than I, a dullard keeps ahead of me. / The rogue has been promoted, but I have been brought low" (lines 35–36). The friend replies, much as will Job's well-intentioned but clueless friends, that it's all the sufferer's own fault: "Your heart has become hardened and you accuse the god wrongly" (line 39)—his mistake is in trying to understand the high mysteries of divine ways. Pressed further, the friend asserts that the gods themselves chose to build injustice into the human condition: "Narru, king of the gods . . . / And goddess Mami . . . / Gave twisted speech to the human race. / With lies, and not truth, they endowed them forever" (lines 61–66). This response seems to comfort the sufferer, who closes with a plea for divine mercy; but what happens if one can't put the blame on a varied and not particularly moral pantheon?

The two psalms given as Resonances (pp. 142–144) show a response parallel to the sufferer's in "The Babylonian Theodicy." The psalmist details his miseries in eloquent terms and then asserts that fear of God's name and faithful praise will restore him. The second psalm makes similar laments but shifts its hope beyond the personal to the national level and to the restoration of future generations—the

Copyright © 2009 Pearson Education, Inc. Publishing as Longman.

sort of psalm likely sung with special fervor during the Babylonian exile, the time when the Book of Job itself was probably written.

Both the psalms and the Book of Job are built out of parallel verses and half-verses. Throughout the study of Job, students can see how the argument proceeds through expansive variation at the level of individual verses as well as larger units like speeches. Hebrew verse didn't use rhyme or set stanza forms or even fixed meters; instead, biblical verses work by parallelism. This parallelism is emphasized in the translation of Job, in which half-lines are set off and indented. The older King James version given for the psalms runs the long lines of each verse without a break, but the parallelism can readily be seen in the way the second half of so many lines restates and expands on the first: "Hear my prayer, O Lord, and let my cry come unto thee" (Psalm 102:1, p. 143). Students can look to see the various effects achieved by these expansive parallelisms, as for example in the fifth line of Psalm 22: "They cried unto thee, and were delivered; they trusted in thee, and were not confounded" (p. 142). The second half of the line rephrases the first half but makes its statement negatively instead of positively: instead of being delivered, the speaker's fathers have more modestly not been confounded, a revision that brings them closer to the speaker's own situation.

The Book of Job uses parallelism in many different ways, sometimes to add vivid detail and bring a point home, sometimes to intensify an initial statement, sometimes to undercut it or ironize it. Consider the opening lines of Job's outcry in Chapter 3:

> "Let the day perish wherein I was born,
>   and the night which said,
>   'A man-child is conceived.'
> Let that day be darkness!
> May God above not seek it,
>   nor light shine upon it.
> Let gloom and deep darkness claim it.
> Let clouds dwell upon it;
>   let the blackness of the day terrify it." (p. 127, lines 3–11)

The parallelisms do several different things just in these few lines. In the first verse, the second statement shifts suddenly back nine months from the day of birth to the day of conception, and reverses time from day to night, at the same time universalizing Job's plight from that of a single person to that of a more general "man-child" (ironically chosen, the term used, *gever*, means a strong youth and is related to the noun *gibbor*, warrior or champion). Next, the normal parallelism is broken by the single, passionate half-line: "Let that day be darkness!" The ensuing lines pair God and light, gloom and darkness, then expand on the physical covering of clouds to an intensely emotional result: "let the blackness of the day terrify it."

The psalms and "The Babylonian Theodicy" show the background of anguished reflection and faithful response out of which—or against which—the

Copyright © 2009 Pearson Education, Inc. Publishing as Longman.

Book of Job was composed. (Appropriately, Job directly follows the Book of Psalms in the Hebrew Bible, instead of preceding them as in the Christian Bible.) The prose frame-tale, presumably an old story taken up by the poet who composed the body of the book, presents a fairly uncomplicated picture of the patient, righteous Job, who refuses all self-pity amid his troubles, perseveres in his confident faith, and is restored and rewarded in the prose conclusion to the tale. This presentation of Job can be compared to the Book of Ruth (p. 178), in which Naomi blames God for killing her husband and sons but perseveres in her faith and is finally rewarded with a grandson by Ruth. The prose frame-tale of the Book of Job responds to the problem of unjustified suffering by turning the question around: If God always rewarded good actions with instant gratification, then "good" would lose its meaning as a real choice. Good deeds should be done for their own sake, not for the sake of bribes. The verse body of the book, however, deeply questions this solution, as Job eloquently details his sufferings and rejects his friends' attempts to excuse God and, increasingly, to blame the victim for his own sufferings.

The selections given here present Job's opening outcry and his friend Eliphaz's first and third attempts to comfort him, with Job's replies in turn and then God's magnificent appearance and response. Students should look to see the progression from Eliphaz's first speech (Chapter 4) to his final one (Chapter 22); having begun by stressing God's inscrutability and the likelihood of Job's eventual restoration, by Chapter 22 Eliphaz is reduced to vicious ad hominem attacks on Job himself. Job's speeches should similarly be examined for their dramatic progression, from his initial outcry of despair (Chapter 3), to his pleas to be heard and receive justice (Chapters 6-7 and 23), to his "negative confession" of the sins he hasn't committed (Chapter 31)—interestingly, just the sort of negative confession that concludes the soul's self-defense in the Egyptian underworld (see *The Book of the Dead*, p. 102).

How are we to assess God's long speech in response (Chapters 38-41), when he speaks out of the whirlwind to silence Job's complaints? Students who come to this book after having read modern writers like Kafka or Beckett may well see the book's ending as a deconstruction of any idea of a just God, or even as the poet's covert declaration of rebellion against religion altogether. Yet the Book of Job has, after all, come down to us because it was preserved as a part of the Hebrew Bible itself, which would never have happened if its ancient readers had seen it as a scandalous, blasphemous work. On the other hand, it's also apparent that the book caused an ongoing discomfort among its ancient readers, which is why (as the introduction to Job in the *Anthology* notes) some ancient editor rearranged some of the speeches (not included here) to give Job more orthodox-sounding lines and abruptly introduced a fourth friend, Elihu, to give a long speech to make up for the three friends' inadequacies.

Noting that Satan here is "the accuser," a sort of prosecutor in God's heavenly court rather than the fallen angel of later accounts, it can be very effective to have students take sides in this case and debate its pros and cons, with a team for the

Copyright © 2009 Pearson Education, Inc. Publishing as Longman.

prosecution and one for the defense. Of course, one question to discuss is: Who's to be defended, Job or God? Some may see Job's final reply at the start of Chapter 42 as a sign of genuine repentance, reflecting a new humility and awareness of his own limitations, whereas others may see it as a masterpiece of thinly veiled sarcasm. Each side should be encouraged to find evidence for or against their view. An understanding of Job's final speech as sarcastic, for example, can argue that this is in keeping with his earlier parodies of language from the psalms (as noted, for example, in footnote 7 on p. 130). An argument for Job's achieving self-knowledge (of his own, Socratic ignorance) could find support in the beginning of the prose conclusion, in which God says that it is Job, and not his friends, who have spoken rightly of him. Perhaps Job's real need never was to have the world's woes magically brushed away, but simply to have the direct confrontation he has sought from the beginning, a wish God does grant.

Both teams can look closely at God's speech to see what he adds to what the friends, and Job himself, have put forward. The survey of the world's beauty and order progresses to—or collapses into?—the long accounts of the monstrous Behemoth and Leviathan. Whether championed by teams of students or set out as aspects of your own presentation, both views can find support in these remarkable chapters of stirring verse.

PERSPECTIVES

Strangers in a Strange Land

This section brings together in a teachable unit two masterpieces of biblical narrative—the Joseph Story and the Book of Ruth—along with two earlier Egyptian texts that give very different kinds of context for the biblical stories of exile and restoration.

The Story of Sinuhe

"The Story of Sinuhe" is like the Joseph Story in reverse: its Egyptian hero flees Egypt and makes a new life in Palestine, then returns to his homeland in old age, unexpectedly called for by his forgiving, fatherly monarch. This story is engagingly told and conveys the sense of an individual personality. It shows, as well, the extraordinary pull of one's homeland as the only place to really live and, best of all, to die and be buried in. Even after he has become rich and prominent in Palestine, Sinuhe says that he still feels "like a stray bull in a strange herd" (p. 149), liable to be singled out for attack at any moment. As artless and direct as the story seems on the surface, it presents two interesting problems to tease out with students.

Copyright © 2009 Pearson Education, Inc. Publishing as Longman.

First, why did Sinuhe really leave? Second, why did Sesostris call him back after so many years and treat him with such exceptional favor? Sinuhe himself more than once expresses bafflement that he ever fled, given that no accusations were being made against him, and he can't believe his good fortune when Sesostris not only calls for him but treats him so well: "There is no commoner for whom the like has been done," as he says in conclusion (p. 153). So why *did* Sesostris do all this for Sinuhe, who had been AWOL for so long?

When Sesostris invites him home, Sinuhe writes back asserting that he fled out of pure "ignorance" and claims that "I do not know what removed me from my place" (p. 151); inexplicably, some god must have willed his flight (p. 152). Yet at the start of the narrative, Sinuhe lets slip a more likely motive: "I believed there would be turmoil and did not expect to survive it" (p. 147). Writing his autobiography back in Egypt, Sinuhe is necessarily circumspect in stating why he might have had this fear, but you can ask students to see if there are any details that might hint at reasons for his fear. Recalling that (as the text's introduction notes) the dead king Amenemhet had founded his new dynasty, his sudden death would have meant a specially precarious time. What is more, the future pharaoh, Sesostris, wasn't even in the capital to take over the kingship. The fact that he has been off subduing rebel tribes on Egypt's border already suggests that this is not a peaceful time, and Sesostris's reaction to the news of his father's death strongly suggests the insecurity of his position. He hastens in secret back to the capital, not even telling his own troops that he has gone, and, significantly, he apparently rushes off in advance of his brothers, who had been with him. Might some of these have been potential rivals to the throne? As for Sinuhe, his fear would not come from any disloyalty to the new king, but on the contrary precisely because he was working for Sesostris's sister and wife, Princess Nefru: if one of the rival brothers got the upper hand, Sinuhe would be swept away along with his masters.

Students can thereby be shown the reasons why Sinuhe might have fled, in an intriguing demonstration of how we can read a text for what it hints but can't say directly. Yet the second mystery remains. Abandoned by Sinuhe at his moment of crisis, why would Sesostris ever have recalled him, still less rewarded him so lavishly? Students can find several possible motives if they look closely at the text. First, having by now firmly established himself, Sesostris may want to make a very public display of generosity to underscore his own security on the throne and to make the point that he doesn't rule by fear: "His majesty said: 'He shall not fear, he shall not dread!'" (p. 153). Second, from the moment he receives Sesostris's invitation to return, Sinuhe makes himself politically useful to the king, exploiting his Canaanite connections to extend the Egyptian king's power in the region, telling him which local leaders he can best bring under his control (see the second paragraph of his letter to the king, p. 151). This can lead us back to the very first sentence of the text, which shows that Sinuhe didn't just relax in the elegant house the king gives him back in Egypt: he has been made "Governor of the domains of the sovereign in the lands of the Asiatics" (p. 146). Like Joseph, Sinuhe has gained royal favor by extending the king's power.

Copyright © 2009 Pearson Education, Inc. Publishing as Longman.

—◦—▪◦▪—◦—

The Two Brothers

"The Two Brothers," the fairy-tale-like story that comes next in this Perspectives section, also involves issues of sibling rivalry and royal authority. Students will find fascinating comparisons between the attempted seduction of Bata by his sister-in-law (pp. 145–155) and the very similar attempt on Joseph by Potiphar's wife (pp. 163–164). Bata's relation to his older brother Anubis can more generally be compared with Joseph's relations with his older brothers. Very different, on the other hand, is the sequence of events that begins when Bata castrates himself. Even though the gods create a wife for him, he cannot have sex with her, "because I am a woman like you" (p. 156), and she ends up marrying the pharaoh and betraying him in turn, repeatedly seeking his death only to be defeated by Bata's limitless ability to transform himself. This sequence ends when he takes the form of a tree, and when she has it felled, he enters his faithless wife's mouth in the form of a splinter, impregnates her, and comes to be reborn as her own son, becoming the heir of his supposed father the Pharaoh. This aspect of the story could be compared to the story of Moses, which directly follows the Joseph Story in the Bible. Moses is raised as an adoptive son by his pharaoh's daughter, in a more restrained and realistic version of this magical tale of transformation.

"The Two Brothers" is probably best seen as a kind of extended tall tale, a dramatic entertainment rather than a carefully wrought work of art, but it provides an effective backdrop from which to assess the Joseph Story's far more searching story of God's hidden power working on behalf of a favored outcast.

—◦—▪◦▪—◦—

The Joseph Story

The Joseph Story was almost certainly composed as a freestanding work before it was eventually incorporated into Genesis. It is structured around several sets of dreams, rather as *The Epic of Gilgamesh* is, and yet its effect is very different. Here it is possible to speak of full character development, in a narrative that traces Joseph's maturation from a callow, self-centered youth to a wise counselor and regent for the Egyptian pharaoh. The story is rich in deep psychological inquiry and insight, and it shows as well the dangerous attractions of life in a wealthy but repressive foreign land.

The likely historical basis for the Hebrews' sojourn in Egypt was the period in which a Canaanite group known as the Hyksos ("foreign rulers," in Egyptian) gained control over northern (lower) Egypt during the period c. 1720–1550 B.C.E. The story very realistically recounts the ways in which Hebrews and other Canaanite groups could be drawn down to Egypt in times of famine at home. The story does not, however, literally represent this hybrid, Canaanite-oriented period,

Copyright © 2009 Pearson Education, Inc. Publishing as Longman.

in which the Hyksos introduced worship of their gods into lower Egypt and emphasized shepherding over the farming traditional in the Nile delta (the Greek historian Manetho, c. 300 B.C.E., labeled them "the Shepherd Kings" as a result). In the Joseph Story, the Egyptians are seen (as they usually were, in fact) as culturally distinct from their northern visitors and contemptuous of their ways. Joseph must make his way in very adverse circumstances.

Hostility begins at home in this story, and it is good to begin by looking directly at the dysfunctional family dynamic elaborated at the beginning of the story (Chapter 37). Remarkably, the great patriarch Jacob (also called Israel) is the first cause of the problem, showing such favoritism to young Joseph that his brothers come to hate him. Joseph's "richly ornamented robe" (p. 160, famous in the King James translation as his "coat of many colors") embodies this favoritism, which is given an added edge of insult by the young Joseph's own boastful recounting of his first prophetic dreams.

Dreams provide an excellent index of the story's development, and students can discuss the overall progression from one set of dreams to the next. As in *The Epic of Gilgamesh* and generally in the ancient world, dreams are shown as a divine means of communication with mortals, and yet they are often ambiguous and need interpretation. Whereas Enkidu dramatically misinterprets Gilgamesh's dreams as they approach the monster Humbaba (see the earlier entry on *Gilgamesh*), Joseph's initial problem is that he all too openly parades his perfectly correct interpretation of his dreams of the sheaves and then the stars, sun, and moon bowing to him (p. 160). The very ability that led to his downfall then comes into play in Egypt to save him, first in prison with the dreams of the cupbearer and baker (Chapter 40) and then with the pharaoh's dreams prophesying years of plenty and years of famine (Chapter 41). These three sets of dreams involving Joseph get most of the story's attention, but there is a final dream that concludes the sequence: Jacob/Israel's dream-vision, direct from God, renewing his covenant with his chosen people at the start of Chapter 46.

The dreams raise a formal question: Why do they keep appearing in pairs? Students should observe that in Joseph's first pair of dreams, the second suggests a hubristic exaggeration, as first the sheaves of grain but then the sun, moon, and stars bow down to him. True, God himself has sent this dream, yet it can be noted that a tendency toward self-glorification persists in Joseph throughout his career. Isn't it a bit of an exaggeration when the successful Joseph tells his brothers in Chapter 45 that God has made him "father to Pharaoh, lord of his entire household and ruler of all Egypt" (p. 171)?

The second pairing of dreams serves to demonstrate the accuracy of Joseph's divinely given intuition: the fact that he has predicted the baker's fall as well as the cupbearer's rise sticks (belatedly) in the cupbearer's memory. Whereas these dreams foretell opposite results, the Pharaoh's two confusing dreams are really "one and the same," as Joseph explains (p. 165): the doubling underscores God's ability to create meaning out of seeming randomness. Students can note how the story can repeat descriptions and speeches word for word, as is commonly seen in

Copyright © 2009 Pearson Education, Inc. Publishing as Longman.

early texts such as *Gilgamesh*, but when Pharaoh recounts his dream of the fat and lean cows, he expansively comments on his own thoughts about what he has seen—a lovely example of the story's novelistic realism.

These pairings of dreams can then lead into a discussion of broader patterns of doubling, repetition, and sheer narrative excess in the story. Two episodes in particular are good to focus on for this purpose. First, why is the tale interrupted by the seemingly self-contained interlude of Judah and Tamar in Chapter 38? Second, why do the brothers have to journey down to Egypt not once but twice, and why does Joseph engage in the doubled ruse of putting money in their sacks, and then money in a silver cup, as they are heading home?

A traditional answer for the insertion of the story of Judah and Tamar is simply that it was there, an anecdote that the biblical writer knew and wanted to put somewhere, so he stuck it in, not worrying about the interruption in his larger narrative. Certainly the Bible often brings together disparate materials, without showing the concern for neat narrative construction that a modern novelist or dramatist would feel. A clear example of a casual suturing of traditions occurs in Chapter 37, where two different accounts of Joseph's betrayal by his brothers have been mixed together (as noted in footnote 5 to the text, p. 161), leading to the awkward shift between Judah and an inexplicably surprised Reuben.

Yet the story of Tamar can also be seen to work well with the overall story's themes, as Robert Alter has argued in *The Art of Biblical Narrative* (1981). Judah is the one who devises the plan to sell Joseph into slavery to the Ishmaelites—a better idea than killing him outright, but not by much, as can be seen in the gruesome charade of the bloody cloak and the deep grief it causes their father. In Chapter 38 Judah himself is caught in a situation in which, like his own father, he is favoring a younger son (Shelah, whom he is shielding from his responsibility to his widowed sister-in-law Tamar), and he is then caught in a trap based on his own sexual self-indulgence. Further, Joseph's demand for Benjamin to be held as a hostage (Chapter 44) leaves a desperate Judah begging to be allowed (as Shelah and the notorious coitus-interrupter Onan should have done) to stand in his brother's stead: "Now then, please let your servant remain here as my lord's slave in place of the boy" (p. 171). The fatherly and brotherly responsibility he withholds from Tamar he now has to take on. In a sense, the Joseph Story could as well be called the Judah Story, particularly given the insistence with which their father is often called by his new name of "Israel." Israel and Judah, after all, were the names of the two kingdoms into which the country split after the brief period of unity that ended upon Solomon's death as a result of a round of sibling rivalry between his sons. As often in the Bible, a family saga has national overtones, and the moral for the reader lies as much in our relation to Israel and Judah as to Joseph.

Students can discuss the doubling of the brothers' sojourns and of Joseph's complex ruses to get his beloved younger brother and their father to Egypt. Why this elaborate cat-and-mouse game? Why the extended hiding of his identity, despite the evident strain it causes Joseph himself and the stress not only

Copyright © 2009 Pearson Education, Inc. Publishing as Longman.

on his brothers but also on his aged father? For all the care the brothers take of their grieving father, it should be recalled that it was Jacob's own preferential treatment of his young son that set the whole drama in motion; in a nice touch, Joseph himself is discomfited when the aged Jacob goes and does it yet again at the end of the story, blessing Joseph's younger son Ephraim—an ancestor of King David—over the first-born Manasseh (Chapter 48). Old patterns are carrying on here, as Jacob himself, with his mother's help, had snatched the blessing that his blind, aged father had intended for his older brother Esau (Genesis 27). Yet an unexpressed desire for revenge is only one explanation for Joseph's behavior; insofar as he is God's agent (as he has told Pharaoh, in a rare moment of modesty), Joseph's mysterious, testy, testing behavior resembles God's typical treatment of his chosen but all too humanly flawed people, and the triumph of younger sons resonates with Israel's election by God over the older cultures of Egypt and Mesopotamia.

Finally, the Egyptian setting of the story is constantly apparent. It is fitting that when Joseph goes to Egypt, he soon finds himself reliving an Egyptian tale, with Potiphar's wife attempting seduction and charging rape just as Bata's sister-in-law had done in "The Two Brothers." Joseph can usefully be compared to Bata, also a figure of divine testing and ultimate favor, to see how the story is adapted to a monotheistic context, and one in which individual reincarnation is superseded by personal growth and by patterned variation across generations. More generally, Egypt is a place both of attraction and of danger. The danger is always twofold: the immigrant may never really be at home, always a suspicious outsider ("like a stray bull in a strange herd," as Sinuhe puts it); or, worse still, the immigrants may assimilate so fully as to lose their own identity. This is a constant temptation for the Hebrews, living among numbers of polytheistic groups in Canaan itself, and culturally and economically overshadowed by the great imperial powers of Egypt, Mesopotamia, and Persia (and, later, Macedonia and Rome). Both sides of this dilemma are seen in Joseph's case. We are twice told that the Hebrews are made to keep their distance from the Egyptians: "Egyptians could not eat with Hebrews, for that is detestable to Egyptians" (p. 169); when they settle in Egypt, the Hebrews must live apart, "for all shepherds are detestable to the Egyptians" (p. 173). Yet Joseph's success in Egypt, conversely, is fraught as well. He is given an Egyptian name and married to an important priest's daughter, surely a doubly problematic situation in the Hebrew Bible, where marrying outside the ethnic group is often the first step toward falling away from God. Here the wife is the daughter of the Sun god, no less! In a telling detail, when Joseph brings his father home to bury him, the local Canaanites name the site Abel Mizraim, "the Egyptians' Mourning"—they think Joseph *is* Egyptian.

Joseph's rise to power in Egypt comes at the expense of the Egyptian people themselves: step by step, as the famine progresses, he sells the Egyptians the grain he has saved up, in exchange for their money, then their livestock, and finally "all the land in Egypt": "The land became Pharaoh's, and Joseph reduced

Copyright © 2009 Pearson Education, Inc. Publishing as Longman.

the people to servitude, from one end of Egypt to the other" (p. 174). On a purely historical level, this tale explores the feudal Egyptian system, strange to the Hebrews, in which the king owned the land and granted its use to his nobility. Yet the emphasis here lies on Joseph's actions in reducing the people to "servitude," an action that will come back to haunt his descendants soon after his death, when "there arose a new king over Egypt, who did not know Joseph" (Exodus 1:8). The new pharaoh enslaves the Hebrews in turn, making their lives "bitter with hard service, in mortar and brick, and in all kinds of work in the field" (Exodus 1:8–14). God's saving activity is constantly at work in the Joseph Story as in the Bible overall, yet the biblical writers set God's work in a human context of always flawed individuals and constant cultural pressures. Strangers in a strange land, the Hebrews must survive the opposed pressures of assimilation and rejection, just as they must navigate the troubled waters of love and jealousy within every family.

The Book of Ruth

The Book of Ruth closes this Perspectives section with a tale of migration, loss, and loyalty from a woman's perspective, seen in the intertwined story of Ruth and her mother-in-law, Naomi. This story is particularly interesting to read alongside the Joseph Story, to which it directly refers in comparing Ruth to Tamar (p. 182, referring back to the episode of Judah and Tamar, Genesis 38, p. 162). Though the Book of Ruth asserts their similarity, the point of this story is actually quite different: to make a case in favor of marriage between Hebrews and non-Hebrews. So often a cause for concern in earlier biblical literature, the issue of exogamous marriage became a subject of intense debate upon the return of the Hebrews from exile in Babylon in and after 538 B.C.E. The exile had not actually involved the entire Hebrew people but the upper stratum of society, brought to Babylon to keep them under control; many peasants and shepherds were evidently left in place during the period of exile. While in exile, religion was a prime bonding force for the displaced Hebrews, but those left behind, deprived of their priestly and secular leaders, began in many instances to shade into the broader, polytheistic culture, often as a result of intermarriage.

In the decades following their return, the exiles reinstated and strengthened the worship of Yahweh, and the prophetic leaders Ezra and Nehemiah promulgated laws forbidding intermarriage and ordering Israelites to divorce foreign wives. As we are told in the book of Ezra:

> While Ezra prayed and made confession, weeping and casting himself down before the house of God, a very great assembly of men, women, and children, gathered to him out of Israel; for the people wept bitterly. And Shecaniah the son of Jehiel, of the sons of Elam, addressed Ezra:

Copyright © 2009 Pearson Education, Inc. Publishing as Longman.

"We have broken faith with our God and have married foreign women from the peoples of the land, but even now there is hope for Israel in spite of this. Therefore let us make a covenant with our God to put away all these wives and their children, according to the counsel of my lord and of those who tremble at the commandment of our God; and let it be done according to the law." (Ezra 10:1–3)

A parallel account in the book of Nehemiah specifically names "women of Ashdod, Ammon, and Moab" who had married Hebrew men, adding that half their children could no longer even speak Hebrew (Nehemiah 13:23–24). This is evidently the context within which the Book of Ruth was written, to assert the cause of a Moabite spouse who was not at all an agent of assimilation but instead was the creator of continuity for the Hebrew people, becoming a direct ancestress of no less a figure than King David.

As in the Joseph Story, doublings serve as an important narrative device. You should ask students to consider why Naomi has two daughters-in-law rather than one, since Ruth alone figures in an active way. Here as often, the doubling dramatizes levels of intensity: the other daughter-in-law, Orpah, at first intends to go with Naomi to Judah, but finally the pull of her homeland is too great, and she stays behind—as Naomi herself fully expects and even urges her to do. It should be pointed out that the attractions of home are shown to be religious as well as familial: she is "going back to her people and her gods" (p. 179). Ruth's devotion—to Naomi, and to Yahweh—is thereby set in relief, and it extends through life and into death itself. Students who have seen Sinuhe's and Joseph's longing to be buried in their homeland will be in a position to understand the force of Ruth's devotion: "Where you die I will die, and there I will be buried" (p. 179).

A further doubling occurs with Boaz's sly upstaging of his kinsman's claim to Ruth, first presenting a simple property transaction that the kinsman is quite willing to undertake, then pointing up the human consequences: a woman comes with the land (Chapter 4). Here again, the message is directed to the writers' audience as much as to the kinsman in the story.

The Book of Ruth turns the tables on the Israelites' own experience as strangers in a strange land, reversing the focus on gender as part of the process, so that we see the story through women's eyes, rather than through male protagonists as usual. The foreign Kingdom of Judah becomes a new and better homeland for Ruth, as it was for the returned Hebrew exiles themselves, almost all of whom would have been born in Babylon during the seventy years of exile. In a final doubling, Ruth is compared in the story's climax not only to Tamar but also to the (again doubled) earlier matriarchs Rachel and Leah, the wives of Jacob, whose sons founded the twelve tribes of Israel, just as Ruth's own son will become the grandfather of King David, the greatest of Israel's kings. Through all these doublings and reversals a seemingly artless tale layers history and expands the boundaries of gender and ethnic identity, to welcome an unexpected stranger into the Promised Land.

Copyright © 2009 Pearson Education, Inc. Publishing as Longman.

Classical Greece

Many students who come to a world literature course will have some idea about ancient Greek and Roman civilization, based on video games, television series, and popular live-action or animated movies centering on such classical figures as Hercules or the gladiator. (One issue to clarify from the start is that there is a very great variety of spellings of classical Greek names, depending on whether or not the translator uses a Romanized form of a Greek name, such as the Latin Ulysses for the Greek Odysseus, or a Roman alphabet approximation of the Greek spelling. Students will probably recognize Hercules but not Herakles.) Students' interest in mythology, even though it may be detached from literature and history, can also draw them into engagement with the questions that preoccupied the ancient Greeks, questions of heroism, of war and peace, of men and women, and of political organizations that might promote human happiness.

Some students will have a sense of what was once upon a time considered the Greek "miracle," the origin of Western civilization among the Greeks. Others may find the origins of the West in the Hebraic-Hellenic fusion. Recent scholarship and this *Anthology* have sought to amplify the mythic nature of such a story of origins and the need to broaden our sense of the complex, multiple beginnings of human civilization throughout the world. Greco-Roman civilization can profitably be seen to be enormously indebted to all the cultures of the Mediterranean basin and beyond. For example, the story of the Flood, so important in the Hebrew Bible, occurs in the Epic of Gilgamesh as well as in stories of Manu, which may look back to Indus valley civilization and precede the culture of the Vedas in India. It also finds its resonances in the flooding of the Nile in Egypt. The Greeks and Romans, although they did not live near great flooding rivers, were influenced by their neighbors' experiences of the Nile, the Tigris and the Euphrates, and the Indus. This contact is registered in one of the origin myths of the Greeks in which, after a great flood, Deucalion and Pyrrha repopulate the earth by "throwing the bones of their mother," that is, the stones of the earth, over their shoulders; the stones become men and women.

Although the Greeks did develop such important institutions as democracy, philosophy, and tragedy, institutions that survive in radically transformed ways throughout the world, they did so in specific historical and geographical circumstances. To understand those circumstances is to understand more fully the ways in which civilizations throughout the world respond to one another as they develop. Greek democracy in Athens, for example, evolved in relation to pressures

Copyright © 2009 Pearson Education, Inc. Publishing as Longman.

from landless citizens and from newly energized rowers in the fleet, who received payment from the Athenian wealth derived from silver mines. And although democracy included all male citizens, it excluded women, Greeks from other cities, all foreigners resident in the city, and slaves. It was a specific institution evolved in specific historical circumstances, and often what later readers consider to be Greek "literature" is in fact polemical intervention in conflicts about who belongs, who does not, in the politics of the city. Consideration of the specificity of Greek democracy can lead to interesting discussion about the nature of democracy in the abstract, other historical examples of democracy, and the role of narrative, dramatic, and historical texts within democracies.

Thus a question that arises is the degree to which we can think of these texts as "literature." Many of them were produced in contexts very distant from today's literary market, with its single authors, huge publishing houses, best sellers, and printed texts. Some works of the Greeks, like the dramas, tragedies, and comedies, formed part of the political and religious life of the *polis*, the ancient city, and are more like political and religious spectacles than plays performed on proscenium stages on Broadway. The wavering distinction between oral and literate composition also marks a difference between our notions of the literary and those held in the ancient past. In fact, some of the genres dearest to postmodernism (e.g., cinema) may offer better analogies to ancient modes of composition than the image of a single author laboring over a manuscript in her or his study. The spontaneous composition of rap and hip-hop in performance are more like ancient bardic oral composition than like Frank Sinatra's singing "My Way." Ancient epic is a genre perhaps formed through accretion, through many generations of composers, often nameless, all telling and retelling familiar stories, not only drawing on traditions indigenous to the Greeks themselves but also owing a great deal to narratives of neighboring peoples.

Polytheism is another issue that sometimes troubles students and provokes discussion. Greek polytheism is not serial monotheism. It may be useful to compare it to the worship of the saints in Christianity. It is important to resist the notion that the natural, inevitable, and superior form of religious worship is monotheism and instead to open up students' imaginations to the possibility that polytheism has its merits and is indeed still practiced in the modern world. Polytheism leaves its mark everywhere on ancient Greek "literary" texts; the quarrels of the gods in the *Iliad* and the *Odyssey*, for example, call into question the notion students sometimes have of a fixed and absolute fate that governs human beings' existence in the ancient world.

The role of fate in ancient societies is another issue that often troubles contemporary students. They sometimes see ancient people as living in a world in which all has already been decided, in which human beings have no independence of action and behave like the gods' puppets. In fact, the question of fate is a difficult one, with a variety of interpretations among ancient thinkers. In Athens in the classical age, some intellectual called into doubt the gods themselves and their capacity to affect the lives of human beings. In general, teaching

Copyright © 2009 Pearson Education, Inc. Publishing as Longman.

the conflicts and debates that energized ancient people calls forth exciting discussion among students. Sophocles, for example, seems concerned about his fellow citizens doubting fate and may have been responding to critiques of more orthodox believers lodged by such philosophical types as the sophists. In *Oedipus Rex*, Jocasta says:

> Why should man fear since chance is all in all
> for him, and he can clearly foreknow nothing?
> Best to live lightly, as one can, unthinkingly. (lines 1041–1043)

Jocasta is expressing not the last word on the question for the ancient audience but rather a position of skepticism that Sophocles' play answers by calling down a terrible fate upon Oedipus. Sophocles' view is obviously generated in a context of debate, of the questioning of traditional values, a situation in which students often find themselves. A discussion of such issues turns the Greeks into three-dimensional human beings, rather than automata governed by omniscient gods. Among those conflicts that persist in classical Greek literature are conflicts between man and woman, between human beings and the gods, between aristocrats and the people, between kings or tyrants and their subjects, between pleasure and profit, between the Greeks and their barbarians, those others who surrounded them and from whom they learned so much.

The most important thing to communicate is the historicity of the Greeks themselves. They are not a static thing, "the Greeks," with a static set of beliefs and practices. They changed and developed over time, and they argued their way through that time, engaged in constant polemic about how to live. *Logos* (at the root of our words *logic, biology, logocentric, dialogue, dialectic*) means "word, reason, account." The men of this society kept talking, arguing, conversing, and it is their conflicts, expressed in words, that we have. We can use these to open up their culture to view and to draw students into debate, argument, and criticism about this world that precedes their own.

Another issue that can prove troublesome for some students is the distance between some Greeks' ideas of public propriety and their own. Some works of art and some literary texts rejoice in a frankness about human bodies and their pleasures and functions that can shock some students and delight others. It may be best simply to make it clear that for the Greeks speaking of such things in public was not considered obscene or even especially provocative, that their ideas about decorum, as about many things, differ from ours, and that their culture is not therefore necessarily inferior to our own. So, you might emphasize connections between the Greeks and the rest of the ancient Mediterranean world, rather than a "Greek miracle," highlight debate among the Greeks rather than "the Greeks" as monolith, and present the history of Greek literature as not "literary" in a post-Romantic sense, but rather as a series of engagements, interventions in all sorts of debates about gods, politics, social life, human existence, and a variety of questions that still consume us in the present.

Copyright © 2009 Pearson Education, Inc. Publishing as Longman.

The Greeks gave names to many of the literary genres that survive into the present and gave us the words *poetry*, *tragedy*, *epic*, *lyric*, and *history*. The Greeks may draw on neighboring cultures for their production of these texts, as the poet Hesiod in his didactic poetry drew on ancient Mesopotamian narratives. They practiced and then also formulated theory concerning their practices, as in the works of Plato and Aristotle. The ideas of tragedy and the tragic, for instance, persist long after the writing of Greek drama. Watching films that stage Greek tragedies is one way of making these issues more vivid for some students; to be recommended especially, and valuable for the tragedies in this volume of the *Anthology*, are Cacoyannis's *Iphigeneia* and Pasolini's *Oedipus* and *Medea*. An excellent source of images, maps, site maps, and other materials can be found through the Perseus Project at Tufts University: http://www.perseus.tufts.edu.

Homer

In terms of the literary questions, students might be led to think about the relations among the epics in the *Anthology* and about "authorship," with its connotations of individual expression, private property, and copyright; such notions are foreign to these early texts. They are often stories of war, linking great families to the gods and considering the place of war in civilization and in definitions of communities. "Homer" is not a man but rather a name for generations of singers whose collective memory stretches back to the fall of a great city. Discussion can focus on how communities define themselves in relation to enemies, how internal hierarchies are established and negotiated, how such communities deal with envy and rivalry, how they experience loss and death of community members. For the Greeks, Homer's work became a sort of treasure trove of rhetorical moves, of ethical ideas, of examples of heroism and cowardice. The tragedies return again and again to the matrix of these stories, known to all, to explore questions that changed as the city developed into a city-state. One of the issues for the classical period is how relevant the old truths of the Homeric poems can be for the changed circumstances of democratic citizens. This too is an issue that can stimulate debate among students in the twenty-first century.

The *Iliad*

Teaching the *Iliad* might begin with a close reading of the very first lines, which establish the themes of the wrath of Achilles, the will of Zeus, and the conflict between Achilles and Agamemnon. (Lattimore's translation names the hero "Achilleus," in a closer approximation of the Greek than the more usual English rendering "Achilles.") The question of fate, then, is already set in motion, without a simple closure; at work are conflicting forces: the emotion of the hero, the god's plan, and disorder between the leaders of the Greek army. The *Iliad* begins with a plague and ends with a funeral. It thus moves from one kind of loss to a consola-

Copyright © 2009 Pearson Education, Inc. Publishing as Longman.

tion for another loss. In the first lines, Apollo has driven a "foul pestilence along the host" (1.10), and men are dying. At the end of the poem stands the funeral of Hektor, "breaker of horses."

The *Iliad* is extraordinary in its treatment of Trojans with Greeks, rather than as barbarians, as the later Greeks would call foreigners. The residents of the Asian city of Troy speak the same language as the Greek invaders, have the same customs (with a few deviations), and are treated with compassion for their suffering. The funeral that ends the *Iliad* is celebrated for Hektor, Trojan hero, and in some sense stands for all the funerals, all the losses of the poem: the plague dead; the many heroes killed in battle; Patroklos, friend of Achilles, whose death eventually plunges Achilles back into the fray; and Achilles himself, who dies not in this poem but later in the legend of Troy when he is killed by an arrow shot from Paris's bow.

Cedric Whitman described the *Iliad* as having a "ring-form"; the larger pattern of deaths and funerals framing the beginning and end echoes throughout the poem with an ABCCBA sort of rhythm. This may have been a mnemonic device for the singing poets. It is one of the great beauties of the *Iliad*, allowing it to move out and then return to its themes of war and loss. The great overarching story of the *Iliad* is that of the hero's withdrawal from battle and his return, a narrative pattern in other epics and in the story of Meleager, told in Book 9 of the poem. Meleager, like Achilles, receives ambassadors who beg him to return to battle. Only the last supplicant succeeds; in Meleager's case, it is his wife. Achilles relents, briefly, when his beloved Patroklos begs him and then finally when Patroklos is killed.

One way to organize the teaching of the poem is to focus on some of its central themes and figures, as discussed in the following subsections.

Achilles

Achilles is the son of a goddess wedded to a mortal so that Zeus could avoid fathering a son with her who would be greater than his father. The wedding of Peleus and Thetis, which all the gods attended, appears on the famous François vase. The portrait of Achilles emerges in contrast to that of Agamemnon; they struggle for domination over the Achaians. Agamemnon appears haughty and arrogant at times, convinced of his pre-eminence, while Achilles insists that his martial prowess should guarantee him status. When Agamemnon takes Achilles' prize, Briseis, Achilles insults Agamemnon and threatens violence. This is a world in which the institutions of the jury trial, for example, have not yet been developed, in which an eye for an eye, blood payment, feuds, and quick violence still reign, where power involves as much an entourage and weapons as economic might, and here too we find analogies in popular music and its culture in the twenty-first century. The difference is that Achilles is not an outlaw but a prince, struggling with another nobleman for domination over an army in which there is a crisis of legitimacy.

Achilles is shown as quick to react and easily offended; he refuses to be shamed by Agamemnon. This is not a world of guilt, in which the characters contain inner lives governed by notions of virtue. Public opinion has immense impact on these heroes, who seek to preserve their followers and their own domination

Copyright © 2009 Pearson Education, Inc. Publishing as Longman.

through harsh words and blows. Yet the tenderness of Achilles arises in relation to his comrade Patroklos, who comes in supplication to Achilles in Book 16, begging him that if he will not recover from his rage, from his withdrawal from the battle, then he will allow Patroklos to fight back in Achilles' armor.

The scene of Patroklos' arming in Book 16 illustrates the formulaic quality of such moments: Patroklos, like all the heroes, first puts on the greaves, or ankle guards, then the corselet for his chest, then the sword, after the shield, and then the "well-fashioned helmet." Then he takes up two powerful spears, mounts his chariot, and goes to his death, in a terrible duel, at the hands of Hektor. The formulaic arming of the hero, with a set sequence in which he dons the various pieces of his weaponry, occurs throughout the *Iliad*, becomes a feature of later epic poetry, and is echoed in the disarming of the hero Marko in the nineteenth-century heroic Serbian song of Kraljevic Marko.

Finally, Achilles, enraged at the death of his comrade and companion, chooses a short, glorious life, marked eternally by fame, over long-lived obscurity. He arms himself in the glorious, divine armor made for him by the god Hephaistos. At times Achilles himself resembles a divinity. He receives the armor made by Hephaistos at his mother's request and participates in battle like a god. He is compared to a force of nature throughout his rush of slaughter, the *aristeia*, of Book 22. He is like fire, like a frenzied god, and he clogs the Trojan river with his victims. The poet sings: "He killed in a blur of kills" (21.235). His enemies beg for mercy, but he is merciless, and he battles the river itself like something beyond a human being. The battle recalls Mesopotamian clashes between the gods, great forces of salt and sweet water, and here draws the Olympian gods into quarrels with each other, as Hera and Artemis fight. Hektor comes out to meet him, to defend Troy; Achilles comes "in full shining, like that star / which comes on in the autumn and whose conspicuous brightness / far outshines the stars that are numbered in the night's darkening" (22.26–28). With the gods on his side, who trick Hektor, Achilles is invincible.

Hektor

The hero Hektor offers another sort of contrast to Achilles. Not only a great warrior, he also is shown at home at Troy, with his brothers and parents and his beloved wife Andromache, herself a war captive. When Hektor goes back to the city after a day of battle, he finds his wife and his son Astyanax, later thrown from the ramparts by the victorious Greeks. He imagines the day when Troy will fall and Andromache will be taken captive:

> it is less the pain of the Trojans still to come . . .
> that is nothing, nothing beside your agony
> when some brazen Argive hales you off in tears,
> wrenching away your day of light and freedom! (6.534–541)

He pictures his wife a slave at the hands of some victor, who will say: "There is the wife of Hektor, the bravest fighter /they could field, those stallion-breaking

Copyright © 2009 Pearson Education, Inc. Publishing as Longman.

Trojans, / long ago when the men fought for Troy" (6.548-550). His son Astyanax, frightened by the father's crested helmet, screams and cries, and Hektor takes off his helmet and lifts his son in the air and kisses him. Later Hektor runs from Achilles and seals the fate of his loved ones. In death, Hektor is protected from corruption, but his wife and family mourn until his body is returned, in the great consolation book at the end of the poem, to his grieving father.

Rhetoric

Logos, the word, so important later in Greek culture, appears first here and is apparent in sometimes elaborate speeches delivered by warriors, kings, heralds, and priests. There are vaunting speeches, elaborate boasts that are meant to destroy opposition and guarantee the respect of enemy and assembly. There are also speeches of persuasion, like that of Odysseus in Book 9, who comes with others to convince Achilles, withdrawn from battle, to return. Odysseus speaks with eloquence of the need for the hero to fight again and offers him rewards, trophies, seven women from Lesbos, the woman Agamemnon first took from Achilles, untouched, along with twenty Trojan women when the Greeks defeat the Trojans, and Agamemnon's daughter, along with a dowry, and seven citadels more. Achilles responds with rage and denounces the rhetorical elegancies of Odysseus's speech:

> I hate that man like the very Gates of Death
> who says one thing but hides another in his heart.

These two positions—elaborate, cultivated speech versus blunt, martial candor—come to define an opposition developed further in Greek society between the political, educated speakers of the city and the taciturn warrior heroes. The differences in style become an issue not only for Greek political debate but also for the history of rhetoric that follows.

Similes

The Homeric simile is a characteristic feature of the epic poems, inherited by later epic poets. The similes often remove the listener from the blood-stained battlefield and remind him or her of the rhythms of nature or of a sometimes violent pastoral or artisanal world that sets the war in perspective. The blood from Menelaus's wound in Book 4 is compared to the purple with which an artisan colors ivory. When in Book 5 Aeneas kills twin Greek brothers, the poem compares them to wild animals:

> Fresh as two young lions off on the mountain ridges,
> Twins reared by a lioness deep in the dark glades,
> That ravage shepherds' steadings, mauling the cattle
> And fat sheep till it's their turn to die—hacked down
> By the cleaving bronze blades in the shepherds' hands.
> So here the twins were laid low at Aeneas' hands,
> Down they crashed like lofty pine trees axed.

Copyright © 2009 Pearson Education, Inc. Publishing as Longman.

This is the same Aeneas who later founds Rome, after the fall of Troy, which Virgil in his *Aeneid*, in an epic simile, describes as a great ash tree crashing to the ground. Aeneas recalls the fall:

> Neptune's Troy is overturned: even as when the woodsmen
> along a mountaintop are rivals in
> their striving to bring down an ancient ash
> hacked at with many blows of iron and ax;
>
> . . .
>
> it gives one last great groan, then wrenches from the ridges
> and crashes into ruin.
> (*Aeneid*, 2.844–853, trans. A. Mandelbaum)

Just to follow similes concerning trees leads to the comparison of a fallen warrior, Simoeisios, in *Iliad* Book 4, who "dropped then to the ground in the dust, like some black poplar," and this famous simile that in a flourish of rhetoric compares human generations to the leaves of a tree. The hero Diomedes speaks to his enemy Glaucus:

> Like the generations of leaves, the lives of mortal men.
> Now the wind scatters the old leaves across the earth,
> now the living timber bursts with the new buds
> and spring comes round again. And so with men:
> as one generation comes to life, another dies away. (*Iliad* 6.171–175)

Similes bring the world of animals, wild and domesticated, of labor, farming, and artistry into the scene of battle; they both locate the struggles of warriors and distinguish them from other human and natural processes. Tracing a particular kind of simile can illuminate war and peace in the Homeric universe.

The Gods

The gods of the *Iliad* are not monolithic, and they do not represent "fate" in any simple way. In the poem's preamble, the song refers to the "will of Zeus" (line 5), but this is a will, a plan developed in time, and it conflicts with other divine wills. The gods take sides in this great conflict, for a variety of complex and sometimes mysterious reasons having to do with traditional worship, perhaps, in various localities of the Greek world. Athena, for example, is a strong partisan of Odysseus and the Greeks, to the extent of tricking Hektor into his death, while Hera, a great enemy of the Trojans, seduces Zeus to distract him from the battlefield and let the Greek forces threaten the city of Troy for a time. Tracing the gods' loyalties and affiliations with various heroes and various sides of the conflict can demonstrate how complex and multivalent polytheism is, and how fate, even though Zeus decides, arrives through a circuitous route. Even Zeus's own dear son, Sarpedon, dies in bat-

Copyright © 2009 Pearson Education, Inc. Publishing as Longman.

tle in Book 16, in a heart-wrenching scene recorded in a famous vase now in the Metropolitan Museum of Art, showing Sleep and Death carrying off the corpse of the beautiful young man, and Hermes ready to guide him to the underworld.

Women in the Poem

The mortal women of the *Iliad* serve almost as precious objects, exchanged and fought over by heroes. Chryseis and Briseis provide the reason for the quarrel between Agamemnon and Achilles. These women serve as war prizes; others are links between great aristocratic families. Helen, stolen from her husband, serves as the ostensible reason for the assault on Troy, and she appears in several scenes lamenting her status as a victim, manipulated by Aphrodite. These women wait, and their fates are decided by conflicts engaged in by the warriors who possess them.

The goddesses, on the other hand, often act with independence. Although ultimately subordinate to Zeus, they have their own favorites and engage in the events of battle, in debates on Olympus, and even in deceiving Zeus in favor of the fall of Troy. Thetis, mother of Achilles, is represented poignantly as the immortal mother of a mortal son, who does all she can to protect him, from supplicating Zeus to providing Achilles with supernatural armor.

The Shield

The shield of Achilles is an extraordinary work of art, produced by the divine artisan Hephaistos, who shares those powers, closely guarded and observed with admiration and amazement and some fear, of the metal workers of the ancient world, who could take stones and earth, make them liquid, and create weapons and works of art. Like Ptah, the creator of the world in Egyptian theology, and other creator gods, Hephaistos makes a world through his divine art. The shield magically shows the earth, encircled by the Ocean River, makes sounds, contains scenes like those of the battlefield of the *Iliad* and its similes, and also sets forth two kinds of city, one in which elders settle conflict and another besieged by an army, beset by Strife and Havoc. The maker of the shield thus sets the situation of the whole poem within this microcosm, later called an *ekphrasis*, a rhetorical figure, the verbal description of a work of visual art. The poem here also alludes to poetry, songs, dancing, and celebration, alternatives to the slaughter of war. Like the similes, the *ekphrasis* becomes a *topos*, a commonplace of the epic genre. It also appears in such poems as Keats's "Ode on a Grecian Urn," which calls attention to the paradoxes of movement and stasis in this rhetorical figure.

Consolation

The poem ends with the magnificent book of consolation, in which Priam travels to Achilles' tent, like a supplicant visiting the god of the dead, to retrieve his son, dead but not disfigured by the abuse inflicted on the corpse by Achilles. Like the World War I soldiers who crossed battle lines to celebrate Christmas together and then returned to killing, Achilles and Priam find a way to console one another in an interval out of time. The scene is fraught with danger and risk, yet Achilles re-

Copyright © 2009 Pearson Education, Inc. Publishing as Longman.

calls Niobe, who lost all her children, and who finally consumed food, after grieving. So the enemies Priam and Achilles, each of whom has lost so much at the
other's hand, eat together and admire one another in a meeting without parallel.

The Fall of the City

The fall of Troy became emblematic for ancient Greeks and Romans of the end
of civilization. In ancient civic life, ceremonies marked the foundation of a city.
Priests ploughed around its boundaries, and ancient cities were fortified, walled,
and protected by gates and towers at their entry points. The city was differenti-
ated from wilderness, from nonhuman space; it had a sacred quality, and analogies were made to rape and violation when the walls of a city were breached. Troy
had special qualities, having been founded in a manner that boded ill for its survival. According to legend, the king Laomedon had hired two laborers to build
Troy and then failed to pay them for their work. They were, unbeknownst to him,
the gods Apollo and Poseidon; thus the city had a tainted foundation.
Nonetheless, Troy's fall came to represent an end to order, the order of sover-
eignty, hierarchy, worship of the gods, protection of women and children, and all
that was valued in human accomplishment.

Especially in an age of terrorism and the effective destruction of buildings,
order, and institutions by enemies, students can appreciate the ways in which the
myth of Troy attempts to come to terms with violent ends. Although the fall of Troy
is not represented in the *Iliad*, it is assumed. All listeners knew the legend of the great
city, its king with his fifty sons and fifty daughters, and its wealth. The fall of the city,
inevitable yet deferred, colors the narrative of the *Iliad*. The scenes of Hektor and
Andromache, of Helen and Paris, domestic tranquility menaced by the invading
army of the Greeks, have an elegiac, poignant quality because of the inevitable sense
of imminent destruction. For the Greeks, there was no replacing Troy. The invasion
of Athens by the Persians at the beginning of the fifth century B.C.E., when the
Acropolis itself, site of a great Athena temple, was burned along with its votive stat-
ues, takes on cultural weight when juxtaposed to the fall of the Trojans' city.

RESONANCE

Filip Višnjić

The Homeric themes associated with the hero and his armor and arming persist
in this selection of Serbian oral epic poetry; Marko faces his destiny. As the
Homeric hero puts on his armor, in a formulaic pattern that recurs, here Marko
disarms, drawing his saber, beheading his horse, breaking his saber, smashing his
lance, casting his mace into the sea. Like the *Iliad*, this selection ends with the burial of a hero, this time in an unmarked grave.

Copyright © 2009 Pearson Education, Inc. Publishing as Longman.

The *Odyssey*

It may be useful to compare the *Odyssey* not only with the *Iliad* but also with other epic narratives of the ancient world, like the *Ramayana* and the *Epic of Gilgamesh*. The poems of the journey, especially to the land of the dead, yield many points of comparison. The *Iliad* represents a striking contrast with the *Odyssey*, since with the exception of the similes and the episodes on Mount Olympus, the *Iliad* takes place entirely on the narrow strand before Troy. The *Odyssey* roams over the entire Mediterranean, touching on societies both known and imagined by the Greeks. The first lines of the poem, like the *Iliad*'s, establish the themes that will be addressed in the course of the narrative. Odysseus is a man of many sorrows, and he is at the center of the poem for most of its length. If the poet of the *Iliad* begins with the wrath of Achilles, the singer of the *Odyssey* starts with "the man," "the man of twists and turns" (1.1). He is wily, twisting, much traveled, a man who finds his way back home only through an elaborate and devious path that echoes the structure of the poem itself. He is a man not of wrath, not quick to anger, but rather a man of wide experience and knowledge: "Many cities of men he saw and learned their minds" (1.4). As Odysseus experiences the variety of beings that inhabit the world his journey maps, so do his listeners come to know the extent, and the limits, of the human.

Scholars differ about which of the Homeric epics came first, but in the world of oral composition, this may be a question the answer to which is without consequence. Nonetheless, the *Odyssey* seems to acknowledge the existence of the *Iliad* story more frequently than vice versa. The Sirens who sing in Book 12 remind the listening Odysseus, the only sailor who can hear them, of the events surrounding the fall of Troy:

> Never has any sailor passed our shores in his black craft
> until he has heard the honeyed voices pouring from our lips,
> and once he hears to his heart's content sails on, a wiser man.
> We know all the pains that the Greeks and Trojans once endured
> on the spreading plains of Troy when the gods willed it so—
> all that comes to pass on the fertile earth, we know it all! (12.202–207)

Circe has warned him of the dangers of this song, so like the epic poems themselves. The Sirens sing, "round them heaps of corpses / rotting away, rags of skin shriveling on their bones" (12.51–52). Odysseus succeeds in passing by the temptations of their song, a self-reflexive warning, perhaps, about the seductions of art and beauty, and a warning that only the most elite of passers-by, the well-defended Odysseus, can survive; Max Horkheimer and Theodor Adorno in *The Dialectic of Enlightenment* later made this scene an emblem of the dangers of enlightenment. The scene of Telemachus's visit to Menelaus and Helen in Sparta also calls up the memory of the Trojan city; Helen, the unfaithful wife, like Clytaemestra, is contrasted in the poem with Penelope, faithful for twenty years to the absent Odysseus.

Copyright © 2009 Pearson Education, Inc. Publishing as Longman.

The *Odyssey* is a poem of *nostos*, return, like other lost poems of the epic cycle, concerning not the return to battle of a hero like Achilles but rather the return of the various heroes to their homelands scattered over the whole of the Greek world. Other such narratives are hinted at in the *Odyssey*, for example, in Menelaus's account of his journey back to Sparta in Book 4 (p. 301), which involves wrestling with the god Proteus on the sands of Egypt.

The *Odyssey* can be divided roughly into three sections: the first part, on the situation in Ithaca and Telemachus's journey; the second, Odysseus's account of his own journey, with the trip to the dead at its heart; and the third, Odysseus's return to Ithaca and his eventual confrontation with the suitors. The poem includes not only an elaborate framing of Odysseus's own narrative of his wanderings but also a coming-of-age story, sometimes called the "Telemacheia" for the younger hero Telemachus, who serves as a representative of youth, as Odysseus's father Laertes, withdrawn to his orchard and no longer a potent leader of his people, limns the elder. The void at the center, in Ithaca, has been valiantly overseen by Penelope, who has attempted to preserve Odysseus's *oikos*, his household and domain, for the absent hero. So the life cycle of the male human being, the story of the hero's return to Ithaca, frames his story of his encounters with the multiple and extraordinary denizens of many different societies or polities.

Varieties of Beings

Scholars have discussed the anthropological nature of Odysseus's wanderings, the ways in which his journey maps the Mediterranean world for an audience that is in the process of exploration and colonization that will extend Greek mercantile power far beyond the Greek mainland. Odysseus encounters monsters and creatures, divine and subhuman, and societies organized differently from his own, including the violent Cicones and the lotus eaters, who offer oblivion. One of the most fully elaborated is the society of the Cyclops, who represent a prepolitical, precultural, precivilized, and therefore monstrous form of community. They know nothing of agriculture or councils or laws, marks for the Greeks of a civilized society. The Cyclops Polyphemos himself eats raw human beings and drinks undiluted wine, two signs of underdevelopment. It is here that Odysseus makes the mistake of revealing his name; after cunningly calling himself Nobody, he falls prey to a desire for fame, for recognition in his brilliant escape from being devoured by the Cyclops. Naming himself brings new pains and guarantees his further suffering at the hands of the Cyclops' father, Poseidon. Odysseus suffers through the encounter with the giant Laestrygonians, like Gulliver later, avoids metamorphosis and entrapment at the hands of Circe, and survives a journey to the dead.

It is in the society of the Phaeacians that Odysseus tells his story, brought to say his name by the bard's song of the wooden horse at Troy. Odysseus weeps as he remembers, "as a woman weeps" whose city has fallen, as she is dragged off into bondage (8.588). In the simile, he takes the place of a woman such as

Copyright © 2009 Pearson Education, Inc. Publishing as Longman.

Andromache, Hektor's wife, who is enslaved at the fall of Troy, a scene that later becomes a favorite of Greek tragedies, especially those of Euripides. After weeping, Odysseus speaks his name, which is etymologically connected to the word for "pain" in Greek; he is the man of pain, and he recounts his stories of pain. The society of the Phaeacians resembles a paradise; the garden of Alcinous (or Alkinoos), described in Book 7, is like a garden of Eden, with its endless bounty. Yet, although the Phaeacians have no enemies and Odysseus could live there as the fortunate husband of Nausicaa, who is likened to the goddess Artemis, he chooses mortality and Penelope once more.

Noteworthy is the fact that many of the most threatening of monsters, including the Sirens, Scylla, and Charybdis, share with the women of the poem like Calypso and Circe a threat to the hero's mobility. Odysseus must keep moving, must encounter all these varieties of threat and difference, finally to return home. Unlike his comrades, he is able to resist the temptations of lotus eaters and Sirens and the cattle of the Sun; he is enabled to resist the transformative power of Circe, the immortality offered by Calypso, the tempting marriage with Nausicaa.

Descent

The descent of Odysseus to the underworld, Book 11, is at the heart of the poem. Some scholars have connected the *nostos*, the return of the hero, with *nous*, or mind, in Greek. The hero must encounter darkness and death and return to the land of the living and to light, to consciousness. Like Aeneas, Jesus, and the Dante of the *Divine Comedy*, Odysseus enters the land of the dead and emerges still living. He comes to terms with his own mortality in the prophesy of Tiresias and must accept the death of his own mother, who died yearning for him. He encounters Agamemnon, the heroic figure most persistently evoked in contrast to Odysseus himself, a man who was killed by the lover of his unfaithful wife on his return from Troy: "she, that whore, she turned her back on me, / well on my way to Death— / . . . there's nothing more deadly, bestial than a woman / set on works like these . . ." (11.481–486). This scene too, of course, returns in Aeschylus's tragedy *Agamemnon*, where Clytaemestra has become herself the killer. Odysseus does not know what fate awaits him back in Ithaca.

In a famous exchange, when Odysseus finds the hero of Troy among the dead, Achilles says:

> By god, I'd rather slave on earth for another man—
> some dirt-poor tenant farmer who scrapes to keep alive—
> than rule down here over all the breathless dead. (11.556–558)

Achilles wants news of his son. Rather than imagine a celestial or infernal existence that continues after death, the Homeric poems focus on life itself and the fame of the heroes; the shadowy persistence of the dead in the underworld offers little attraction to the hero who is still capable of exploration and conquest in his life among other mortals.

Copyright © 2009 Pearson Education, Inc. Publishing as Longman.

Yet Odysseus, in his encounter with Tiresias, comes to terms with his own mortality. Tiresias prophesies his future and promises him a peaceful fate. Unlike Achilles, Odysseus will die at home surrounded by his loved ones:

> And at last your own death will steal upon you . . .
> a gentle, painless death, far from the sea it comes
> to take you down, borne down with the years in ripe old age
> with all your people there in blessed peace around you. (11.153-156)

Return

In his return, Odysseus exhibits the crafty, wily intelligence the Greeks called *metis*, a cunning intelligence that values the skillful story, the lie, the plot, over brash physical strength. He shares this cunning intelligence, a shifting, mobile, inventive mind, with the goddess Athena, his protector and guide. She is the dominant divine presence in the *Odyssey*, engaged in a deflected duel with Poseidon, Odysseus's enemy, over the destiny of the mortal hero. Odysseus is a man of many "turns," full of stories and lies and fictions, and thus he becomes both a hero for a rhetorical strain in Greek culture and, for some later, a villain for his willingness to engage in what are seen as dubious, mercantile negotiations by another more aristocratic strain. Although Odysseus demonstrates his heroic capacities, his skills with weapons, and his willingness to shed the blood of his enemies, in his final encounter with the suitors, he cunningly defers his confrontation with them until he has enlisted allies, including his son (who has reached a certain maturity), and until he has set up the ambush of the enemy to his satisfaction. His slaughter of the suitors resembles an *Iliad* in miniature, with all the relish of bloodshed and killing worked out with such delight in variation in the *Iliad*.

In the concluding books of the poem, Odysseus makes his return as son, with Laertes, as he becomes a father to Telemachus, as he reasserts his dominion over his house, lands, and slaves. And he returns to his wife, in a beautiful scene in which he, the great trickster, is tricked by Penelope, herself capable of wonderfully devious and deceitful behavior with the suitors. In Book 23, the scene of the bed, rooted in the earth, the great marker of home and domestic happiness, shows the appropriateness of the match between these two and makes them exemplars of marital contentment. The tree, which in the *Iliad* has signified the body of a warrior, cut down, or the great family, with its many generations, here stands at the heart of this marriage. The poem uses a famous "reverse simile" to show the ways in which man and wife are bound together:

> Joy, warm as the joy that shipwrecked sailors feel
> when they catch sight of land—Poseidon has struck
> their well-rigged ship on the open sea with gale winds
> and crushing walls of waves, and only a few escape, swimming,
> struggling out of the frothing surf to reach the shore,
> their bodies crusted with salt but buoyed up with joy

Copyright © 2009 Pearson Education, Inc. Publishing as Longman.

as they plant their feet on solid ground again,
spared a deadly fate. So joyous now to her
the sight of her husband, vivid in her gaze,
that her white arms, embracing his neck
would never for a moment let him go . . . (23.262–272)

Odysseus has survived a shipwreck and been washed ashore, but here it is Penelope, safe at home all the years of his absence, who embraces and greets him as a shipwrecked sailor finds dry earth once again. Odysseus has come home, and there is, as in the *Iliad*, this moment of reconciliation before he sets off again on another journey, to find a place where an oar is unrecognizable, far from the sea, where the worship of Poseidon can be extended, as the colonies of the Greeks were to be extended in the centuries that followed. The elaborate structure of the *Odyssey*, narratives within narratives forming a sort of labyrinth with the land of the dead at the center, becomes paradigmatic for narratives of journeys, romances, and tales of enlightenment.

RESONANCES

Franz Kafka, George Seferis, and Derek Walcott

These excerpts from modernist writers show the persistence of the myth of Odysseus and his wanderings in the global imagination. Kafka reminds us of the haunting possibility of the Sirens' silence, looking at Odysseus from their perspective and producing an uncanny scene. The Greek Seferis conjures up the wanderer, the exile, for himself. The passage from Walcott's *Omeros* brilliantly extends the wanderings of Odysseus to the Caribbean, widening its geography to include not only Greek myth, and James Joyce, but also the African diaspora.

ARCHAIC LYRIC POETRY

Some scholars believe that lyric poetry may have ties with the world of Vedic poetry and may be older or contemporaneous with the epic tradition, as is seen in the song sung to the lyre on the shield of Achilles. The lyrics we have, however, date to a later period, after the great period of epic composition, and are remarkable for their reference to the epic world, for their relationship to the values of that world, and for their assertion of a more individual voice than that of the epic singer, who represents himself as the conduit of true stories, beholden to the muse for inspiration and content. The lyric singers belong not so much to the world of archaic

Copyright © 2009 Pearson Education, Inc. Publishing as Longman.

princelings shown in epic scenes of celebration like that of Demodocus's song in the *Odyssey*, where Odysseus weeps, but to complex negotiations of dependence on tyrants or aristocratic groups in the gradually emerging city-states of the Greek world. If Odysseus travels over the sea, visiting the farthest western and eastern limits and imagining life even beyond these, the lyric poets themselves traveled, sometimes seeking patronage or fleeing internal political strife in their own cities.

Arkhilokhos

Arkhilokhos has a shocking, original and personal voice, especially when contrasted with the self-effacing, almost invisible Homeric singer. He uses the first person singular freely, and he defies the warrior code that stands as the traditional ethical orthodoxy for aristocrats. He celebrates his sexual desire with a language remarkable for its frankness and also contrasting dramatically with the decorum of the Homeric poems, where Odysseus and Penelope's reunion is cast in very different terms. Arkhilokhos is lustful, sometimes harsh and insulting. He sells himself as a warrior, unmoved by the drive for fame that motivates Achilles in his return to the battlefield.

Most notorious of all is Arkhilokhos's lyric about abandoning his shield. The shield would have weighed him down, so he dumped it and ran, and will get another. In the strict warrior code, a man who abandoned his shield was a coward, fleeing; the canonical Spartan mother reportedly told her son either to come home with his shield or on it, that is, dead.

Sappho

Sappho wrote what are believed to be monodies, songs sung by a single voice, and choral songs, for groups. She is remarkable as the only ancient Greek woman poet whose work, other than minor fragments, remains; she was celebrated in antiquity as the tenth muse. She, like Arkhilokhos and Alkaios, writes from the matrix that is the epic tradition. Some of her poems, in lyric meters rather than epic dactylic hexameter, take up mythic themes related to those of epic; others, like the one celebrating the bridegroom, may have been composed for a wedding.

Scholars differ about whether the other poems reflect a personal voice or perhaps a more ritual situation. The first poem here, "Rich-throned immortal Aphrodite," exhibits a traditional hymnal form, a request for divine assistance that begins with the naming of the god, including honorific epithets, or naming the haunts of the god, proceeding to recall to divine attention previous acts of generosity, and then moving to the prayer for help. This poem stands out for beauty of composition among other such hymns; Sappho brings the goddess down from Mount Olympus in a chariot drawn by sparrows, birds known to the Greeks for their sexual connotations. Sappho sets the chariot in motion, recall-

Copyright © 2009 Pearson Education, Inc. Publishing as Longman.

ing the "dark earth" of the Homeric poems. The interview between the first person singular of the poem and the goddess, set in the past, reminds the listener of the goddess's special favors, teasingly, affectionately given. The moment invoking pursuit and flight summons up epic moments like Achilles' deadly pursuit of Hektor but turns the martial situation into an erotic one; this trope, of pursuit and flight, dominates erotic discourse for centuries, as well as the paradigmatic duel of the later Greek law courts, where a defendant is called the *pheugon*, "the one fleeing." In Sappho's poem, the object of desire is revealed to be female; the goddess will turn the one in flight into a pursuer. The erotic situation of dominance and pursuit, of inequality of desire, seems more characteristic of Greek eros, even between women, than one of mutual desire. This poem ends with a prayer; the poem asks that the goddess "help me to victory," that she fight by her side, and this plea too turns the poem away from Homeric, epic concerns of the battlefield to the domain of eros.

The poem "Come, goddess" is also a prayer, summoning Aphrodite, goddess of desire and its fulfillment. This poem is remarkable for its invocation of the senses and for the creation of a paradisiacal space that might be compared to the garden of Alkinoos in the *Odyssey* or the garden of Eden in the Hebrew Bible.

"Some think a fleet," like the first poem, transmutes the valence of the epic's conflict to love. This poem participates too in a more general cultural tendency in this period toward philosophical generalization and definition. Rather than naming a particular martial sight as the most beautiful, the poet gives a general definition and then moves to an example as proof. Helen, who in the *Iliad* appeared as a toy of Aphrodite, taken from one man and awarded to another, regretting her manipulation, here abandons husband, child, and parents and sails away, led astray by the power of love or by Aphrodite herself (the text is fragmentary). In any case, the poem stresses Helen's action, her subjectivity, rather than her passive exchange, as the most beautiful thing in the world. Then the poem moves to name a particular, Anactoria, the beloved woman, whose walk and face delight the speaker; the poet returns beautifully at the end to the martial powers of the first lines, horse and arms, refusing the trappings of battle, choosing her beloved.

The poem "He looks to me to be in heaven," later translated by Catullus into Latin and altered significantly by its heterosexual setting, has occasioned much scholarly debate. Some scholars claim that it depicts a wedding party, others an anxiety attack, others a poem of praise that draws on Homeric tropes of the god or hero who terrifies and paralyzes an onlooker. In Greek, the line "my tongue is paralysed" has a "hiatus," a collision of vowels usually avoided for a lack of euphony; some have translated it as "my tongue cracked." The poem depicts a physical collapse, dissolution of the body into pieces, perhaps resembling the psychoanalytic model of the preverbal child's recollection of a body in pieces, or the strange collection of limbs that is the Homeric body.

"Honestly, I wish I were dead" establishes a mood of loss typical of much Sapphic verse, in which the poet recalls yearningly a past now recoverable only through the agency of the poem. This poem imagines a community of women, and

Copyright © 2009 Pearson Education, Inc. Publishing as Longman.

of sexual pleasure that they shared, and ends with the painful "no grove," "no festive dance," simultaneously recreating community as it laments its passing. ". . . she worshipped you" similarly recalls a woman lost. Here, as in other poems, Sappho marks the proximity of her island, Lesbos, with Lydia, a kingdom in nearby Asia Minor, site of luxury and associated with a voluptuous and Easternizing, Asianizing tendency among the archaic period's aristocrats. Here the woman is compared to the moon, in a simile recalling the Homeric use of this rhetorical figure. Here the moon, unlike the sun that presides over the fertile fields of the incipient city, later compared to the bodies of citizen women, encourages the growth of flowers, associated with erotic pleasure and expenditure.

⚜

RESONANCE
Alejandra Pizarnik

Alejandra Pizarnik's lyrics belong in the Sapphic tradition, with their rhetorical address in the second person singular, sense of ritual and ceremony, presence of flowers, longing, and mood of intimacy. "Meaning of His Absence" might be read alongside Sappho's "He looks to me to be in heaven."

⚜

Alkaios

The comparison between Sappho and Alkaios is instructive. In the fragments that remain, Alkaios focuses on public, political issues, without the ritualistic and intimate details characteristic of Sappho's verse. He also, significantly, interprets the figure of Helen very differently from Sappho. Helen in the *Iliad* appears to be relatively passive, an innocent victim of Aphrodite and of the men who control her existence; in the *Odyssey*, she tries to emphasize her aid to Odysseus but is reminded that she had tried to lure the Greeks from the wooden horse by imitating their wives' voices. Gradually the portrait of Helen shifts, and she herself becomes the subject of her infidelity, not an example of someone choosing desire, as in Sappho's poem, but rather the one guilty of having caused the agonizing war for Troy. Alkaios represents Helen as crazed with desire for the Trojan Paris and responsible for the deaths of young men. He compares her to Thetis, the faithful mother of Achilles; Helen is gradually being demonized in a complex process whereby the aristocratic women of the archaic period are replaced by the universally subordinated citizen women of the classical *polis*.

Alkaios also touches on the politics of the island of Lesbos; he celebrates the armory of his confederates, building on the themes of armor and arming in the Homeric cycle. And he works out the metaphor of the ship of state, the extended

Copyright © 2009 Pearson Education, Inc. Publishing as Longman.

analogy made between the city and a ship at sea, beset by storm and flood, taken up later by political writers such as Solon and by other statesmen who represent themselves as fit captains for a state besieged.

Pindar

Pindar inherits the glorious riches of archaic lyric, the agonistic strain of Homeric epic, and a new situation in the city-states that emerged from the scattered towns and households of an earlier age. Although the other archaic lyric poets may have been dependent on the patronage of such tyrants as Polycrates of the island of Samos, Pindar had the delicate task of negotiating a new relationship between patron and poet. In a role that might usefully be compared to that of the poets of the Elizabethan age, he praised tyrants and aristocrats. Most of his poems center on athletic victories won through the sponsorship of men of great wealth, in a world that included not only the newly prosperous cities of the Greek mainland but also and especially the rich colonies in such distant but still Hellenized regions as Sicily. Pindar typically, in a dense and highly wrought style, names, praises, and alludes to past glories, including familial connections with the gods, while locating the victory in an almost ecstatic space, temporally both specific and eternal, in contact with divinity and yet rooted in a system of poetry for payment.

"First Olympian Ode" was composed to celebrate the victory in a chariot race of horses owned by the tyrant Hieron of Syracuse, in Sicily. This is one of the greatest of Pindar's poems, difficult but rich in allusion. The "turns" in the translation refer to the movements in the dance, performed by the chorus as they sang this song of celebration.

The first lines can usefully be compared to Sappho's question, "What is most beautiful?" Here the process of definition has advanced further a philosophical posing of such questions. Here, in an elaborate *prooimion*, or preface, the poet lists the best things, water among liquids, gold among solid substances, Olympia among the great games that also included Nemean, Delphic, and Isthmian games, all celebrated in particular localities in honor of the gods. The Olympian games, supposedly founded by Herakles himself, honored Zeus, the pre-eminent of the gods. So the poet names Olympia, then Zeus, and then Hieron. Then the poet focuses on the site of the victory, the Olympian sanctuary, by the river Alpheos, in Pisa, the district around Olympia, in the "land of Pelops," the Peloponnesus, that is, the "island" of Pelops, who was fed to the gods. Demeter consumed his shoulder, which was replaced with one of ivory.

Then, in a characteristically abrupt shift, Pindar casts doubt on the marvelous story, pointing to a spectrum that stretches from truth to deception to lies; he wants not to give credence to this story of divine cannibalism and prefers stories that cast the gods in a more noble light. This move can be contrasted to Plato's "noble lie" in *The Republic*, which he seems to consider a more appropriate story for mortals to hear. Pindar tells another version of Pelops's story, that Poseidon, over-

Copyright © 2009 Pearson Education, Inc. Publishing as Longman.

whelmed by desire for Pelops, took him to Olympus, as Zeus had carried the boy Ganymede from Troy to be his cupbearer. In this version of the story, mortals, envious of Pelops's good fortune, concoct a false story about the eating of the boy. The focus then moves to Tantalos, father of Pelops, he who allegedly fed his son to the gods to test them; students could look at the passage in the *Odyssey*, where Tantalos appears in the underworld. Pindar shows him threatened by a great boulder, while Homer shows him standing in water, tantalized eternally by water and fruit that hangs just above his reach. He had committed various crimes against the gods, including stealing the gods' divine food, *ambrosia*, and their drink, *nektar*, making himself immortal, and feeding these to his friends as well. In retribution, his son, Pelops, was sent back to the company of mortals.

Then follows the account of Pelops's courtship of Hippodameia, represented in a famous sculptural group that adorned the temple of Zeus at Olympia; this is a local version of the story of the foundation of the Olympic games in 776 B.C.E. The contest for the girl resembles other such ordeals practiced among the Indo-Europeans, including the contest with the bow in the *Odyssey*, and even such an ordeal as that in Puccini's *Turandot*. As in many of these contests, failure results in the hero's death. The father of Hippodameia has already killed thirteen of her suitors, but Pelops seeks the help of Poseidon and wins the contest. (In another version of this myth, Pelops disables the chariot of the father Oinomaos by bribing his charioteer, and the father loses, and as he dies curses Pelops. The sinister aspects of this story, too, Pindar suppresses, in a rather ostentatious omission that leaves an aura of danger.) He recalls the worship of Pelops, including the race and including the victor in days of contentment, "as far as contests can assure them" (line 136). That is, these are fragile victories, ephemeral, and shadowed by those versions of the myth that lie concealed behind a surface of celebration.

The ephemerality (literally, "of a day") of blessing occupies the poet next. The mortal's highest good is this single day, in a move that alludes to the first lines of the ode. He returns to the patron Hieron, acknowledging his power, but again, allowing a shadow of menace to color his praise and celebration. A god watches over Hieron; "If he does not abandon you soon" (line 149), sweeter will be the triumph. This is the doubt that protects from overconfidence and hubris but also threatens the security of the blessed, the wealthy and powerful. The poem thus ends on a somewhat tenuous note. The poet warns against looking too far into what mortals cannot know, into the beyond. He wishes that Hieron will walk on high, but he ends with himself, target of the Muse's arrow, with hopes for his place among the victors and confident of his skill. Thus he in some sense sets himself as pre-eminent, like water, gold, Olympia, Hieron, the victor, pre-eminent even among those, skillful like the charioteer. Poetry requires skill, and he has it, and he celebrates himself in a move that is followed by Ovid at the end of the *Metamorphoses*, when he boasts that his poem will outlast the Roman empire. Pindar is neither the anonymous conduit of the Muse, like Homer, nor has he the situated voice of a character like Arkhilokhos. He is rather both, an agent of the divine message and an individual who prides himself on his poetic achievement, in its own way not un-

Copyright © 2009 Pearson Education, Inc. Publishing as Longman.

like the athletic victory, in some sense making him superior even to the vastly wealthy and powerful tyrant whom he celebrates here.

RESONANCES

John Keats and Rainer Maria Rilke

The "epinician" or victory ode has a long history, including Roman poets like Horace. The ode is practiced by Jonson, Marvell, and Keats, the latter represented at this point in the *Anthology* with "Ode on a Grecian Urn." Keats echoes Pindar's theme of human ephemerality and the glorious survival of works of art. Rilke's selection, "Archaic Torso of Apollo," in a complex play of address, sees a call for transformation in the fragment of ancient statuary that survives from antiquity.

Aeschylus

Like the other tragedians, Aeschylus is deeply indebted to the epic cycle for the materials he fashions into tragedies celebrating the god Dionysos in the newly democratic city of Athens. One question raised in recent scholarship addresses the possible misogyny of Aeschylus: Does the portrait of Clytaemestra, the accusations directed at Helen, and other representations in this play and others exhibit the persistent strain of fear and dread concerning women in this culture? Another line of debate centers on whether or not the three plays of this trilogy should be read as an allegory of Greek history up to the time of Aeschylus himself, with the foundation of the Areopagus court as the climax of democratic reform. Some scholars read *Agamemnon* as a play concerning tyranny and the illegal usurpation of power, *The Libation Bearers* as a play about aristocracy and its corruption, and *The Eumenides* as a representation of the triumph of democracy. Another argument stresses the aristocratic ties alluded to throughout, the ways in which the plays serve to affirm and produce a network of aristocratic families bound by blood and loyalties that transcend citizenship in particular cities. All these debates situate the plays not just as literary texts but as interventions in ongoing cultural debates about gender, power, and politics.

   Agamemnon, part of the only trilogy that survives, recalls incidents from the *Iliad* and the *Odyssey* but recasts them into an intensely dramatic spectacle. The play begins with an ordinary man, a watchman; the scene serves as a prelude to *Agamemnon* and to the trilogy as a whole. The watchman watches the stars, dynasties like those of the great warriors whose stories dominate the epic legacy; he, on the other hand, has remained behind with the women, in a state subject to grave disorder. He alludes circumspectly to a world upside down, "a lady's / male strength of heart" (lines 10–11). Then, suddenly, he sees the beacon announcing

Copyright © 2009 Pearson Education, Inc. Publishing as Longman.

the fall of Troy. Some scholars believe the production used the sunrise over the theater of Dionysos as the herald of victory in the East.

The entrance of the chorus, and the first great ode, set up themes for the trilogy; these songs, in lyric verse forms, contrast strongly in Greek with the more prosaic language of the characters. The ode recapitulates the story of Troy, the departure of Menelaus and Agamemnon; they are likened to eagles, in a deepening of the Homeric simile. The attitude toward war differs dramatically from that of *Iliad*, where it is an occasion for immortal fame; Aeschylus's chorus of Argive elders blames Helen:

> for one woman's promiscuous sake
> the struggling masses, legs tired,
> knees grinding in dust,
> spears broken in the onset. (lines 61–65)

These are old men, frail like children, unpersuaded by the call to fame. They address Clytaemestra and then recall the omens of war, invoke the sacrifice of Iphigeneia, who died a victim to Artemis, to bring the winds to Aulis. They use some of the images that will recur through the plays, figures of curbing, netting, trapping, of corrupted sacrifice, and invoke Zeus, "whatever he may be":

> Zeus, who guided men to think,
> who has laid it down that wisdom
> comes alone through suffering. (lines 170–172)

The plays work out this truth, and good of a sort does win out in the end, with the burying of the Furies-Eumenides under the earth. In this play, however, we see only the suffering, Iphigeneia killed, "she struck the sacrificers with / the eyes' arrows of pity, / lovely as in a painted scene" (lines 228–230). The chorus reiterates its message: "Justice so moves that those only learn / who suffer . . ." (lines 238–239).

Clytaemestra imagines the journey made by the fire announcing victory at Troy, leaping across mountaintops from Asia to Argos. She describes the scene of victory, and the dramatist thus expands his representation to include not just the palace and the dancing floor but also this ancient fallen city and all the geography in between. The chorus responds with reflections on *Ate*, "Ruin." They use the image of the net and also a new language of the touchstone and the money-changer, seeing war as a heart-breaker: "in place of the young men / urns and ashes are carried home / to the houses of the fighters" (lines 420–422). The herald too, who announces Agamemnon's imminent arrival, speaks to the chorus of suffering: cramped quarters, foul beds, soaking clothes, lice, and Menelaus missing.

The chorus then sings a great ode on Helen, her name echoing the Greek for destruction: "Who is he who named you so fatally in every way? . . . Helen, which is death" (lines 663–669). The lion cub that plays with children becomes a lion, bringing blood and death, drawing on a complex system of analogies between

Copyright © 2009 Pearson Education, Inc. Publishing as Longman.

characters in the legend of this house and eagles, lions, and bulls, animals associated with predation and slaughter. Helen in the *Iliad* had been a passive object of exchange, for Sappho one who chose her desire, for Alkaios an agent of destruction. Aeschylus's ode completes the process; Helen has become a wild, destructive, wanton beast. The magnificent imagery of this ode assembles all the complexity of the lyric tradition in its denunciation of this "dream of calm / and the wind dying, . . . / the blossom that breaks the heart with longing" (lines 716–720), which turns, bitterly, and blights. The chorus ends contrasting pride with righteousness, and Agamemnon enters.

Clytaemestra greets her long-absent husband with consummate hypocrisy and prefigures his end with her allusion to the many stories brought to her concerning his fate:

> Had Agamemnon taken all
> the wounds the tale whereof was carried home to me
> he had been cut full of gashes like a fishing net. (lines 840–842)

He tries to resist here, claiming that the carpet she has laid down for him is too delicate, too Asiatic; it might call down on him the jealousy of the gods, and he is a mortal man. But she prevails, and he surrenders, fearfully, claiming to feel shame at such extravagance.

As they enter the palace, Cassandra, Agamemnon's war-captive, is left behind, and suddenly the chorus sings of its fear. She has a dazzling scene, swept away by her Apollonian prophetic powers; she imagines for the audience, in a brilliant *coup de théatre*, the slaughter of her lover. Image clusters that were established earlier recur: the net, the trap, the corrupted sacrifice, the tainted, cannibalistic family of the Atreidae. The mythic past of the city enters, as Cassandra's words are layered upon the chorus's odes; she recalls the feast of Thyestes, eating his own children, and Aegisthus as the strengthless lion who has seduced Agamemnon's queen. Cassandra, daughter of the doomed house of Priam, has entered another cursed palace; having wrestled with Apollo, but not bearing a child, she delivers prophecy, ecstatic, but to no avail. She sees Clytaemestra as a fawning bitch, a viper, and as Scylla, all dangerous female monsters who dare to strike down the male, as a woman-lioness who sleeps with a wolf. Cassandra smells the butchery occurring within the house and exits into the palace, resigned, calling herself "one simple slave who died, a small thing, lightly killed" (line 1294).

Agamemnon cries out as he is killed, and the chorus is impotent and dithering, in a scene that was mocked later. And then Clytaemestra enters, to play out a stunning scene of victory that lies at the heart of the play. She describes how she slaughtered her husband, using the language of nets, once metaphorical, now made literal. Reading this speech aloud, or having the students act it out, brings it to chilling life. She strikes him three times, in a scene that echoes the theme of failed sacrifice; he is like an animal being offered to the gods. And in a horrific image, Clytaemestra suggests that she is the earth receiving blood as an offering:

Copyright © 2009 Pearson Education, Inc. Publishing as Longman.

as he died he spattered me with the dark red
and violent driven rain of bitter savored blood
to make me glad, as gardens stand among the showers
of [the] god in glory at the birthtime of the buds. [translation modified]
(lines 1357–1360)

This moment would repay comparison with the *Odyssey*, the garden of Alkinoos in its benign plenty, and the scene of reconciliation between Odysseus and Penelope, when she finally brings him to reveal his identity. Clytaemestra's is not a benign paradise, nor their bed a rooted part of the hero's homeland. This is a polluted family, cursed with ancient crimes that seem to spin on forever in cycles of vengeance. And it is this matter, of the bloody absence of reconciliation, mediation, and the law, that brings at the end of the trilogy the invention of the law court in Athens, with its jury and persuasion and the divine intervention that seemingly interrupts the endless chain of murder. This is an important subject for students who have seen the consequences of unmediated vengeance in Ireland, the Middle East, and Africa, and an increasing commitment to punishment even in their own society.

Clytaemestra goes on to justify her murder, boasting, reminding the chorus of Agamemnon's sacrifice of their daughter Iphigeneia and exposing her rage at taking Cassandra from Troy. She, who was excited by the blood that shot from him as she killed him, who in a perverse distortion saw his blood as fertilizing rain, now expresses a twisted pleasure in seeing his lover dead:

. . . she who swanlike cried
aloud her lyric mortal lamentation out
is laid against his fond heart, and to me has given
a delicate excitement to my bed's delight. (lines 1412–1415)

Scholars have written about a Greek misogyny that dreads above all else the sight of women armed. In actual sacrifices at women's festivals, the priestess could not perform the rite of animal slaughter. Only the man, the priest, could wield the knife that slit the ox's throat. The myths of the women of Lemnos, who killed their husbands, of the fifty Danaids, forty-nine of whom killed their bridegrooms in their wedding beds, bear witness to a cultural fantasy that is realized fully in this scene of Clytaemestra's triumph. She vaunts her victory like a man and marks the terrible disorder and taint in this place. She resembles Helen, whom the chorus recalls: "Alas, Helen . . . / . . . for the thousand lives / you killed under Troy's shadow" (lines 1423–1425). The chorus is appalled at Clytaemestra's arrogance; she is drunk on her husband's blood:

Standing above the corpse, obscene
as some carrion crow she sings
the crippled song and is proud. (lines 1439–1441)

Copyright © 2009 Pearson Education, Inc. Publishing as Longman.

The horror of a world gone awry is condensed into this scene, and the chorus laments, acknowledging that nothing is done without Zeus, that this act too must have the blessing of the god. A performance of *Agamemnon* staged this scene, in which the actor who played Clytaemestra appeared costumed like an ivory Minoan figurine, with flounced skirt, bare breasts, snake bracelets, and an animal head-dress; this was an extremely effective presentation of what became a nightmare figure for the Greeks, the anti-Penelope, the vengeful woman who lies in wait and murders her husband.

Finally the strengthless lion Aegisthus enters, sole survivor of the cannibalistic feast of Thyestes, which he invokes; he has corrupted the bed of the house of Agamemnon, and these two adulterers and murderers control the city. Aegisthus threatens the old men of the chorus with fetters and with starvation, as they accuse him of womanly cowardice, of avoiding the war. The effeminate man in this society is one who spends too much time with women, eroding his masculinity with heterosexual lust, in contrast with the martial hero whose masculinity flourishes in homosocial comradeship with other soldiers. Like a tyrant, Aegisthus threatens all the citizens; he and Clytaemestra end the play with threats, as the chorus calls him a rooster with his hen.

The first tragedy of the trilogy, then, leaves the audience with this monstrous spectacle, of the wife who has slaughtered her husband, in company with her weak but menacing lover. This is a world upside-down, tyranny, gynecocracy, women's rule, a horror that sets the stage for the two plays that follow, in which this disaster must be set right. In *The Libation Bearers*, Orestes returns from exile and kills his mother, only in turn to be tormented by the Furies, avengers of mother-right. Clytaemestra had killed her husband because he killed their daughter and brought another woman into their bed. Orestes kills his mother perhaps because he sees himself as his father's son, his mother's body as merely the incubator of his father's seed. In the final, climactic play, Orestes is acquitted, in Athens, by a jury that reaches a tie vote concerning his guilt but is overruled by Athena, who chooses the side of the father, having been born herself from her father's head. The Furies become the Eumenides, the Blessed Ones, and bless Athens as they are buried beneath Athena's shrine on the Acropolis. Aeschylus thus represents the birth of law, persuasion, deliberation, and argument, celebrating Athens, site of this monumental moment in human history.

All of this can excite passionate discussion in the classroom concerning revenge, shame and guilt, juries, judges, punishment. Who decides guilt? Is it an internal psychological experience or an external social phenomenon? What is the place of the surviving members of a family in the deliberations concerning punishment? How can seemingly endless, vicious cycles of revenge be broken? How abstract should the law and punishment be? Should there be fixed penalties for crimes? Can confinement "pay" in some sense for crime, or is the goal rehabilitation? How does the death penalty figure in this set of arguments? Is it vengeance? Even without the whole trilogy, and its resolution in the foundation of the homicide court, discussion can take up the ways in which this play, a dramatic, religious,

Copyright © 2009 Pearson Education, Inc. Publishing as Longman.

political celebration of the god Dionysos, puts on stage an unforgettable spectacle of female power and bloody vengeance, thus embodying these questions of law, guilt, and punishment at the beginnings of the formation of the state.

RESONANCE
William Butler Yeats

William Butler Yeats's poem "Leda and the Swan," written in 1924, shows the enduring power of the myth of the house of Agamemnon. He realizes vividly the beginning of the catastrophe, in a scene influenced by Ovid's many representations of rapes. He makes very strange the violent encounter between the human and the avian species, and between mortal and immortal. He points to the act's consequences, including all that is represented in the *Iliad*, in the fall of Troy, the *Odyssey*, and *Agamemnon*, the train of violence that follows from the union of Leda and the swan that is Zeus. The cruelty and indifference of the gods to mortal suffering mark the limits of this intercourse.

Sophocles

Many students will already have encountered this masterpiece, *Oedipus the King*, in high school courses. Things to emphasize might include how the king curses himself, unknowingly. The drama evolves as a kind of boomerang, in which the determination to find the killer eventually implicates the very one seeking the truth. Oedipus is like a detective who discovers himself to be the greatest criminal. The truth is revealed gradually, in an agonizing process, as details slowly emerge concerning the murder of Laios and as Oedipus gradually comes to know himself as son of Jocasta and Laios—husband of his mother, murderer of his father, the bearer of plague to the city of Thebes, which had celebrated him as its savior and king. Like the *Iliad*, the play begins with a plague: "a deadly pestilence is on our town" (line 30).

Oedipus the King ends not with the funeral of a hero, like Hektor's, but rather with the revelation of a hero's shocking disgrace, his public humiliation, the loss of his shamed mother/wife, and the utter wretchedness of his blinding. It is probably not necessary here to go through the details of the tragedy, so familiar to most readers. The play ends with words very close to those spoken by Solon to Croesus in Herodotus's *Histories*: "Count no mortal happy till / he has passed the final limit of his life secure from pain" (lines 1598-1599).

The most interesting scholarship on the play has focused on two issues. One is the context of the play. There are multiple references to a new intellectual, philo-

Copyright © 2009 Pearson Education, Inc. Publishing as Longman.

sophical, religious, and political climate in the city and allusions to mathematics, to innovations in navigation, to medicine, to rhetoric, to anthropology, and to other domains of human progress. These have been interpreted as recognition of the growth of human knowledge of a more scientific sort in this period, a source of human pride, therefore, and in Sophocles' view perhaps dangerous in their power to turn men away from devotion to the gods and to traditional ethics and morality. As in the famous ode on man, sung by the chorus in *Antigone*, Sophocles reminds his audience members of their fragility in the face of the immortality and power of the gods:

> Many are the wonders, none
> is more wonderful than what is man . . .
> Only against death
> can he call on no means of escape . . .
> (*Antigone*, lines 368, 398, trans. D. Grene)

Oedipus has been imagined as a savior, as an almost divine figure, perhaps born from a god, but he meets a most human and ignoble fate.

Another critical question has been whether or not the tragedian meant the fall of Oedipus as a warning concerning the arrogance and innovation of the city of Athens itself. It may be helpful to link, as scholarship has, the fate of Oedipus with two illuminating practices of the city. One is the institution of ostracism, which cast out of the body of citizens any man who seemed to be overreaching, attracting too much attention, and therefore, perhaps, endangering his fellow citizens through the threat of either tyranny or divine punishment. The other civic institution is the *pharmakos*, or scapegoat ritual, in which the poorest and most wretched of men were selected, sometimes from prison, driven through the city, and beaten with onion bulbs, in an ancient fertility ritual that combined expulsion of the "low" with insult and humiliation. Oedipus has been compared to the central characters of both these institutions; he rose too high, challenging the gods and behaving tyrannically, and fell too low, a crippled and blinded beast at the end of the play. Is Oedipus an allegorical figure for the city of Athens itself, a representation of the human condition, human beings between gods and beasts? Or is the play a political message for the assembled citizens of Athens, urging them to accept their place in the middle, to "know themselves"?

It would also be useful to connect the play and its hero's downfall with other cultural artifacts of the period. Some have argued that the portrait of Athens in Thucydides, a city driven by impulse through the mechanisms of democracy, resembles Oedipus in its glorious prime and in its fall into catastrophe and defeat by the Spartans. Other possibilities for fruitful comparison include the representations of Teiresias here and in the *Odyssey*, where the seer's prophesies are accepted without question or hesitation.

Another issue of interest is Freud's fascination with this play. Does it, as he argues, present an inevitable and universal problem of human beings, the desire

Copyright © 2009 Pearson Education, Inc. Publishing as Longman.

to sleep with the parent of the opposite sex and murder the other parent, the rival? Classical scholarship has frequently rejected this argument, claiming that this drama is only one of many Greek tragedies that present a great variety of human dilemmas and contending that in fact Oedipus did not desire to sleep with his mother and did all he could to avoid killing his father. Freud would argue that the play records the truth of the unconscious desire. Others have made the point that in the cultural context of the ancient city, with its metaphorical systems, the desire to sleep with one's mother is interpreted as a desire for domination of territory, not as an incestuous impulse.

As for the question of fate and destiny in the play, many readers find a confirmation of their view that human beings are mere puppets in the hands of the gods. It is important to remember that Sophocles' play was written and produced in a time of crisis in the history of Athens and that he wrote polemically to intercept what he might have seen as radically impious and dangerous new currents in the intellectual and political life of the city. If Jocasta urges Oedipus to disregard the traditional, more conservative lessons concerning the gods, oracles, fate, and destiny, the play itself serves as a warning against such skepticism.

Not all Greeks, especially various pre-Socratics and sophists, shared Sophocles' anxiety about the path of intellectual development and political expansion in the period. Even the three tragedians whose work survives took differing positions concerning democracy and what has been called a period of "enlightenment" in the city of Athens. Aeschylus expressed optimism about the city and its institutions, Euripides radical skepticism about the gods and traditional morality.

Sophocles' *Antigone* appeals to young students; it often reminds them of the tragic love story of Romeo and Juliet. Its two young protagonists are torn in ways students can recognize, between obligations to family and the duty to a greater community. They often identify with Antigone as a noble heroine, sacrificing herself for love of family. She resists the tyrannical commands of Creon and dies for her beliefs. She has been read as a romantic figure resistant to tyranny (see Jean Anouilh's *Antigone*) or as the representative of ancient, women's law, the laws of blood that precede the law of the city.

The play is structured in such a way as to exemplify the agonism, the structures of contestation that characterize other institutions of the Athenians, including the law courts, the ritualistic pan-Hellenic competitions like the Olympian games, and indeed, politics itself in the city. The play is structured as a set of agonistic encounters, first Antigone against Ismene, then Creon, followed by the tyrant's debate with his son Haimon, and finally his angry, anxious exchanges with Teiresias. Antigone disappears early; some critics have pointed to the "diptych" form of this tragedy. The messenger speech describing the scene at Antigone's live burial spot concludes the drama, which is a tragedy in our sense, unlike some Greek tragedies. It ends in terrible loss for all who participate, in the scene where Haimon, discovering Antigone's corpse, hanged, tries and fails to kill his own fa-

Copyright © 2009 Pearson Education, Inc. Publishing as Longman.

ther and then stabs himself, spewing blood in a ghastly parody of the marriage bed's deflowering.

Another way to read the drama is to see *Antigone* as the site of ideological struggle, putting into play a conservative ideology rooted in devotion to the gods, blood ties, and identified with women's powers of mourning, and set against the secular ideology of the tyrant, who defies the gods and asserts his own power. A third term, expressed by Haimon in his speech urging Creon to yield, like the trees that grow beside a river (affinities here with Taoist ideals) can represent the synthetic ideology of the democracy, based on *logos*, debate, and the flexibility of the assembly. If the two principal characters in this drama were capable of listening to one another, instead of clinging stubbornly and absolutely to one point of view, there might have been another resolution. But Antigone, in an almost incestuous way, is focused on her brother to the complete exclusion of her betrothed, and Creon is furious at being resisted by a woman.

There are two great myth cycles in Athenian tragedy, neither of them about Athens itself. Yet implicit always is a contrast with Athens, with the first audience sitting in the theater in Athens, watching, always part of the drama. The themes of the Mycenaean cycle, concerning the family of Helen and the Trojan War, include cannibalism and adultery. The Theban saga concerns annihilating contact with the gods, repetition, and the sterility of incest. Sophocles tells this story in a complicated way, beginning with *Antigone*—toward the end of the myth—and makes it a tragedy about irreconcilable differences, the price paid for rigidity, the inflexibility of both Antigone and Creon. Sophocles followed *Antigone* some years later with *Oedipus Rex* and ended his life with *Oedipus at Colonus*, putting on stage the transcendence of worldly politics in this last tragedy, written by an old man, about passage beyond politics into metaphysics, preparing the way for Plato and philosophy. This story haunted Sophocles throughout his career and provides a way for telling the story of the fifth century in Athens, with mid-century optimism turning to anxiety, and then to the need for escape from a world of defeat.

Among the greatest of lyric passages in all of Greek tragedy is the so-called "ode on man," about which the German philosopher Heidegger wrote so eloquently. It celebrates the magnificence of human civilization, human beings' powers of domination over sea and earth, animals and the creatures of the sea, and speech and thought; yet this wondrous being cannot conquer death, and he needs law, in the chorus's words, and piety. Another magnificent passage is the song of Antigone herself as she goes to her death; note the power of the negative—she is unwept, unwed, friendless, and her very name signifies the opposition of generation.

Sophocles feared that the experiment that was democracy would be destroyed by men's arrogance. He seems to express in this tragedy his life-long fear of secular abandonment of the traditional ways, the dangers of disregarding women's powers, and the gods, for the sake of man's daring, audacity, and his intellectual accomplishments. All must be tempered by respect for the gods, or the consequence will be the terrible dead end that is Antigone's tomb.

Copyright © 2009 Pearson Education, Inc. Publishing as Longman.

RESONANCE

Aristotle

Plato's character Socrates wanted to expel the tragic poets from his ideal city, suggesting that imitation of women, for example, on the part of tragic actors, weakened them, and that a tearful response to a tragic scene on the part of the audience also encouraged unwelcome feelings:

> And so in regard to the emotions of sex and anger, and all the appetites and pains and pleasures of the soul which we say accompany all our actions, the effect of poetic imitation is the same. For it waters and fosters these feelings when what we ought to do is to dry them up, and it establishes them as our rulers when they ought to be ruled, to the end that we may be better and happier men instead of worse and more miserable. (*Republic* 10, 606e)

Aristotle takes a very different position, arguing that the purging of pity and fear experienced by the tragic spectator provides benefits. Scholars have differed about whether this "purging," or catharsis, refers to a medical model of expulsion or a ritual cleansing. In any case, for Aristotle, the effects of the spectacle are positive and therapeutic, and so he writes this manual, the *Poetics*, on how best to compose a tragedy, arguing in fact that poetry, or fiction, a made-up thing, *poiesis*, is superior to history. History records what happened, while poetry represents what ought to have happened, or what was most likely, most believable, and therefore more instructive, most useful to the reader, spectator, listener who is seeking a balanced, contented life. Aristotle also reveals his preference for the sort of tragedy written by Sophocles, in which the greatest concision of plot occurs. His admiration for *Oedipus the King* and a belated formulation of how to write a tragedy (e.g., limiting it in time) had their effects on later productions of tragedy, for which writers followed his prescriptions rather than the more open and various practices of the ancient tragedians themselves, who had written a century before Aristotle sought to describe and prescribe.

PERSPECTIVES

Tyranny and Democracy

The passages in this section of the *Anthology* can be tied back to scenes from the *Iliad* and the *Odyssey*, in which political systems are addressed. On the shield of

Copyright © 2009 Pearson Education, Inc. Publishing as Longman.

Achilles in Book 18 of the *Iliad*, for example, one of the two cities represented has councils of elders and a system of justice based on judges, while the other must resort to violence and war to counter its enemies. The conflict between Achilles and Agamemnon touches on a struggle between monarchy and aristocracy, rule by one or rule by the best. Among the variety of social arrangements explored in the *Odyssey* is the world of the Cyclops, without agriculture, laws, or assembly, all of these signs of civilization for the Greeks.

In these early texts, the question of the best form of government is being investigated, in part through fictions of difference. The Cyclops can in retrospect be seen as a parodic version of a tyrant; the king of the Phaeacians, Alkinoos, with his magical garden, the exemplar of a benign sovereign; Ithaca, without Odysseus, a society without leadership, falling into chaos. From the very beginnings of Greek culture, perhaps because of the many centers of power and many city-states vying with one another for power, with Achilles' army fighting alongside Agamemnon's Argives, vigorous debate about political forms characterizes Greek civilization. The arguments concerning tyranny and democracy of the fifth and fourth centuries B.C.E. carry on this tradition and focus on the recent past of the cities, on the innovations of democracies, and on the always-present challenge of monarchy, one-man rule, sometimes stigmatized as tyranny.

Solon

Solon has been seen as a more workmanlike poet than the luxurious aristocrats Sappho and Alkaios. He seems concerned with defending his policies, taken to protect the city of Athens, a growing and important mercantile center, from internal dissension. In the poem "Our state will never fall," he argues for lawfulness, in language that may recall the scene on the shield of Achilles in the *Iliad*. Solon's poetry is notably addressed to the Athenians, his constituency, rather than broadly to all those concerned with the deeds of the epic heroes, those aristocrats who may have traced their genealogy to the gods and heroes of the epic world. He is imagining a community of Athenians protected from disorder not only by Athena, not by a great man, but rather by the abstraction that is a transcendent law. His poetry marks the crucial juncture between monarchy and tyranny, and a new vision of a community governed by the body of citizens.

"The commons I have granted" even more directly speaks of Solon's own accomplishments as savior of the Athenian state and as law-giver. He seems to be suggesting that he tried to find a middle way, between pleasing the aristocrats, or the wealthy, and the "commons," the people; yet he acknowledges the dissatisfaction in a familiar sentiment: "Hard to please everyone in politics" (line 11).

"Those aims for which I called the public meeting," like Solon's other poems, stands in sharp contrast to Homer and to the aristocratic lyric poets of Lesbos. Solon deals with matters of history and law, and he boasts of having

Copyright © 2009 Pearson Education, Inc. Publishing as Longman.

lifted boundary-stones; this is probably a reference to markers that indicated sale of traditionally held lands by the poor to the rich, in a gradual process of impoverishment that led to civil unrest. Solon was reputed to have ended this system of indebtedness, in which citizens mortgaged their land, sharecropped it, and then lost it entirely. He also here claims to have made illegal the enslavement of citizens for debt and to have called those sold back to Athens, restoring their privileges and a community that ideologically construed itself as autochthonous, born from the earth of Attica. This poem ends with a metaphor that recalls the similes of the Homeric epic: the wolf at bay, attacked by hounds, and the themes of pursuit and flight at the heart of the analogy between love and war. Here the statesman, like the captain of Alkaios's ship of state, finds himself assaulted, in a gesture that points to the harsh adversarial politics of the ancient city.

Thucydides

Thucydides' celebrated predecessor Herodotus came from Asia Minor and may have been influenced by the cultural and intellectual heterogeneity of his world, on the unstable borders between Greek and Asian cultures; he claims to have visited Egypt and offers extensive accounts of Scythian, Babylonian, and Egyptian civilizations, with ethnographic and magical elements intertwined with his attempt to account for the mutability of the destinies of cities and empire. Thucydides, an Athenian, comes to the writing of history with a very different set of intentions, in part because he follows Herodotus and seeks to differentiate himself from the earlier writer, whom he sees as unreliable. In Thucydides' preamble, he stresses accuracy in his account of a new war, not waged between barbarians and all the Greeks but rather *among* Greeks, between the Peloponnesians and the Athenians.

Thucydides begins by going back in time to situate the conflict on which he will focus, but rather than stories or "myths," he attempts to trace economic and political forces that affected the events of the war. He describes differences among the Greeks and draws an analogy between earlier Greeks and contemporary barbarians. He tries to bring his analytic and critical powers to bear even on the historical elements of the Homeric poems. His reasoning often relies on quantitative assessments, as when he evaluates the numbers of ships sent by various Greek cities at the time of the Trojan war: the length of the siege of Troy was due, for example, to "shortage of money." He sifts and discards information he finds untrustworthy, applying new standards of proof: "For men accept one another's accounts of the past, even about their native countries, with a uniform lack of examination." He applies a higher standard.

Thucydides also defends his technique of presenting the often highly rhetorical speeches of various important political and military figures of the Peloponnesian War. He claims to have heard some speeches himself and to have

Copyright © 2009 Pearson Education, Inc. Publishing as Longman.

consulted informants about others. He reports that he used criteria of authenticity to compose the speeches in his history, "with the closest possible fidelity . . . to the overall sense of what was actually said." This too represents a new standard of truth-seeking, relying not on the Muse, divine inspiration, or tradition, but on some proximity to the events, which allows for a different kind of text, one based on new principles.

Thucydides writes in a style marked by the work of the rhetoricians of the fifth century B.C.E. and by philosophical developments of the period as well. He is skeptical concerning evidence, and his conclusions can usefully be compared to contemporaneous thought in which questions of responsibility, blame, and guilt are being worked out, both in the courts of law and to some degree in tragedy. Thucydides composes tense, antithetical, elliptical sentences of difficult brevity. He is not interested, at least overtly, in pleasing and flattering, in stroking Athenian patriots and in congratulating his own city on its superiority to others. His attitude is one of unflinching truth-seeking, adherence to fact and evidence, and pessimism about human nature. It can offer insights into the truths of human conduct for the future, and here too Thucydides stands apart from poets and earlier historians. He calls his work a *ktema es aei*, "a possession for all time," in a phrase that resounds with Pindar's claims about his own poetic gifts. But Thucydides distinguishes himself from poets engaged in contests; his is a work that perhaps is conceived of as a case study, an exemplary history, rather than as a narrative giving the last word on particular events.

His analysis of the causes for the Peloponnesian War may seem very modern; he names "increasing Athenian greatness and the resulting fear among the Lacedaemonians." Rather than a mythic explanation, one relying on natural difference or ancient and traditional hostilities, Thucydides' explanation has been affirmed by some historians of ancient Greece, who share his assessment of an economic and political aggression on the part of the Athenians. This is both like and unlike the paradigm of Greek tragedy that seeks the cause of catastrophe in hubris and over-reaching. Thucydides' Athenians are not the victims of divine envy, yet they fall from wealth and glory as surely as does Croesus.

The funeral oration of Perikles in Book 2 has the characteristics Thucydides attributed earlier to his recording of such speeches: he gives us "what was especially required in the given situation." Whether an eyewitness account or not, this speech has long stood as a sort of manifesto for the Athenians' sense of their greatness and their mission. This is an "epideictic" speech, a speech of praise, display, and exhortation for the immediate audience and for eternity. Acknowledging the losses of the year, the men who died in battle, Perikles, the great statesman, heir of a distinguished noble family, urges emulation rather than envy on his audience. He praises the ancestors of the Athenians and then moves to their form of government. Perikles in Thucydides' text praises the Athenian democracy because it allows privacy to individuals and encourages law-abiding behavior in its citizens. He discusses the openness of the city and the frugal admiration of beauty that accompanies a manly wisdom. Sentences like this one reveal the rhetorical compres-

Copyright © 2009 Pearson Education, Inc. Publishing as Longman.

sion and aphoristic quality of this speech and of the text as a whole: "Rightly would they be judged strongest in spirit who recognize both dangers and pleasures with utmost clarity and are on neither account deterred from risks." The brevity and compactness of such expressions combine for an effect that had great impact on subsequent oratory and rhetoric.

Perikles reaches a climax in claiming that "our city as a whole is an education for Hellas." That is, all the Greeks look to Athens as an example of power, self-sufficiency, and attractiveness; like Thucydides' history, Athens will be admired by future generations. The city requires no poets, leaving monuments of its power, in a very Greek formula, good to its friends, harmful to its enemies. He returns at the end to praise of the fallen, again urging emulation rather than envy on the part of his audience. His penultimate remarks concern the women listening, about whom he delivers a famous phrase that sums up the role of the Athenian citizen's virtuous wife: "Your renown is great through keeping up to the standard of your basic nature, and if your reputation has the least circulation among men, whether for virtue or in blame." That is, the good woman is invisible, causing no comment, attracting no attention to her master, father, husband, or brother.

The last selection from Thucydides, from Book 3, portrays the decay of language in a moment of civil war and has been compared to George Orwell's analysis of the disintegration of language in the "doublespeak" of the twentieth century. Thucydides' pessimism about human nature finds expression in the collapse of order on Corcyra and in the regression of its citizens to bestial behavior, which could interestingly be compared to that of the Cyclops Polyphemos in the Homeric *Odyssey*. Civil war is of course a part of American history and figures prominently in the headlines of the twenty-first century as well. Lies and the liars who tell them, manipulating language and reversing its customary meanings, as well as the arts of propaganda in general, are tellingly anatomized by Thucydides. He condemns both sides in the struggle in Corcyra—the mass party called its program "political equality," the aristocracy called theirs "moderation"—and both parties committed atrocities. Thucydides sees law, an abstract set of principles that curbs passions and revenge, as necessary to human civilization, which is fragile and vulnerable to explosions of impulse, envy, fury, savagery, and greed. This portrait of humankind finds its like in later formulations such as Hobbes' and can also be compared to the eruption of murderous rage in the *Iliad*, when Achilles, like a homicidal beast, a raging forest fire, sweeps against the Trojans and chokes the river with corpses. For Thucydides the corruption of language marks a similar annihilation of the bonds that allow human beings to live together.

Plato

Although we do not know the chronological order of the composition of Plato's writings, most readers assign the *Apology* to the earlier period of his work. The

Copyright © 2009 Pearson Education, Inc. Publishing as Longman.

Apology, or "defense" of Socrates, is Plato's version of Socrates' speech in court before he was condemned to death by the Athenians. Like the speeches of Thucydides in his history, it is an artful piece of writing rather than a transcript. Some historians trace Plato's rejection of democracy, apparent in *The Republic* and elsewhere, back to this moment in Athenian history when, after defeat in the Peloponnesian War, according to some due to democratic excesses, the city killed Plato's friend and teacher. This speech, notably not a dialogue, as are the other texts of Plato, addresses the jurors in the second person plural and goes beyond the circumstances of the law court to offer a defense of Socrates' life. It resembles other extant courtroom speeches by the Attic orators. It is also a remarkable biographical text, perhaps the first extended treatment of an individual's life not embedded in a historical account. Plutarch's *Lives*, written much later, begins a more formal biographical tradition; Augustine's *Confessions* also makes a useful point of comparison. This is an interesting question to discuss with students; it is only with a stress on individualism and a new relationship to life spans, birth, and death, that biography seems important and necessary. Achilles' and Odysseus's life stories are told in very different generic situations and concern communities as much as individuals.

Socrates, speaking in the first person singular, begins by acknowledging the convincing nature of his accusers' arguments, stressing, however, that they lied. It is important to note that the state did not itself prosecute Socrates; in the Greek system of law, other citizens brought defendants before juries, and there was little or no state apparatus of prosecution. The speeches that have survived from classical trials exhibit features of vendetta, of jockeying for power in a volatile political situation, and of the management of anger in a close-knit social organization. Socrates dismantles the claims of accusers by going back to rumors circulating about him for many years. In the first set of accusations, brought by Meletus, Anytus, and Lycon, they say that he meddles, that he inquires into things below the earth and in the sky, that he makes the weaker argument the stronger and teaches others to follow his example. He cites Aristophanes' play *Clouds*, in which Socrates was represented as an impostor and fraud, a likely source of many citizens' false impressions of the philosopher. Another common misapprehension was that Socrates numbered among the sophists, or those natural philosophers now often called the pre-Socratics, who were interested in physical questions. While acknowledging an early interest in Anaximander, Socrates here denies sharing these thinkers' preoccupations and points to the crucial distinction between him and the sophists: he did not accept money for teaching, but rather conversed with friends.

Greek legal defense often relied not so much on the refutation of charges as on the establishment of a good reputation, and this sometimes involved the presence and support of well-known and respected friends and associates. Socrates cites not only his friends but also the oracle at Delphi, which said not that he was the wisest of men but that no one was wiser than he. He doubts, but his investigations confirm this assessment. Socrates questioned his fellow citizens and gath-

Copyright © 2009 Pearson Education, Inc. Publishing as Longman.

ered around him elite young men. This may indeed have been a source of resentment against him, since some of his friends were involved in anti-democratic political groups.

Socrates addresses another set of accusations, concerning his corruption of the young and belief in new gods. In this section of the oration, Plato offers a cross-examination of Meletus that resembles the dialogical form of other Platonic works. He trips up Meletus in his own answers. In an early statement of what becomes an important principle in Platonic philosophy, Socrates shows that no one would do wrong intentionally. He would not harm the community in which he lives, just as later he argues that no one would willingly injure his own soul by doing wrong. And in an important literary citation, Socrates quotes Achilles in the *Iliad*, defending the choice of honor over death.

Socrates, who has braved death in battle, is not afraid of dying at the hands of the Athenians, and he explains that he will not repent nor cease practicing what he calls philosophy, questioning and examining and testing others. This, in his eyes, is not corruption. Putting Socrates to death will be a crime on the part of the jury. He has been attached to the city, by the god, as a "gad-fly," and without him the city will fall asleep again. He surveys his behavior in the time of "the thirty," the oligarchic coup, and proves his difference from the conspirators, who killed and confiscated the property of others.

The jury convicts him and then refuses his suggestion of a mild penalty, choosing death, perhaps in reaction to his unwillingness to accept chastisement. What follows is the most philosophically complex part of the oration. Socrates mentions the voice that prevents him from erring. This has been seen as the development of a new sense of an interior self, different from the other-directed, shame-based self of Homeric culture. Here is a new kind of subject, characterized by an internal dialogue, pushed further in an image used later in the Platonic dialogues, of the soul as a charioteer driving two horses that must be tamed and governed by the soul's best part. This part of the *Apology* also begins to explicate Plato's ideas concerning death, that it is not to be feared but rather perhaps to be welcomed as a deliverance from the fetters of the material body. Later Plato writes more explicitly of the immortality of this soul. Socrates ends here with an optimism about his fate that marks the history of philosophy and Christian theology; no one can know death, therefore no one can know if death is superior to life.

Some scholars who look into the circumstances of Socrates' friendships and associations, his links with the oligarchy that briefly seized power in 411 B.C.E., for example, think that the city was justified in condemning Socrates to death. This raises interesting issues concerning treason, freedom of speech and conscience, and the right of the state to execute, all matter for discussion. This speech can usefully be mined for rhetorical shape, techniques of persuasion, and creation of an *ethos*, or "character" in words, which had by this time become a focus of legal speeches; a speechwriter who wrote for others focused on *ethos*, on producing a distinct, trustworthy, honorable "character" in words for his clients to deliver before the jury.

Copyright © 2009 Pearson Education, Inc. Publishing as Longman.

This *Apology* offers a striking contrast with Perikles' portrait of Athens as an "education" for Hellas. As for Thucydides, perhaps, the history of Athenian democracy is an "education" only as a negative spectacle, a disaster to be avoided. For Plato, the democracy made a monstrous error in killing its best citizen, and in so doing provided a founding martyr for the new discipline of philosophy.

Euripides

One question that preoccupies current critical work on Greek tragedy concerns the degree to which difference is present in the texts and whether we can say that there is a "democratic" openness to many voices in the plays. Some critics point to the variety of speakers in tragedy, including women, slaves, and barbarians; such persons would not have been publicly vocal in the assemblies of the ancient cities, yet they have their place in drama, and, the argument goes, they therefore make tragedy an almost "utopian" space, imagining a wider democracy than once conceivable in actual political practice. Others respond that tragedy finally takes a conservative, regressive line on these questions, affirming not just the network of aristocratic families that defines a Panhellenic world (as in Aeschylus) but also a paternalist, even patriarchal universe in which kings, and Zeus, rule and know best. The latter argument may hold for the work of Aeschylus and Sophocles, but it is more difficult to sustain in the case of Euripides.

Euripides has been seen as a bad man, dangerous to know. His work partakes of the philosophical experimentation, rhetorical developments, and excesses of the fifth century B.C.E., as well as skepticism about the traditional divinities and about the founding myths of the Greek cities. He has been called an absurdist, a melodramatist, a feminist, a metatheatricalist, and worse. When in Aristophanes' *Frogs* Dionysos goes to the underworld to bring back a tragedian to rescue Athens, he leaves Euripides behind among the dead, preferring Aeschylus for his patriotism and superior artistry.

Euripides is a playwright of many moods; his plays have surreal aspects, perfunctory moments, profound irreverence toward the gods, sophistry, and the unlikely return to ecstatic Dionysos worship at the end of his career, in the *Bacchae*. He gives more place in his tragedies than tragedians usually do to the voices of slaves and women and to the representation of everyday life. He exhibits a more sympathetic concern for the currents of intellectual challenge in the fifth century B.C.E., currents of skepticism, impiety, and secular humanism addressed with some alarm by Sophocles.

The Medea is an especially intriguing example of the confrontation between the Greeks and their "others," the barbarians who surrounded them and helped them define themselves through opposition. In his portrait of the Colchian princess from the distant eastern coast of the Black Sea, Euripides represents an exotic sorceress with occult powers. The first speech of the play points to her origin far away and her previous crimes, alluding to her murder of her own brother

Copyright © 2009 Pearson Education, Inc. Publishing as Longman.

and her murder of Pelias. She has bestial qualities, is not quite human, and is seen as dangerous from the start, injured by Jason and volatile: "No more than either a rock or surging sea water / She listens when she is given friendly advice" (lines 28-29).

After having established the exoticism, the otherness, the barbarism and difference of Medea, Euripides brings her on stage, where she delivers a speech that not only examines the trials suffered by foreigners, strangers in the Greek city, but also catalogs the sufferings of the Greek wife:

> We women are the most unfortunate creatures.
> Firstly, with an excess of wealth it is required
> For us to buy a husband and take for our bodies
> A master; for not to take one is even worse. (lines 229-232)

She goes on to complain about her life, enclosed in her master's house, without the distractions a man can seek, other friends or lovers. And she laments the pains of childbirth: "I would very much rather stand / Three times in the front of battle than bear one child" (lines 248-249). Although the evidence is inconclusive concerning the attendance of women at Greek tragic performances, this speech is certainly calculated to evoke the sympathy of an audience with the plight of women, especially a foreign bride. And of course, any bride in this culture was in some sense "foreign" to the family, imported from her father's house into the household of her husband and new master and thereby sharing to some degree Medea's sense of otherness. The chorus in the ode "Flow backward to your sources" seems to respond to her pleas for understanding as they lament a world in which men, not women, have become the deceitful ones. Also important in the tragedy is the representation of Medea's nurse, a slave who exhibits concern for her mistress and dreads the outcome of Medea's rage: She likens her to "a lioness guarding her cubs," and her character is developed more fully than that of slaves in the works of other tragedians. The husband Jason, like certain other Euripidean heroes, including the husband of Alcestis, shows the decline of the heroic. If Greek tragedy inherits the stories of such supermen as Achilles, a cowardly, whining creature like Jason demonstrates the exhaustion of such ideas of aristocratic masculinity.

Even as her rhetoric calls for sympathy from the chorus and from the audience, something rings false; Medea complains that she has "no mother or brother, nor any relation" (line 255), but her own actions have brought her to this pass. With Jason she fled her own country, her brother in tow, and in one version of the myth she chopped her brother in pieces and threw his dismembered body into the sea in the wake of Jason's ship, so that her grief-stricken father, in hot pursuit, would stop to gather up the corpse.

Euripides seems in this play first to seek to capture the audience's sympathy for this woman seduced and abandoned and then to make it impossible for that audience to maintain its adherence to Medea's cause. Some readers disagree with

Copyright © 2009 Pearson Education, Inc. Publishing as Longman.

this interpretation, seeing Medea as sympathetic throughout, as justified in her behavior, as heroic in her vengeance. However, her violent retribution, taken not only against the bride-to-be but also against her own children, seems to make her monstrous. Like Hecuba, in the eponymous tragedy of Euripides, who kills her enemy's children and then stabs out his eyes, Medea's acts of vengeance seem driven by motives of cruelty and excess, of bloody sacrifice, that go beyond the heroic into a zone of female barbarism and bestiality.

There are many powerful scenes in the play. Among them are the interviews between Jason and Medea, in which she defends herself against his long-winded and hypocritical arguments. He reminds her, for example, that she should be grateful to him, that "instead of living among barbarians, / You inhabit a Greek land and understand our ways, / How to live by law instead of the sweet will of force" (lines 524–526). She has fame, when she would be unknown (to Greeks) had she remained at home. All of this is of course small consolation for a woman about to be deserted, much as Jason argues that his new marriage will benefit their children and that she is blinded by eros.

Euripides then, having given the audience an aggrieved wife, a marriage on the verge of collapsing into a horror show, now moves further into melodrama with Medea's pathetic address to her children, who do not speak.

> Why, children, do you look upon me with your eyes?
> Why do you smile so sweetly that last smile of all?
>
> . . .
>
> How delicate the skin, how sweet the breath of children! (lines 1014–1048)

This is a great scene, a soliloquy, a *tour de force* for an actor playing a woman scorned, a murderess bent on killing her own children to punish their father.

The next stunning scene is the messenger's speech, which describes, with a lurid sensationalism, the death of the bride and her father:

> . . . From the top of
> Her head there oozed out blood and fire mixed together.
> Like the drops on pine-bark, so the flesh from her bones
> Dropped away, torn by the hidden fang of the poison. (lines 1172–1175)

After these horrors, Euripides piles on more. The father, trying to save his daughter, is dragged into the poison, "ripping his aged flesh from his bones" (line 1191). For students raised on horror movies, this scene has its interest. The Greeks found it more decorous, and perhaps even more terrifying, to have the messenger describe these events than to represent them on stage.

The play ends with Medea triumphant, above the stage on a crane, a chariot drawn by dragons, with the dead bodies of her children alongside her. She has become a mythic creature, the children an object of cult, in an etiological twist that returns the play to the domain of religious celebration:

Copyright © 2009 Pearson Education, Inc. Publishing as Longman.

> . . . In this land of Corinth
> I shall establish a holy feast and sacrifice
> Each year for ever to atone for the blood guilt. (lines 1355–1357)

Medea's final exchange with Jason performs a reversal in which she vaunts herself as the arrogant victor, as he has become a bereaved father, the pitiful victim of her violent revenge. Euripides has twisted the sympathies of his audience in a move that finally condemns the barbarian princess precisely for her barbarism. And in a final turn of the knife, Medea is headed for Athens, where the tragedy's first audience sits. If the end of the *Oresteia* trilogy represented the foundation of law and the burying of the now beneficent Eumenides under the Athenian Acropolis, this play ends with barbarism, otherness, the vengeance of the betrayed wife all still to be embedded irrevocably inside the household and the city. Euripides brings home otherness and shows the barbarism at the heart of civilization.

⌀

RESONANCE

Friedrich Nietzsche

Friedrich Nietzsche's *Birth of Tragedy* must be situated within the intellectual climate of nineteenth-century Germany. His radical and original reading of the Greeks and their art-forms was influenced by his experience of the revelations of Wagnerian opera and by what he saw as insipid and false interpretations of the Greeks by contemporary classicists, some of whom condemned him viciously after the publication of his first book, the one excerpted in the *Anthology*.

Nietzsche sees the birth of tragedy in the primitive chorus that celebrated the god Dionysus (Dionysos). The chorus is the ideal spectator, the only beholder of the visionary world of the scene on stage. The fusion of the Dionysian chorus and its music with the Apollinian world of images and dreams creates tragedy, a paradoxical opposition of styles. Euripides, in Nietzsche's view, destroyed tragedy first by bringing the spectator onto the stage, forcing the everyday upon the fragile synthesis and dialectic of tragedy, abandoning Dionysos for Apollo. For this crime, Apollo abandoned Euripides, and Greek tragedy died tragically, by suicide. Nietzsche associates this catastrophe not only with Euripides but also with Socrates, for whom Euripides performed as a mask. Euripides had become a thinker, not a poet, bringing the masses onto the tragic stage and writing only out of consciousness, rather than in an artful, poetic fusion of the Apollinian and Dionysian. And he had voiced Socratic cheerfulness, the optimism apparent in such Socratic views as are expressed in the *Apology*, for example, that no man intentionally harms himself, that the only error is ignorance. Socrates appreciated only the Aesopian fable, the neat little tale with a moral attached. In Euripides' hands, the chorus atrophies; in Socrates' hands, philosophy becomes theoretical

Copyright © 2009 Pearson Education, Inc. Publishing as Longman.

optimism. Nietzsche calls this the death of tragedy, of that extraordinary terrain in which tragic insight, the possibility of simultaneous pessimism and affirmation, had once been possible because it was protected by art.

Thus for Nietzsche the very features of Euripides' tragedies that may most appeal to modern and postmodern readers—his giving voice to women, slaves, and barbarians, his representation of everyday life, and his interest in philosophical and rhetorical currents of the late fifth century B.C.E.—destroyed the institution of Greek tragedy and led to the insipidities of New Comedy. Nietzsche's arguments, although rejected by the discipline of classics, have had a long life, especially in his analysis of the Apollinian and Dionysian strains of tragic art, and influenced twentieth-century thinkers such as Martin Heidegger.

Aristophanes

Instructors must remember to brace students for the Greeks' notions of propriety and decorum, possibly very different from their own. Translations of Aristophanes have often bowdlerized and sanitized the Greek text, which deals very frankly with bodily functions, sexual and excremental. Aristophanes and his audience clearly took great pleasure in laughter and in the enjoyment of ridicule of public figures. There are analogies in the present day that can be invoked to situate ancient comedy, but the institution of a publicly funded and richly obscene comic drama seems remote and marks a difference between the Greeks and contemporary culture, one that should always be taken into account in representations of the Greeks that have tended to idealize them as founders of democracy and philosophy, ignoring these aspects of ancient culture.

Lysistrata is not the most chaotic or obscene of Aristophanic comedies. And other comedies have been mentioned as having bearing on other texts presented here, including the *Frogs*, which features a journey to the underworld, and a literary critique of the tragedies of Aeschylus and Euripides, and *Clouds*, starring a Socrates with his head in the air. *Lysistrata*, however, concerns the Peloponnesian War very directly, and a fantastic sex strike proposed to end it. Other Aristophanic comedies deal with the war, and in the *Acharnians* the hero Dikaiopolis actually strikes a separate peace with the Spartans.

Lysistrata was first performed at the height of the war, in 411 B.C.E., the year of an oligarchic coup in Athens, when the Athenians were at war, when the war seemed to have turned decisively against them. Scholars have differed on how to take it; is it an antiwar manifesto on Aristophanes' part, a plea for a Panhellenic politics that anticipates tendencies of the fourth-century B.C.E. alliance against the Macedonians, a sign of his adherence to a Spartanizing conservative party in Athens (itself nostalgic for the old Persian War alliance among the Greeks), a diverting fantasy that signifies how literally impossible such a plot would be?

Copyright © 2009 Pearson Education, Inc. Publishing as Longman.

To read *Lysistrata* after *The Medea* is revealing; at the end of the fifth century, women in these dramas are represented as powerful and willful, in roles that seem to contradict the evidence about Athenian women's sheltered existence in their husbands' and fathers' houses. Lysistrata herself, the central character in Aristophanes' comedy, controls her band of women assembled from all the warring states of Greece and leads them in a two-pronged attack, first to deny their husbands sexual gratification until they negotiate an end to the Peloponnesian War, and second to seize the Acropolis and the monies used to wage the war. Her name means "undoer of armies," and also perhaps alludes to an epithet of eros, *lusimeles*, "limb-loosener." A contemporary inscription found in Athens refers to a priestess Lysimache, a name similar to that of the heroine, "undoer of battle." Aristophanes' heroine cleverly devises the conspiracy, enlists enemy women, and directs her forces, encouraging them when they weaken.

The Panhellenic utopia, the community of women joined by their opposition to war, speak to the exhaustion and pessimism about the war that belie Perikles' words about the city of Athens, supposedly uttered some twenty years earlier. The comic writer's invention has its humorous side but also provides Aristophanes with the opportunity to imagine a new community, one that includes all the Greeks, who once upon a time saw themselves as a unified body struggling against a Persian invasion. The idea of women forming a political group may have seemed comical, since many women lived private, domestic, and isolated lives resembling that described by Euripides' character Medea, who complains of her life inside the house. But the fantasy betrays a political impulse that goes beyond other Aristophanic texts in which the protagonists dream simply of peace, prosperity, and eels to be eaten. The ambition of this play in its depiction of the heroine and her comrades makes it extraordinary in the Aristophanic corpus.

The chorus includes cynical veterans, no longer moved by patriotism but rather by gain, characterized like all the men in the play by their phalluses, and women who have served the city in religious institutions, encompassing the cults of the city's goddesses Demeter, Artemis, and Athena. Cultic references abound in the play, including the allusion to the actual priestess of the Acropolis cult of Athena, to the worship of Adonis by the women of the city, and to Sabazios, a Phrygian god worshiped by women and slaves. Rod refers to marital intercourse as "Aphrodite's holy mysteries." The strike ends with praise for the goddess Athena, "who's won a total victory."

Key scenes include Lysistrata's explication of her plan, the arrival of the Spartan delegation, her exchange with the magistrate, and the seduction scene between Myrrhine and Rod. "Rod" is actually called Kinesias in Greek, the verb *kineo* referring to sexual intercourse; the desperately engorged husband arrives and orders his wife to satisfy his frustrated desire. He even brings their child with him, to excite Myrrhine's maternal feelings, but in the end, after having teased him mercilessly, she leaves him still painfully erect, a condition he shares with the arriving Spartan herald.

Copyright © 2009 Pearson Education, Inc. Publishing as Longman.

Aristophanes uses the customary comic slurs, that women were desperate for sexual satisfaction, something alluded to more decorously by Jason in *The Medea*. Lysistrata says, "Oh what a low and horny race we are!" Although she expresses disappointment in her co-conspirators, some of whom seek to betray the cause by sexual backsliding, she rallies them by reminding them of what is at stake, and they are inspired and enlisted in the cause of peace to suppress their voracious sexual appetites. Like other political conspirators, they swear an oath, this time upon a wine cup, a signifier of women's allegedly bibulous tendencies. The magistrate adds to the implicit critique of women's ways when he condemns his fellows for mismanagement of their wives: "When we ourselves abet our wives' misbehavior and teach them profligacy, these are the sort of schemes they bring to flower!" He cites the goldsmith invited to fit a prong in a hole, a shoemaker urged to loosen up his wife's shoe, both notorious despoilers of women's virtue, and the women themselves seen as eager participants in their ruin. Lysistrata's elaborate speech on reform of the *polis* uses the analogy of carding wool, women's traditional work, and urges a fine new cloak made of all the various flocks, the tribes of the Greeks:

> First you wash the
> city as we wash the wool,
> cleaning out the bullshit. . . .
>
> . . .
>
> Now you're ready: weave a brand new
> suit for all the citizens. (2.199–218)

Weaving was women's work, as is seen in the *Iliad* and the *Odyssey*, for example, where Penelope's weaving serves as a delaying tactic, allowing her to defer her marriage. Carding and weaving by the women of the house provided clothing and cover for its inhabitants. This hilarious extended analogy, treating the tangled city like a fleece, calls up much more serious treatments of the fabric of the polity, its warp and woof, discussed by Plato with gravity, the fabric seen as the work of the great god Zeus, or like the new *peplos*, or garment, offered to Athena in ritual and represented in the frieze of the Parthenon. Here women's work mimics the expulsion of the *pharmakos*, the scapegoat, and the ostracism, in the rituals and institutions that inform *Oedipus the King*. Like *The Medea*, yet even more explicit, Lysistrata offers a compelling commentary on gender relations, women's customary roles, and marriage in the ancient city and depicts the first comic heroine, the clever, witty, and successful Lysistrata.

Possibilities for comparative reading among the Greek texts abound. The women can be seen to resemble a Sapphic group, recast in a comic and robustly heterosexual vein: Calonice vows, "I will not raise my Persian slippers toward the ceiling." They form a parodic version of a polity, described in various texts, including those by Solon, Thucydides, and Plato. Their community can be read

Copyright © 2009 Pearson Education, Inc. Publishing as Longman.

against Plato's version of the ideal republic. The fantastic utopia, a universalist enterprise that yields a successful strike for peace, has a long history in the utopian literature of the West. The focus on war and militarism, so characteristic of many Greek texts from the *Iliad* onward, movingly invoked in Aeschylus's *Agamemnon*, here meets an undermining, pacifist strain of Panhellenism, a prelude to the enforced unity of the Greek cities under the domination of the Macedonians, first Philip, then Alexander the Great and his heirs, then finally, under the Roman empire, which incorporated the Hellenistic kingdoms into its vast territory.

Copyright © 2009 Pearson Education, Inc. Publishing as Longman.

Early South Asia

Although curiosity in the United States about the history, cultures, peoples, and politics of South Asia has perhaps never been higher than it is today, and more and more instructors are called upon to teach the literatures of South Asia, many find this to be a somewhat forbidding task. For new readers all that is strange and difficult about South Asia seems encapsulated in the very names of the characters, which strike them as not only impossible to pronounce but even to keep straight. And they're right—it's not easy. There are *three* different and important Ramas: Parashu Rama (Rama with the Axe), a Brahman (priestly) ascetic who destroyed the Kshatriyas (warrior) order twenty-one times over; Dasharathi Rama (Rama son of Dasharatha), the hero of the epic *Ramayana*; and Bala Rama, the brother of Krishna. Brother, that is, of one of the *three* different and important Krishnas: Vasudeva Krishna (Krishna son of Vasudeva), the friend and advisor to the Pandavas in the epic *Mahabharata* (and the brother of Bala Rama); Krishna Dvaipayana Vyasa, the author of that epic and a character in the story; and Draupadi, wife of the Pandavas, who sometimes bears the nickname Krishna. And if one and the same name can refer to many different characters, one character can bear many different names. Vasudeva Krishna himself has dozens of epithets (Hrishikesha, Shauri, Madhava, Narayana, and so on) in the epic and in its most popular section, the *Bhagavad Gita*, or "Song of the Blessed One"— Bhagavan being yet another one of these epithets. And since Krishna in this text and elsewhere in the *Mahabharata* is considered to be an earthly incarnation of the god Vishnu, he is capable of being referred to by any of the *thousand* names of that deity—and that there are at least a thousand is proved by the *Vishnu Sahasra Nama*, or "The One Thousand Names of Vishnu," a well-known devotional Sanskrit text from medieval India.

Of course, every tradition, even those we might consider to be our own, confronts us with obstacles to understanding. Once we become familiar with a few of the main points on the compass of early South Asian literature, we can begin to find our way to the riches it has to offer us. Works like the *Mahabharata* and *Ramayana*; the lyric poetry in Tamil, Prakrit, and Sanskrit; or the Upanishads and the Discourses of the Buddha may seem strange and confusing at first, may violate every conviction we hold about authorship, textual unity, plot, or character. But these are not violations but simply different ways of dealing with character, plot, unity, and authorship. And in many instances the texts you will be reading with your students embody the collective reflection of generations of some of the most

Copyright © 2009 Pearson Education, Inc. Publishing as Longman.

powerful minds the world has ever known grappling with many of the core problems of human existence. Students will quickly see that the effort to understand
these great works is worth the trouble.

The Mahabharata of Vyasa

While both the *Mahabharata* and the *Ramayana* can be taught separately, it makes
a good deal of sense to teach them together—indeed, a unit on the old epics can
be even more rewarding. Drawing out the similarities among the Indian and Greek
epic traditions, for example, can point up the shared concerns that many early peoples had for producing, as Hegel put it (in his *Lectures on Aesthetics*), texts that
sought to communicate the "national story," a kind of summary of a community's
core concerns and primary ways of being in polity and society (its "world-outlook"
and "concrete existence," as Hegel said). The *Iliad* and the *Odyssey* in fact provide
astonishing homologies to the *Mahabharata* and *Ramayana*; if selections from all
four texts were taught in a single unit, students could be asked to explore the various similarities. For example, the *Iliad* and the *Mahabharata* are overwhelming
tales of war, wounded pride, treachery, betrayal, each a kind of grand anthem for
doomed youth. In both, the unmanageability of power seems to be the one truth
constantly vindicated. The *Odyssey* and the *Ramayana*, by contrast, while not in-
different to central political issues—the suitors who threaten the power of the absent Odysseus, the brother Bharata at home in Rama's Ayodhya who was used in
his mother's grab for power that first drove Rama into exile—are far more focused
on the family unit, the relationship between separated husband and wife, the pain
of homesickness and the desire to get home.

The *Iliad* and the *Mahabharata* are terrifying in their realism, and they are pervaded by a deep sense of despair. Consider just two famous speeches of the pathos
of doom foreseen. The first occurs late in the *Iliad*, when Achilles, having re-
entered the battle, refuses an enemy soldier who is begging for life:

> . . . You see, don't you, how large
> I am, and how well-made? My father is noble,
> a goddess bore me. Yet death waits for me,
> for me as well, in all the power of fate.
> A morning comes or evening or high noon
> when someone takes my life away in war,
> a spear-cast, or an arrow from a bowstring.
> (*Iliad* 21.107–112, trans. Fitzgerald)

The second speech comes near the end of the fifth book of the *Mahabharata*, when
Karna takes leave of Krishna, spurning Krishna's offer of kingship at the price of
abandoning those who had shown him kindness:

Copyright © 2009 Pearson Education, Inc. Publishing as Longman.

Will I see you, great-armed Krishna,
escaping with my life from the great war
that brings death to soldiers?
Or will we meet in heaven? Yes, I am sure,
it will be there, blameless Krishna,
that we will meet again.

(Mahabharata 5.141.45–46, trans. Sheldon Pollock)

The *Odyssey* and the *Ramayana*, by contrast, are far less concerned with realistic portrayals of men struggling for power on the field of battle. Instead, they share elements with what can be thought of as the romance genre: the movement into another world or antiworld, the quest for reunion with a beloved, the adventures with unearthly beings. And they end, not in the despair of Pyrrhic victory, but in reunion and resolution. (Such parallels do not require us to posit a genetic relationship among these epic texts, though this has long been a favored mode of analysis. See, for example, the various works of Georges Dumézil, such as *The Stakes of the Warrior*, 1983; a grand synthesis of evidence in favor of an Indo-European literature is now available in Calvert Watkins, *How to Kill a Dragon: Aspects of Indo-European Poetics*, 2001. Still very worth reading, so long as the reading is critical, is Hegel's comparative study of the epics in his *Aesthetics: Lectures on Fine Arts*, trans. T. M. Knox, 1998.)

The *Mahabharata* and the *Ramayana* can also be taught profitably as a comparative unit in themselves—or perhaps better put, as a "connective" rather than "comparative" unit, for in the case of these two works there is no doubt about their historical interaction; their interrelationships are sustained, sometimes even dizzying. The *Mahabharata*, for example, contains in its third book (a massive collective of supplementary narratives) a complete short version of the *Ramayana*. And the *Ramayana* makes frequent allusion to the *Mahabharata*; indeed, there is no doubt that the central story and the overall structure of the *Mahabharata* is known to the creator of the *Ramayana*. Not only is the general theme the same—the transfer of royal power and the struggle between brothers that this transfer provokes or would be expected to provoke—but so is the overall architecture and even the structure of specific books. Students can be asked to think about the similarities between, say, the second book of the *Mahabharata*, the "Book of the Assembly Hall" that contains "The Friendly Dice Game," and the second book of the *Ramayana*, the "Ayodhya Section." The very urban, even familial environment (before both sets of heroes are exiled to the forest) offers material for comparative analysis. Students can reflect profitably on the central role of the women, Draupadi in the one case, Sita in the other—and on how and why, here and throughout the epics, the problem of political power so frequently expresses itself by the gendered metaphor of the violation of a woman. (The place of Helen in the *Iliad*, Dido in the *Aeneid*, perhaps also Eve in *Paradise Lost*, might be added to usefully complicate the discussion.)

Copyright © 2009 Pearson Education, Inc. Publishing as Longman.

Yet each of the epics also presents its own particular interpretive challenges. "The Friendly Dice Game" that opens our selection from the *Mahabharata* raises several problems of interpretation that have to do with the ritual or mythical context of much early South Asian literature. Why, for example, does Yudhishthira gamble on the way he does? (Students shouldn't worry about the curious nature of the game; we simply don't know how it was played.) Some scholars have argued that, according to the ritual handbooks of the Vedic epoch, part of the ancient initiation ceremony of new kings was a ritual gambling with their rivals (suggested first by J. A. B. van Buitenen, "On the Structure of the Sabhaparvan of the *Mahabharata*," in *India Maior*, eds. J. Ensink and P. Gaeffke, 1972). According to this view, Yudhishthira is compelled, so to speak, by ceremonial tradition to do what he does. In the discourse of the epic itself, however, Yudhishthira is warned by Vyasa that the thirteen years to come would be difficult for the Pandavas because of Yudhishthira himself, and so he vowed never to refuse a request lest he provoke a quarrel. This leaves him vulnerable to Duryodhana's invitation. At the same time, today's readers will find it very hard not to conclude that some inner compulsion is also at work in the scene—after all, the usher who goes to get Draupadi after she has been lost as a wager describes Yudhishthira as having become "mad" with dicing. And the compulsion is of the sort that suggests power is a gamble (to be sure, a possible signification in the Vedic rite itself) and absolute power, the object of the *Mahabharata* war, an absolutely corrupting gamble. Yudhishthira's problematic character is in fact a theme to which the epic returns again and again. He may be a paragon of honesty and truthfulness, core values of kingship and precisely what enable Yudhishthira, alone among the Pandava brothers and their wife Draupadi, to enter heaven in bodily form at the end of the epic. But there is no question that he is often represented as weak and indecisive, incapable either of resisting evil with force or of renouncing power with indifference. It was precisely such implications in the epic that made a deep impression on later South Asian writers, not one of whom ever turned Yudhishthira into a hero of Sanskrit drama or courtly epic, in stunning contrast to Rama. So the interpretation of the "Dice Game" remains a conundrum. As for the salience of the Vedic background, doubts may well be entertained. All peoples preserve an inheritance of archaic culture while knowing little and caring less about original meaning. How many of us, after all, understand the original significations of the ancient Germanic custom we inherited of placing candles on birthday cakes? And so, without discounting the possibility that archaic ritual contributed something to the structure of "The Friendly Dice Game," for readers and writers in traditional India it had fallen into complete oblivion—to be remembered only by modern Western scholarship. The complications of Yudhishthira's behavior won't be unraveled by so simple a method.

Few passages in the epic can move modern readers as much as "The Temptation of Karna" in Book 5 does—and in this they are just like their premodern predecessors in India, who have always treasured the scene. Abandoned at birth by his unmarried mother, raised by a low-caste couple and shown kindness

Copyright © 2009 Pearson Education, Inc. Publishing as Longman.

by the sons of Dhritarashtra, Karna refuses to abandon his benefactors and ally himself with his real brothers, the Pandavas, whatever the reward, even if it be the kingship itself. Our sympathies are naturally with the man who acts so honorably, but again there are serious uncertainties about the moral implications of this scene. Is Karna's social status as a low-caste man, something of which we are reminded repeatedly in the course of the epic, meant to suggest a capacity to honor the claims of gratitude and fealty that higher-caste people might be prone to ignore, indeed people like Krishna himself and Karna's biological mother, Pritha, both of whom try to persuade Karna to repudiate those claims? Are we really being told that low castes are better than high—better and wiser in fact than God, whom Krishna represents? And, since caste is a matter of bodily substance, is there an implication that nurture is stronger than nature? Or does the *Mahabharata*'s repeated insistence on the "subtlety of *dharma*," the openness or even undecidability of the moral order, presuppose that Karna's choice to remain loyal to Duryodhana could be the morally correct choice? (On some of these tensions see Aditya Adarkar, "Karna's Choice: Courage and Character in the Face of an Ethical Dilemma," in *The Mahabharata: Whatever Is Not Here Is Nowhere Else*, ed. T. S. Rukmani, 2003.)

Radically at odds with this view, however, as well as with our natural sympathies and understandings, are the traditional interpretations of this scene. These argue consistently that (to quote one commentator from medieval Bengal):

> Because of a fate sent by the will of God the politically wrong ideas among Duryodhana, Karna, Shakuni, and Duhshasana were such that they couldn't be changed through even a thousand teachings on the part of men as wise as Brihaspati, counselor to the gods. Thus, although Krishna imparts wisdom to Karna in private by arguments that are filled with *dharma*, the instruction has no effect on him. Karna and the rest have been struck down by a more powerful fate, and they cannot be cured by any remedy whatever.

This is a wonderful example of the potentially radically different views of what Stanley Fish famously named "interpretive communities" and their historical constitution (*Is There a Text in This Class?: The Authority of Interpretive Communities*, 1980). An even better example is provided by the *Bhagavad Gita*.

In the case of the first few chapters at least, the *Gita* is the sort of text that almost teaches itself, at least in the sense that it immediately confronts us with arresting questions. The *Gita* comes in the sixth book of the great epic, after the embassies and counter-embassies sent to avert war have all failed and after, as a last-ditch effort, Krishna has tried to win over Karna to the Pandava side. When the drama of the impending violence has built to a fever pitch, and the two armies at last are arrayed facing each other in battle, we are given a long disquisition on life and death, *karma* and *samsara*, and the ways of God to man and various justifications of them. Generations of Western scholars, like Moriz Winternitz (author of the standard reference work on early Indian literature in the last century), declared

Copyright © 2009 Pearson Education, Inc. Publishing as Longman.

that this philosophical interlude violated all dramatic propriety and were ready to lop off this or that portion of the *Gita* as "interpolations" that "deformed" the text. "It is scarcely imaginable that an epic poet would make his heroes hold a philo- sophical conversation of 650 verses in the midst of the description of a battle" (Moriz Winternitz, *History of Indian Literature*, 1983–1985, p. 439). But there is no reason to insist that the authors of the ancient *Mahabharata* honor certain canons of realism as these developed in nineteenth-century Europe. The *Mahabharata* is filled to overflowing with such elaborations as the *Gita*, and clearly the philosophi- cal and the dramatic were not in conflict in the epic aesthetic.

Far more problematic than its contextual propriety is the *Gita's* moral argu- ment. Even when coupled with the ethics of disinterested action that lie at the heart of the *Gita*, the injunction to obey, to do one's duty however abhorrent, to kill since only the body dies and not the soul, has troubled many Western critics. "There is no murder or act of violence," to quote Winternitz one last time, "which could not be justified by this miserable sophistry" (*History of Indian Literature*, p. 412, n. 1). Many modern South Asian readers, however, like Mohandas Gandhi, the founder of nonviolent resistance in colonial India, have argued that the *Gita*, indeed like the *Mahabharata* as a whole, is not actually a tale of war at all, not a historical work in any sense. Instead, "under the guise of physical warfare, it de- scribe[s] the duel that perpetually [goes] on in the hearts of mankind"; the narra- tive of actual warfare is brought in "merely to make the description of the internal duel more alluring" (M. K. Gandhi, *The "Bhagavad Gita" According to Gandhi*, 2000). Much of the epic, as well as the history of the epic's reception in premod- ern India (where the reality that an actual war had occurred was never doubted), militates strongly against such an allegory. But a classroom discussion of this kind of reading offers an opportunity to explore with students such issues as perspec- tivism in the constitution of textual meaning and the plurality of interpretations, the criteria of their validity—what makes some stronger, better able to account for more of the text, than others—as well as the longing, as in Gandhi, to find a use- able past in the often problematic traditions bequeathed to posterity, especially when that posterity bears the postcolonial psychic scars left by an Orientalism all too sure of the inerrancy of its own views.

❦

RESONANCES

Kautilya and Ashoka

These two works (Kautilya's *The Treatise on Power* and Ashoka's *Inscriptions*) can be taught together to suggest the remarkable spectrum of social theory in early South Asia—this was no monodimensional "Asiatic despotism"—and indeed, the kinds of contexts within which the political discourse of both the *Mahabharata* and the *Ramayana* recover something of their historical signification. The contrasts between the two texts, which pertain to almost every feature, are especially productive.

Copyright © 2009 Pearson Education, Inc. Publishing as Longman.

Although Chanakya, alias Kautilya (or Kautalya), is associated with the founding of the Mauryan dynasty in the last decades of the fourth century B.C.E., the text that has come down under his name cannot be older than the second or third century C.E. (Hartmut Scharfe, *Investigations in Kautalya's Manual of Political Science*, 1993). What parts are to be ascribed to Kautilya, and what, accordingly, his doctrines actually were, cannot easily be determined. By contrast, we know almost exactly when Ashoka wrote—from the 260s to the 230s B.C.E.— and we have a very good idea of his views on polity. Kautilya presents a vision of the political world where the acquisition and preservation of power, *artha*, is the ultimate good. (Not all parts of the *Treatise* share this vision, however, and so the often-drawn comparison with Machiavelli's *Prince*—see Vol. C, p. 233—is not entirely correct.) Thus, his treatment of princes is entirely pragmatic and devoid of all sentimentality.

Just this Kautilyan ethos was embodied in the young Ashoka when, as legend has it (John Strong, *The Legend of King Ashoka*, 1983) he returned to the Mauryan capital as his father lay dying and slaughtered all possible rivals to his succession to kingship. It was after his war against Kalinga (on the southeast coast of India) around 260 that the dramatic moral transformation occurred, which Ashoka recounts in a personal confession (the opening of this Resonance section) that has no equivalent in the ancient world. The revision of political ethos comprised, in essence, the replacement of *artha* by *dhamma* (*dharma*) as the core value of his political beliefs, but what exactly does *dhamma* mean for Ashoka? Although there is no doubt that the emperor became a lay Buddhist, scholars have long recognized that, aside from nonviolence, there is not a great deal in the *dhamma* edicts addressed to the populace at large that strictly aligns with the teaching of the Buddha. What Ashoka's *dhamma* offers is, to put it almost simplemindedly, a new vision of political goodness—recognition of others, respect, tolerance, generosity— one that is best understood within the context of an apocalyptic *Machtpolitik* of the *Mahabharata*, and in line with the radically different vision to be presented in the *Ramayana*. The fact that this was a vision based on a profoundly paternalistic conception of power—"All people are my children"; "All children must obey their mothers and fathers"—might offer a point of departure for classroom discussion of how and why obedience, even unfreedom, have so often been asserted as the price of social stability and political peace. (A concise discussion of Ashoka's inscriptions is offered in Romila Thapar, *Early India*, 2002, pp. 200-204.)

The Ramayana of Valmiki

The doctrine of obedience that Ashoka demands in his new political ethos appears to have profoundly shaped Valmiki's *Ramayana*. If the *Mahabharata*, which is admittedly about many things, may be said to be about any one thing, it would be

Copyright © 2009 Pearson Education, Inc. Publishing as Longman.

the paradox of power, the apparent necessity to kill in order to live. If the *Ramayana*, too, can be said to be about any one thing, it would be precisely the resolution of that paradox in a new conception of kingship and of social and political morality. That the moral dimension of the poem has long had powerful effects on the behavior of real people in southern Asia has been noted in the introduction to the *Anthology* section on Early South Asia (p. 804). Rama, Sita, Lakshmana, and the others have constantly been held up as models of behavior, unlike the heroes of the *Mahabharata*, Yudhishthira, Draupadi, even Arjuna, to say nothing of Bhima. To this day public performances of the *Ramayana*, regardless of the version, often revolve around moral questions: Why did Rama do this? Was Sita right to do that? Indeed, there even developed a small subgenre of texts known as the "List of Doubts" cataloguing moral quandaries in the story, and public recitation and exegesis are often developed on the basis of such lists (Linda Hess, "Lovers' Doubts: Questioning the Tulsi Ramayan," in *Questioning Ramayanas*, ed. Paula Richman, 2001, pp. 25–47; Philip Lutgendorf, *The Life of a Text: Performing the Ramcaritmans of Tulsidas*, 1991, pp. 177, 393 ff.).

Students could be asked to map the problem of authority and obedience in the selection from the "Book of Ayodhya." The dynamic is explored everywhere and from every angle—in Rama's relations with his father, Dasharatha; his brother, Lakshmana; his mother, Kausalya; his wife, Sita; and in Kaikeyi's relations with her husband, Dasharatha, and so on. But almost everywhere we look there are ambiguities and obscurities. Most striking is the very premise of Rama's behavior in obeying his father: Though Dasharatha may have been tricked into granting a wish he once promised Kaikeyi, Rama feels compelled to preserve his father's honesty and so must go into exile rather than accept the kingship. The very injustice of the cause seems to magnify Rama's sacrifice. But we learn later in the same book that the bride price required of Dasharatha, if he was to gain the hand in marriage of the beautiful young princess of Kashmir, was pledging the kingship to Kaikeyi's future son. If Rama knows this at the end of the book, mustn't he, at the beginning, be colluding with his father in cheating Kaikeyi out of her due? But what Rama must know at the end if he is to convince his brother Bharata of the reasonableness of his refusal to return to Ayodhya—the fact that Dasharatha had made a marriage agreement—is precisely what he cannot have known at the beginning if he is to ensure that his father remain true. This contradiction, and there are others like them throughout the poem, seems irreducible. It is rather the necessity of the obedience that the poem aims to emphasize, rather than the quality of the authority that demands it. To obey is not always as straightforward as it might at first appear to be.

Not unrelated in its moral orientation and ethical ambiguity is what for many readers new and old is one of the most problematic scenes in Valmiki's poem, the fire test of Sita in Book 6. (Its enduring impact is indexed in Madhu Kishwar, "Yes to Sita, No to Ram! The Continuing Popularity of Sita in India," *Manushi* 98 [January/February 1997]; also available online at http://www.manushi-india.org/pdfs_issues/articles/Yes%20to%20Sita,%20No%20to%20Ram.pdf.) To what de-

Copyright © 2009 Pearson Education, Inc. Publishing as Longman.

gree, and on what grounds, should we be prepared to accept or reject the text's own justification, that Rama is not just a man but a king whose own moral standards and those of his wife must be beyond reproach? This problematic reaches the breaking point in the seventh and final book of the epic (not included in the *Anthology*), when in order to silence the malicious gossip in Ayodhya that Sita has lived with another man, Rama has Lakshmana take her away from Ayodhya, pregnant and unsuspecting, and abandon her in the forest. This whole subnarrative of the epic offers a good opportunity to discuss the relative weight of public versus private welfare, if those terms may be used here without anachronism, and the vexing problem of the relativity of moral standards between historical epochs.

(For a complete translation of *The Ramayana of Valmiki*, along with detailed introductions and commentary, consult the series under the general editorship of Robert P. Goldman, published by Princeton University Press, 1983–, five of seven volumes issued to date.)

∞

RESONANCES

A Public Address and Daya Pawar et al.

The *Ramayana* sometimes seems like a language in its own right, which various peoples across Asia have used to tell tales of consequence for their everyday lives. One powerful motif in the Valmiki text seems to lie in a two-fold move. The first is to semi-divinize the hero, for Valmiki the terrestrial king is really a "god who walks the earth in the form of a man." The second, which is correlative to the first, is to demonize the enemy:

> Not only are these two thematics the defining thematics of Valmiki's epic, they are two of the most powerful conceptions of the social-political imagination. The first proclaims that the order of everyday human life is regulated by the active, immanent presence of the divine; the second, that those who would disturb or destroy that order must be enemies of God and not really human. (Sheldon Pollock, "Rama and Political Imagination in India," *Journal of Asian Studies* 53:2 [1993], p. 281)

A direct historical line connecting Valmiki's poem with any of the many later redeployments of these thematics is not easy to draw, but redeployments there have been in history, most recently in the town of Ayodhya, India, in 1992, when a mosque built on what is thought to be the birthplace of Rama was destroyed by militant Hindus. (See, e.g., Peter van der Veer, *Religious Nationalism: Hindus and Muslims in India*, 1994, pp. 1–24; or Richard H. Davis, "The Iconography of Rama's Chariot," in *Contesting the Nation: Religion, Community, and the Politics of Democracy in India*, ed. David Ludden, 1996.) Contested places, the contested histories of those places, the processes of manufacturing memory and producing po-

Copyright © 2009 Pearson Education, Inc. Publishing as Longman.

litical action through those histories and memories are questions that confront people everywhere, from Jerusalem to Kosovo and beyond. And how we deal with these places and memories can become issues of pressing urgency, which students need to confront.

Often of equal urgency, too, is the fact that one community's culture can be another community's barbarism. The *Anthology* does not foreground this kind of literature—let's call it the literature of indignation, for lack of a better name—in part perhaps because it is uncommon outside of areas with continuous literary traditions preserved over a long term across vastly changing social and political landscapes. India is particularly rich in this sort of literature, however, and the *Ramayana* has been an especially productive catalyst. (See *Questioning Ramayanas*, ed. Paula Richman, 2001, for a number of good examples.) One way to frame this issue for classroom discussion is to avoid the problem of "positivism"—what was Valmiki really talking about when he was talking about "monkeys"? (something we cannot really ascertain anyway)—and focus on reception. How is it that some people have come to believe that when Valmiki was talking about "monkeys" he was talking disparagingly about them? What students should try to grasp is that only a specific mode of reading and a specific history of humiliation have made it possible to draw such conclusions.

PERSPECTIVES

What Is "Literature"?

When we think about the status of literature in the ancient world, in classical Greece, for example, our thoughts are likely to turn to Plato. In Plato's dialogue *Ion* or in the opening books of the *Republic* what is at stake in the philosopher's critique of literature is the problem of knowledge—or rather, of ignorance. Poets compose poetry through inspiration or imagination, Plato argues; they do not possess analytical skills or true knowledge of what they are doing. Literature is, accordingly, not a form of reason. Philosophy, or *logos*, the rational account of something, and poetry, or *mythos*, a figurative account, are in irreducible opposition to each other in the Platonic conception. (See, e.g., Penelope Murray, *Plato on Poetry*, 1996.)

In early South Asia, by contrast, literature was never thematized as a particular way of knowing. Indeed, the very idea of an opposition between poetry and philosophy is alien to this thought world, where many of the greatest systematic minds were also poets. Every thinker did of course understand that literature was different from philosophy, but not because it was inferior, confused, or unknowing, let alone deceitful. It was different because what they called its "emphasis" was different. The emphasis of holy texts, they said, is the words themselves. (Mantras

Copyright © 2009 Pearson Education, Inc. Publishing as Longman.

after all exercise their power even if what they say is not understood, something many participants in a Catholic mass where the Latin liturgy is used, or a Japanese Buddhist ceremony where Sanskrit *sutras* are chanted, will readily acknowledge.) The emphasis in a text on philosophy, history, law, or the like is the meaning rather than the verbal formulation. In literature, however, the emphasis is on words and meaning both. Scholars in early South Asia all agreed on these distinctions; where they disagreed was how precisely to understand the specific nature of the literary emphasis, and this disagreement proved to be one of the most fertile in Indian intellectual history, producing a range of texts over more than a millennium that pointedly ask, and try to answer, the question: What is literature? The three selections in the Perspectives section offer, each in its own quite different way, answers to this question.

⊷ ⹁⧖⹁ ⊶

The Ramayana of Valmiki

Few works in the classical literary history of Greece, Rome, or China thematize their own newness, and none, so far as we can tell, claims to be the very first work of literature. (This is so even where we know for certain that a work did play that role; such was the case with the writings of Livius Andronicus, who invented Latin drama and epic around 240 B.C.E. in Rome.) Very different is the case with writers during the "vernacular revolution," where the problem of beginnings is everywhere made present. A figure like the English poet Caedmon is emblematic of new local writing in a world dominated by global Latin, and many comparable instances can be found in medieval South Asia (see "The Vernacular Revolution" in Vol. C of the *Anthology*, and especially the remarks on the Marathi poet Tukaram in the *Manual*, p. 247). Valmiki, the author to whom the *Ramayana* is ascribed, makes this claim of priority, and it is one that needs to be taken seriously. Why should a work call itself the first poem? How is the poem that makes such a claim thought to have come into being? And what is the relationship between these two facts in the mind of the poet himself?

These are the kinds of questions that will present themselves naturally to students as they read the account of the birth of poetry in the first book of Valmiki's *Ramayana*. To help answer them it will be useful to keep in mind a couple of culture-specific issues and some that are more widespread. For example, the god whom the poet encounters during his creative experience is Brahma, the four-headed creator deity who is forever simultaneously chanting the four Vedas (the source of all knowledge and thus the blueprint for cosmic creation), the very epitome of Sanskrit textuality. It is hard to avoid drawing the inference that Brahma's presence in this scene has something to tell us about the *language* in which Valmiki is to compose the work. And in fact a cogent historical argument can be made that the *Ramayana* was among the first texts to be used for composing "literature" in Sanskrit.

Copyright © 2009 Pearson Education, Inc. Publishing as Longman.

What this category "literature"—*kavya* in Sanskrit and other Indian languages—refers to in the logic of the story will become clearer if we reflect on some of the other concerns of the narrative. Valmiki is asked to compose the complete story of Rama on the basis of a short version of the *Ramayana* he received from the wandering sage Narada (this bare-bones epitome is provided in the first chapter of the first book and is omitted from our selection). Again, it is not much of a stretch to infer that literature is being constituted as something different from the simple unadorned stories—the mere "meanings"—of a historical-legendary account. The poet also invents a new form for the work, in the shape of a quatrain consisting of eight-syllable lines, of the following sort, the very first that Valmiki composed:

> *ma nishada pratishtam tvam / agamah shashvatih samah /*
> *yat kraunca-mithunad ekam / avadhih kama-mohitam /*

> > Since, Nishada, you killed one of this pair of krauncas, distracted at the height of passion, you shall not live for very long. (trans. Robert P. Goldman)

And he fills it with emotion—his own emotion, or *rasa*—stimulated when he encounters an act of pitiable violence in the everyday world, not the mythical world of the Vedic seers, the locus of most pre-"literary" textuality. He then is shown to teach his poem orally to two young reciters. In this scene orality is reflexively represented in a way that, it could be argued (as it has in fact been argued for analogous scenes from other traditions, such as Caedmon's orality), would have been impossible in a world ignorant of writing. Indeed, the work shows none of the standard traits of oral composition. Thus what marks literature may have been the fact that it was what came to be committed to writing when that skill was first made available in India in the mid-third century B.C.E. Thus, *rasa*, meter, textual complexity, Sanskrit, and, implicitly, writing seem all to function as diagnostic of what was thought, by Valmiki, to mark something as "literature"—precisely characteristics that would figure in any later definition of the category in South Asia.

—•—≡◆≡—•—

Rajashekhara

A very different vision of the creation of literature is offered by Rajashekhara, an early-tenth-century scholar and poet of north-central India. (One of his plays, the *Karpura Manjari*, or "Bouquet of Camphor," has been translated often; a large number of his lyrics are preserved in the *Subhashita-ratna-kosha*, rendered into English by Daniel H. H. Ingalls as *An Anthology of Sanskrit Court Poetry*, 1965.) "Poetry Man [Kavya Purusha] Weds Poetics Woman [Sahitya Vidya]," a chapter

Copyright © 2009 Pearson Education, Inc. Publishing as Longman.

from the one surviving book of what was planned as an encyclopedia of poetry, is a charming origin myth of literature. Teachers interested in developing a comparative unit to include this text might consider a selection from the early portions of Martianus Capella's fifth-century allegory, *The Marriage of Mercury and Philology*. (There is no reason to believe, however, that this text, extraordinarily influential though it was in western Europe from the moment of its composition through at least the twelfth century, could actually have been known to Rajashekhara.) One can understand well how the god of interpretation and the mortal lady of grammatical learning (or for some interpreters, Speech and Reason) could have fallen in love with each other. It is a little less obvious what we are to understand from the marriage of Poetry Man and Poetics Woman.

As is well illustrated by the central motif of the myth, which is a playful parody of its Vedic prototype, for Rajashekhara—and in this he is representative of a widespread view—a key feature of literature is its geographical specificity. *Kavya* is something that occurs in a particular world and nowhere else. When Poetry Man, the beloved son of the Goddess of Speech, moves across the cultural landscape to create regional styles of literary expression, it is through the landscape of the subcontinent he travels. To be sure, real people in the tenth century were familiar with spaces far beyond the subcontinent. Indians traveled widely, from Central Asia to China, for example, and across Southern Asia as far as Java—indeed, carrying Sanskrit poetry with them, so that the vernacular literature of Java, for example, newly invented during the vernacular revolution, is closely related to Indic models. Rajashekhara himself was interested in concrete geography; he claims to have written a separate book on the subject and alludes to geographical information repeatedly in his *Inquiry*. But for him literature is very much a subcontinental phenomenon. However many its local variations, these are variations on a theme occurring within this finite space.

As for the relationship between Poetry Man and Poetics Woman—or, if we can unpack the allegory, the right relationship between literary practice and literary theory—we might not want to formulate too definite an answer. If Indian writers were among the most technically sophisticated in the ancient world, they also knew that poets were born more often than made. Poetry leads, and Criticism, though she clearly has something to contribute, follows behind.

Anandavardhana

We enter a completely different conceptual universe from that of Valmiki or Rajashekhara when we come to the work of Anandavardhana, the most innovative thinker in the history of Sanskrit literary theory. While the old understanding that literature emphasizes word and meaning conjointly was hardly to be challenged, the apparently simple but actually profound question that Anandavardhana (often affectionately known as "Ananda") asked—what is meant

Copyright © 2009 Pearson Education, Inc. Publishing as Longman.

here by "meaning"?—changed the course of the history of reflection in India on what makes literature literary. His answer, in the most basic terms, is that literary meaning is specifically the meaning that is *not* said but rather is heard "echoing" in the background of the utterance.

Ananda's exposition of this idea moves from the simple to the very complex. Students don't need to come to terms with that complexity; it is enough if they get the basic idea. In a metaphor, say, "to suffer / The slings and arrows of outrageous fortune, / Or to take arms against a sea of troubles," we can hear some echoes or suggestions of the kind Ananda is talking about if we pause to listen: How Hamlet saw the events in his life as a series of nothing but sorrowful episodes, varying only between the dull ache and the piercing pain; how these troubles overwhelmed and threatened to drown him, and against which he wants, quite irrationally, to use weapons—of the kind that fortune uses against him?—irrationally because you cannot stop a flood by shooting it with arrows. These are some possible unsaid meanings in the passage that make themselves known when we stop to ask why the poet wrote precisely in the way he did. When we proceed to some of Ananda's narrative examples, we quickly find that even the single, straightforward verse has potentially limitless layers of meaning. Consider Ananda's very first example of suggestion:

> Go your rounds freely, gentle monk;
> The little dog is gone.
> Just today from the thickets by the Godā
> Came a fearsome lion and killed him.

When we look into the anthology of Prakrit poems from which Ananda took this example, these four lines of the poem are all we find. The poem is meant to be complete in itself; there is no narrative context, no frame story, nothing but these four lines. Since the verse appears in a poetry collection we know right away that this cannot be an utterance of someone merely giving information to a wandering holy man. We know intuitively (though how we know Indian critics don't say) that people don't write poems to that end. "Suggestion" begins when we get ready to hear more than what is said. But we also need to know how to listen, which means knowing some of the conventions of Indian poetry. And here things can get complicated. This is how a twelfth-century commentator understood this verse:

> A certain loose woman is always leaving her house, under the pretext of fetching water from the river, in order to meet her lover in a thicket on the bank of the Godā. She regards a certain mendicant as an obstacle in that he destroys the thicket by gathering flowers for his religious rituals. And though she is a clever woman she speaks here like an ingénue: "The dog," that is, the one that used to harass you whenever you entered our compound, was careless and, to our good fortune, was killed today by a

Copyright © 2009 Pearson Education, Inc. Publishing as Longman.

fierce lion. The lion will not bother you here in the village, since it is "making its lair," that is, constantly staying, in a thicket on the banks of the Godā. You may therefore continue to wander without worry.

According to this commentator, the mendicant's begging rounds in the town had been interrupted by the woman's dog, and he is being invited to continue his rounds in the town now that the dog is dead. One of the things suggested is a prohibition against his visiting the riverside, where he often goes to gather flowers, thereby stripping bare the dense camouflage on the bank.

It is only by familiarizing ourselves with the conventions of a literary system that we come to know that riverbanks in Prakrit poetry, especially densely overgrown riverbanks (and they are always densely overgrown in Prakrit poetry), are places where lovers go, that is to say, unmarried couples who have no other place to be alone together. But couples who are not married cannot, in Prakrit poetry, licitly be together (though of course they are always together in Prakrit poetry). But calling attention to a desire to preserve the privacy of the rendezvous spot by use of a direct prohibition ("Don't go there!") would be tantamount to revealing the illicit liaison itself. The very linguistic form prompts us to ask who would make such a statement, and it is only from familiarity with the larger social text that we can know it is the woman in the illicit relationship. The gender relations that constitute the social world of Prakrit poetry demand that it is always the woman, never the man, who organizes adultery. Only when we know such social-literary facts does the real suggestion behind the poems become available. The very formulation of the statements—meaning without saying, communicating by not communicating—suggests that the woman speaker is sophisticated and clever and ardent to preserve her place of lovemaking. And in a way, once we know all this, our own reading becomes a satisfying exercise in the revelation of our own sophistication, since not only can we understand the meaning of the clever woman's statement but we understand something that the holy man necessarily cannot; the whole point is artfully to allay his suspicions about the place of rendezvous while keeping him away.

The most accessible brief account of Anandavardhana's ideas is found in the introduction to Daniel H. H. Ingalls et al., trans., *The Dhvanyaloka of Anandavardhana*, 1990; see also Sheldon Pollock, "The Social Aesthetic and Sanskrit Literary Theory," *Journal of Indian Philosophy* 29 (2001): 197–229, from which the analysis of "Go your rounds freely" is adapted.

LOVE IN A COURTLY LANGUAGE

A number of the complexities about the poetry of early South Asia have been addressed in Volume A of the *Anthology* and this *Instructor's Manual* (see the "What Is 'Literature'?" sections in each). The following notes on the lyrics presented in

Copyright © 2009 Pearson Education, Inc. Publishing as Longman.

the "Love in a Courtly Language" section in the *Anthology* are intended to supply some of the literary conventions and the "social text" that are often presupposed by these poems.

The Tamil Anthologies

"Dear man from the city": The opening selection offers a perfect example of the classical theory of Tamil poetry. The woman's lover is described as the man "from the city / of portia trees," and what is said of the city subtly comments on the lovers' situation. In terms of traditional Tamil criticism, the lovers of the poetry moved within a natural world that is emblematic of their relationship, from first meeting to postmarital infidelity. The mention of the rice fields places us in the agrarian land where, we are told, the man tires of settled life and seeks the company of prostitutes. In early Indian poetry, the heron is a proverbial figure of deceit, for it builds the trust of the fish that swim around its feet before devouring them; similarly, the man has seduced not merely one but many women, a point made explicit in the final line of the poem. So great was the betrayal, the woman no longer knows whom she can trust.

"As they carry the white paddy": The "white heron" links this particularly complex poem with the preceding, but to significantly different effect. Again, there is a suggestion of infidelity, elevated here to the level of sexual excess. The twin mention of the "Seashore man" and the "water lily" points to the seashore landscape, where the woman anxiously awaits the man's return. This compound image is set against what seems on the surface to be the unrelated opening lines. This device is known to the tradition as the "confusion of landscapes," where elements from several regions are juxtaposed, creating a descriptive and emotional collage. Coming from the agrarian country (as above, the landscape of infidelity), the salt merchants barter rice paddy for the salt of the seashore, where the woman awaits the man's return. Unlike the man, the merchants have nothing to hide and bring their families along with them. Coupled with the herons, this suggests the girl friend's awareness of the cause of the man's delay.

"'O your hair,' he said": This poem, along with the following two, falls largely outside the realm of affective naturalism described in Tamil poetic theory. Compiled in a separate anthology, these poems take the form of dialogue (or, as here, a monologue embedding another's speech) that may have originally provided a script for a performance. Within the frame of the text itself, the knowing explanation of the woman conveys a wry sexual sophistication, something rare in Tamil love poetry. The obvious play with the conventions of love poetry raises the question of the courtly audience of the poem and its ability to enjoy this kind of self-reflexive play.

"O you, you wear flowers of gold": A commentator describes this poem as an example of "saying what really happened"—in this case, in order that the woman might prompt her family to arrange her marriage. The real-time picture of seduc-

Copyright © 2009 Pearson Education, Inc. Publishing as Longman.

tion and consummation seen here is in keeping with the transgressive tone in the previous poem, but there's no trace of ironic distance here. The final line, a piece of sententious wisdom appended to the poem's outright sensuality, might seem odd, but the promise of continued sexual satisfaction is one of the principal motives that drive the Cankam couples to marriage.

"Friend / like someone who gets drunk": The mention in this poetic dialogue of the "goatherd lover" and the jasmine flowers hints at the pastoral landscape, that of waiting patiently for marriage. The slight disjunction of the woman's anxiety in light of her being found out may thus be intended for humorous effect.

"In encampments": This verse is the only among this selection that draws its images from the other main genre of old Tamil literature, the poetry of the "exterior," of war and public life. Such martial poems normally praise the victorious king; here we see instead a warrior crossing back over the divide between war and settled domestic life. The woman's pallor is one of the principal signs of lovesickness in Old Tamil verse, and its hypostasis, as here, is frequently encountered.

"On beaches washed by seas": The final poem is attributed to a woman poet, one of several in the Cankam anthologies. Although the sentiments are conventional, there is no reason to dispute the authenticity of a woman's voice in the poem. Tamil writers and readers of centuries past lived lives made significant by the conventions of art, just as we do now.

The Seven Hundred Songs of Hala

"At night, cheeks blushed": The speaker must be the young woman's husband, for lovers are rarely shown to spend the whole night together, and when they do, it's typically to emphasize their painful parting at dawn (common in the *aubade* genre of European poetry). He is describing his newly married wife, one of three main varieties of female protagonist in Prakrit and Sanskrit poetry, the other two being the moderately experienced woman and the fully experienced woman. (Women are also classified as one's own, another's, and a common woman, or prostitute.) Girls are often described as being married at a very young age, in fact sometimes before puberty, though the marriage would not be consummated until afterward. The new bride is always described as clueless about sex and embarrassed to be alone with her husband. But once the wheel of passion begins to turn, as Vatsyayana puts it in the *Kamasutra*, her natural skill in the arts of lovemaking is revealed, and she is almost transformed, as here, into a completely different person—only to vanish again in the light of day. Part of the charm in the verse is its implicitly overturning the typology of female characters: passion can suddenly reveal the ingénue to be the sophisticate.

"After a quarrel, / The breath suppressed": Indian literary theory divides the erotic *rasa* into two main varieties: love enjoyed and love frustrated. The former is

Copyright © 2009 Pearson Education, Inc. Publishing as Longman.

illustrated in the previous verse. In the present one, the topic is one of many sub-varieties of love frustrated—as one literary critic in early India points out, there are many more ways to be frustrated in love than to enjoy love, so it's a far richer genre for poets. The love quarrel is almost never meant to be serious in Indian poetry; it's rare to hear the voice of real sadness, though we'll see in the Amaru selections that some of the most moving verses communicate just this melancholy. The plot of a love-quarrel poem is typically the woman's wounded pride and her feigned anger and the lover's genuine repentance. This verse is slightly unusual in that both the man and the woman are pretending to be angry (he is no doubt angry at her anger, not at any infidelity on her part). And it is precisely the pretense, masking the real love and passion that are waiting to be manifested, that constitutes the charm.

"His form / In my eyes": Another species of love frustrated results from actual separation. (This was to become a major theme of religious poetry, where the devotee's separation from God would be represented as the separation of two lovers, to be overcome only by their mystic union.) The man is often away on business, and the woman is at home pining for him, as in fact he is shown to pine for her. (In suffering the pain of separation, at least, there is complete gender equality in Indian poetry.) This woman has come to realize that her fixation on her lover is such that he is not really gone from her when he is gone. An Indian commentator might find a deeper "suggestion" here: the very fact of bringing to awareness the negation of separation indicates that she knows he's not really there.

"Though he's wronged me": The verse exhibits a figure of speech known as "adducing a parallel instance," or corroboration, of the case in hand, typically from everyday life, which sometimes approximates a proverb. Vatsyayana uses these in his *Kamasutra* when discussing love: We don't refuse to plant seeds just because birds might eat them or refrain from cooking dinner just because a beggar might show up and demand food, so we shouldn't forgo pleasure just because something might go wrong (1.2.38). In poetry the parallel instance itself needn't, and typically doesn't, connect narratively with the matter under discussion except in a general way. Here, however, the poet nicely links the two. We continue to use fire even though devastating fires can break out; similarly, the woman, though "burned" by her lover, needs him still—indeed, so it seems to be suggested, she needs him almost elementally.

"Tight lads in fields": Prakrit poetry is not what we would call folk poetry in any sense. It is poetry written by sophisticated, urbane, and for the most part probably court poets, who were projecting a fantasy vision of rural life meant to stand in contrast to urban life. Prominent in this idealized inversion is the moral laxity of the country girl, whether the woman welcoming a traveling salesman, the girl tending the village well who gives visitors more than just water, or the unspecified *asati*, or loose woman, of the present verse. Nothing of this sort would ever be said of a woman in Sanskrit poetry, married or unmarried, unless of course she were a prostitute (though in that case the moral tone is entirely different, for after all, it is the *dharma* of the prostitute to show equal affection to all her customers). Indian

Copyright © 2009 Pearson Education, Inc. Publishing as Longman.

commentators would also note, in this verse, the "stimulant causes," or the scenic and other material elements represented in a literary work that contribute to the production of the *rasa*. For the erotic mood, these include a male appropriate in age to the woman, the springtime (or the rainy season), and the requisite stimulants, such as betel (as in a verse below), or here, country liquor.

"**He finds the missionary position / Tiresome**": The female in early Indian poetry often has a girlfriend who can function as a go-between (and one not always to be trusted) or as in this verse simply as a device by which the interiority of a character can be communicated. (Sanskrit drama does have stage directions to represent such interior dialogue with the self, but it's not used in poetry.) Here we have a good instance of the sort of echo Anandavardhana would hear behind the explicit meaning of the verse. The problem in a woman's suggesting other ways to make love with her husband is that the only way for her to have learned these new ways is to have made love with some other man. Yet another echo, perhaps, is that she does know other ways and therefore is making love with another man, precisely because her own husband, even though he is bored, is by implication too uninventive and unexciting to come up with something new.

"**When she bends to touch / Her mother-in-law's feet**": See the introduction to this section in the *Anthology* (pp. 937–938) for some remarks on this verse.

"**As though she'd glimpsed**": Most early South Asian poetry is G-rated, if often highly erotic—the poets appreciated the fact that, as the great eighth-century dramatist Bhavabhuti put it (and Hindi filmmakers still understand), a wet sari can be far more exciting than no sari at all. Yet there are verses, especially in Prakrit, as this one, that reveal a very earthy, unconstrained exuberance in sexuality. Sometimes, however, the social text offers yet another layer of meaning in an erotic poem that has little to do with its eroticism. Here the mother's joy may lie less in the fact that her daughter is in love than in the evidence that the girl has reached puberty (other verses in the collection point in this direction; her pubescence is implied by her interest in sex) and so is ready to be married off. And though it may seem to be pressing too far, it's probable that the "pot of gold" refers not to what it seems to refer (only a lover would use the simile in that way, not a mother) but to the bride-price that the family would acquire at the marriage.

The Hundred Poems of Amaru

The Sanskrit poems from the *Amaru* collection do not present quite the same interpretation issues as Hala does. But there are things to know that will help in presenting the poems to a class.

"**She is the child, but I the one of timid heart**": This verse is ascribed in many anthologies to Dharmakirti, the great Buddhist logician of the seventh century. And not improbably, since the poem plays upon logical difficulties in the causal process, which constituted one of the great problems in early Indian philosophy. The verse also offers a catalogue of "poet's conventions" about female

Copyright © 2009 Pearson Education, Inc. Publishing as Longman.

beauty, such as are visible in any example of classical Indian sculpture (see the illustration, Vol. A, p. 798).

"You will return in an hour?": A good instance of the erotic genre of love frustrated, which turns on the figure of the new bride, the ingénue who hopes against hope that the separation from her husband will be anything but what she fears it will be.

"As he came to bed the knot fell open of itself": The verse is ascribed in anthologies to a woman poet, which there is no reason to dispute (though it is massively in evidence that male poets wrote often in a female voice). It invokes a common motif of the overpowering nature of real passion. Women who are able to describe to their friends exactly what happened during their lovemaking couldn't have *really* been making love at all. Real passion blinds us so much that our very self-identity dissolves.

"The sheets, marked here with betel": Betel leaf is smeared with limepaste and wrapped around an areca nut to make what in India is known as *pan* (pronounced *pahn*). It is a very mild intoxicant and a standard accoutrement of pleasures, whether sexual, gustatory, or other. Aloe (or more often sandalwood) paste was used to cool a woman's breasts, and lacquer (more usually called lac) refers to a kind of red paint used to adorn a woman's feet.

"At first our bodies knew a perfect oneness": This verse is also ascribed, again entirely credibly, to a woman poet. As noted earlier, there is a pervasive sense of conventionality to much Sanskrit poetry, where scope for individual creativity was narrowed and where as a consequence the capacity to invent within the limits of convention was all the more prized. Verses on love frustrated thus follow a typical pattern, often revolving around the wounded pride and feigned anger of the heroine. But the present verse hardly fits the norm. It is completely unadorned by any figure of speech (many Indian critics argued explicitly that figuration was not an essential component of poetry, and to prove their point cited verses like the present one), and it has a very individual ring in expressing the loss of passion in the banality of everyday conjugality.

"Your palm erases from your cheek the painted ornament": It's the lover, of course, who in lovemaking would erase the design that a woman in Indian poetry typically has painted on her cheek, and drink the nectar of her lips, and fondle her breasts. The idea of nursing—falling in love with—one's own anger has perhaps never found such happy expression.

"They lay upon the bed each turned aside": A Sanskrit version of the love-frustrated theme found also in Prakrit poetry, as in "After a quarrel, / The breath suppressed," discussed earlier.

"If you are angry with me, you of lotus eyes": It's easy to imagine that this could be an English translation of a Sanskrit translation of a lost Latin poem by Catullus (see, e.g., "Lesbia, let us live only for loving," in Vol. A, p. 1246), different only in the element of personalization (see the introduction to "Love in a Courtly Language" in Vol. A, p. 930). Such parallels show that, for all their local conventionality, we often do encounter texts of Sanskrit and Prakrit poetry that somehow slip their local moorings for some wider sea of human meaning.

Copyright © 2009 Pearson Education, Inc. Publishing as Longman.

"You listened not to words of friends": The poem depends on understanding the Sanskrit poetic conventions regarding the "stimulant causes" of the erotic *rasa*: love enjoyed will often take place on a moonlit night, and as the lovers embrace, the sandalwood paste used to cool the woman's breasts will be smeared onto her lover's chest, and the night of lovemaking will seem to last but a moment. In love frustrated—here prompted by a woman's wounded pride and anger over her lover's infidelity—all these stimulants produce precisely their opposite effects. "Incongruity" (*vishama*) is a common figure of sense in Sanskrit poetry.

"At day's end as the darkness crept apace": See earlier, on "You will return in an hour?", which raises similar issues.

"She let him in": Compare with "At first our bodies knew a perfect oneness," discussed earlier, for the unadorned directness of the poem. Here and in the following two texts, the well-known poet and translator W. S. Merwin, seeking a more contemporary form, throws the quatrain structure of Sanskrit poetry to the winds. Here it might be worth raising with students the problem of translation, which of course runs through much of what they will be reading in the *Anthology*. Indian poets strove very hard to meet the demands of form. Should their translators? Is it better to be beautiful or faithful? A live sparrow or a stuffed eagle?

"Held her / tight to me": On the idea that real passion leads to the dissolution of the self, compare this poem with "As he came to bed the knot fell open of itself," discussed earlier. What is distinctive here is that the voice is male.

"Lush clouds in / dark sky of tears": Key to the verse, though almost hidden, is the image in the first two lines: Love frustrated can of course occur at any time of the year, but it is especially painful in the rainy season, when travel is difficult and men are supposed to be at home with the women they love—and if they are not, their absence is unbearable. Clouds are full ("lush") when the monsoons begin and white when they end in the autumn.

Kalidasa

If we are inclined to explore the problem of literary interpretation, we can do this with any text, of course, though those from distant times and places pose the problem more insistently than do texts from our own period. *Shakuntala* is a particularly good work to read with a class to demonstrate the various contingencies to which literary understanding is subject. For one thing, we have a long and interesting history of reception of the text, and each response to the work can be shown to bear the stamp of its particular context. Selections of several of these are given in the Resonances section for Kalidasa. (A fuller account of the reception history of the work has recently been made available in *Sakuntala: Texts, Readings, Histories*, ed. Romila Thapar, 1999.) Rabindranath Tagore's moralistic interpretation from late-colonial India, for example, might be viewed as articulating the new moral order that the great Bengali poet felt was necessary for the new postcolonial political order whose birth was imminent. Goethe, at the beginning of a new age of world litera-

Copyright © 2009 Pearson Education, Inc. Publishing as Longman.

ture—a conception appropriate for the new world market of colonial capitalism, to which nothing could be alien—easily assimilated *Shakuntala* into his literary categories, almost as if the play were a straightforward middle-class European romance, a sort of *Young Werther* on the banks of the Ganges, though with a happy ending. (For more on Goethe, who adapted the introduction of *Shakuntala* for his dramatic epic *Faust*, and on the history of German Romanticism, with which the image of nature in *Shakuntala* and natural love transcending class distinction seemed to conform so closely, see Vol. E of the *Anthology*, p. 84.) What we must today find astonishing is that neither Tagore nor Goethe showed the least doubt about the correctness of their respective interpretations, never paused to ask whether there might be historical or cultural forces at work in the constitution of the play that serve to distance it from the thought-world of twentieth-century colonial India or eighteenth-century bourgeois Germany.

The eleventh-century Indian critic Kuntaka raises a whole range of different questions in his critical account of the play. Kuntaka starts from the problem of the revisions that the dramatist introduced into the epic story of "Shakuntala" as found in the *Mahabharata*. (The full tale is available in *The Mahabharata: The Book of the Beginning*, trans. J. A. B. van Buitenen, 1973.) His analysis is based squarely, and not unreasonably, on the aesthetic doctrine that prized the cultivation of *rasa*, or the emotional dimension of the work, above any other literary element such as characterization or narrative verisimilitude. Indeed, if we consider the changes Kalidasa introduced into the epic story, we can see how profound these were. Consider only the transformation in the character of Shakuntala: Her remarkable autonomy, power, and presence have almost completely disappeared from the drama. But character change and other alterations seem to be related to, and even a consequence of, a far more fundamental revision, which Kuntaka singles out: Kalidasa has introduced a whole new, defining narrative element—the sage's curse and the ring of recognition—according to Kuntaka, in order to account for a "mystery left unexplained in the original *Mahabharata*": why the hero Dushyanta fails to recognize Shakuntala. "Forgetting his wife without any reason," according to Kuntaka (p. 1011), would have tarnished the play as much as it tarnishes the epic. And that kind of blemish (a very serious loose end in the narrative that could cause the whole to unravel) is precisely the sort of thing that inhibits the listener's entrance into the emotional world of the play, into its *rasa*.

Western scholars typically speak of the *Mahabharata* as an "epic," but it calls itself an account of things "as they really were" (a literal translation of the Sanskrit term *itihasa*, which there is no reason not to translate as "history"), and it purports to tell the whole truth about the past. Our natural assumption is that playwrights would have hesitated to depart from the truth of such history. But in fact the kind of rewriting we find in Kalidasa is the norm rather than the exception. Indian critics themselves were fully aware of the transformations necessitated by the passage from epic to theater, and they praised plot changes, however "unhistorical" they might be, that contributed to the enhancement of the aesthetic mood of the play. Here is how a ninth-century critic put it:

Copyright © 2009 Pearson Education, Inc. Publishing as Longman.

A poet when writing a poem must concentrate with all his soul on the *rasa*. If he observes some state of affairs in the historical fact that goes against the *rasa*, he should eliminate it and invent some other story appropriate to the *rasa*. No purpose is served in a poet's providing merely the historical facts. That task is accomplished by historiography itself.

As for the nature of *rasa* itself in Kalidasa's play, a detailed if rather technical account based on the traditional commentaries is given in Edwin Gerow, "Plot Structure and the Development of Rasa in the Sakuntala," *Journal of the American Oriental Society* 99 (1979): 559–572, and 100 (1980): 267–282.

However, if we are willing to grant more narrative coherence than Kuntaka does to the epic narrative and to examine it more charitably, we could argue that the king's failure to recognize Shakuntala is hardly a mystery left unexplained. The key dramatic revision that Kalidasa introduces into the epic plot concerns the theme that constitutes its hinge, the "bride-price consisting in the kingship." As we observed when considering the second book of the *Ramayana* of Valmiki and its narrative inconsistencies, this motif refers to a promise made by a royal groom to the bride's family to award the kingship to the son she would eventually bear, in preference to any other heir the king may have from other wives. (The theme structures a number of *Mahabharata* subnarratives, including the story of grandfather Bhishma's own father, Shantanu; to honor Shantanu's promise to his father-in-law-to-be, Bhishma took a lifelong vow of celibacy.) In the epic version, the king's refusal to acknowledge Shakuntala as his wife is entirely a function of this agreement. He requires the validation of a divine voice to prove to all concerned that her son is in fact his own and therefore merits the status of heir apparent, and this validation he eventually compels from the gods by his adamant refusal in public to accept the woman.

Far more than the question of *rasa* is likely to have been at stake in Kalidasa's revision. The flattening of Shakuntala's character in the play is partly a consequence of the removal of the bride-price motif, for her assertive protests to the king at the climax also contribute to the provocation of the divine voice and become unnecessary once that motif is removed. But the dramatist is also concerned with representing Shakuntala as something far more than a strong-willed country girl, a sort of Indian Lotte. She has a unique lineage, part heavenly, part terrestrial: She is the daughter of a divine nymph and Vishvamitra, the sole Kshatriya ever to transform himself into a Brahman. In addition, and as a consequence of this lineage, throughout the play she is shown to be a kind of primal force of nature. Dushyanta, too, is not just a king—no early Indian king was just a king—but rather an earthly embodiment of the great god Shiva. As such he is called upon by Indra, the king of the gods himself, to defeat the demonic forces threatening the universe (end of Act 6)—precisely the task of Shiva. Shakuntala will carry "Dushyanta's potent seed / for the good of the world" (Act 4, v. 4), that is, the birth of the boy Bharata, who will eventually become universal emperor (Act 7, v. 33), just as Parvati will carry Shiva's seed in

Copyright © 2009 Pearson Education, Inc. Publishing as Longman.

the *Birth of the War God Kumara* (*Kumarasambhava*). This courtly epic of Kalidasa's tells the story of the union of Shiva and Parvati, Daughter of the Mountain (Himalaya), who join in marriage to produce a son, Skanda Kumara, in order to destroy the demonic forces of the world. *Shakuntala* may be understood as a this-worldly version of this divine narrative, where the good of the world is also at stake and subject to the intervention of cosmic forces. Given these kinds of narrative objectives, the old-fashioned motif of the bride-price agreement no longer has relevance.

This cosmic design to ensure the birth of Bharata is objectively correlated with the formal design of the play, by which the action of the different scenes, indeed, the very language, is linked by a kind of concentric design. Consider only Acts 1 and 7: Both begin with a description of violence (the hunt/war) and a description of the motions of Dushyanta's chariot, followed by the king's desire to pay homage to a sage (Kanva in Act 1, Kashyapa in Act 7), his entrance into a peaceful hermitage, the appearance of omens and remarks on fate, the blessings for a son in Act 1 and gaining a son in Act 7, and his meeting with Shakuntala. The opening invocation in Act 1 to Shiva in his cosmological forms is echoed in Act 7 by a closing invocation to his saving grace. This kind of echoing can be perceived in Acts 2 and 6, and 3 and 5 as well, knitting them together at almost every level. Wherever we look in the play, from the nature of the characters to the structure of their actions, we find evidence of design in every sense of the term.

Traditional readings of the *Shakuntala* tend to highlight the sentimental education of a young woman, the drama of personal separation and recovery, the dynamics of intimate social relationships between father and daughter, husband and wife, father and son, and friends, especially women friends. These features undoubtedly mark the work and need not be seen to be in conflict with, let alone mutually exclusive of, the range of different meanings suggested by the play's unambiguous architecture, the divine stratagem behind the union of two supramundane beings, or the parallels with the tale of Shiva and Parvati. It is a truism that great literature is great in part because of its capacity to allow meanings to proliferate, and few works of Indian literature demonstrate this as well as *Shakuntala*.

The capacity to make a text one's own, the way Tagore and Goethe made *Shakuntala* their own or the way religious readers make scripture their own (as Paul Riceour once said, "Saint Paul's Letters were written *to me*"), is no doubt some good thing. For it occurs when the text is part of living culture, rather than presented to us as a pickled specimen in a lecture hall. *Shakuntala* was alive in this sense for both Tagore and Goethe. Yet such a mode of appropriation also seems to force the text to adjust to our needs, rather than inviting us to adjust ourselves to its needs. *Shakuntala* challenges students to discipline that sort of lazy homogenization of otherness by an exercise in slow reading—working out the subtle allusions to Shakuntala as a force of nature, for example, or mapping the carefully if unobtrusively constructed formal symmetries of the play—where concerns of a literary world potentially very different from their own can eventually make themselves known.

Copyright © 2009 Pearson Education, Inc. Publishing as Longman.

China: The Classical Tradition

The Book of Songs

"No one today reads the *Shi jing* without help—lots of help" (Willard Peterson, "Reading *Sheng min*," in *Ways with Words: Writing about Reading Texts from Early China*, eds. Pauline Yu et al., 2000, p. 31). This wry comment on the challenges presented by this sixth-century B.C.E. anthology, the *Book of Songs*, alludes both to the sheer linguistic difficulties of reading a text compiled almost two millennia ago and to the daunting burden of commentary it acquired over the centuries. Many poems in the anthology contain words or phrases that rarely appear in any other early text and whose meanings are therefore difficult to ascertain by standard philological methods of textual comparison and triangulation; hundreds are *hapax legomena*, or unique usages found nowhere else. Like all classical Chinese writing, their language also typically suppresses the grammatical subject and does not specify tense, gender, number, or case. Most poems, like later classical poetry in general, are so brief that their basic situations are sketchy at best. Titles assigned well after the fact are singularly uninformative, generally consisting simply of two words drawn from the first line of the poem.

Thanks to canonical status conferred at the beginning of the first millennium C.E., the poems have been further buried in layers of interpretation that may, not surprisingly, conceal as effectively as they reveal. Generations of scholars were expected to master and contribute to this literature, and the resulting accretions (of exegesis, gloss, and commentary), the debates among them, the intellectual and political grounds for such contentions, and the trajectories of such disputes resemble the fates of scriptural texts in other cultures. (See Steven van Zoeren, *Poetry and Personality: Reading, Exegesis, and Hermeneutics in Traditional China*, 1991.)

Modern translators have generally chosen to cut through these layers, happily or not, but students are well advised to keep in mind both the existence of a rich hermeneutical tradition surrounding the *Book of Songs* and the reasons for its development. That China's pre-eminent sage, Confucius, was—according to one legend—said to have compiled the anthology was crucial to this process, and that he commented on its utility more than once in his *Analects* made its status even less assailable (see the Resonances for these comments, which themselves are worth discussing). Other early historical texts depict conversations in which lines from over two hundred poems are cited as means of conveying possibly controversial political opinions obliquely but effectively. Such evident respect for the didactic efficacy of the *Book of Songs*, as well as the fact that some pieces did record actual

Copyright © 2009 Pearson Education, Inc. Publishing as Longman.

historical events and figures, led many early commentators to argue that the entire collection functioned in this way. Individual songs were therefore viewed as documents of a particular time and place, whether as reflections or allegorical critiques of contemporary circumstances. However far-fetched some of these interpretations may seem, they did serve to maintain the revered status of the text and also shaped enduring assumptions that any literary text was a response to external conditions and required a full understanding of its context, its background and sources, its audience and reception, and its interpretive tradition. These notions are best articulated in an early preface, attributed to Wei Hong, to the first poem in the collection that became known as the "Great Preface" to the entire group, included here in the Resonances.

Most of the poems in the selection here are "Airs of the States," arranged (with scant discernable basis) according to the various feudal states of the Zhou dynasty. Evidence of their oral provenance (such as the use of stock phrases like the cypress boat in poems 26 and 45 and the pear tree in poems 119 and 123, discussed by C. H. Wang in *The Bell and the Drum*, 1974) links them to folk songs and ballad traditions elsewhere, with which they may be fruitfully compared. Typical formal features include a four-word line, three four-line stanzas, heavy use of reduplicative phrases, and reliance on repetition with slight variations. In most cases the songs' situations are immediately apparent: courtship, seduction, trysts, separation, abandonment, and the like. The fondness for enumeration—of things or of phases of a process—suggests that some poems function as cultural ledgers or almanacs (e.g., poem 154, "The Seventh Month"). Early twentieth-century scholars have mined the songs for their information on rituals and festivals of ancient China, ignoring what must have been the purely literary or musical factors in their composition. Nonetheless, many prevalent concerns of Zhou dynasty culture can be gleaned thereby, and in particular the importance—and fragility—of human bonds, loyalty, solidarity, and fertility.

The other types of poems in the anthology, "Lesser and Greater Elegances" and "Hymns," are increasingly linked to a ritual or liturgical function, perhaps being explained or recorded for the benefit of future generations. ("Elegance" is a translation of the term *ya*, but its meaning as a generic category is unclear. The word may derive from Xia, the name of the dynasty that was said to have immediately preceded the Shang, the Zhou's predecessor.) Most of those works are longer and less easily appreciated than the "Airs of the States" poems and are therefore not well represented in this selection. However, poem 245, "Birth to the People," is a "Greater Elegance" whose account of the legendary founder of the Zhou dynasty, "Lord Millet," bears telling resemblances to origin myths from many other cultures that are well worth exploring.

The *Book of Songs* provides many glimpses into early Chinese culture—its predominant concerns, its nuggets of wisdom, and the lessons it wished to impart through illustrative vignettes, images, and admonitions. The collection can also be used to illustrate the vast differences among both commentators and translators, and alternative versions of three songs have been provided in the Resonances.

Copyright © 2009 Pearson Education, Inc. Publishing as Longman.

Poem 23 is especially interesting to consider, in light of the early commentary traditions. According to one, this is an appeal by a virtuous girl to her lover for a dead deer as a betrothal gift, while another thought it expressed disgust at the lascivious manners that had flourished during a period of political disorder and the emergence of reformed practices under a new enlightened rule. (See James Legge, *The Chinese Classics*, 1892.) The varieties of modern Western translation are equally productive of discussion.

Confucius

The middle of the first millennium B.C.E. was termed by Karl Jaspers the "Axial Age" (in the "The Axial Age of Human History," *Commentary* 6.5 [Nov. 1948]), a period when lively intellectual debates inspired by similar social and economic transformations emerged almost simultaneously in Greece, India, China, the ancient Near East, and Iran. With respect to China, it would be difficult to overemphasize the role of Confucius in this history, as well as his impact on all subsequent cultural developments. As Bryan van Norden suggests, "Imagine a person who has an influence on his native tradition comparable to the *combined* influence of Jesus and Socrates on the Western tradition. Such a person was Confucius." Drawing upon a comparison developed by Jaspers, van Norden continues:

> Although all three were literate, perhaps all highly so, neither Confucius, nor Jesus, nor Socrates left behind any of his own writings. We know each only through the later writings of his admirers and detractors. In addition, each had a distinctive, charismatic, and complex personality. These three common features have made each the object of love, hatred, admiration, denigration, and debate for over two millennia. ("Introduction," *Confucius and the* Analects, 2002, p. 3)

In the case of Confucius, the textual basis for this role is a slim one, the *analecta* or "selected sayings"—an apt translation of the Chinese title *Lun yu*—collected by his disciples and their students, whose own emphases may have been as disparate as the differences among their personalities that emerge from the text. That the collection does not present an utterly coherent worldview owes much to these likely factional squabbles. Equally important, however, is the fact that Confucius showed little interest in the extended systematic, logical argumentation and search for classification and definition that so intrigued his peers in other cultures. Students are thus well advised to pay attention to the stylistic features of the text, which—beyond the explication offered by their provenance—reflect both Confucius's intellectual predilections and the expectations he set out for his students. Rather than being primarily concerned with the truth, falsity, or logic of a statement or belief, his interest was in its behavioral implications: How would someone act if he or she believed this? And instead of engaging in abstract, meta-

Copyright © 2009 Pearson Education, Inc. Publishing as Longman.

physical speculation, he focused his attention on observations about particular people and their qualities; concrete images and examples were crucial to argumentation, rather than discursive elaboration. Moreover, the terse, laconic nature of his statements owes much to intrinsic features of classical Chinese, but it reflects with equal salience his expectation that a listener ought to get the point without having it spelled out in detail.

The performative, imagistic, and didactic inclinations of *The Analects* locate it properly within an anthology of literature by its very example, not to speak of its influence on all later critical and hermeneutical practice and the seamless boundary between philosophy and literature for much of Chinese history. How it compares with philosophical and religious texts elsewhere can generate much lively discussion. How it differs from other texts concerned specifically with ethics is equally interesting. As van Norden points out, unlike Plato and Aristotle, for example, "Confucius never bothers to organize systematically or justify his list of virtues," nor does he feel obligated "to justify the virtuous life." Students might be asked to explore why and also to turn the question around to ask why Western philosophers have "been so obsessed with justificational issues in ethics" as well. (See van Norden, "Unweaving the 'One Thread' of *Analects*: 4:15," in *Confucius and the Analects*, p. 216.)

According to one oft-cited passage from *The Analects*, Confucius did not think he was doing anything new: "I transmit, I invent nothing. I trust and love the past" (7.1). His paragon was the Duke of Zhou, uncle of the dynasty's founder, whose descendants had lost both legitimacy and power and—by Confucius's time—ruled in name only. As was the case much later during the Holy Roman Empire, itinerant scholars began to offer their advice on how to regain this power to anyone who would listen. Reflecting his likely origins in a scribal wing of a class committed to studying and preserving ancient ritual and serving as custodian of cultural traditions preserved in state archives, Confucius dedicated himself to instructing people how to recover those lost ways. While he failed to secure the political appointment he sought, he did succeed in establishing himself as China's first scholar-educator.

Confucius's exemplars are historical personages, rather than divine or supernatural beings, and his world is a resolutely sociopolitical one: There is no salvation beyond this life, and he is in fact utterly uninterested in anything beyond this world. The Way (*dao*) he speaks of can be viewed quite literally as a path, a set of behaviors and practices that will lead to social and political order. Society and the body politic are the sum of a set of relationships and attendant roles. As Chad Hansen notes, "To Confucius, an isolated individual means that some disaster has occurred; the natural, healthy state of humans is in social structures" (*A Daoist Theory of Chinese Thought*, 1992, p. 60). At the center of this order is the filial piety to be demonstrated by a son to his father, which may reflect a transference of the practice of ancestor worship to living families. The importance of this virtue, the nature of which would in fact be spelled out later in a work entitled the *Classic of Filial Piety*, should not be underestimated. Voltaire, for example, is said to have be-

Copyright © 2009 Pearson Education, Inc. Publishing as Longman.

lieved that "One need not be obsessed with the merits of the Chinese to recognize that the organization of their empire is in truth the best that the world has ever seen, and moreover the only one founded on paternal authority" (quoted by Derk Bodde in "Dominant Ideas in the Formation of Chinese Thought," in his *Essays on Chinese Civilization*, 1981, p. 137, n. 16). In later formulations this would be amplified by four other pairs to constitute what were termed the Five Relationships: ruler–subject; father–son; elder brother–younger brother; husband–wife; and friend–friend. All but the last, it should be noted, are hierarchical in nature; three are centered in the family; and all involve mutual obligations. How this has affected notions of heroism that elsewhere are based on an individual's often violent transcendence of sociality has been much debated. For Confucius, the task is to act in accord with one's role, to make the name accord with the reality (see, e.g., 12.11 and 13.3). While slippage has occurred, requiring one to "rectify the names," he is nonetheless much more optimistic than his Greek and Indian counterparts about human nature and its capabilities.

In *Analects* 4.15, one disciple declares that reciprocity, along with loyalty, is the "one single thread" weaving Confucius's teachings together, and elsewhere it is formulated as a kind of negative Golden Rule, not to do to others what you would not want them to do to you. Little else is provided to flesh out this evidently key term, and students might be advised rather to ponder instead the meaning of another tem, "humanity" (*ren*), which is similarly defined and discussed with much greater frequency. "Defined" is something of a misnomer, for Confucius typically only recognizes it in action or presents us with specific, local features of how it works. *Analects* 12.1 provides one of the few direct clues to what he means by this central concept: "tame the self and restore the rites," and suggests that "humanity" is an internalization of the ritual that is the key to proper behavior and social order. The true gentleman is not necessarily born into the ruling class but earns that right thanks to his learning and virtue, and this principle of social mobility is central to Confucius's teachings. Education and moral character, in turn, exert their transformations by the power of influence and example, rather than coercion.

It should be noted that finding this Way is hard work. There is a repeated stress in *The Analects* on the need to examine new things on the basis of old knowledge and to be willing to constantly correct oneself. Unwittingly or not, then, the fragmented form of *The Analects* forces the reader to engage in a restless pursuit of understanding that would surely have pleased the Master.

PERSPECTIVES

Daoism and Its Ways

The texts in this section embody attitudes and arguments that are often presented in stark contrast to the moralistic and sociopolitical focus of Confucianism, but it is important for students to realize that throughout Chinese history these schools

Copyright © 2009 Pearson Education, Inc. Publishing as Longman.

of thought were regarded more typically as complementary rather than contradictory. Daoism (the school of the *dao*, or Way) and Confucianism offered guidelines on how best to get along in a world fraught with disorder and perils that differed profoundly in their premises and goals. For any individual, however, the advice of both could be followed without wholesale rejection of the other, according to circumstances. A proper Confucian official by day, for example, might hang up his cap of office and whistle a Daoist tune in the evening. Neither school, in other words, required adherence to an exclusivity characteristic of monotheism. Nonetheless, the primary concerns of each emerge most clearly when juxtaposed to each other in class.

Dao De Jing

As Chad Hansen has pointed out, of the many contradictory and no doubt fanciful legends surrounding the origin of this text, one in particular yields an important insight into the *Dao De Jing*—that it was dashed off at the behest of the Keeper of the Pass into India as Laozi was leaving China. "The point is that he had no intrinsic motivation to write. He does so under mild duress but also does it quickly and without deliberation" (Hansen, *A Daoist Theory of Chinese Thought*, 1992, p. 211). This account is a salutary reminder of the provisional and contingent nature of many of the text's assertions, its profound skepticism about language, and a corrective to a reading that would overemphasize its metaphysical and mystical aspects.

Taking the *Dao De Jing* as an only loosely integrated collection of strategies for finding one's way in the world and, indeed, surviving in it, makes it much more approachable than it might otherwise prove to be. The term "reversal" that appears at the beginning of this selection is key to understanding its fundamental opposition to the moral vision of Confucius (even more clearly seen in passage 62 / XVIII). Morality may be just a conventional structure of names by which society trains us to make distinctions; distinctions in turn create desires that make us vulnerable to both harm and unhappiness. We can, on the one hand, undo the power of these conventions by valuing what is traditionally disvalued, hence the *Dao De Jing*'s elevation, for example, of the weak, submissive, dark, female, and unlearned, whose unexpected virtues common experience can confirm. On the other hand, however, it is important not to take these opposites as fixed values either, since in a world of constant flux anything can be turned upside down.

Confucians, of course, did not regard their human, social Way as unnatural, but Daoists focus on "that which is naturally so" (69 / XXV). Taking "no action" does not mean doing nothing, but rather doing nothing contrary to nature and responding spontaneously to universal change. Later Chinese emperors would typically draw from this text to encapsulate their ruling policy as "Doing nothing, nothing is left undone." Students might be asked to compare the *Dao De Jing*'s

Copyright © 2009 Pearson Education, Inc. Publishing as Longman.

statements about government with those in *The Analects*: What are the similarities, and where the differences?

Hansen urges us to keep in mind the naturalistic, rather than metaphysical, impulse of Daoism, which "contrasts starkly with the Platonic and Kantian myths of transcendent realms of being" (*A Daoist Theory of Chinese Thought*, p. 27). Students can be asked to consider how the language of oneness and undifferentiation in this text compares, then, with that of mystical teachings in other traditions. On another theme, how do the text's apparent primitivistic inclinations compare with those of later Europeans wishing to return to nature?

Zhuangzi

Like the *Dao De Jing*, the *Zhuangzi* is associated with an individual (in this case historically attested to) but was more likely compiled over the course of two or three centuries. Still, the sense of a personality emerges much more powerfully from the thirty-three chapters in this text, whose irreverent, drop-out protagonist, along with the numerous characters in his parables, have both delighted and perplexed countless generations. Moreover, "it is no exaggeration to say that the [*Zhuangzi*] has influenced Chinese artistic sensibility more profoundly than any other single book," thanks to "its ideas about self-oblivious contemplation of Nature leading to intuitive union with the Tao" (James J. Y. Liu, *Chinese Theories of Literature*, 1975, p. 31).

The *Zhuangzi* explores the implications of the linguistic skepticism that is largely tacit in the *Dao De Jing*, both explicitly and to a much greater extent. Scholars agree that the second chapter, "Discussion on Making All Things Equal," is central to this effort, though the seventh chapter, "Autumn Floods," may provide more concrete illustrations of the earlier chapter's abstractions. You may wish to start with "Autumn Floods," where the long dialogue between the Lord of the River and Jo of the North Sea demonstrates both the relativity and the endlessness of all distinctions and values, whether of size, time, knowledge, or language. The chapter's answer to the logical next question about the value of the Way, however, that it will help one to understand how to deal with things and thus keep one from harm, is less than satisfying, although the concern with self-preservation is central to Daoism.

The second chapter offers the better, if more difficult, answer. A. C. Graham, who prefers to translate its title as "The Sorting Which Evens Things Out," observes that it contains the "most philosophically acute passages" of the entire work, "obscure, fragmented, but pervaded by the sensation, rare in ancient literatures, of a man jotting the living thought at the moment of its inception" (*Chuang-tzu: The Seven Inner Chapters and Other Writings from the Book*, 1981, p. 48). The series of enigmatic fragments and anecdotes, moreover, seems designed to destabilize all traditional habits of reading and thinking. In the end, one finds

Copyright © 2009 Pearson Education, Inc. Publishing as Longman.

that analyzing the notion of distinctions out of existence fails, for the very concept of analysis itself must be questioned as part of the habit of mind that leads to discriminating in the first place. Depending on one's perspective, all distinctions may be wrong, or they may be right. What are the consequences of such sustained skepticism for knowledge and action? Take a look at the anecdote in the excerpt from a later chapter, "The Secret of Caring for Life," about Cook Ting—one of many exemplary craftsmen in the text who have succeeded in stilling their minds—for one possible answer.

Liezi

A much later Daoist text, the *Liezi* presents similar material to the *Zhuangzi* but in a more coherent and straightforward manner. The story of the boy and the seagulls, for example, illustrates the risks of abandoning a spontaneous relationship to nature. Other anecdotes further explore the *Zhuangzi*'s interest in the nature of dreams and the border between reality and illusion. Particularly influential have been the *Liezi*'s anecdotes about communication, and especially pertaining to the relationship between an artist and his or her audience. Note from the last two stories presented in the *Anthology* how music can literally evoke a natural scene, and how important it was for a work to be heard and understood by sympathetic listeners. Po Ya's lament for the loss of someone who grasped his meaning was replicated endlessly by writers seeking someone who "knew their music" (*zhi yin*).

Xi Kang

Whether or not he actually wrote this letter to reject the urgings to enter the bureaucratic life, Xi Kang surely entertained thoughts similar to those expressed in his letter to Shan Tao. Like the other "Seven Sages of the Bamboo Grove," Xi saw the wisdom of adopting a Daoist-inspired retreat from political engagement during perilous times, although his eventual execution suggests that he did not succeed in extricating himself from such predicaments entirely. Students can look for evidence of the *Zhuangzi*'s influence on Xi's position, though they should also note the fact that this does not entail a wholesale rejection of courtly or Confucian values.

Liu Yiqing

From Liu's anecdotes about their unconventional behavior, Ruan Ji and Liu Ling, two of the "Seven Sages of the Bamboo Grove," could be viewed as iconoclastic individualists who rejected all social norms. It is important to keep in mind, how-

Copyright © 2009 Pearson Education, Inc. Publishing as Longman.

ever, that their drinking and nudity do not necessarily mean a fundamental questioning of the basic values or hierarchical structure of their society, but rather the extent to which they should be expected to conform. Students might be asked to consider how their attitudes compare with those of individualists or iconoclasts in other cultures.

Copyright © 2009 Pearson Education, Inc. Publishing as Longman.

Rome and the Roman Empire

In contrast to Greek literature, which students are likely to have encountered in some form during high school, Roman literature will feel at first like unknown territory. It will not take long before they discover that its contents are in fact far less a *terra incognita* to them than the Greek tradition its authors inherited and appropriated. Students know the names of the gods in their Roman form, if only from astronomy—Jupiter, Saturn, Neptune, Pluto, Mars, Venus, Mercury—and from NASA—Apollo. What acquaintance they have with classical mythology will almost certainly have been filtered through Ovid's retelling in the *Metamorphoses* of the legends of Midas, of Icarus and Daedalus, of Theseus and the Minotaur, of Phaethon, or of Ariadne, and from the many movies based on that retelling. Their language, their political system, their sense of such notions as virtue, patriotism, stoicism, and self-sacrifice are all legacies of ancient Rome. And, of course, the Christianity they have either grown up or learned to coexist with began and eventually flourished under the auspices of the Roman empire. Gian Biagio Conte's encyclopedic volume, *Latin Literature: A History* (1994), provides the best contemporary introduction to all aspects of the literature of Rome.

Conte makes the valuable point that the familiarity of so many of the categories of classical thought should not blind us to what is irreducibly alien about ancient cultures. This refers not so much to what prior generations would have referred to as the "primitive" qualities of Rome—its cruel circuses, its merciless tactics in warfare, its animistic religion and deification of ancestors, generals, and emperors—as to conceptions of sexuality, of physiology, of interpersonal relationships, and especially of psychological motivation wholly distinct from those of the post-Enlightenment West. Studying the literature and culture of ancient Rome is a compelling exercise in unraveling the intertwined strands of the familiar and the unfamiliar.

Unlike Homer in ancient Greece, the *Beowulf*-poet or Chaucer in England, or Dante in medieval Florence, there was no founding literary monument of Roman literature. Nor was there even much of any distinction drawn between literary and nonliterary texts; writing was either practical and professional or private and for pleasure. From its beginnings in the third century B.C.E., Roman literature was based on the imitation of and translation from the Greek tradition. Until at least the time of Virgil, Roman poets labored under an inferiority complex comparable to that of nineteenth-century American writers faced with the English tradition, or medieval writers faced with the Bible and classical antiquity: nothing they wrote could come close to the revered texts of their peers.

Copyright © 2009 Pearson Education, Inc. Publishing as Longman.

What made the case of Rome special was the fact that it had subjugated the culture its citizens emulated; their Greek teachers of philosophy and rhetoric were conquered subjects of colonial expansion. It would be a long while before Augustine in the late fourth century C.E. could complain about his childhood distaste for Greek and pretend never to have learned it. Even his disparaging comments, however, were the subtle strategy of a former instructor of rhetoric striving to promote the stylistic simplicity of scripture over what he argued was the decadent ornamentation of classical form and the immoral behavior encouraged by pagan culture. Even in the republican era before the empire and before the rise of Christianity, a similar contrast was drawn between the rugged, rustic virtue of the Italian tribes who had settled Rome and the urban sophistication of the growing city. In a maneuver common to national ideologies, one set of qualities seen to define the Roman character was labeled as indigenous—what became known as the *mos maiorum*, the austere code of behavior of one's glorious ancestors—and another set of qualities attributed to foreign influence—a love of display, excess, sophistication, and expansion. Catherine Edwards's excellent book-length essay *Writing Rome* (1996) provides numerous examples and a lucid analysis of this phenomenon, especially during the principate of Augustus.

All Roman authors were well versed in both aspects of their national identity. Still, while self-consciously modernist and cosmopolitan poets such as Catullus and Ovid highlighted the Hellenistic influence on their representation of Roman culture, poets close to the circle of Augustus such as Horace and Virgil stressed the local past. Virgil's ethos, like that of many later Romans under the empire, was grounded in an application of the tenets of the fourth-century B.C.E. Greek philosophy of Stoicism to the local traditions of the *mos maiorum*. The Stoics had argued that virtue was sufficient for happiness, that only virtue was good, and that emotions led to unhappiness. The most celebrated Roman Stoic, the second-century C.E. emperor Marcus Aurelius (who gloried in his descent from Numa, the most virtuous of the legendary early Roman kings), devoted himself to the perfection of his character and conduct. In his *Meditations*, a collection of sayings and maxims derived from the Stoics and written in Greek, Marcus Aurelius argued that, "The person to whom the only good is what comes in due season, to whom it is the same to have done more or fewer acts according to right reason and to whom it makes no difference to view the spectacle of this world for a longer or a shorter time—for this person death is nothing to be afraid of" (Book 12, Meditation 27). That an essential goal in life was to surmount the fear of death through rational thought and self-reliance was a belief shared with adherents to Epicureanism, whose philosophy was summarized by Lucretius in his epic poem, *De rerum natura* (On the nature of things). Although they may have disagreed on many other issues, it was their adaptability to the ethical tradition of the *mos maiorum* that made these philosophies endure in the everyday life of Rome.

For Catullus and Ovid, by contrast, poetry and, by extension, life, was to be devoted to the transient pleasures of sex, eating, passion, wit, and art. Rather than regard their writings as a stark opposition to the measured piety of Virgil's *Aeneid*

Copyright © 2009 Pearson Education, Inc. Publishing as Longman.

and Horace's *Odes*, however, it is important to note the give-and-take of poets responding to each other. The behaviors and philosophies of life they present are as much a rhetorical inflation of a single side of the doubleness of Roman character as they are a heartfelt gesture of autobiography. Rome was a flamboyantly rhetorical society both in its perversions and in its piety. The same play of extremes can be glimpsed in the dual response to the instability of the first- and second-century empire by Petronius on the one hand and Luke and Paul on the other. The pagan writers depict a roiling and fascinating city of corruption and dissolution with refined irony; the early Christians address that same corruption by utter repudiation. One of the qualities that makes Augustine's *Confessions* so revealing to read at the end of a unit on Roman literature is the way it syncopates these two extremes into the before (the decadent pagan Roman) and after (the pious ascetic Christian Roman) of its formal structure of conversion.

Note that this section has been written to avoid overly duplicating material in the introductions and annotations presented in the *Anthology* itself. Consequently, where biographical material or fundamental aspects of a particular text, such as its prosody, are covered elsewhere, they are not repeated here. Similarly, while specific critical sources are singled out where relevant, no attempt has been made to cover again what is in the bibliographies at the end of each volume of the *Anthology*.

Virgil

Virgil and Homer

The best introduction to Virgil's *Aeneid* is the *Iliad* and the *Odyssey* of Homer. And while few of us can hope ever to achieve the extraordinary intimacy with these Greek epics possessed by Virgil and many of his Roman contemporaries, the more familiar we are with them, the more rewarding the experience of reading his poem. Like the epics attributed to Homer, Virgil's *Aeneid* was regarded as a religious and historical document more than as a poem. But as with everything else between Homer and Virgil, there is an important difference as well, for Virgil self-consciously composed his poem as a literary artifact that would take on religious and historical significance for Augustan Rome. The primary mode of representation used in the Homeric epics, as Erich Auerbach established in *Mimesis* (1946), is to maintain a pretense of an eternal present, a sense that each moment is self-contained and self-explanatory. Virgil, by contrast, gave his poem a structure that reflects his borrowing from and commentary on Homer. Everything in the *Aeneid* is intended to be read doubly, in terms of the ancient past and the imperial present, in terms of Greek versus Trojan/Roman, and in terms of fate versus chance.

Traditionally, the *Aeneid* has been divided into its first, "Odyssean" half and its second, "Iliadic" half, with the first half, like the epic it copies, the more popular and accessible of the two. Books 1–6 have romance, adventure, and a descent to the underworld; Books 7–12 are a dark and nearly hopeless depiction of civil

Copyright © 2009 Pearson Education, Inc. Publishing as Longman.

war. In the account of how Aeneas gets to the site where Rome will be founded, Virgil rewrites Homer's *Odyssey* in several ways. In a quite literal fashion, Aeneas actually revisits places and characters Odysseus passed, including the Cyclops, Scylla and Charybdis, and, after a fashion, the underworld. As in the case of the desperate Greek warrior abandoned by Odysseus (now Latinized as the more familiar "Ulysses") on the island of Polyphemus, the humanity of Aeneas in rescuing one of the enemy is starkly contrasted to the action of Ulysses toward one of his own men. Reversing the sympathies of the prior poem, Virgil not only sets his epic apart from Homer's but also makes the act of drawing comparisons second nature for the reader.

Because the *Aeneid* was composed many centuries after the *Odyssey* but is set in the same archaic period, Virgil was also able to play with a time gap between events and composition that, while it existed in the *Odyssey*, had subsequently become an expected way of making meaning. The time of the *Odyssey* is explicitly the time of ancestors and origins, and their ways are seen as admonitory (Ulysses) and exemplary (Aeneas) while also simultaneously analogous to the present day and alien to it. On the one hand, the god Neptune calms the winds in Book 1 like "some dedicated public man, a veteran" in the center of "a great city" (lines 194, 199); on the other hand, he is an Olympian god with powers very few Romans would have expected to appear in such a proactively human context. Similarly, in Book 8, Evander's tribe of herdsman in the wild hills where Rome will be bears a close resemblance to the pastoral lifestyle depicted in Odysseus's Ithaka in the *Odyssey* but very little to that of contemporary Rome. Still, because they saw themselves as descended both from the rustic Latin locals and the exotic cosmopolitans from the East, Virgil's readers could see themselves reflected in both. Whereas the Homeric poems negatively contrast the cosmopolitanism of the Trojans with the rustic simplicity of most of the Greeks, the *Aeneid* presents positive and negative examples of both qualities.

Virgil was not content simply to rewrite each epic in six books, for the first half of the *Aeneid* actually recounts material from the sphere of the *Iliad*—the fall of Troy—while the second half closely echoes Odysseus's slaughter of the suitors at the end of the *Odyssey*. And Virgil introduces a different sort of complexity in the paradoxical quality of Aeneas's journey. Like Odysseus, Aeneas is seeking to return home, but to a home he does not know, fleeing another home that has been irrevocably lost. Odysseus seeks to restore the status quo of a stable kingdom, symbolized in his faithful wife and the deeply rooted tree of their marriage bed. Aeneas's quest is deeply historical, grounded in a sense of past and future and also in a conception of national identity based on abstract ideas as much as on return to one's native land. Rome will be Aeneas's home because he carries the essence of Troy with him in his father, his son, his household gods, and himself. In analogous fashion, the battle with Turnus in Books 7–12 echoes the *Iliad* in that an invading army is seeking to occupy a settled land, but in Virgil's hands the invasion feels like a homecoming and the locals akin to the usurping suitors on Odysseus's island. Rome is both Troy and not Troy, the Romans are both Romans and not

Copyright © 2009 Pearson Education, Inc. Publishing as Longman.

Romans, Aeneas is both home and not home. Such dualistic conundrums were integral to the poetics of Roman literature; Virgil's genius was to adapt them to the matter of Homeric epic and of imperial Rome.

Reading Laterally

Read as a straight imitation of Homeric epic, the *Aeneid* pales in comparison to its predecessors. There is little of the dramatic unity and intense tragedy of Achilles and Hector in the *Iliad* and little of the narrative flair and charm of the *Odyssey*. Piety, the epic epithet applied to Aeneas, makes for an uncompelling hero. Students coming to the *Aeneid* from Homer are often left cold and remain so until they discover that the drama and passion of the poem lie in the comparison of interwoven texts, events, and situations more than in self-contained character and action. Just as Virgil developed a complex dialogue with Homer within the poem, so do the characters and events accrue power and depth in relation to one another. Virgil expected his readers to be adept at reading laterally, skipping back and forth to draw ever more comparisons within the text, with the republican past, and with the imperial present.

All three epics are deeply concerned with lineage and tradition; in the *Aeneid*, this concern takes primary form as a series of pairs of parents and children. Aeneas is introduced in Book 1 as the child of the goddess Venus. His character is defined by the famous image in Book 2 of the Trojan hero fleeing the sack of his native city, leading his son Ascanius by the hand while his aged father Anchises rides on his back. In exemplary fashion for a Roman matron, his wife Creusa, lost in the flames, begs him through her ghost to escape with the patrilineage intact, leaving her behind, in the past. The account of the fall of Troy given by Aeneas in Book 2 casts the losers as exemplary parents and honorable warriors, and the Greeks as impious thieves. Pyrrhus not only slaughters Priam's son Polites in front of his father and the family altar, killing the patriarch in the bargain, but his disgraceful actions contrast markedly with the conclusion of the *Iliad*, where his father, Achilles, is moved by recognition of Priam's courage and tragic loss to let go his own wrath toward the slain Hector.

Once the scene moves to Italy in the second half of the poem, we find the contrasting pairs Evander and Pallas, benevolent ruling family at the site that will be Rome, and the tyrant Mezentius with his son Lausus, positive and negative images of patriarchal behavior in the future republic. Meanwhile, civil war begins when the weak king Latinus is unable to back up the promise of his daughter to Aeneas, outflanked by his wife, Amata, and by Turnus, young ruler of the neighboring Rutulians. Whereas the Trojan past and the Homeric epics before them were a matter between men, the action in Italy is awash with unruly women. Indeed, the *Aeneid* provides a sustained meditation on the relation between women and power, the general conclusion of which is that bad things happen when they mix.

In addition to analogous sets of related characters, Virgil invites his readers to compare characters and situations in terms of repeating motifs. The positive force of the poem is symbolized in the sequence of cities—lost, failed, incorrect, and pos-

Copyright © 2009 Pearson Education, Inc. Publishing as Longman.

sible—that punctuates the poem, especially in its early books. Each city raises a specific set of questions regarding the best way to found and preserve a city (and, by extension, a nation). Aeneas and Dido are first presented not as possible lovers but as types of rulers; the downfall of Dido is paralleled by the changing status of her city of Carthage, eventually doomed by her inability to control her emotions, to eliminate her female qualities. (The ruler Dido was long known as a type of the virago.)

Dido's fall is characterized by imagery of storms and of fire, externalizing the unmasterable emotions that Roman culture identified with feminine irrationality. Virgil both epitomizes Roman misogyny and suggests the limits of its validity, starkly dividing his characters' choices between self-denial to preserve the commonweal and the destructive indulgence of private desires. Flares of passion are marked by imagery of fire and flames. Whenever it appears that the masculine qualities of order and self-control have preserved Aeneas's mission, passion will burst out: Dido's funeral pyre, the women's burning of the ships in Book 5. In the second half of the poem, this imagery becomes linked to that of the serpent wielded by the Fury Allecto to inflame the passions of Amata and Turnus. The poet establishes a set of contrary patterns: the teleology of fate dictated by Jove and the power mustered by raging Juno to thwart that teleology, or at least to delay it as long as possible. After all, this, too, is a civil war: a battle between husband and wife, brother and sister.

Gods and Passions

The key motif linking the action of all the characters is the question of choice. Rather than present his characters as psychologically rounded and autonomous individuals, Virgil depicts them as torn between or driven by abstract forces. One set of these forces is represented by the gods, who are neither the full-fledged characters of the Homeric epics nor the abstract personifications they would become in the Middle Ages. Virgil's gods, especially his Juno, are terrifying because they are neither abstract enough to be reliable as natural forces nor human enough to negotiate with. Students may be confused by this equivocation, tending to prefer to allegorize their actions and eliminate any element of free will in the actions of Aeneas and the other characters. This underestimates both Virgil's subtlety and the sophistication of ancient cultures. Just as modern society attributes causes both to genetics and to environment and regards psychological motivation as simultaneously outside of a person's control and something for which he or she is held responsible, so Roman literature used the gods to give dramatic form to conflicts and philosophical issues for which there existed no simple answer.

Both Jove and Juno represent forces that profoundly affected society, neither of them comprehensible in purely human terms. Scholarship on Virgil has long been split between those who see the *Aeneid* as a celebration of the victory of imperial order, Jove as the divine authority bestowing its blessing on Aeneas cum Augustus, and those who see an unending series of catastrophes ironically undercutting every effort to establish that order. There is no question that the Olympian forces of social order and the chthonic forces of passionate chaos dominate the

Copyright © 2009 Pearson Education, Inc. Publishing as Longman.

poem's form and thematics, and determining which reigns supreme by the end can make an excellent talking point in discussions. Students should be encouraged to resist quick conclusions, however; recent scholarship on Roman literature has tended to stress the love of ambiguity and doubleness, the desire to use literature to raise questions and try out social issues rather than settle them. And, certainly, from the time of Augustus on, there was little to be gained by making direct social criticism and much to be said between the lines for an audience so versed in lateral reading.

The complex forces embodied in the figures of the gods are somewhat different from the straightforward personifications of such figures as Rumor, which function as conventional literary tropes. There can be ambiguity even in such figures, though; take Venus and Juno, who as Love and Marriage preside over a momentary truce that unites Aeneas and Dido in Book 4. It is impossible wholly to distinguish this straightforward allegory of the progress of love from the personal motivations of the two goddesses, plotting and counterplotting with the two humans as pawns. Nor does Virgil quite allow us to forget that Aeneas and Dido remain recognizably human in the ways they act out their parts in the allegory. Aeneas may be compelled by Mercury to recall his duty, but the speech with which he breaks with Dido is a textbook example of male sophism (deeply indebted, as is much of the imagery of female rage, to the tragic crack-up of Jason and Medea's relationship in Euripides' tragedy).

Ecphrasis

The characteristic way to incorporate mixed levels of symbolism into the texture of ancient narrative was through *ecphrasis*, the verbal description of visual artifacts. The ecphrastic archetype was Achilles' Shield in the *Iliad*. In Roman poetry, ecphrasis was both a means of demonstrating verbal virtuosity and a programmatic statement about poetry and society themselves. The longest poem in Catullus's collection, for example, is almost entirely occupied by a fiendishly complex description of a marriage quilt. Because what it described almost never actually could exist as described, the ecphrasis often stood as well for the relationship between the poem and the world to which it referred. In a poem like Virgil's, occupied as it is with defining the character of Roman history and its modern identity, these were key moments. In Book 1, Aeneas and Achates, freshly arrived at the new city of Carthage, are awed by the images of the Trojan war on the façade of a temple dedicated to Juno. What Aeneas cannot know, as he weeps at the memories and takes solace in the fact that he is known to these distant people, is that he has misread the meaning of the images, dedicated as they are to a goddess who supported the Greeks and gloried in his downfall.

The façade of Apollo's temple at Cumae is more enigmatic and much exercised Virgil's late antique and medieval exegetes. Attributed to a failed father, Daedalus, and dedicated to his travails in Crete (matters included in the selections from Ovid), the dark tale breaks off, the father unable to bring himself to sculpt his son Icarus's fall. Unfinished, too, is Aeneas's viewing, cut short by his need to

Copyright © 2009 Pearson Education, Inc. Publishing as Longman.

see his own dead father. More fully realized is the third and most celebrated ecphrasis: Virgil's revision of the Shield of Achilles, bracketed in Book 8 by the visit with Evander. Forged by Vulcan, Aeneas's shield also shares with its model the depiction of an entire cosmology. Rather than the timeless vision in Homer, however, this shield details once more the triumphs of Rome, concluding with an inventory of the bounds of a specific land, the empire of Augustus. The reaction, again, is key: Aeneas hoists the shield on his shoulder without an inkling of the meaning of its images. He may lead his people to the promised land, but he will enjoy none of it. Instead, the only artifact he is able to read correctly is the tragic sword belt given by Evander to his son Pallas. Taken by Turnus when he slays the young ward of Aeneas, the sword belt flashes its horrible meaning at Aeneas at the moment of his triumph in Book 12, as Turnus begs for mercy and the end of civil strife. There is no complex allegory here, though, only "the relic of his anguish" that infects Aeneas with anger, the same divine *ira* that infected Juno at the start of the epic, driving him to conclude the poem with an act of rage and revenge.

The World Below

The peak of the poem's combination of allegory, religion, typology, and ideology is Book 6, the book that won Virgil his posthumous reputation as a magician and philosopher and his poem that of a holy book of prophecy. The underworld is a feminine realm in Virgil's depiction: Aeneas's guide is the Sibyl of Cumae, the goddess Hecate presides over it, and in its hells reside those mythological souls who refused to control the dictates of their desires. And yet, the Sibyl's bouts of ecstatic inspiration are dictated by the god Apollo, and within the confines of the underworld also lie the Elysian Fields, home of Aeneas's father, and where the son receives a prophetic vision of the long sequence of Roman rulers that his own son will initiate. Even in the heart of this vision of peace and order, all Aeneas can think about is the horror of returning to the world above and to his task of instantiating that vision. Rather than a teleology with a glorious end, he suggests, his endeavor is a fruitless repetition of eternal suffering.

Just as the pain of the Sibyl's possession by the wisdom of the god Apollo questions the value of the trade-off, so Aeneas's stoic demeanor cracks at times to reveal the cost of what he is doing. "So hard and huge a task it was to found the Roman people," runs the conclusion to the proem in Book 1.48-49—this can mean either that the suffering was worth it in the end or that it was not. That this might remain an open question is raised by the continuing presence of chthonic forces within the world Aeneas is endeavoring to tame and control. One of the frightening aspects of the series of encounters between Aeneas and the figures of his past—Trojans, Greeks, and Carthaginian Dido—is that death causes pain and separation but assuages and changes nothing. Even in the paradise in which he meets his father, Aeneas is unable actually to embrace him.

Perhaps the most famous moment in the *Aeneid* is the enigmatic image of the two Gates of Sleep through which dreams pass out of the underworld, true ones from the gate of horn, false ones from the gate of ivory. Readers have long

Copyright © 2009 Pearson Education, Inc. Publishing as Longman.

debated the significance of Aeneas's departure through the gate of false dreams. If nothing else, Virgil chose to stress the tenuous nature of prophecy, or at least of those prophecies contained within the medium of poetry. The *Aeneid* is built around prophecy, which is the mode of signification of Jove and fate in the same way as serpents, fire, and passion are the *modus operandi* of the chthonic forces invoked by Juno. Nearly all of the prophecy in the poem is typological; that is, it functions within history as earlier events come in retrospect to prophesy later ones: the fall of Dido pointing toward the destruction of Carthage, the vertiginous vision in Book 8 of Rome before it existed, the civil war of the later books looking forward to those recently won by Augustus. Virgil also exercises a more explicitly retrospective prophecy, his historical vantage point allowing repeated prophecies of events to come in the history of Rome. Control over the meaning of the past, the poem makes clear, will go a long way toward control over the meaning of the present and future. One of the enduring fascinations of the *Aeneid* is the unrelenting manner in which it dramatizes the battle over the control of history and so compellingly dramatizes not only the pain of the losers but the cost to the winners.

The *Aeneid* in Context and in History

Virgil knew tremendous success during his life and moved in the highest circles of power. His immediate patron was Octavian's minister, Maecenas; Virgil reportedly gave a preview reading of the *Georgics* to Octavian himself; and the *Aeneid* was composed as the foundational epic of the era inaugurated by Octavian's assumption of the principate as Augustus. The Horatian ode dedicated to Virgil (Ode 1.24, included in a Resonances section in the *Anthology*) provides a good starting point for a discussion of the role of patronage in Roman poetry. Virgil had introduced his younger friend to Maecenas. If this ode constitutes a form of payback, it has been beautifully disguised in the rhetoric of a shared philosophy and an homage to the importance of their association. Horace's Satire 1.5 can give students a looser sense both of the day-to-day life of these poets and their nonliterary duties. Poetry was regarded neither as something above the concerns of everyday life nor as a wholly instrumental means of advancement and social lubrication. The selections from Horace and Catullus in the Perspectives section demonstrate the range that could be taken by the poem as the most polished form of conversation. It was a highly supple tool of communication and persuasion that also could give rise to artistry of the highest level. Epic was expected to be less explicit in its relation to the exigencies of everyday life in Rome. Rather than eliminating such relations, however, the distance simply gave rise to a different rhetorical stance, as evidenced by the complexity of the *Aeneid*'s oblique but pointed commentary on Augustus and his reign.

As Conte succinctly puts it, "Virgil's *Nachleben* is Western literature" (*Latin Literature*, 1994). The Resonances selection from the *Saturnalia* of Macrobius (late fourth to early fifth century) gives a good sense of Virgil's high standing and the various ways in which later Roman readers approached the poem. Literary analysis

Copyright © 2009 Pearson Education, Inc. Publishing as Longman.

took the form primarily of explication of difficult passages or ambiguities—one of the participants in the banquet is Servius, author of the most influential of the classical commentaries on the *Aeneid*. Macrobius was involved in the pagan revival in Rome, and the invocation of Virgil as a philosopher-sage and his poetry as wisdom literature possessing the truth of doctrine shows the degree to which the *Aeneid* and its author had quickly come to personify the ideology of imperial Rome. Early Christians could not afford to dismiss this poetry the way they could less politically charged works such as Ovid's *Metamorphoses*. Instructive in this context is Saint Augustine's vexed and ambivalent reckoning with Virgil in the *Confessions*, representative of a Christian reception that rejected the pagan poet and his epic but accepted the Fourth Eclogue as a prophecy of the coming of Christ.

Christian ambivalence continued to mark Virgil's reception through the Middle Ages. Domenico Comparetti's venerable study *Virgil in the Middle Ages* (1908) is dated in many of its assumptions but fascinating in its comprehensive history of how the poet and his poetry were regarded through to the Renaissance. *Virgil in English* (ed. K. W. Gransden, 1996) provides an annotated selection of translations from the Middle Ages to the present. Theodore Ziolkowski's *Virgil and the Moderns* (1993) surveys the substantial presence of the Latin poet in the twentieth century, in both literature and popular culture, and ways in which he continued to represent, for better and for worse, the legacy of the Roman empire and all that was associated with it. An excellent introduction to Virgil in Western culture and to a series of contemporary critical views on his writings can be found in *The Cambridge Companion to Virgil* (ed. Charles Martindale, 1997).

Ovid

While the *Aeneid* has passed through the European tradition as a great monument to the Roman empire, Ovid's *Metamorphoses*, like most of its hundreds of characters, has been scattered and transformed beyond recognition. Nevertheless, its influence has, if anything, been the greater, and the protean form Ovid gave to the myriad myths of the classical world has persisted. To this day, it is as impossible to consider classical mythology outside of Ovid's *Metamorphoses* as to consider Christian hell without the form given it by Dante's *Inferno*. Reading these selections from the *Metamorphoses* is generally a pleasurable experience of recognition and familiarity for students; the challenge in teaching them is to defamiliarize the stories enough so that students can recognize the artistry of the poet in molding them into a single flowing epic poem and in fixing the ways we still think of them today.

Myth and Metamorphosis

There is much debate over the degree to which the citizens of Augustan Rome continued to believe in the truth of the ancient stories told of their gods, goddesses, and ancestors. Certainly, public display continued to invoke the sanctity

Copyright © 2009 Pearson Education, Inc. Publishing as Longman.

of key deities such as Jupiter, Juno, and Minerva, just as rulers and generals would be deified and worshipped in rituals. The expected comportment of the ruling class made piety and reverence its central component. Still, just as there was no single dominant deity, so too there was not a single document carrying the weight of scripture—the *Aeneid* in later years was as close as it got. The degree of Ovid's reverence toward his subject has been much discussed; what is certain is that few poems could be as wholly contrary to the teleological history of the *Aeneid*'s principal narrative trajectory as the *Metamorphoses*' lack of any overarching structure beyond the insistence on incessant change, the lack of any structure to history.

This is not to say that nothing about the *Metamorphoses* is conventional; rather, it takes every convention of epic and of myth and tosses it into the maelstrom of poetry. A primary role of religion is to define what is human by categorizing what is not, and classical myth is no different. In Homer, the gods function primarily to explore what it means for humans to be mortal by depicting a pantheon of deities human in nearly every quality except their immortality. In Virgil, the gods embody primarily the question of fate: To what degree are men and women in control of the choices they make, of their destinies in history? Ovid, too, queries negatively what it means to be human. Men and women are the only inhabitants of the world who are unable to control their own transformations. Gods and goddesses are able to transform themselves and others at will; animals transform as part of their nature—hence the importance of the skin-shedding serpent as a motif in the poem. Humans are characterized by tears, by speech, and by taboo (including the desire to be a god), but their essence for Ovid seems to be a sensation of being trapped in a world outside of their control. As in Virgil, passion is seen as transformative, ecstatic, and able to dissolve identity completely. In Ovid's world, however, there is no alternative to passion, and its effects are ambivalent rather than wholly negative. In this, Ovid shows his debt to his own erotic poetry and that of Catullus, both of which depict a world ruled by the pursuit of desire. The difference is that in that erotic poetry, the world was circumscribed to Roman society; the *Metamorphoses* expands that world to the cosmos and to the epic matter of history and religion from which Virgil had rigidly excluded it.

The principle of metamorphosis works on many levels in the poem. First of all, as Ovid announces in his proem, it is the subject matter and structuring motif: "Of bodies changed to other forms I tell" (1.1). No single character's deeds are to be sung, but those of what appears to be a philosophical principle. Metamorphosis also functions in the poem as an organizing metaphor. Rather than linking his episodes according to action, Ovid does so in terms of imagery and association. The basic stuff of poetry is to transform reality with words, to make connections between apparently unrelated things and concepts. Ovid creates a compendium of ways of linking one story or one transformation to the next, many of them flagrantly arbitrary in any narrative sense. Phaethon is introduced because he is "peer in pride and years" (p. 1208, line 6) of Epaphus, son

Copyright © 2009 Pearson Education, Inc. Publishing as Longman.

of Io, who had previously been transformed into a cow by Jove; Narcissus because of a prophecy recalled of Tiresias; Arachne's story is told by Minerva in response to the Muses' tale of their contest with the Pierides, nine daughters of Pierus, turned into magpies for their presumption. Or Ovid uses a frame-tale to contain a series of other stories, sometimes thematically linked, sometimes not. The two parts of Orpheus's story are interrupted by the stories he sings to the trees in lament of those who refused marriage, of Eurydice, of Ganymede Jove's cup-bearer, of Hyacinth beloved of Apollo, of Pygmalion in love with his own marble creation, of Myrrha enamored of her father.

Ovid was also a master of linguistic metamorphosis. The poem is replete with witticisms, wordplay, and misprision. Garth Tissol provides many examples in *The Face of Nature* (1997). Tissol argues that the poem is characterized by the rhetorical figure of syllepsis, or zeugma—a word of various meanings used without distinguishing between them or an ambiguous word used to signal several things at once. The story of Echo and Narcissus is exemplary here. Unable to create her own words, Echo can only make meaning by transforming the intent of the words of her beloved. Classical scholars were long exercised by what they saw as the bad taste of Ovid's failure to clarify his meaning or to make infelicitous combinations, as in the description of Jupiter's blasting of Phaethon in the chariot of the sun: "animaque rotisque / expulit," "Struck Phaethon from the chariot and from life" (p. 1217, line 354). This refusal to adhere to the rules of high epic style and of poetic decorum is consistent with the apparent irreverence of Ovid's treatment of the rules of structure, not to mention the figures of the gods.

Structure

There is a rough chronological trajectory to the *Metamorphoses* as it moves from the Creation through the Four Ages and the Flood to the earliest generations of mortals, who still lived in close proximity to the gods. For Ovid, this proximity entails for the most part being subject to rape and other types of assault, the results of many of which are the creation of demigods and heroes. In the middle books, Ovid deals, if sometimes obliquely and with extensive digressions, with the primary heroes of classical mythology: Perseus, Jason, Theseus, Hercules. They do not always come off much better than the gods did, and again it is difficult to believe Ovid is not sometimes parodying the heroic tradition—after all, his subject matter is sex, not battle. Still, his tone remains unpredictable enough throughout that one cannot pin him down as a straightforward parodist either. Sometimes, as in the pious midpoint story of Baucis and Philemon, the elderly couple who, like Lot in Sodom, are the only persons saved when their wicked land is destroyed by the gods, he appears to have gone straight. Often it appears as if he is intent on proving his mastery of every style and genre in the classical repertoire—there are episodes of pastoral, of the epyllion (miniature epic), and, in the latter books, of what is known as the "Little Aeneid," in which Ovid summarizes the matter of the Trojan War and Virgil's epic in three quick books (12–14),

Copyright © 2009 Pearson Education, Inc. Publishing as Longman.

condensing the Dido episode to five lines, Anchises's prophecies in the underworld to one, and devoting much of the space to digressive episodes that have nothing to do with the founding of Rome. The majority of the Iliadic material, for example, is replaced by a four-hundred-line reminiscence by an apparently senile Nestor, who concludes with the confession that he has distorted his story because he hates Hercules.

The epic concludes with a philosophical disquisition by the Greek philosopher Pythagoras on vegetarianism and the belief in the transmigration of souls. Critics remain in violent disagreement as to whether the Pythagorean doctrine that all is change, nature ceaselessly in flux from one form to another, is the summa of Ovid's poem and the keystone of its thematics or an ironic *reductio ad absurdum* of his own principle of metamorphosis. Ovid is certainly slippery enough as a poet to have meant both meanings at once. Similarly, the poem concludes with a final transformation, the apotheosis of Julius Caesar, and then asserts, again wholly paradoxically, that, while he may have established that all is changeable, this poem has assured that "My fame shall live to all eternity."

Poets, Singers, and Artists

While Ovid tends to play fast and loose with the heroic tradition and the epic conventions that accompany it, he often renders poets, singers, and artists as tragic characters, doomed by their insistence on challenging the gods: the Pierides in song, Arachne in weaving, Marsyas with the flute, Daedalus and Pygmalion in their art, and Orpheus with his lyre. Moreover, Ovid devises storytelling units that tend to derail the forward thrust of the chronology just as his digressions confuse the traditional focus of the narratives he retells. Sometimes, as with the Muses' account of the stories sung in their competition with the Pierides, there are stories within stories within stories. The longest of these is the tale of Orpheus, which occupies all of Book 10 and part of the next and highlights the storyteller/poet (who had his own mystery cult in the classical world) as a central figure in Ovid's poem. Like Aeneas, Orpheus descends to the underworld, but he does so for love, and he fails in his quest, returning empty-handed. He is a transgressive figure, able to reanimate the natural world, the trees and plants once transformed from human form by the gods; he sings of taboos broken by mortal figures; he is punished for his nonconformity and mourned by nature as his singing head floats down the Hebrus river. Lest we be overly moved by his story, however, Ovid concludes it with an irreverent grace note. Reunited as shades, Orpheus and Eurydice play at the lack of faith that caused their separation: "Sometimes he follows as she walks in front, / Sometimes he goes ahead and gazes back— / No danger now—at his Eurydice" (11.78–80).

Ovid was a voracious synthesizer, and his poem incorporates innumerable earlier sources, both known and unknown. Rather than making his rewriting transparent, as Virgil does with Homer, Ovid transforms his sources, mixing them without regard for any sense of fidelity. In her introductory volume, *Ovid* (1988), Sara Mack provides a good summary of Ovid's use of different genres and of the way he

Copyright © 2009 Pearson Education, Inc. Publishing as Longman.

treats his many different sources (see also the *Cambridge Companion to Ovid*, ed. Philip Hardie, 2002). As he does with the *Aeneid*, he begins and ends wherever he chooses, often elides key events, and changes the order of the story he tells. Most students will not have the background to do much comparing of this sort, and space constraints prevented us from including Ovid's version of the Trojan War. Nonetheless, students will be able to discern Ovid's changeable, slippery voice and the unique way in which he tells a story that sweeps readers along without ever letting them be sure where they are going.

Because of its virtuoso demonstration of the power of poetic language and imagery, Ovid's *Metamorphoses* has especially appealed to later poets. In the Middle Ages, Ovid's short poetry was taught in schools, and the tales in the *Metamorphoses* were interpreted as Christian fables. Dante may have chosen Virgil for his guide to the underworld, but Ovid is the poet he used most to depict the realm of Paradise, although he seldom credited the poem he transformed. The Penguin collection, *Ovid in English* (ed. Christopher Martin, 1999), samples translations of Ovid through the centuries; *After Ovid: New Metamorphoses* (eds. Michael Hofmann and James Lasdun, 1994) is but the most recent version of poetic reimaginings of the myths made immortal by Ovid's hand.

The Culture of Rome and the Beginnings of Christianity

This Perspectives section groups together fairly diverse material from the two centuries around the birth of Jesus in order to assist students in getting a sense of the intertwined nature of the culture of ancient Rome and the early documents of the Christian religion. The sophisticated and worldly poetry of Catullus and Horace predates Christianity and establishes both the sensuality of life in Rome and the philosophical mind-set of its elite. Petronius wrote his *Satyricon* in a changed society, but the keen observation of behavior and fascination with the stuff of everyday life have not changed; they have simply become more cynical. While Catullus and Horace will help students understand why so many Romans felt no need for Christianity, the later Petronius captures well the sense of empty excess and meaningless show that seems to underlie the turn to asceticism of so many of the religious cults of the time. It should also be observed that Trimalchio is a provincial merchant, just as Judaea was in the far reaches of the empire. Rome never quite lost its own seductive flavor, as Juvenal observed with irony in his *Satires*. Those on the margins had far less to lose. Read in conjunction with the literature of Rome contemporary to them, the writings of Luke and Paul lose none of their power as records of Christian doctrine but gain much in historical texture and context.

Copyright © 2009 Pearson Education, Inc. Publishing as Longman.

+· ≍♦≣ ·+

Catullus

The shock of reading Catullus is to discover just how modern he feels. It was an effect that he cultivated with great effort. Most prominent of the "neoteric" poets, Catullus made his verse an assertion of newness and a rejection of the past and the tradition of Rome, particularly the local weight of the *mos maiorum*. Rather than the heavy and stodgy literature of their elders, the neoterics promulgated a poetics borrowed from the Hellenism of cosmopolitan Alexandria that privileged a combination of slightness, polished concision, and great learning. They characterized their poetry as *urbanus*, *elegans*, *lepidus* (charming, witty), *salsus* (salty, witty, clever), and *venustus* (charming, graceful, pretty, neat), and they had little truck with the timeworn qualities of *gravitas* and *virtus*. The poetry that resulted was thus light and brief, rooted in everyday life but honed to the perfection of the perfect dinner-party epigram—one of the forms of which Catullus was a master. Accompanying the poetics is a first-person persona who lives according to the same qualities, devoting himself to the joys of private life: the pleasures of the flesh, of the table, of companionship, of conversation, and of writing, all conducted with the utmost suavity.

It is a philosophy of life that resonates with many students, raised as they have been on the enduring dictums of romanticism, but it comes with a sharp and inalienably Roman edge in Catullus's poetry. Take the apparently anodyne lyric 5, "Lesbia, let us live only for loving." The sentiment is familiarly romantic: Abandon the opinions and mutterings of the outside, adult world and lose yourself in the private realm of innumerable kisses. As the translator Charles Martin shows in his book, *Catullus* (1992), however, one extended metaphor compares their love to the natural eternity of the sun; the other to bookkeeping and economics. Private and public are held in tension, as are the elegant and the everyday, the philosophical and the financial. Their love cannot in fact escape the envy of their fellow Romans, the social context in which it takes place. Catullus's poetry enacts again and again the tension between the isolation of the lyric and its status as a dialogue, a communication with another person in the real space of Rome.

One of the fascinations of Catullus's verses is the way they are simultaneously pure artifacts (or linguistic confections) and words with a social purpose. In one lyric (40), Catullus threatens "Poor little Ravidus" that he will "be shafted by my sharp iambics" for "loving my darling." The threat is simultaneously literal and figurative, carried out by the very wit of the conceit. Sometimes the anger that motivates the ingenious invective is purely social, as in lyric 12, where he berates one Asinius for stealing the linen napkins sent Catullus from Spain by his friend Fabullus. Sometimes it is seduction rather than anger, as in the following lyric, where he promises said Fabullus a marvelous dinner, provided he bring everything—the feast, like the revenge on Asinius, is already there in the verses.

Copyright © 2009 Pearson Education, Inc. Publishing as Longman.

The better part of the time, however, it is either a literary quarrel, as in lyric 16, or one of love, usually, but not exclusively, concerning Lesbia. Although it is widely considered that Lesbia refers to the powerful Roman matron Clodia, and it is quite possible that Catullus carried out an affair with Clodia, it is impossible to know the degree to which the situations he depicts actually happened. (Cicero's speech "In Defence of Marcus Caelius Rufus," who was accused of attempting to poison her, contains a memorable character assassination of Clodia.) What Catullus does achieve, however, is to bring to those situations an emotional reality that has indubitably been derived from experience. One way to elucidate this paradox for students is to provide a selection of translations of the same poem, with recourse to the Translations feature, showing how many different poems and personalities can be drawn from a single report of an apparently lived experience. Shakespeare amplified the torn concision of lyric 85 into a ten-line narrative in *Cymbeline* (3.5.69ff). Thomas Carew rationalizes Catullus's irrational split between love and hate as a battle of love and reason: "But if my constant love shall faile to move thee, / Then know my reason hates thee, though I love thee." The seventeenth-century poet Richard Lovelace ("I hate and love, wouldst thou the reason know? / I know not, but I burn and feel it so.") and the nineteenth-century poet Walter Landor ("I love and hate. Ah! never ask why so! / I hate and love—and that is all I know. / I see 'tis folly, but I feel 'tis woe.") preserve the paradox of the Latin but lose the play between passive and active voices. Twentieth-century translators have striven for more literal renditions. Ezra Pound ("I hate and love. Why? You ask me but / It beats me. I feel it done to me, and ache") and Peter Whigham (1966) give a highly Anglo-Saxon syncopation to the flowing feel of the Latin, but Whigham's "and I'm torn in two" manages to capture the full violence of *excrucior* (derived from the verb "to crucify" and cognate to the English "excruciating"). The version by Martin in the *Anthology* gets the strange length of the Latin and the interplay of verb forms, and "it shivers me" is a fine invention for the feel of Catullus's conclusion (for the Latin see p. 1249 of the *Anthology*). But each translator has imported a bit of his own period and culture's attitude toward uncontrollable passion, and this in turn suggests that Catullus's brilliant dissection of his own behavior reflects Roman opinions on love as much as it does the man's despair toward his Lesbia.

With one exception, the 113 poems that constitute Catullus's known oeuvre come to us from a single thirteenth-century manuscript in his hometown of Verona. Scholars continue to debate whether Catullus himself was responsible for the order of the poems and whether the manuscript includes all or simply part of his production. As it stands, it falls into three fairly clear parts: lyrics 1–60, the "polymetric" or varied meter poems (mostly hendecasyllables), are fairly brief and mostly private or incidental in subject matter; lyrics 61–64, the four long poems, include two marriage hymns, an epyllion (or miniature epic) on the marriage of Achilles's parents, Peleus and Thetis, and a bizarre portrayal of Attis, who castrates himself in worship of the goddess Cybele; the remainder of the poems rehearse, in elegiac couplets, much the same material as the first part of the collection.

Copyright © 2009 Pearson Education, Inc. Publishing as Longman.

There have been many attempts to unravel hidden structural schemes—a distinct possibility given the propensity of Alexandrian poetry and of Roman rhetoric to prefer symmetrical patterns—and many critics have preferred to rearrange the Lesbia poems to make a conventional sequence running from passion through betrayal, recrimination, dismissal, and reunion. But other characters also recur: the friends Furius and Aurelius, the youthful lover Juventius, the enemy Mamurra, the beloved brother whose death Catullus mourns in lyric 68. There are also adaptations from the Greek: of the Alexandrian poet Callimachus (lyric 66) and of Sappho (lyric 51).

✐

RESONANCE

The Priapea

Obscenity, as William Fitzgerald explains in his excellent study, *Catullan Provocations* (1995), had a fixed place in Roman society, in ritual and in invective. This place was generally a private one, like the garden in which the phallus which narrates the poems in the *Priapea* is planted. Convention in ancient Rome categorized sexuality according to active versus passive roles rather than the gender of the participants. There were three verbs of penetration: *futuere* (vaginal), *pedicare* (anal), and *irrumare* (oral). Roman sexual mores privileged power and control, so the passive role in all three forms of intercourse was considered disgraceful, while the active was not. According to Fitzgerald, words and oratory were sacred, and the key locus for obscenity in Roman culture was the impure mouth.

Richard Hooper's introduction to his translation of the *Priapea* is a useful resource here. The fact that the 80 *carmina Priapea* that constitute the main corpus of poems dedicated to the guardian god Priapus were long attributed to Virgil suggests the degree to which the Romans distinguished between the sacred and the profane far differently than does the modern West. These are modest but clever doggerel, on the level of high-quality bathroom graffiti, but all the more revealing and entertaining for being so. They can also serve to show just how accomplished and ambitious, in comparison, the invective poems of Catullus are. Note that while the conceit of the neoterics was that their poems were dashed-off bits of witticism, they were instead a challenge to the poet's virtuosity to make a masterpiece out of *nugae*, nugatory bits of joking around. "In your honor, Lord Priapus," by contrast, is content to be nothing but a clever bit of scribbling, although here, too, the poet makes it clear that he (presumably) knows he is slumming. Moreover, the poet demonstrates a mastery of rhetoric even here: his threat to thieving boys in "The law . . ." is formulated as a chiasmus around the word "garden; his argument in "You ask why . . ." uses the tools of logic and the figure of anaphora to argue that it is only fitting that he be obscene, for therein lies his only power.

Copyright © 2009 Pearson Education, Inc. Publishing as Longman.

Similarly, when Horace turned his hand to a priapic poem in Satire 1.8, he ran through the familiar tropes, but quickly bent the form to his own devices. He locates the garden both spatially and temporally, amplifying the opening contrast between the past existence of Priapus as wood and his present state as a god: the garden once was a common burial ground, now it is Maecenas's elegant garden in the now-exclusive Esquiline quarter of Rome. Whereas Catullus's invective and the threats of the standard Priapus are divinely potent, Horace's is a self-deflating figure of modest powers. He is terrified of the witches that used to haunt the neighbourhood, and he chases them away, not with the force of his phallus, but with the noise of an involuntary fart.

Horace

The poetics of Horace shares many qualities with those of his predecessor Catullus: the striving for brevity, the *labor limae*, or work of the file, honing his words down to a finely polished gem of verse, and the focus on the personal and the everyday, even when approaching the great events of the time. These were the generic conventions of the short forms in which both poets wrote. The ethos that Horace expressed through that verse, however, could not have been more different. The now commonplace phrases coined by him, such as *carpe diem* ("seize the day") or the *aurea mediocritas* ("golden mean") suggest a poetic voice far removed from the passion and swagger of Catullus. As a glance through the collection of translations *Horace in English* (eds. D. S. Carne-Ross and Kenneth Haynes, 1996) demonstrates, Horace has always been a favorite of gentlemen of letters, worldly seekers after stability and balance in their lives. As such, his poetic conservatism makes an excellent counterpart to the transgressive modernism of Catullus, a counterpart that also helps to contrast the life of a self-made man near to the center of imperial power with that of a comfortable aristocrat in an unstable republic. In his poetry, Catullus and his friends engage in obscene banter, riotous carousing, sexual escapades, and all-night bouts of poetic composition; Horace and his friends are content with "humble Sabine" in "modest cups" (Satire 1.22), "olives and chicory and mild mallows" (1.31) on the country farm bestowed on him by his patron Maecenas, the modest dining, simple company and calm described in Satire 2.6, which concludes with a version of the parable of the country mouse and the city mouse.

Horace's poetry is characterized by a gift for understatement extended to the level of a poetic credo. When in Satire 1.5 he recounts a trip he undertook as part of a key diplomatic summit between the warring factions of Octavian and Brutus, Horace prefers to describe the petty discomforts, the various inns, his sore eyes, a mock duel between two buffoons, a failed tryst, and the wet dream that followed

Copyright © 2009 Pearson Education, Inc. Publishing as Longman.

thereafter. Brundisium, the site of the meeting, is the end rather than the beginning. Along the way, Horace insinuates his point that the journey *is* the point and that the point of the journey is being able to laugh at its discomforts and appreciate its pleasures: the fellowship of friends (such as Plotius, Varius, and Virgil), the ties of the native land ("Apulia—my Apulia"). To be with friends in a state of simplicity with one's basic needs met—that, for Horace, is the nearest to godliness that any man can come.

Like Catullus, Horace weaves autobiographical events and personal emotions into his writings, but never in a precisely revelatory manner. Events are included because exemplary of the lessons to be learned from life, usually couched negatively, for what they reveal is what Horace is not rather than what he is. He fought on the wrong (republican) side of the battle of Philippi in 42 B.C.E. and for a long time afterwards suffered from the consequences of his choice. What he tells us of it in Ode 2.7, however, is that he threw down his shield and fled; what he chooses to memorialize in the poem is the joy of surviving and of happening upon a friend, more valorous, who also survived. So, in Ode 2.13 Horace rages not at the vicissitudes of fate but at a tree on his Sabine farm that nearly fell on him. The poem continues in a negative mode, detailing all that he has *not* seen because he escaped the tree: the visions of the underworld, the epic tales of war sung there below by the valorous who did perish, forgetting all their many cares in the transports of the vatic poet's lyre. But Horace survives, lives simply on his farm, and writes poetry that would conjure up in its very themes and structures for all who read it the life it is too modest to celebrate directly.

Friedrich Nietzsche famously wrote of Horace:

> The mosaic of words, in which every word, every sound, by placing, and by meaning, spreads its influence to the right, to the left, and over the whole; this minimum in extent and number of symbols, this maximum thereby achieved in the effectiveness of the symbols, all this is Roman, and believe me, elegant par excellence. (*The Twilight of the Idols*, 1895, "What I Owe to the Ancients," no. 1)

Like the essays of Montaigne, Horace's *Odes* at first glance appear to meander without a clear sense of where they are going until they arrive. Two odes on the subject of *carpe diem*, Ode 1.9 and Ode 2.14, both begin in a sublime register, the first with a calque of the archaic Greek lyric poet Alcaeus (who also appears singing in the underworld in Ode 2.13), describing the white snow on Mount Soracte, the second with a lament on the swift passing of the years. As they wend their way through their theme, however, both poems conclude on immediate and concrete images of the everyday: the scarcely resisting wrist or finger of a girl in the Campus Martius in Rome; the Caecuban wine of Postumus staining the pavements of his estate after he is gone. "Seize the day," for Horace, is not so much a matter of indulging in the present as of inhabiting it fully, turning one's gaze away from the

Copyright © 2009 Pearson Education, Inc. Publishing as Longman.

sublime vision of the distant peaks and the underworld and onto the attainable pleasures of the here and now. "*Iam satis est,*" runs one of Horace's favorite phrases: "now/already [it] is enough."

Perhaps what made Horace so influential as a poet, especially in the pre-Romantic era, and what made him quintessentially Roman, as Nietzsche argued, is the perfect meshing of form and content in his poetry. Just as for Catullus to skewer an enemy on his iambics was to raise poetry to the level of deed, so for Horace to write well was to live well, and if one could make one's life an expression of one's poetry, one would be a fortunate man indeed.

❖

Petronius

Like Horace, Petronius was deeply implicated in and close to the center of political power in Rome. Unfortunately, there was a considerable difference between being a poet under the patronage of Augustus and being the "Arbiter" of the taste of the emperor Nero's court. While Catullus, Virgil, and Horace left considerable traces of themselves, their poetics, and their ideologies in their writings, Petronius and his *Satyricon* have remained quite an enigma. Rather than simply the language of literature, the *Satyricon* includes a range of idioms—each character speaks as his or her character would have spoken in reality. This linguistic variation is difficult to capture in translation; a useful exercise would compare J. P. Sullivan's eminently readable rendering in standard English, which we use in the *Anthology,* with recent efforts by P. G. Walsh (1996) and Sarah Ruden (2000) to render the full flavor of the original in contemporary terms. Erich Auerbach saw in the style of Petronius an unprecedentedly non-stylized record of a social milieu, and, indeed, much of what goes on at Trimalchio's dinner is attested to in other sources. Still, as Walsh argues in *The Roman Novel* (1970), this does not preclude the presence of many conventional types, especially those of farce and low theater. And, as Emily Gowers demonstrates in her marvelous study of satire, *The Loaded Table* (1996), the very rituals of the banquet, and especially their literary representation, were replete with symbolic meaning.

Students are less likely to be shocked by the decadent and amoral behavior of the characters in the novel than by the author's apparent lack of concern over that behavior. Classicists have long debated whether the *Satyricon* is a realistic depiction without any moral judgment on its characters, a document of approbation, or a deadpan satire. Fuel for various theories has come from the tenuous state of our knowledge of the novel. It survives only in a highly fragmented and corrupt form from late antiquity; the best-known and most complete episode—"Dinner with Trimalchio"—came to light only in the seventeenth century in Trogir, a town in Dalmatia. The *Cena Trimalchio* probably comprised most if not all of Book 15; parts of Books 14 and 16 also survive. No one knows how far it continued after-

Copyright © 2009 Pearson Education, Inc. Publishing as Longman.

wards; those who posit a moral underbelly hypothesize a final conversion scene, as in the later *Golden Ass* of Apuleius.

Most critics, however, assume that the picaresque narrative—random, chaotic, episodic—and its random, unstable characters who appear and disappear without explanation or motivation would appear so even if we had the full extent of the mammoth original text. As Froma Zeitlin puts it in "Petronius as Paradox: Anarchy and Artistic Integrity," in *Oxford Readings in the Roman Novel* (ed. S. J. Harrison, 1999), we as readers should "accept its paradoxes, its inconsistencies, its ambiguities, its absurdities, and its incongruities as integral elements of a world view." In Zeitlin's reading, the *Satyricon* is intentionally a radically anticlassical work of literature, lacking unity of tone, stylistic purity, and any sort of focus. Whether or not such an anticlassical stance was an active choice or the consequence of the world Petronius chose to depict, there is no question that this world is as representative of ancient Rome as the one we can glimpse in the poets of the early empire. It overlaps with that world—here too we find members of the elite, if an elite with an entirely different set of values than those described by Catullus or Horace, for there is little of comradeship or wit at Trimalchio's table. And the world that Encolpius moves through exhibits a lawlessness and inhumanity of Hobbesian proportions. It makes an instructive comparison to the milieu of fishermen, prostitutes, and slaves among which Jesus first preaches in Luke's Gospel; and the allure of the certitude offered by the Messiah stands out all the more clearly against the background of Encolpius's misadventures. The intimacy and simplicity of the Last Supper in the Gospels are particularly striking when set against the saturnalian tradition of the Roman symposium.

There was a fixed etiquette to the seating arrangement at the *triclinium*, the set of three low couches used for the Roman *convivium* (the evening meal). The hard couches were set around a central table, with the lower end left open to allow servants access to the table. Seating was for nine persons. To the left was the *lectus imus*, the lowest couch, where the host sat on the inside, then his wife, and then another member of his family, such as the eldest son. On the outside of the right-hand couch, the highest, or *lectus summus*, was the chief place for the lower of the two guest's benches, with two more places for guests above it. The top, or middle couch, the *lectus medius*, was also known as the *locus consular* and was reserved for the guest of honor, in the third place next to the host's couch, along with his wife or others of his party. Guests reclined on cushions on their left arm, with the right arm free for eating. For more on classical dining and its representations, see Gowers and also the essay collections, *Dining in a Classical Context* (ed. William J. Slater, 1991) and *Sympotica: A Symposium on the Symposion* (ed. Oswyn Murray, 1990).

Thematically, "Dinner with Trimalchio" is especially concerned with appearances and performance. Trimalchio's tastes are defined by elaborate practical jokes and punning deceptions, from the warning of *cave canem* on the door, to the trick dishes presented to his less than amused guests, to the performances derived from mime and low theater. While certainly concerned with gaining prestige for himself

Copyright © 2009 Pearson Education, Inc. Publishing as Longman.

and improving his tenuous social standing—a standard motivation for giving a banquet—Trimalchio is also marked as an individual by his obsessive need to stage-manage every aspect of the festivities, striving to maintain control over the smallest details as well as the largest, as in the mock funeral that brings the banquet to a confused close. While Horace in Satire 2.8 regaled a social climber analogous to Trimalchio with a series of fortuitous disasters—the ceiling collapses, the servants drop everything, the dishes are all burned—Petronius gives his host rope enough to hang himself without resorting to external forces. Trimalchio's conversation revolves around sex, food, and money, in each case his own; when he attempts to enliven his party with talk about literature, he manages only to expose his ignorance. Not that Petronius is any more or less generous with the guests, who are spongers and hangers-on every one. For all his absurdity, it is also difficult not to be a little bit charmed by Trimalchio's sheer vitality.

Paul

Students usually focus on the abstractions of the Epistle to the Romans and the familiar points of its doctrine; it may be helpful to defamiliarize these aspects by approaching the text first from those aspects it shares with the literature of ancient Rome: its rhetorical form and its audience. It is customary to teach the New Testament from a religio-cultural point of view, but what if we expand that point of view to ponder the fact that Paul, classically educated in Hellenistic Tarsus, was addressing his letter to a congregation of Romans whose contemporaries included Petronius, Lucan (the brilliant young author of the *Pharsalia*), and Lucan's uncle, the philosopher and tragedian Seneca. All four men, after all, died at the hands of Nero; all four were highly educated citizens of the Roman empire. Moreover, while we do not know Petronius's place of birth, the Córdoba of Lucan and Seneca was quite a bit farther and at least as isolated from the capital city as Paul's Cilicia.

Like any good rhetorician, Paul tailored his letter to his audience. Writing to Jewish-Christians in Galatia, he would argue that living "under the law" was a prerequisite for salvation; addressing the Greeks of Corinth, he would focus on the spiritual—freedom from the law was a sign of one's salvation. Tailored to converts practicing in the heart of the empire, Romans directly tackled the place of Jewish law within a universally defined Christianity by arguing through a series of paradoxes that the law continued in full force, but with all of its meaning transformed by the Christ event: the birth, life, crucifixion, and resurrection of Jesus. As Paul makes clear in 1:15, the main purpose of the letter is to pave the way for him to come to Rome to preach the gospel; consequently, he must establish his authority to do so and diminish the authority of others. Following the salutation (1:1-7), he makes a prayer that also states the purpose of his letter (1:8-15). He concludes the first chapter by introducing the letter's theme: the changed circumstances involved in living after Christ and the precise relation of this life to the laws that governed

Copyright © 2009 Pearson Education, Inc. Publishing as Longman.

life under God before the Incarnation. He begins Chapter 2 with a statement of his own authority to establish doctrine, before moving into his argument, the gist of which is that salvation was open to Gentiles who did not follow the law as well as to the community of Jews who did. Paul's teaching that justification now comes from faith rather than adhesion to the law continues through Chapter 11; Chapters 12-15 shift to admonitions on how to live in the shadow of the end of the world; and Chapter 16 wraps up the epistle with a series of personal salutations.

The rhetorical figure for which Paul's Epistle to the Romans is justly famous is paradox, which allows Paul to reformulate the strictures of the law while discarding the literal adherence to it that would have limited its application to Jews alone. On circumcision, for instance, he teaches that, "he is not a real Jew who is one outwardly, nor is true circumcision something external and physical. He is a Jew who is one inwardly, and real circumcision is a matter of the heart, spiritual and not literal. His praise is not from men but from God" (2:28-29). "Circumcision of the heart" is wholly paradoxical, for circumcision is a categorically physical procedure, performed on the flesh. Paul's genius as a rhetorician is to coin his paradoxes on the very mystery of spirit made flesh and flesh made spirit that was the credo of the new religion. The paradox could not be unraveled through logic, through the letter of the law, even though its structure depended on it; the mysteries of Christianity had to be accepted on faith, but a faith that was so fundamental that it marked its adherents as permanently and as physically as a circumcision, woman and man, Jew and Gentile alike.

In an analogous manner, Paul amplifies the mystery of the resurrection to teach that as its consequence, all men and women are dead to sin but alive to God (6:7-11) and hence in a state of grace. In the midpoint of the letter, Chapter 7, Paul uses paradox to reverse the meaning of law: the literal words of law are equated with death and sin, while the state of grace requires a new spiritual law that, although simplicity itself, is far more exigent than those of the Jews. To follow it is itself a question of grace: "For I do not do the good I want, but the evil I do not want is what I do" (7:19). The admonitions of the final chapters revolve around the need to be adequate to the state of grace and to control the recalcitrant body and the physical laws that would bind it. Here, Paul invokes the third mystery, the Trinity, three in one and one in three: "So we, though many, are one body in Christ, and individually members one of another" (12:5). Nature, too, submits to the figure of paradox, for what may appear to be obscure and unintuitive can be formulated in the simplest of terms. Sleep becomes a metaphor for sin, and the time of destruction to come signifies not death or an end but awakening and salvation (13:11). The Christ event is thus the spiritual image of the rising sun—and these are the hortatory words that would later complete the conversion of Augustine in the garden of a house in Milan: "The night is far gone, the day is at hand. Let us then cast off the works of darkness and put on the armor of light; let us conduct ourselves becomingly as in the day, not in reveling and drunkenness, not in debauchery and licentiousness, not in quarreling and jealousy" (13:12-13).

Copyright © 2009 Pearson Education, Inc. Publishing as Longman.

Whereas Paul dismisses the binding power of the Jewish law, likening it to the dark night of sleep or carousing, he is more sanguine of that of Rome, arguing in the phrase that became famous, "Pay all of them their dues, taxes to whom taxes are due, revenue to whom revenue is due, respect to whom respect is due, honor to whom honor is due" (13:7). Still, as his martyrdom and those of so many others were intended to demonstrate, rendering to Caesar the things of the flesh and of this world was, to the new Christians, nothing more than discarding a shell as empty of meaning in the new light as the laws of the Jews. Let Jews and Romans attend to whatever laws they like, Paul asserted; in the end, they had binding force only in the meaning he could give them through the illumination of faith.

Luke

Of the four authors of the canonical Gospels, the author of Luke and of Acts strove most to reincorporate the teachings of Paul into the Jesus movement. The chronology of Paul and Luke can be confusing because in the New Testament the Epistles follow the Gospels and Acts even though historically the Epistles constitute the earliest surviving documents of the Jesus movement. Moreover, their doctrinal focus seems logical as a consequence of the events narrated in the earlier books, whereas in fact it is the other way around. Just as Luke molded the events he recorded many decades after the fact into a cohesive narrative with a particular agenda, so did the other authors filter the (mostly) same received events through a specific standpoint while purporting to recount the origins of the movement. It may help to remind students that it is as possible to use the same set of facts to produce divergent accounts as it is to fabricate different versions; the way you structure and narrate history affects the result, just as Paul's rhetoric guides what we take from his Epistle to the Romans. Hence, when Luke in his Gospel tells us that, "Inasmuch as many have undertaken to compile a narrative of the things which have been accomplished among us . . . it seemed good to me also, having followed all things closely for some time past, to write an orderly account for you, most excellent Theophilus" (1:1-3), he is neither discrediting other accounts nor conceding their precedence over his—all are true, but his is more accurate, because of his close acquaintance with the events and because of his historical mode of narration.

It was customary in classical literary criticism to distinguish between history and epic not so much by their greater or lesser veracity—the *Aeneid* was held to be no more nor less true than Livy's *History*—as by whether they recounted events in chronological order (history) or began *in medias res* before returning to the beginning (epic). History and epic were two distinct ways of making sense of things that had happened, but both employed the typological structure of events familiar from the *Aeneid*. Luke wrote his Gospel primarily in the mode of Jewish history, closely related to Roman and Hellenistic historiography but with a highly developed sense of ways in which, rather than open-ended, history was eschatological, the begin-

Copyright © 2009 Pearson Education, Inc. Publishing as Longman.

ning connected to the end through the will of the Lord. As John Drury writes in his essay on Luke in *The Literary Guide to the Bible* (eds. Robert Alter and Frank Kermode, 1987), Luke's Jesus is first and foremost a prophet. This means that he is a historical figure who possesses the ability to relate the different stages of the history of the world to one another, to know the meaning of the present because he understands what has passed and is aware of what is to come. The events of his life are both the moments when the identity of Jesus as the Christ, or Messiah, is revealed and when as narrator Luke can relate those events typologically to those of the Hebrew Bible as fulfilled by Jesus.

The long list of generations in 3:24-38, held back until Jesus has reached adulthood, thus establishes his royal lineage (the Messiah had been prophesied to descend from King David) all the way back to Adam, "the son of God." Jesus is the legitimate outcome of a divine plan stretching back to the creation. Luke takes pains to establish the place of Jesus within Jewish tradition and the narrative style of the Hebrew Bible; his is the only of the four Gospels to devote time to the families of John the Baptist and Jesus, to describe them in the language of the patriarchs—"And they were both righteous before God, walking in all the commandments and ordinances of the Lord blameless" (1:6)—and to recount the births of John the Baptist and of Jesus. The parallelism of Jesus and his prophet John is simultaneously typological (recalling the many Hebrew Bible prophecies that had been fulfilled) and political—Luke takes care to set his history "in the days of Herod, king of Judea" (1:5) and to mention all the relevant authorities, from the emperor Tiberius through the governor Pontius Pilate, through the local authorities of the regions, to Annas and Caiaphas, the high priests. He also includes a discussion of whether Herod or Pilate has jurisdiction over the prisoner Jesus, Herod's interview with him, and the alliance made between the two authorities at the prisoner's cost (23:6-12). Moreover, only in Luke do we find described the circumcision of Jesus according to the prescriptions of Leviticus 12:3-4. Jesus himself proves to be an adept reader, citer, and exegete of the Hebrew Bible. Luke is unique in giving Jesus his first words as a twelve-year-old when his parents find him in dialogue with the rabbis in the temple. Unlike the other three Gospels, his first words as an adult are to refute the temptations of Satan in the desert: "It is written, 'Man shall not live by bread alone'" (4:4; the passage also appears in Matthew). Preaching at the synagogue in Nazareth (an episode exclusive to Luke), Jesus reads from the book of the prophet Isaiah (4:18), commenting only, "Today this scripture has been fulfilled in your hearing" (4:21).

As the narrative of the founding of a people, the Gospel makes a fascinating comparison with Virgil's *Aeneid*. Both regard the present day as the fulfillment of long-past events; both recount a record of miracles and the persecution of a subjugated people. Their protagonists are semidivine, semihuman figures destined to perform heroic deeds whether they will it or no—recall the touching words of Jesus at Gethsemane, asking, "Father, if you are willing, remove this cup from me; yet, not my will but yours be done" (22:42). The differences are equally illuminating, beginning with the generic distinction between history and epic. The presence of the Lord

Copyright © 2009 Pearson Education, Inc. Publishing as Longman.

is evident only through the words and deeds of Jesus, whereas in the *Aeneid* the gods are active and direct participants in the action. Most striking perhaps, and profoundly involved in the grassroots appeal of early Christianity, is the difference in the cast of characters. Jesus may have an illustrious heritage, but his family is of a low estate, as are the disciples he calls to him, most famously the fishermen Simon Peter, James, and John. Jesus eats with publicans and sinners, consorts with prostitutes, and preaches that the kingdom of God is reserved for the poor. He is crucified alongside common criminals. Appearing resurrected to two disciples on the road to Emmaus, he proves he is not an apparition by the simple expedient of eating a piece of fish. As opposed to the high, ornate style of epic, simplicity is the hallmark of the style later called *sermo humilis*, and the simplicity of the imagery of everyday life used in the parables and the miracles is matched by what classical readers viewed as a poverty of rhetoric. To find a way to make poverty into a virtue was a task that plagued not only would-be Christians but also classically educated writers such as Augustine who strove to convert the sophisticated members of the Roman elite.

The Acts of the Apostles purports to pick up the history precisely where Luke's Gospel had left off, beginning with Jesus's ascension and the subsequent descent of the Holy Spirit into the Apostles at the Feast of Pentecost. Acts is concerned with the spread of the gospel of Christ by his apostles; its central protagonist is Paul. Paul may not be the first convert, but in Luke's telling, his dramatic conversion on the road to Damascus bears all the hallmarks of the conversion narratives that would epitomize Christian autobiography for ever after. The calling of the disciples in the Gospels is swift and gentle; that of Paul is violent and extreme. It is not accidental that Paul, compared to Jesus and his apostles, is a privileged insider in the empire. He is not only a Roman citizen but also a Pharisee and an active persecutor of the Christians. Blinded by an apparition of Christ, Saul (Paul's name in Hebrew) must humble himself and wait for a disciple to heal him so that he may become the "chosen vessel" (9:15), as he was known thenceforth. As Augustine would make clear in the *Confessions*, Paul's entire career was read as an allegory of the spread of Christianity enacted by the man himself, beyond the local and low appeal of its origins, all the way to Rome, where, following much persecution and martyrdom, it would eventually take over the empire. Just as Aeneas and his Trojans melded with and supplanted the Italians, so Paul and his Christians infiltrated Rome and remade it in their image.

Roman Reactions to Early Christianity

The early Christians left a collection of accounts telling us how they perceived themselves and how they wished to be perceived by posterity, but we seldom consider how they might have looked to their contemporaries and rulers (beyond, of course, the villainous Roman and Jewish authorities portrayed in the New Testament). The fairly limited number of accounts of the first hundred years of

Copyright © 2009 Pearson Education, Inc. Publishing as Longman.

Christianity from the outside suggests that it was the religion fated to dominate Europe only from the biased point of view of the staunchest believers. To historians such as Tacitus and Suetonius and authorities such as Pliny and Emperor Trajan, they were mostly one fanatical nuisance among many, one more consequence of the syncretic nature of the Roman empire. Rome was an eminently practical empire in its day-to-day activities, and the concerns that emerge here are predominantly those of order and governance. In that sense, the assimilationist impulse of Paul and the Pauline tradition can be seen to be far more suited, and consequently far more of a threat, to Roman religion and its traditions than were the sectarian Jews, who had no interest in making converts.

These selections can also give students a taste of two of the most prominent and important genres of Roman literature: historiography and letter writing. Suetonius and Tacitus were the two great practitioners of the former genre during the early empire, Pliny a prominent figure in the latter. Suetonius, whose sensational and racy *Twelve Caesars* furnished the basis for Robert Graves's novel, *I Claudius* (and the highly entertaining 1970s BBC series adapted from it), was a master of the narrative biography. Tacitus, by contrast, excelled in analytical history, no less ideological, but organized around a chronological sequence of events, although his characters, too, are sharply observed. His selection also gives students a glimpse of one of the most infamous episodes in Roman history, Nero and the great fire of Rome. Pliny is known as one of the first to write letters intended for publication, as a recorder of everyday life in the first century, and as an eyewitness of the eruption of Mount Vesuvius.

Augustine

Paul was the first Christian figure to make a significant connection between Christianity and Rome; it was Augustine who made this connection a fundamental aspect of his theology. The *City of God* was his magnum opus, a monumental exegesis of world history with the goal of proving that Christians were not responsible for the collapse of the Roman empire. The image of the two cities that structures this world history has proved enduring in Christian iconography, both in the persistent representation of the metropolis as a place of evil and corruption—the earthly city—and as the image of heaven itself—the Rome where Christ is Roman, as Dante put it (*Purgatorio* 32.102), or the city on the hill, as it became known in the political rhetoric of late-twentieth-century America.

What is easy to overlook in focusing on the afterlife of the allegory of the two cities is how completely they are intertwined in Augustine's writing even as theologically they must remain totally severed from one another. After all, they are also an allegory of the relationship between mind and body already shown by Paul to exist in intimate but mortal conflict with one another. In the lexicon of the *City of God*, Rome the earthly city is the body and Rome the heavenly city is the mind—itself an allegory strongly indebted to the Hellenistic philosophy of Neoplatonism.

Copyright © 2009 Pearson Education, Inc. Publishing as Longman.

Neoplatonism was based on the idea that the divine soul was sent down from the heavens to be imprisoned in the body; its goal was to free the mind of the weight of the body, its desires and needs. In their doctrine, Augustine's writings were all about achieving the separation of earthly and heavenly on the level of history and at the level of the individual. In their *modus operandi*, however, his thought, style, and argumentation were an influential synthesis of both, of the classical and the Christian, of pagan literature and Christian scripture, of high style and the *sermo humilis*. Like Paul, Augustine wanted Christianity to appeal to the high and mighty as well as to the poor and lowly, targeted by Jesus.

The Ages of Man and the Ages of the World

The analogy between macrocosm—the universe—and microcosm—the human body—was a fundamental tenet of both Aristotelian and Platonic thought. Augustine was the first to combine the Roman tradition of describing the history of the empire in terms of the life of an individual with the Judeo-Christian millenarian tradition of dividing the world into seven millennia modeled on the seven days of creation in Genesis. *Infantia* (0-7 years) describes history from the creation to Noah; it passes through its boyhood (*pueritia*, 7-14 years) from Noah to Abraham; the covenant signifies its *adulescentia* (14-28 years), when the individual must learn to follow the rules of society; youthful prime (*iuventus*, 28-50 years) is achieved with David, the height of the world's temporal glory; the age of the world's *gravitas*, or decline (50-70 years), occurs in the age of the prophets; the life and death of Christ occur in the *senectus*, or old age of the world (70+ years), which will continue for the time remaining before the end of the world and resurrection on the day of rest. The life of Christ is the linchpin of the analogy between macrocosm and microcosm. Just as each individual may achieve salvation by modeling his or her life on that of Christ—the *imitatio Christi*—so did the chaos of history become orderly and meaningful when seen as the imitation of Christ through its events by the city of God in its pilgrimage toward salvation at the end of time.

In the figural reading of history already evident in the New Testament, in Luke's Gospel and Paul's Epistle to the Romans among other places, and systematized by Augustine, the Christ event constitutes a conversion on the macrocosmic level, a transformation of the world from a sinful entity performing an apparently random and meaningless set of deeds to a salvific entity whose every act is bent toward final salvation. To the convert, every seemingly pointless gesture performed in the past becomes in retrospect saturated with meaning—if it has led to the salvation of conversion, it had to have happened as it did. As in the parable of the prodigal son, a favorite image of Augustine's, it was necessary to hit bottom before being able to find the right way back. And if, as the Neoplatonists believed in a material sense and Christians in a more symbolic one, the soul emanated from the heavens, fell to earth, and spent its life either wallowing in fleshly desires or finding its way back to the heavens, then the life of every individual was in fact a narrative of conversion, either failed or achieved. The lessons of history (that all

Copyright © 2009 Pearson Education, Inc. Publishing as Longman.

earthly cities fall to dust while the immaterial community of the city of God finally makes its way to celestial Rome) are thus also the lessons of the individual life: All earthly desires are evanescent and hence unsatisfying; the only true satisfaction is the rest to be found in returning to God.

Conversion Narratives

To this end, Augustine gave the *Confessions* a double structure, allowing the reader to experience both the confusion and yearning of the sinning Christian and the certainty and knowledge that could only come after conversion. The dual perspective of "what I didn't know then, what I do know now" has become such a fundamental aspect of not only spiritual autobiography but first-person narrative in general that it can be difficult even to notice it for the innovation it is here. Close attention to this structure can help clarify not only Augustine's sometimes arbitrary-seeming choice of which events to include but also the recondite opening paragraphs and even the attitude he takes toward classical culture. (For an excellent introduction to Augustine's life and works, see Peter Brown's 1967 biography, *Augustine of Hippo*.) The primary intention of the book may have been to confess his own experience of conversion so that others may imitate his imitation of Christ, but its secondary concern was to convert classical culture itself, to take its sinful form and content and give them a new meaning in the light of Christ.

For Augustine, as for Paul before him, the convert gains an extraordinary authority from the inspiration of his conversion. His life may be exemplary, but it is also, paradoxically, unique because of his ability to compose it into an artistic document applicable to others. In particular, the convert has gained the grace of seeing himself and the world not only from the flawed and limited human perspective but also from the omniscient and eternal perspective of God, a perspective that has been recorded in scripture (as in each human life, and as in the events of world history) for all to see if they possess the vision to discern it clearly. Pre-conversion, Paul strove to block the divine will; post-conversion he realized he was its "Chosen Vessel." Augustine similarly posits himself as a conduit for God's truth, both in the lessons of his sinning and in the insight granted by his salvation.

The *Confessions* is composed as a tissue of citation from the Bible, weaving the matter of Augustine's life into God's words. Generically, Augustine identifies it as a psalm, a song of praise; hence the predominance of the book of Psalms in the opening paragraphs. Rather than announcing his theme directly, Augustine poses it as a series of questions and quandaries, mysteries that his readers, like himself before them, must resolve: To praise the Lord you must know where to find him; to find him you must know where to look for him; to look for him you must open up the essential theological paradoxes of Augustine's time. Did anything exist outside of or before God and his creation? What was the point of creation if God is/was already perfect? If God is omnipotent and good, how can evil exist?

Copyright © 2009 Pearson Education, Inc. Publishing as Longman.

God as Rhetorician and Poet

The solution, elegant if perhaps disappointingly rhetorical to our pragmatic and materialist age, is there at the beginning: "You stir man to take pleasure in praising you, because you have made us for yourself, and our heart is restless until it rests in you" (1.1.1). The entire creation is a song of praise sung by God for his own pleasure through the chorus of his creation. The aim of man is to perform his part well; doing so will give him the pleasure he seeks, rest in God. The role of evil in general and of sinners in specific within this great psalm is to supply rhetorical counterpoint, to be the coloring that makes the grace notes emerge more perfectly. As Augustine put it in the *City of God*, "God would never have created a man, let alone an angel, in the foreknowledge of his future evil state if he had not known at the same time how he would put such creatures to good use, and thus enrich the course of world history by the kind of antithesis which gives beauty to a poem" (4.11.18). The final selection of the *Confessions*, from Book 11, outlines this sense of existence as a performance and the epistemological fireworks made possible by it. This can be a useful starting point in teaching the bedrock structure of the book. Rather than conceiving of time in terms of past, present, and future, as human minds generally do, the divine perspective exists in an eternal present, neither outside of history nor contained by it. In 11.28.38, Augustine finds in the recitation of a psalm a material analogy for this divine paradox: "Suppose I am about to recite a psalm which I know. Before I begin, my expectation is directed towards the whole. But when I have begun, the verses from it which I take into the past become the object of my memory." For Augustine, the same holds true for any fragment of the psalm, as well as for "the entire life of an individual person, where all actions are part of a whole, and of the total history of *the sons of men* [Psalms 31:20] where all human lives are but parts." For those unfamiliar with God's compositions, they seem random and unfolding in time, but for those who have learned to recite them, both past and future exist in their memory and inform their sense of the present moment, wherever in the recitation that may be.

Augustine contends, then, that one has always known God, because he is the origin and the endpoint of every part of the universe. One spends one's life seeking him blindly everywhere. Hence the events of the *Confessions*, recording a stumbling toward knowledge from one false hope (petty theft, dissolution, Cicero, Manicheeism, Neoplatonism) to another, each one providing a distorted piece of the puzzle because part of it, but none able to provide either intellectual or emotional satisfaction. Only when the desperate Augustine, sitting in a garden, is able to listen to the voice of a simple child, to hear in it a divine order, and to open scripture at random and see in its words a voice speaking to him—only then is he able to convert by finding God where he had always been, in him and everywhere around him. Returning to the origin of mankind (Eden) and the origin of the individual (the child), Augustine is able to discover the thread that gives sense to his own life.

Copyright © 2009 Pearson Education, Inc. Publishing as Longman.

Augustine as Rhetorician and Poet

For a classically trained rhetorician like Augustine, as for most classically educated Romans, to regard God as a poet and singer and his creation an act of
rhetorical genius was not a cop-out; it was the highest praise that could be bestowed on him. The concept of the vatic or prophetic poet hearkens back to the
figure of the blind Homer and the cult around the singer Orpheus. It had been
given a contemporary Roman inflection by Virgil and the worship surrounding
him and his poetry. It may help to remind students that poetry in particular and
linguistic production in general were still conceived of orally even when written
down. Memorization was an important skill to be mastered and an essential component of knowledge. Oratory was a fundamental part of Roman society and the
sermon even more essential to Christian culture, as is clear in Augustine's record
of his experience in hearing bishop Ambrose preach in Milan. The practice of
confession began as a public pronouncement of one's conversion. Book 8, in
particular, is concerned with the difficult final step from private to public conversion at a time when being a Christian could entail, at the least, professional
difficulty, and in the extreme, death.

This is not to say that Augustine did not trade equally in the denigration of
rhetoric, the art of the *venditor verborum*, or seller of words. As traders in the surface meanings of language, he likened such persons to the Jews, worshippers of the
letter of the Hebrew Bible, not the Old Testament text revealed in its figural meaning by the New. Augustine reports on first hearing Ambrose that "My pleasure was
in the charm of his language" (5.13.23), which opened his heart to him, but he is
swayed when the truth of the speech reaches him, as "first one, then another, then
many difficult passages in the Old Testament interpreted figuratively, where I, by
taking them literally, had found them to kill" (5.14.24; 2 Corinthians 3:6).
Augustine appealed to his educated contemporaries with a dual argument.
Contrary to standard opinion, scripture could become classically eloquent in the
right hands—Augustine's writing, even more than that of Paul, is full of rhetorical
figures, wordplay, antithesis, paradox, chiasmus. At the same time, its deceptively
humble appearance was itself a powerful rhetorical device, making it accessible to
the most simple but still compelling even to the most learned, as Augustine wrote
of scripture in the *Confessions* (6.5.8).

Food and Lodging

Augustine's language may be classical in its figures, but the imagery he favors is essentially Christian—the simplest elements of life such as food and shelter. The imagery of the house punctuates the narrative from the opening inquiry into God's
dwelling place, through the image of modesty adapted from *Aeneid* 8 to reflect his
early confusion ("The house of my soul is too small for you to come to it. May it be
enlarged by you" [1.5.6]), through the refrain of "knock and it shall be opened," to
the houses of conversion in Book 8, personifying both the dwelling place of the soul

Copyright © 2009 Pearson Education, Inc. Publishing as Longman.

and the house of the world. Through it all resonates the mystery of the incarnation, God's choice to be born as his son in the poor earthly hut of a body. In the process of conversion, Augustine thus cleanses his house, accepting its poverty rather than trying to glorify it, and ridding it of the dirt of sin. His mother Monica, too, is closely tied in with the domestic imagery, remembered by Augustine for her peccadillo of sneaking wine from the cask but also memorialized for the glimpse of eternity shared by them just before her death, seated on a window sill overlooking a garden, at the threshold between the things of this earth and those of the next (9.10).

Food is as central to the Judeo-Christian tradition as to the Roman. In the latter, it appeared in religious ceremonies as sacrifice to the gods, especially in the archaicism of the *Aeneid*, but it was primarily a means of social symbolism, as in the satire and its commentary on philosophy through analysis of food. The Christians responded to what they saw as the decadent banqueting of the Romans and the intricate dietary restrictions of the Jewish law with a poetics of simple food that makes even Horace's philosophical diet look gluttonous. Rather than reaching the divine through opulence or complexity, Christian writers maintained that only the simplest of bodily needs were adequate to provide a glimpse of the peace of salvation. Augustine uses food both metaphorically, as when he describes the "empty trifles" produced by "the tender vine of my heart" as a result of being force-fed on poetic fictions (1.17), and literally, as in the famous episode of the pear tree in Book 2, which Augustine retells as a perverse imitation of the process of conversion and of the fellowship of man—performed from a correct desire improperly directed, for no material purpose (they are not hungry, the pears are unripe) but only out of desire for camaraderie. The imagery resonates both with the forbidden fruit of the garden of Eden, rehearsing Augustine's explanation for the fall, and with the parable of the prodigal son, who comes to himself only when reduced to eating sops with the pigs. As with all of Augustine's imagery, as it recurs it accretes new associations and different meanings. In its final iteration, we find the same fruit ripened to perfection for blessed souls like angels, who see the "fruit concealed" in the "dark thickets" of scripture, "to which they fly in delight, chirping as they seek for it and pluck it" (12.28.38).

Pick Up and Read

In the final analysis, the *Confessions* is a book about reading, and every one of its natural images has been filtered through the language of scripture and the language of pagan Greek and Rome. Most of its pages are concerned with what Augustine has read, and when he does delve into carnal sins, they are always interpreted as faulty reading, the incorrect application of the correct impulse. Find the correct book, and read it correctly, he tells us, and you will be saved. The *City of God* purports to reread history, and it is as a primer in reading one's self and the world that the *Confessions* has been most influential over the last millennium and a half and has maintained its influence over a secular readership who no longer have much interest in the thorny theological questions of the origin of evil and the

Copyright © 2009 Pearson Education, Inc. Publishing as Longman.

conflict between free will and predestination. Augustine has endured because he provided a possible structure for finessing these questions rather than what was impossible, a final, noncontradictory, and unparadoxical resolution of them.

For Michel de Montaigne and Jean-Jacques Rousseau, as shown in their selections in the Resonances section, reading becomes both a metaphor and a valid description of the search for self-knowledge and the means to represent that search to one's peers. For both writers, too, the rhetoric of simplicity retains its power and cloaks a complexity of motive and effect of which they were well aware. Montaigne plays on the disparity between the discovery of the New World and the conventional wisdom of Christianity, Rousseau on the gap between Enlightenment secularism and Christian rhetoric. Arrived in heaven, he will present his book to his Lord as his confession.

Copyright © 2009 Pearson Education, Inc. Publishing as Longman.

Volume B
The Medieval Era

---◆◆◆◆◆---

Medieval China

WOMEN IN EARLY CHINA

The readings in this section of the *Anthology* consist both of didactic texts that were designed to provide models for emulation and rules of conduct for women and also of literary works composed by or about women as key protagonists. It is important to keep in mind that these selections span a period more than a millennium in length and that they spring from and speak to a spectrum of social classes. As Sharon Shih-jiuan Hou has pointed out, the underrepresentation of women's literature "in the larger context of China's literary history may be attributed to the many and varied restrictions imposed on Chinese women." At the same time, there was a deep-seated belief "that a nation's prosperity or adversity" could be highly influenced by them ("Women's Literature," in *The Indiana Companion to Traditional Chinese Literature*, eds. William Nienhauser, Jr., et al., 1986, pp. 176-177). In some instances it is interesting to see how the various literary representations confirm the lessons of the didactic texts, whereas others raise questions about whether they are seeking actively to counter the latters' guidance or—for whatever reasons—are simply heedless of them.

Liu Xiang

Like earlier Chinese biographers, Liu Xiang organizes his subjects into categories that are in his case clearly morally inflected. Of the six virtues he illustrates (on the basis of evidence that is probably at best legendary), the section on wise mothers, understandably, comes first. After all, of the three roles available to women (the other two being daughter and wife), that of the mother was the one with the greatest power. That Liu Xiang credits the mother of Mencius, who may be considered the first Confucian, with having set him straight is no small tribute. Students should consider what her priorities are represented to be, how they relate to the precepts of Confucius's *Analects* (see Vol. A, pp. 1046-1060), and how she is depicted as conveying them to her son.

Copyright © 2009 Pearson Education, Inc. Publishing as Longman.

Ban Zhao

There are obvious comparisons to be drawn between Ban Zhao's *Lessons for Women* and those of conduct books for women in other cultures. A woman of considerable education herself, Ban Zhao asserts that right for the daughters in her family, but the exercise of that learning was reserved, evidently, for the household, rather than in some public sphere. On the issue of whether sexual difference was innate or constructed, there is no question where she—along with the entire Confucian tradition—stood. Ask students to think about the motivations and fears behind her advice, and the values and goals it might have sought to uphold. What insights into the psychology of social relations and possible strategies for survival does it reveal? Remind students that the self-deprecating language, as well as the presumption that the principal obligation of any individual was to fulfill the expectations of a social role, were shared by men and women alike.

Yuan Cai

One thousand years after Ban Zhao, the opportunities for women had become more, rather than less, constrained, thanks to an increasingly prudish interpretation by dominant Confucian thinkers of proper sexual behavior and relations. Yuan Cai's guidelines for his own family are responding to an evidently widespread disregard for the fate of women in the social unit, especially those who had lost the husbands or fathers who had given them leverage. (In later centuries, widows were often expected to eliminate themselves as problems and preserve their "chastity" by simply committing suicide.) Among other features of the text, note the influence of a burgeoning commercialism during the Song dynasty on Yuan's concerns.

Voices of Women

The first two sets of poems included here are anonymous and were probably written to musical tunes. The "Willow Bough" series is traditionally regarded as the work of a woman from the upper classes, whereas the "Midnight Songs" are attributed to a courtesan of uncertain virtue, but the evidence for authorship in both cases is largely based on the poems themselves. Both series treat with relatively disarming directness intimate relationships between a woman and her lover, and the fact that "silk" and "thoughts" are homophones in Chinese plays a key role in each. Otherwise, it should be noted that imagery in the "Willow Bough" series of pines, cypress, and chrysanthemums draws on a cultural lexicon shared with male literati poets (see, for example, Tao Qian), whereas "Midnight Songs" employs much more daring diction and deploys the mercantile values attendant to her commodified position. For the next millennium, a large majority of the few

Copyright © 2009 Pearson Education, Inc. Publishing as Longman.

recorded female authors were women of uncertain virtue, who provided often highly cultivated entertainment to young men outside their households.

The remaining two poems, also anonymous, are probably of male authorship and depict two very different roles for women. When discussing "A Peacock Southeast Flew," ask students to consider the relationship of the poem's story to the prescriptions of the texts at the beginning of the section. The disempowerment of both lovers reflects, among other things, that "marriage in China was not so much the alliance of two individuals as that of two families" (Sharon Shih-jiuan Hou, "Women's Literature," in *The Indiana Companion to Traditional Chinese Literature*, eds. William H. Nienhauser, Jr., et al., 1986, p. 175). You may also wish to compare the situations of its protagonists with those of Pyramus and Thisbe as well as Romeo and Juliet. As for "The Ballad of Mulan," Anne Birrell has suggested that the gender transposition of Mulan (whose legend was revived in a twentieth-century Disney movie) may have mythic counterparts in "goddesses of sacral violence" depicted in an early collection of legends entitled the *Classic of Mountains and Seas* (see her essay "Myth," in *The Columbia History of Chinese Literature*, ed. Victor Mair, 2000, p. 68). Her performance is *so* unusual, however, that other scholars have speculated that the story comes from non-Chinese sources.

Yuan Zhen

Student response to this very enigmatic tale is likely to be lively, with discussion centering on how to explain and pass judgment on both the events recounted in the story and the narrator's apparent perspective on them. Recurring questions are likely to include the following: Why does Chang do what he does? Why does Ying-ying do what she does? Why is this called the story of Ying-ying if it is told from Chang's perspective? Is Chang's behavior sensible, laudable, or reprehensible? What does the narrator think of Chang? What should we as readers think of him? The story's reticence with respect to motivation at key moments and the perplexing and (in some eyes) frustrating closure invite multiple readings. Whether or not Yuan Zhen was writing about his own experience, discomfort with which might have led to the peculiarities and omissions in the account, consumed the attention of Chinese critics for centuries, but contemporary students are unlikely to find this autobiographical interpretation of any great interest.

Cultural stereotypes of mysterious encounters with divine women and of the bewitching, "kingdom-toppling" female were there to be called upon, and we might view this story as exploring the delights of infatuation, only to reject it for proper ritual order. The word "disorder," in fact, appears close to a dozen times in the text, and it is no accident that the interesting action takes place in a marginal, and one of the few public, spaces available in Tang China, a monastery, and during a time of political disturbance. Literary historians have also noted that other works written during these middle to late periods of the Tang similarly explored scenarios that mirrored the increasing destabilization of the dynasty itself. But is

Copyright © 2009 Pearson Education, Inc. Publishing as Longman.

Ying-ying simply a femme fatale whose marital clutches Chang was wise to elude? Keep in mind that as maternal cousins with different surnames, they could certainly have been married to each other.

"The Story of Ying-ying" offers excellent material for discussing issues of point of view and narration. As Stephen Owen has observed, it "is undoubtedly the most problematic narrative of the Tang" because, among other reasons, it sustains at least "two opposing points of view, each of which tries to take control of the story and compel judgment in its favor. . . . The story begs us to pass judgment" ("Conflicting Interpretations: 'Yingying's Story,'" in his *The End of the Chinese 'Middle Ages': Essays in Mid-Tang Literary Culture*, 1996, pp. 149–150). And this judgment is to be passed at several levels—on the protagonists, the narrator, and an imputed audience. Few other stories test as successfully as does "The Story of Ying-ying" what it means to play a role. Remembering the Confucian conviction that it was the responsibility of the individual to, in a sense, internalize a socially mandated role, we might well wonder where the boundary between virtue and performance might lie. Whether or not students agree with Owen's conclusion that "we are left with no secure ground to decide between them" is well worth discussing.

Note, finally, the central role played by literary texts such as letters and poems in moving the story forward. The degree of agency ascribed to them, each of which, quite typically, is further laden with layers of other texts, suggests a high degree of self-referentiality within the story itself to its own status as a written work. These internal texts are not only performative but also literally performed, read aloud to appreciative audiences within and outside the text itself. Such acts cannot but call attention to the fact that their medium itself is a site of performance, and one within which social order could be all too easily destabilized. Indeed, some scholars have speculated that the risks created by Ying-ying's demonstrated ability to write may have been partially responsible for the pervasive sentiment in later imperial China that a woman's morality might, in fact, be inversely proportional to her literacy.

⚬⚭⚬

RESONANCE

Wang Shifu

The appeal of Ying-ying's story is reflected in the fact that over the course of centuries it was reworked in several other literary forms, of which the most popular was the play *The Story of the Western Wing* by Wang Shifu. Look ahead to *The Story of the Stone* five centuries later (see Vol. D, p. 74), and you'll see in Chapter 23 its appeal as the paradigm for romances between "brilliant students and talented beauties" that captivated generations of readers. Regarded as a "lover's bible," it was "happily devoured by innumerable young men and women who easily recognized themselves in the protagonists of the play" (Stephen H. West and Wilt

Copyright © 2009 Pearson Education, Inc. Publishing as Longman.

Idema, "Story of the Western Wing," in *Masterworks of Asian Literature in Comparative Perspective*, ed. Barbara Stoler Miller, 1994, p. 347).

The Story of the Western Wing's version of the relationship between Chang ("Student Zhang") and Ying-ying (referred to as "Female Lead"), of course, is different in both form and outcome from that of the original tale. Expanded into an operatic play with five acts, within each of which one character sings all the principal arias, it added new characters and enhanced significantly the role of Ying-ying's maid, called Crimson in Wang Shifu's work, as matchmaker. Most importantly, the play changed the ending, which now brings the student and his first love together in happy matrimony.

Tao Qian

The respect for Tao Qian as a noble "recluse" (the category under which his biography is recorded in dynastic histories) preceded and has endured even after his validation as a poet. As a consequence, most traditional discussions of him center on his philosophical position, in particular on whether his actions and his poetry were inspired more by Confucian or by Daoist inclinations. Counting up the textual allusions in his poetry, scholars have noted that references to the Daoist works *Zhuangzi* and *Liezi* come in first and third in terms of numbers, with those to Confucius's *Analects* placing second, yet Confucius as an individual emerges with much greater force. (See Donald Holzman, "A Dialogue with the Ancients, Tao Qian's Interrogation of Confucius," in *Culture and Power in the Reconstruction of the Chinese Realm 200–600*, eds. Scott Pearce, Audrey Spiro, and Patricia Ebrey, 2001, pp. 81–85.) It is well to keep in mind that adherence to one school of thought did not require rejection of the other, and Tao Qian's indifference to the "dusty" world and its values thus co-exists—however uneasily—with a Confucian sense of service and moral duty. As James Robert Hightower suggests, Tao Qian "reflects the conflicts and contradictions of the period, and his poetry best expresses the dilemma of the man of good will born into the troubled times of medieval China" (*The Poetry of T'ao Ch'ien*, 1970, p. 1).

The impulse to interpret poetry as biography is one that goes back to readings of the first anthology, the *Book of Songs*, whose preface explicitly stated that poems should be read as expressive responses to the particulars of an individual's experience and context. Tao Qian further reinforces this impulse, thanks both to his dating of several poems (he was the first known poet to provide such information) and to his brief autobiography, so unusual in the early written tradition that he presents it as a biography. You might ask students to consider how he presents himself there and how that picture tallies with what can be drawn from the poetry.

The language and diction of Tao's poems are as simple and direct in the original Chinese as they are in translation, a style that went against the grain of

Copyright © 2009 Pearson Education, Inc. Publishing as Longman.

contemporary tastes for ornateness and allusiveness. His poems are rich with textual references, of course, but to ones that his peers would have easily recognized. Note the recurrence of the word "return" and the repeated mentions of simplicity and freedom. "The Peach Blossom Spring" is interesting to consider in this context. How does it compare to accounts of utopias elsewhere, and what is the relative importance of the nature of the journey itself? What does wine, the "Thing in the Cup" in "Finding Fault with My Sons," mean to him in this context?

Tao Qian has traditionally been characterized as the founder of the poetry of "fields and gardens," which has been likened to both pastoral and nature poetry in Europe. It is worth considering, however, how far the comparison can be taken. How much do we see of the actual beauties of the landscape around him? How important are the symbolic associations of pines, chrysanthemums, and mountains, all of which evoke thoughts of longevity and mortality? What is the nature of Tao's reclusion, and how does it compare to images of eremetic life in other cultures?

Han-shan

Given the impossibility of identifying these poems linguistically and historically with one individual, it is probably best not to think of them in terms of authorship. The difficulty of establishing that link, along with the highly colloquial and often irreverent nature of their language, probably led to the general lack of attention on the part of Chinese literary historians to these Cold Mountain poems until the twentieth century, when an interest in developing a new vernacular revived a focus on premodern antecedents. The account by an unidentifiable official that depicts Han-shan as a Buddhist monk is spurious at best, but it reflects an attempt to provide some biographical flesh to a legend.

The poems were better preserved in Japan because of their use of Chan (Zen) concepts that played a much more influential role in Japanese literary traditions than they did in China. Chan was a distinctly Chinese (as opposed to Indian) strain of Buddhism that came to prominence during the eighth century. It stressed the importance of meditation—as opposed to faith, good works, or the study of scriptures—as a means of attaining enlightenment. Note the significance of the word "sit" in these poems, which in the Chan context evokes meditative practice. A key goal of the exercise would be to realize that Buddha-nature and enlightenment already lie within the self, and the importance of being able to transcend such distinctions as that between a state before and after enlightenment is also crucial to understanding these poems. Still, the question remains as to whether one can speak from that state and if the persona here is doing so. Many poems not included in the *Anthology* resort simply to "rhymed sermonizing" (Burton Watson, *Cold Mountain Poems*, 1970, p. 11). Watson feels that efforts of some scholars, especially in Japan, to see Han-shan as a fully enlightened Zen layman have led to

Copyright © 2009 Pearson Education, Inc. Publishing as Longman.

forced and one-sided readings of the collection. He prefers to "read the poems as a chronicle of spiritual search—rewarded at times by moments of wonderful contentment, but at other times frustrated by loneliness and despair—rather than as a pat report of success" (p. 14).

Translations by both Gary Snyder and Burton Watson offer a glimpse into the possibilities of translation that are well worth discussing. If Han-shan's mountains in Snyder's hands resemble more closely the crags of the High Sierra than the worn slopes of southeastern China, his choice of diction may nonetheless be entirely apt.

POETRY OF THE TANG DYNASTY

Given the likely remoteness of poetry from the daily lives of most students today, it may be difficult for them to understand the extent to which it was a truly integral part of culture, society, and politics for the educated classes of pre-modern China. It is a point, nonetheless, that needs to be made as persuasively as possible. Note the extent to which the poems in this section reflect their important and varied roles as a means of emotional and philosophical communication and a medium of sociality, commentary, and critique. Poets could assume that their audiences were familiar with the same body of literature, and the free use of allusion was therefore a game whose rules everyone understood. Students may be grateful for the fact that shared conventions of exchange and expectations for on-the-spot composition led to the predominance of rather short poetic forms.

The best discussion of Tang poetry between two covers is Stephen Owen's *The Great Age of T'ang Poetry* (1981), which includes excellent chapters on Wang Wei, Li Bo, and Du Fu.

Wang Wei

Frequently characterized as a nature poet, Wang Wei clearly did not engage in exhaustive description of the landscapes he loved to traverse, a fact that is interesting to consider in light of the fact that he was also known for his paintings, often of those very same scenes. Because of this connection, intriguing questions arise about how the imagery in Wang Wei's poems functions. What are its characteristics, and how is it organized within a poem? Is it intended to be visually informative or precise? Stephen Owen has noted that Wang Wei appears to be interested in stressing a balanced geometry of natural forms, a tendency fostered by the form's demands for parallelism, as well as in calling attention to the nature of perception itself. (Consider, in this connection, the sixth line of "Zhongnan Retreat," which speaks of watching "the time when clouds rise.") Both of those interests

Copyright © 2009 Pearson Education, Inc. Publishing as Longman.

would presumably work counter to an impulse to descriptive fidelity. It may be worth considering how appropriate an epithet like "nature poet" is, after all, for Wang Wei and how his work may be compared with that of the Romantics and Imagists in the West.

It is equally clear that symbolic associations, whether conventional, religious, or personal, were important in his choice of imagery. White clouds, for example, which figured prominently in Tao Qian's poems, appear frequently in Wang Wei's work as well. In earlier poetry they were emblems of transience or illusoriness, as of fame. Here they may be suggestive of the Buddhist notion that all phenomena have no fixed reality or are "empty," a term that also appears a number of times in these poems. The larger significance of both is well worth discussing.

Wang Wei was certainly familiar with Buddhist doctrine, but it is difficult to determine the extent to which he meant his poems to be read as religious statements. "Visiting the Temple of Gathered Fragrance" describes a literal ascent up a mountain to visit a monastery, but whether it should be read as an allegory of enlightenment is not clear. A comparison with the poems of Han-shan on this question might be useful.

Note the social setting of many of these poems, especially the first set of quatrains written at various sites of Wang Wei's country estate in tandem with his good friend Pei Di. Scholars have discussed at great length whether or not Wang's poetry exemplifies an unusual and distinctive stance of impersonality or detachment, and if so, the extent to which it may be explained by his known commitment to Buddhism. Given the fact that Wang held office virtually without a break until he died, a discussion of the last couplet of "In Response to Vice-Magistrate Zhang" provides a typically complex answer to the question about his degree of commitment to the bureaucratic career: Is it something he would like to reject, in favor of a life in nature like the fisherman's; something that has made sense given the circumstances, following the advice of the Chu fisherman's song; or something else entirely, perhaps an enigmatic image meant to stimulate his friend's imagination? None of the answers to any of these questions ought, in the end, be considered mutually exclusive. For further reading on this issue, consult Pauline Yu's *The Poetry of Wang Wei* (1980).

Li Bo

According to an inscription written by a later poet on Li Bo's tomb, he was a "banished immortal" whose poetry "could make gods and ghosts weep" (Stephen Owen, *The Great Age of T'ang Poetry*, 1981, p. 120). That Li Bo made a strong impression, both as personality and as poet, on his contemporaries seems clear. He shared with them a total mastery of the literary tradition and, as far as preferred genres and forms were concerned, his choices were relatively conservative ones. Unlike them, however, he appears to have resisted—for any

Copyright © 2009 Pearson Education, Inc. Publishing as Longman.

number of reasons—submitting himself to the rigors of the civil service examination and a bureaucratic career track, and his poetry offers an unprecedented array of displays of inventiveness, bold diction, and interplays between sound and sense that resist translation.

"Drinking Alone with the Moon" provides a good example of his imaginative engagement with the natural world, seen also in the quatrain "Sitting Alone by Jingting Mountain." No other Tang poet would have claimed such a personal and exclusive relationship with either the moon or the mountain, and whether this distinctiveness is childlike or arrogant has been the subject of much critical discussion. It is certainly unique in the tradition. Wine is an important part of Li Bo's world as well, as it was with Tao Qian, though Li seems to consume it with greater intensity and abandon than earlier well-known drinkers. The attendant risks of such heedlessness were summed up in the legend (one of several) that he drowned while drunkenly attempting to embrace the reflection of the moon in a lake. While surely unfounded, the story does raise the interesting possibility that China's most literally egocentric poet sought desperately to escape from that self.

As a craftsman, Li Bo has been described as "backward-looking" (Burton Watson, *Chinese Lyricism*, 1971, p. 141) because he preferred to imitate established models of anonymous folk songs rather than experiment with newer and more demanding regulated verse forms. The long narratives here are examples of these reworkings, which are characterized by standard themes (antiwar critique, carpe diem, etc.) and typically uneven line lengths. Even these revisions, however, involve new visions. Stephen Owen notes that the violent energy and exuberance of "Bring in the Wine" far exceeds what would be conventionally expected (*The Great Age of T'ang Poetry*, p. 126), shifting attention thereby from the theme to the speaker. Li Bo's contemporaries were especially perplexed by "The Road to Shu is Hard." Though there were antecedents of descriptions of ecstatic journeys and visionary flights through the cosmos in early shamanistic songs, Li Bo's poem still impressed a Tang anthologist as "strangeness upon strangeness" (Owen, p. 123), both because of its unusual auditory effects (Vikram Seth's rhymed translation succeeds in conveying a sense of the importance of sound) and its extreme imagery.

Not all of Li Bo's poetry, of course, flirts with such extremes. Ezra Pound's versions of two folk songs ("The Jewel Stairs' Grievance" and "The River Merchant's Wife") written in a woman's voice capture with disarming directness the implicit lament of abandoned women. And "In the Quiet Night," which captures without overt statement a traveler's homesickness, is probably the single most famous Tang poem, one of the first that all children have had to memorize for centuries. Chinese students in your classes are likely to be able to recite it.

Li Bo has thus far resisted being studied extensively as poet in a Western monograph. Arthur Waley's *The Poetry and Career of Li Po* (1950) focuses on his biography, and the author's evident disapproval of his subject's life unfortunately colors his presentation of the material.

Copyright © 2009 Pearson Education, Inc. Publishing as Longman.

Du Fu

Du Fu was Li Bo's junior and during his lifetime clearly in his shadow, but within a century his reputation had begun to outstrip that of his more unconventional contemporary. Although the contrast between the two poets is probably overdone, it is true that Du Fu's appeal grew especially as different and later generations increasingly came to admire his high moral tone and the greater formal complexity of his work. Whereas both poets were clearly masters of the entire poetic tradition, Du Fu focused his readers' attention on that command and became in turn a resource for others seeking similar inspiration and models. In an inscription on Du Fu's tomb the writer Yuan Zhen (779–831) wrote that "He attained all the styles of past and present and combined the unique, particular masteries of each other writer" (Owen, *The Great Age of T'ang Poetry*, p. 183). Later critics therefore came to refer to him as the "Great Synthesizer."

For the Western reader unfamiliar with the tradition and unimpressed by its mastery, it is sometimes difficult to appreciate the significance of Du Fu's accomplishment. Translation of the poems into English has vexed many an expert hand. The two most important early monographs on Du Fu (William Hung, *Tu Fu: China's Greatest Poet*, 1953, and David Hawkes, *A Little Primer of Tu Fu*, 1967) did not even attempt to put the poetry into English verse, settling rather for prose renditions. A. C. Graham, who has produced magnificent versions of some of Du Fu's late poems, discusses some of the challenges in his introduction to *Poems of the Late T'ang* (1965), which also provides an excellent overall discussion of general issues encountered by the translator of Chinese poetry (pp. 13–37).

That said, this selection of poems should convey some of the reasons for Du Fu's exalted position in the Chinese poetic canon. Many poets wrote antiwar laments, but Du's "Ballad of the Army Carts" reaches a conclusion—on the advantage of having girls rather than boys—whose surprising irony injects more convincing sentiment into a conventional theme. Du Fu was much admired in general for his ability to integrate the personal and the political, and to write directly and to great effect on topics that had previously been considered routine. "Moonlit Night," for example, is unprecedented as a tribute to his love for his wife, and thanks to its witty extension of familiar tropes (the moon uniting two separated individuals, descriptions of a courtesan's body), it avoids the hackneyed and sentimental.

Both "Spring Prospect" and "Traveling at Night" move in scope from large to small, from the political and cosmic to the figure of Du Fu himself, almost comical in one, and probably tragic in the other. This is characteristic of many of his poems, which address major contemporary issues and wonder with anguish and frustration at his ability to play a role in resolving them. In "Yangtse and Han," perhaps, we can see some acceptance of both his limitations and his possibilities. The series of eight "Autumn Meditations" takes advantage of space afforded by a poetic sequence to an otherwise short form to explore the relationships between Du Fu and his contemporaries, and between his time and the past. Situated in exile from a capital at war, he reflects both on his own relative failures and on the failure of

Copyright © 2009 Pearson Education, Inc. Publishing as Longman.

the Tang empire to sustain the brilliance attained by the Han dynasty five hundred years earlier. In addition to A. C. Graham's *Poems of the Late T'ang*, Tsu-lin Mei and Yu-kung Kao's "Tu Fu's Autumn Meditations: An Exercise in Linguistic Criticism" (*Harvard Journal of Asiatic Studies*, 28 [1968], pp. 44–80) offers a detailed discussion of the sequence.

Bo Juyi

"A Song of Unending Sorrow" was to become Bo Juyi's best-known poem, though he would have preferred to be remembered for his trenchant critiques of contemporary social and political abuses. The Tang emperor Xuanzong's infatuation with one of his palace ladies, Yang Guifei, was blamed for the downfall of his reign, which in turn irrevocably weakened the dynasty itself. More precisely, the fault was placed on her, adding her to the long line of femmes fatales responsible for any number of calamities.

Bo Juyi departs here from the previously moralizing and censorious interpreters of the relationship, however, to depict it as one based on apparently genuine mutual affection. The emperor did have to order the execution of his beloved, and he did seek to make contact with her after her death through various means. Note the echo of the anonymous folk song, "A Peacock Southeast Flew" (see Vol. B, pp. 41–49). The success of this effort described here is, of course, Bo's embellishment on history, but it succeeded in associating Yang Guifei's best-known dance tune, "The Rainbow Skirt and the Feathered Coat," with all subsequent loves. It also allowed the relationship between the emperor and his concubine to be memorialized in a major seventeenth-century drama, *The Peach Blossom Fan*, by Kong Shangren (1648–1718).

PERSPECTIVES

What Is Literature?

As was the case in other traditions, the earliest writings on literature in China were intimately connected with specific texts, intended to provide guidelines on how to read them. Confucius in his *Analects*, for example, offers brief comments on the usefulness of studying the poems in the *Book of Songs* as part of a program of personal cultivation and education. The "Great Preface" to the anthology (see Vol. A, pp. 1045–1046) has been considered to be the most important early statement on the sources, purposes, and effects of poetry, but it is important to remember that it was written not as an abstract theoretical statement but rather as part of an explication of the collection's first poem. The main points of the "Great Preface," however, did establish principles that were never seriously questioned by later crit-

Copyright © 2009 Pearson Education, Inc. Publishing as Longman.

ics—that a poem was an expressive response to circumstances (whether natural, political, or social) in the world and that a poem could in turn effect a transformation in the world of its audience.

The works collected in this Perspectives section begin with this premise but focus on different corollaries deriving from it. The first three excerpts are taken from longer works that encompass many literary genres in their purview. Subsequent considerations of the nature of literature, like the final two examples, tended to focus on poetry alone, which by the Tang dynasty had emerged as the most distinguished literary form. In later dynasties, however, discussions of poetry were couched usually as informal and only loosely organized collections of ad hoc comments, with sustained and systematically argued treatises a rare exception.

◆━━◆ ━☰◆☰━ ◆━━◆

Cao Pi

This is part of what was evidently a much longer work, most of which has not survived. When reading this essay, students should keep in mind that Cao Pi is speaking from the throne of the emperor, an Olympian (if precarious) perch from which he (as a "superior person") can view the squabbling of literary men at court vying for his attention and eager to belittle each other. Much of the essay (omitted in this selection) consists of lists of those individuals, with comments on their relative strengths and weaknesses.

What is important here is Cao Pi's attempt to analyze literature as an aesthetic object, thus laying a foundation for quasi-belle-lettristic thinking. Like other early writers, however, he includes works we would not now consider "literary," such as memorials to the throne and other official documents; these were all considered to be part of the literary (wen). Cao's interest in the multivalent term ch'i (qi) is regarded as his distinctive contribution to Chinese literary theory. As David Pollard explains, "In Chinese cosmology, ch'i is what the world is made of, the 'vapor' out of which sensible things condense, primordial matter-energy. In relation to human beings it is the 'breath' we breathe out," which can then stand for "physical vitality" or "inherited constitution." Furthermore, when made manifest, this ch'i is perceptible as "'atmosphere,' 'climate,' 'manner,' or 'style,' depending on the scale: in the Confucian view of things the 'climate' of a time means particularly the state of morale . . . of the people; persons from a certain place were recognized as sharing local characteristics . . . ; and the bearing or manner of an individual was also described in terms of ch'i" ("Ch'i in Chinese Literary Theory," in Chinese Approaches to Literature from Confucius to Liang Ch'i-ch'ao, ed. Adele Rickett, 1978, p. 45). Both concrete and ineffable, this element is what roots a literary work to both person and place and determines its power to transcend the limits of human mortality.

Copyright © 2009 Pearson Education, Inc. Publishing as Longman.

Lu Ji

Students may take heart that writer's block has been universally feared, and this work is notable for its evident interest in the mysteries of the creative process. However, it's important to keep in mind that in his *Rhymeprose on Literature* Lu Ji is interested in much more than that, too. Like Cao Pi, he is taking all forms of writing under discussion. Moreover, the expectations of the "rhymeprose" or rhapsody as genre dictate the lavish catalogs, ornate descriptions, and parallel constructions; a contemporary mania for evaluations and rankings of all sorts is reflected here as well. The stanzaic breaks and subtitles, it should be noted, were provided by the translator.

Daoist notions of an ideally undifferentiated unity of the subjective and objective lie at the heart of Lu Ji's conception of the creative process, which he describes in images that became commonplaces of the tradition. Notice that writing has its sources both in the stimulus of the external world and in the literary tradition itself and that Lu Ji calls upon a panoply of analogies to describe it, ranging from natural phenomena to human activities. It is interesting to consider the oscillation between the consciously crafted and what appears to be beyond the writer's control throughout Lu Ji's discussion. To what extent is the poet in command of the process and to what extent a vessel or midwife to something beyond him? Lu Ji draws on an existing critical vocabulary that had been developed to talk about music to discuss concrete features of literary works, but in the end he is forced to acknowledge the true ineffability of both inspiration and effect.

Stephen Owen provides an alternative translation as well as extensive line-by-line annotation and exegesis to the entire work, translated as "The Poetic Exposition on Literature," in his *Readings in Chinese Literary Thought* (1996, pp. 73–182).

Liu Xie

Like Lu Ji's *Rhymeprose on Literature*, Liu Xie's fifty-chapter work *The Literary Mind: Dragon-Carvings* is unique in the Chinese tradition as a comprehensive, theoretical discussion of all forms of writing. The influence of Lu Ji on Liu Xie is especially evident in these two chapters, each of which leads off the two sections into which *The Literary Mind* can be divided. In general, the first half discusses various genres, whereas the second half focuses on aspects of style.

The title of the first chapter could be translated either as "Tracing Literature to the Dao" or "Literature Originates from the Dao." Liu Xie's manipulation of the multivalence of the term *wen*—calling upon its reference to astronomy, topography, civilization, and literature—is a true *tour de force* that embeds writing in the cosmic order. As James J. Y. Liu writes:

Copyright © 2009 Pearson Education, Inc. Publishing as Longman.

By linking literature (*wen*) with the configurations (*wen*) of natural phenomena, Liu is able to trace the origin of literature to the beginning of
the universe, and to elevate literature to a status of cosmic significance.
Drawing his ideas from the *Book of Changes* and other ancient works, he
evolves the theory of multiple correspondences between cosmic order
and the human mind, between mind and language, and between language and literature. (*Chinese Theories of Literature*, 1975, p. 22)

Students might be asked to compare these grand notions with claims made about literature and its aspirations in other traditions. In China they were to prove enduring.

Chapter 26, "Spirit Thought," bears the imprint of Daoist thinking, especially
that of Zhuangzi, to which it alludes more than once. Like Lu Ji, Liu Xie describes an
initial phase of the writing process that appears to involve a transcendence of the self
in a state of stillness that enables a spontaneous responsiveness to the external world.
Many of Liu's analyses and descriptions of this process borrow from Lu Ji's *Rhymeprose*.
Again, Stephen Owen's discussion of both Lu Ji and of this chapter in his *Readings in
Chinese Literary Thought* (1996, pp. 73–182, 201–210) is an invaluable reference.

Wang Changling

The authors of the comprehensive theoretical works just discussed were obviously
as interested in the fine points of the creative process as in more abstruse speculation on its sources and effects, so it should come as no surprise that later writers
might choose to focus on the nitty-gritty of the former. Wang Changling's
"Discussion of Literature and Meaning" appears to have been one of many works
that were essentially manuals for aspiring poets, who—in the face of the development of increasingly regulated forms of verse—were in need of concrete advice on
how to negotiate the new challenges.

Much of Wang's text consists of very specific details about what works and
what doesn't, with examples of felicitous and less successful lines drawn from the
tradition. His very down-to-earth suggestions on how best to let the creative juices
flow were surely also of some comfort to those poets otherwise easily daunted by
the mysteries of the process.

Sikong Tu

Whether or not these poems were actually the work of Sikong Tu, their Daoist-
inspired vision exerted an important influence on later literary theory. In most
cases it is difficult to specify what is the precise referent—poet, poetry, poetic experience, perhaps the Dao itself—and the point seems to be that one should

Copyright © 2009 Pearson Education, Inc. Publishing as Longman.

strive to transcend such distinctions and achieve a state of nonassertive tranquility and spontaneity.

The importance of suggestiveness is clear and is reiterated in two of Sikong Tu's oft-cited letters, which urged friends to achieve a "meaning beyond flavor" and to evoke an "image beyond the image, a scene beyond the scene." This poetics of implicit meaning served to nuance the strongly didactic tendencies of the tradition.

Copyright © 2009 Pearson Education, Inc. Publishing as Longman.

Japan

Man'yōshū (Collection of Myriad Leaves)

Given the dense allusiveness of these poems, we've included our commentary on them directly in the anthology itself (Vol. B, pp. 134–146).

Murasaki Shikibu

The Tale of Genji has often been called the world's first psychological novel, a notion reinforced by Arthur Waley, who transformed *The Tale of Genji* both stylistically and socially into a Victorian novel in his noted translation. The label of "novel" is obviously meant to be a compliment, but it can be misleading. First of all, it is hard to read *The Tale of Genji* from front to back as a single monolithic work. *The Tale of Genji* was not conceived and written as a single product and then published and distributed to a mass audience as novels were in the twentieth century. Instead, the chapters were issued in limited installments to a small aristocratic audience, possibly to a single reader (the empress). Furthermore, the chapters probably did not appear in the order that we have them today. In all likelihood, *The Tale of Genji* began as a short story, and in response to reader demand, Murasaki Shikibu produced another story or sequel.

The Tale of Genji is probably best appreciated as Murasaki Shikibu's corpus, as a closely interrelated series of texts that can be read either individually or as a whole, the product of an author whose attitudes, interests, and techniques evolved significantly with time and experience. It is thus possible to read only a part of *The Tale of Genji* and still appreciate many of its finer qualities. Murasaki Shikibu, whose focus evolved radically as she wrote, altered the significance of the existing text, or body of texts, not by rewriting it but by adding and interlacing new sequences. To take a larger example, love, glory, and courtliness, the secular ideals of the earlier chapters, are placed in relative and ironic perspective in the later chapters by the emergence of their opposite: a deep-rooted desire to renounce the world and achieve detachment.

The fact that *The Tale of Genji* is an evolving narrative, however, does not mean that Murasaki Shikibu ignores or forgets the earlier stages of the narrative. The author links many of the women by blood or physical appearance, in the form of surrogate figures. For example, in the opening chapter, after losing the Kiritsubo consort (Genji's mother), the emperor finds consolation in Fujitsubo, a lady of similar countenance. Genji, longing for his deceased mother, is likewise drawn to his fa-

Copyright © 2009 Pearson Education, Inc. Publishing as Longman.

ther's new consort. Frustrated by Fujitsubo's stiff resistance and the barriers that separate them, he eventually finds a substitute and a wife in the young Murasaki, who is Fujitsubo's niece and almost identical in appearance. In each case, the loss of a woman leads the man to find a surrogate, who is similar in appearance, or closely related, or both. The notion of the surrogate lover enables Murasaki Shikibu not only to explore one of the great themes of *The Tale of Genji*—the pseudo-incestuous nature of male/female relationships—but to move smoothly from one new sequence to the next.

Gender and Genre

The tenth and eleventh centuries were a remarkable period of cultural production for aristocratic women in Japan. Perhaps the single most important factor was the political ascendancy of the Fujiwara regents, who married their daughters to the emperor and surrounded them with coteries of highly educated ladies in waiting. These ladies in waiting, who came from the middle rank of the aristocracy, wrote in a variety of genres in *kana*, the native syllabary: essays (such as *The Pillowbook* by Sei Shōnagon), literary or poetic diaries (such as *The Kagerō Diary* by the daughter of Michitsuna who never went to court but was married to a Fujiwara regent), private poetry collections, and tales or prose fiction (*monogatari*), such as *The Tale of Genji*.

As various texts such as the *Genji ippon kyō* (*Genji One Volume Sutra*, 1176, by Priest Chōken) reveal, a genre hierarchy existed from the tenth century through the medieval period. The most highly regarded genres were Buddhist scriptures and Confucian texts (such as the *Book of Songs*), followed by Chinese genres of history (such as *Records of the Historian*) and poetry (such as *Wen Hsuan*, Anthology of Literature), and then, at the bottom, *waka* (Japanese classical poetry) and *monogatari* (vernacular tales) and various writings in the native syllabary.

The difference between the four genres at the top of the hierarchy, which were all in Chinese prose or the "man's hand" (*otoko-de*), and the bottom two, which were in *kana* (vernacular syllabary) or the "woman's hand" (*onna-de*), is evident in the material presentation. The texts written in Chinese format, which were related to religion and public affairs, were usually presented on large sheets of new, thick paper. The texts in *kana*, by contrast, were usually in small size, the equivalent of a small paperback, often on recycled wastepaper or on the backs of used documents. The prestige of the Chinese writing system was such that works in *kana* were usually unsigned, while those in Chinese almost invariably bore signatures. The only *kana* or vernacular texts of importance were those related to the 31-syllable Japanese classical poem, which grew in prestige and was widely practiced by men and women. There was a considerable drop in prestige from the Japanese classical poem to the *monogatari*, which was considered a frivolous pastime, mainly written for women and children who did not have access to the higher genres. Of particular interest here is that in Murasaki Shikibu's day even the vernacular tales were written by men. So while the two vernacular genres at the bottom of the genre hi-

Copyright © 2009 Pearson Education, Inc. Publishing as Longman.

erarchy were associated with women, all the genres were in fact dominated by male writers, whether scholars, priests, or government officials.

Another key element in this genre hierarchy was cultural identity. The top four categories, the most prestigious genres, were of foreign origin, identified primarily with China. (The Buddhist texts often originated in India but came to Japan via China.) The two bottom genres, by contrast, were identified with native culture (with Yamato or Japan). In the "Fireflies" chapter of *The Tale of Genji* there is a famous passage, sometimes referred to in English as the "defense of fiction," in which Genji talks to Tamakazura, whom he is trying to seduce, about the nature of the *monogatari* (Vol. B, pp. 190–192). The passage is often seen as a metacommentary by Murasaki Shikibu on *The Tale of Genji* itself, on the new role that she envisions for the *monogatari*. Genji first takes the standard male position toward the *monogatari*, commenting on its frivolous nature, on how full of fabrication it is and how it leads to deception, particularly for naive women readers. Genji then switches to what we might call a feminist view of the *monogatari*: he attacks *The Chronicles of Japan*, an official history written in Chinese and one of the most publicly esteemed texts, for being a mere fragment of the truth, mere surface. Instead, it is the *monogatari*, or vernacular romance, that reveals the inner truth, the way things actually happen in the world. In a passage reflecting *waka* poetics, Genji notes that the author of the *monogatari* expresses experiences or observations that are too deep to keep within oneself. Furthermore, he argues that the use of fiction—and here he is referring to a new vision of the *monogatari* as opposed to the older romances—is like that found in the Buddhist parables, a means of conveying a higher truth. In other words, *The Tale of Genji* is equal to if not better than the genres at the top of the hierarchy: the Buddhist sutras, the histories in Chinese, and *waka* poetry, not to mention the older *monogatari*. *The Tale of Genji* never attained the status of Buddhist or Chinese texts, at least prior to the Edo period, but it did, due to its highly poetic nature and over eight hundred poems, attain the status of *waka*, or Japanese poetry, becoming a source of diction, of allusion, of cultural and seasonal associations. In the late twelfth century, Fujiwara Shunzei and his father Teika, two of the leading poets of the day, claimed that *The Tale of Genji* was indispensable for *waka* composition.

It is important to remember that Murasaki Shikibu not only turned to a genre of low status, she turned to a genre dominated by male writers. The extant *monogatari* that came before *The Tale of Genji*—such as *The Tale of the Bamboo Cutter*—were probably all written by men, in all likelihood male scholars who drew heavily on Chinese literature for inspiration. Murasaki Shikibu incorporated some of the conventions of these vernacular tales into *The Tale of Genji*. The most obvious example is the narrative of the amorous male hero who has a series of relationships with women, one after another. Here the male reader can identify with the male protagonist, while the female reader can identify with the various women who have the fortune of encountering a noble of such charisma and high rank. This narrative paradigm, which is also found in *The Tales of Ise*, another Japanese classic from the Heian period, forms the foundation of the first part of *The Tale of*

Copyright © 2009 Pearson Education, Inc. Publishing as Longman.

Genji. Another pattern, found in *The Tale of the Bamboo Cutter*, is the courtship, in which men compete to win the hand of a daughter, with the woman being the ultimate prize.

Perhaps the most pervasive narrative paradigm, however, is the evil stepmother motif, which is familiar to us in the form of the Cinderella story. The Heian aristocracy had a deep interest in the stepmother motif because of the particular structure of aristocratic society, which combined a semi-matrilineal social order with male polygamy. Men were in the position of power, but inheritance was still largely determined by the standing of the mother or the maternal relatives, at least for aristocrats. In the regency system of the time, political power was attained through one's daughters: if a daughter could bear the emperor a son, then one could become a regent, a powerful maternal grandfather of the emperor. Most of the heroines in *The Tale of Genji* have lost their mothers and are in dire circumstances until the hero discovers them. Genji becomes a hero not simply because he is a great lover but because he is also a father, or surrogate parent, a guardian and teacher at the same time. We thus have, on the one hand, the woman's need for a guardian/father, and on the other hand, the man's political need for a daughter. Both needs are fulfilled and symbolized by the Rokujō Villa, which is constructed at the climax of the first part (the first thirty-three chapters) and which brings together all of Genji's wives and daughters.

The polygamous ideal of the Rokujō Villa begins unraveling at the end of Part I and comes to a tragic climax in the "New Herbs" (*Wakana*), leading to the death of Murasaki, Genji's great love. This process of disillusionment with love and marriage, especially polygamous marriage, is anticipated by earlier women's writings. The most outstanding example of Heian women's writing prior to *The Tale of Genji* is probably *The Kagerō Diary*, by Michitsuna's mother. In contrast to the contemporary tales, which generally come to a climax when the man and woman are married, *The Kagerō Diary*, which grew out of disillusionment with the story told in these tales, explores the tribulations of polygamous marriage, separation, old age, and death. Generally speaking, the author of the Heian woman's diary attempts to integrate herself not with men, whom she ultimately finds disappointing, but with a deeper self, which the literary or poetic diary explores. This same process occurs in the course of *The Tale of Genji*. Significantly, *The Tale of Genji* moves from a male-centered narrative, typical of earlier *monogatari*, in which the primary relationship is between man and woman, toward a world outside of marriage. The grand arch of *The Tale of Genji*, in its full fifty-four chapters, moves from narrative focused on secular concerns to narrative focused on spiritual issues and the concern for individual salvation.

The Tale of Genji also differed from the earlier tales in the use of poetry, poetic diction, and the accompanying sense of internalization. Instead of pushing the plot forward, moving from action to action, as frequently occurs in earlier tales, *The Tale of Genji* moves inward, dwelling on the time, on memory, on the interpenetration of past and present. As in the Heian diaries by women, there is a constant sense of time passing—the passing of seasons, the passing of one's life, the

Copyright © 2009 Pearson Education, Inc. Publishing as Longman.

minute passage of time (as in the dew drying on the leaves of the bush clover)—which is mixed with memory of times past.

PERSPECTIVES

Courtly Women

For nonspecialists, it may be useful to approach *The Tale of Genji* in the context of gender (women's writing), genre (the novel/tale), or court literature. As a masterpiece by a woman and as novel-esque fiction, that is, as a psychologically oriented, realistic, character-centered narrative, *The Tale of Genji* was a major innovation in world literature. In contrast to poetry, which is relatively portable and has emerged in a variety of cultural situations, the novel, which generally deals with the individual or family in larger society, has been closely related to urbanization, the rise of the bourgeois, print culture, money economy, mass education, and large public audiences—the characteristics of early modern society. There are, however, at least two major exceptions: late-tenth- and early-eleventh-century Japan, and seventeenth-century France. In both cases, women's writing took the lead and the novel/*monogatari* became one of the primary genres. *The Tale of Genji* is often compared to the modern nineteenth-century British or French novel (a typical comparison is to Marcel Proust), but these are not the most appropriate historical models. English women's literature began as early as the late sixteenth century, but it did not come to a peak until the nineteenth century, with Jane Austen (1775–1817) and others, until after the genre of the novel had already been established by male writers. The growth and development of English women's writing in fact parallels the growth of the modern English novel.

In France, by contrast, women's writing emerged early and came into full bloom immediately in the 1660s. By the eighteenth century, when English women writers were coming into their own, French women writers were fading and, with some exceptions, such as George Sand, they reached their nadir in the nineteenth century. The key socioeconomic and cultural factor here is that in France, the first generation of women writers, in the 1660s, were of predominantly aristocratic status (either aristocrats or bourgeois who frequented aristocratic milieus), giving them greater independence and resources than their English counterparts. Significantly, after the French Revolution this aristocratic women's tradition in France declined significantly. In other words, women's writing in France flowered under the most absolute monarchy, during the reign of Louis XIV, the Sun King.

The rise of Heian women's writing bears a surprisingly close resemblance to that of France in the seventeenth century. Like the French women's writing, it comes very early, in the tenth century, shortly after the widespread use of *kana*, beginning with *The Kagerō Diary* (974), and plays a critical role in creating the genre of prose fiction (*monogatari*). The women's writing comes to a peak in the eleventh

Copyright © 2009 Pearson Education, Inc. Publishing as Longman.

century, when the northern branch of the Fujiwara clan (led by Fujiwara Michinaga, Murasaki Shikibu's patron) was at the height of power. This was not a monarchy but a regency, although the structure of power was similar, being concentrated in the body of one person, Fujiwara Michinaga, who reigned much as Louis XIV did, creating a highly sophisticated court culture. The peak of women's writing lasted for about a hundred years, from the mid-tenth to the mid-eleventh century, tapering off in the thirteenth and fourteenth centuries and disappearing almost entirely by the fifteenth century. After the peak in the eleventh century, only those women such as the authors of *Sanuki no suke nikki* (1108), *Izayoi nikki* (1280), and *Towazugatari* (Confessions of Lady Nijō, 1306), who were closely associated with either the imperial court or the nobility, continued to write works that survive today. The fate of female writing parallels the fate of the aristocracy, which ceased to be a major cultural force by the late medieval period.

If, as in England, the fortunes of women's literature climbed with the novel, we would have the rise of women's prose fiction in the early Edo period. Ihara Saikaku's prose fiction (*ukiyo-zōshi*), such as *Life of a Sensuous Woman* (see Vol. D, p. 545), in the late seventeenth century—which was fueled by the same kinds of socioeconomic and technological conditions found in Europe in the early modern period—represents the archetypal early modern novel, with parallels to be found in Daniel DeFoe (1660?–1731) and other early novelists. But due to the low social, legal, and economic status of women in the Edo period, women's literature, except for occasional classical poetry and haiku by women, did not really appear until the early nineteenth century, with the earliest signs being Tamenaga Shunsui's *Shunshoku umegoyomi*, which he wrote for a female audience with the aid of a woman writer and which, significantly, focuses on working women surrounding the Genji-like figure of Tanjirô. (Women poets managed to write throughout the history of Japan, but only in certain periods were women writers able to write novelistic fiction.) It is only with the Meiji period and the arrival of modern society, which gave women greater opportunities for cultural production, that women novelists emerged, beginning with those such as Higuchi Ichiyo. In short, in both France and Japan, the socioeconomic and cultural base of the nobility was critical to women's writing, particularly for novelistic forms.

Significantly, in both the French and Japanese cases, a women's literary movement emerged before the establishment of a mainstream vernacular genre (the novel and the *monogatari*, respectively), creating women's writing with a distinct language and style. Both of these cultures created what we would now call *women's space*, specifically, literary salons created and run by women. The women writers who emerged in the mid- to late seventeenth century in France—such as Madeleine de Scudéry, Madame de Sévigné (Marquise de Marie de Rabutin-Chantal, 1626–1696, perhaps France's greatest letter writer), and Madame de Lafayette (Marie-Madeleine Pioche de La Vergne, 1634–1695, the author of *La Princesse de Clèves*)—share much in common with the mother of Michitsuna (*The Kagerō Diary*), Sei Shōnagon (*The Pillowbook*), Murasaki Shikibu, and the daughter of Takasue (*Sarashina Diary*). They either were from aristocratic families or interacted with no-

Copyright © 2009 Pearson Education, Inc. Publishing as Longman.

bility, mixed in court circles, and had close contacts with male scholars and men of *belles lettres*. In both cases, the luxury and protection of a highly refined, aesthetically oriented aristocratic society gave these talented women the opportunity to not only write but also to be highly innovative.

Not by coincidence, both of these women's movements created the first "novel" in their respective traditions. Lafayette's *La Princesse de Clèves* (1678) is widely considered to be the first psychological novel in the West, while *The Tale of Genji* (early eleventh century) is considered to be not only the first great *monogatari* but the world's first novel. Significantly, both were the cumulative result of at least a hundred years of women's aristocratic writing that had come before it. Both share two striking characteristics: their sociocultural milieu and psychological interiority.

Scholars have described salons such as that of Madame Scudéry as hotbeds of cultural activity in which the participants (mostly female) collaborated in literary production, with members providing feedback and helping to write different parts of the same novel or work. *La Princesse de Clèves* in fact was the result of group composition, with Madame de Lafayette as the principal author. A parallel phenomena occurred with the literary salons of Empress Teishi and of Empress Shōshi, which produced Sei Shonagon's *Pillowbook* and Murasaki Shikibu's *Tale of Genji*, respectively. As in the French situation, the members of Teishi and Shōshi's salons helped directly in the production, particularly in supplying the precious paper and in the laborious copying of the manuscript. Without the salon and the support of the empresses, who functioned as the salon hosts, there would have been no *Tale of Genji* or *Pillowbook*. We do not know if other women helped Murasaki Shikibu write *The Tale of Genji*, but there is no doubt that the close interaction and feedback between Murasaki Shikibu and her circle of readers were critical in producing *The Tale of Genji*.

Both *The Tale of Genji* and *The Princesse de Clèves* are set about a hundred years in the past compared to the time of their composition. The first part of *The Tale of Genji* echoes the Engi-Tenryaku era (early tenth century), while *The Princesse de Cleves* is set in the age of Henri II (1519-1559). At the same time, both texts draw heavily on contemporary society, and each has been considered a *roman à clef*, with particular characters suggesting specific contemporary individuals. Most important, however, both novels broke from their generic predecessors in interiorizing the romance—an aspect that derives in large part from the kind of writing done by women prior to these two prose masterpieces.

In seventeenth-century France, women wrote in various genres, diaries, memoirs, letters, and novels, but it was the epistolary style, especially the letters of Madame de Sévigné, that achieved canonical status. Likewise, it was the poetic diary and the poetry collection, both epistolary forms, that fueled the first phase of women's writing in Japan. Murasaki Shikibu built on her female predecessors, such as the mother of Michitsuna, to give the *monogatari* an interior dimension that had never been seen in the genre before. Madeleine de Scudéry and Madame de Lafayette likewise brought to the novel a psychological realism—a probing of the

Copyright © 2009 Pearson Education, Inc. Publishing as Longman.

inner emotions and thoughts of the characters—hitherto unrealized. In both cases, the psychological realism focused on personal relations, marriage, and love.

It could also be said that in both works the characters are in an enclosed, almost claustrophobic, stage, in which they become prisoners of their own high status. Both *The Tale of Genji* and *The Princesse de Clèves* focus on the position of the woman in marriage, on the woman's control or lack of control over her own destiny in a highly constrained social system. Scudéry's heroines desire to live their lives unconstrained by marriage, while Lafayette's women seek to win increased control over marriage as an institution—themes that are echoed in both *The Kagerō Diary* and *The Tale of Genji*. Indeed, Lafayette's *Princesse de Clèves*, the story of an aristocratic woman (Madame de Clèves) who becomes disillusioned by a seemingly ideal marriage, rejects erotic love (with the attractive Monsieur de Nemours), and finally becomes a nun, in fact bears a striking resemblance to *The Tale of Genji*, particularly to the last ten chapters (called the Uji chapters), in which women (Oigimi and then Ukifune) turn their backs on marriage and men and seek out an alternative world. Thus, while the women writers in both cultures emerged at the apex of court culture, they implicitly held perspectives that were critical of that society.

In both the French and Japanese cases, the women's writings that result from the first blossoming were later read and prized by both male and female readers, and they were eventually granted recognition or canonical status by a largely male critical establishment. In seventeenth-century France, the novel was held in such low esteem that Madame de Lafayette publicly denied authorship of her greatest work, *The Princesse de Clèves*. Likewise, in early-eleventh-century Japan, the *monogatari* stood at the bottom of the genre hierarchy, but by the early thirteenth century, *The Tale of Genji* would be canonized by Fujiwara Shunzei and Fujiwara Teika, just as *The Princesse de Clèves* was canonized by later French writers.

Tales of the Heike

Tales of the Heike deals mainly with the struggle for power at the end of the twelfth century between the Taira (Heike) clan and the Minamoto (Genji) clan. Under the leadership of Kiyomori, the Taira rose to power at the expense of the Minamoto. At the end, however, the Minamoto, under Yoritomo and his brother Yoshitsune, were successful in defeating the Taira. The decisive battle occurs at Dannoura, the end of which is described in "The Drowning of the Emperor" (p. 360). *Tales of the Heike* focuses primarily on the Heike, the defeated clan, and its many fallen heroes and women.

At the risk of oversimplifying this epic narrative, we could say that there are two broad themes at the heart of *Tales of the Heike*: Buddhism and the warrior (samurai) ethic. These two themes reflect the manner in which *Tales of the Heike* was constructed and the audience for which it was produced. *Tales of the Heike* depicts a turning point in Japanese history, when Japan was transitioning from an aristocratic civilization to one that would be dominated by a new warrior class. In

Copyright © 2009 Pearson Education, Inc. Publishing as Longman.

this regard, *Tales of the Heike* marks the decline of aristocratic values, which the Taira/Heike still cling to, and the emergence of this new warrior ethic, embodied most dramatically in the Eastern warriors under the Minamoto/Genji. *Tales of the Heike* is thus excellent material for examining warrior attitudes and values (such as devotion, concern for family name, acceptance of death at any moment, and courage), which differ significantly from the aristocratic attitudes and values found in *The Tale of Genji*, written in the early eleventh century. *Tales of the Heike* was probably initially written by an aristocrat who incorporated classical *monogatari* (tale) elements, but it was reworked by Buddhist priests and chanted by blind minstrels to a wide, often illiterate audience. The result is a work that has a strong Buddhist cast, that could be used for preaching the Buddhist way, and that had an audience of commoners that never existed for *The Tale of Genji*.

For the purposes of teaching, you can divide the selections into Buddhist/religious stories (such as "Giō," "The Death of Kiyomori," and "The Death of the Imperial Lady") and those that deal with warrior life (such as "The Death of Lord Kiso"). "The Death of Atsumori" represents a mixture of the Buddhist and warrior themes.

The Opening Passage

The bells of the Gion monastery in India echo with the warning that all things are impermanent. The blossoms of the sal trees beneath which the Buddha died teach us through their hues that what flourishes must fade. The proud do not prevail for long, but vanish like a spring night's dream. The mighty too in time succumb—all are dust before the wind. (p. 346)

The standard phrase, "all that lives must die," is replaced by "what flourishes must fade." That is to say, the focus is on human fate, particularly the history of individuals. This applies to both the Heike as a clan and to particular individuals such as Kiyomori, Yoshinaka, and Giō, each of which rises only to fall.

The Buddhist law evoked in the opening lines can be broken into four fundamental elements. The first is the impermanence of all things (implicitly, all that lives must die). This is demonstrated in the lives of the many warriors who die in the course of the narrative. The second element is that all that flourishes must decline. This is a variation on the law of impermanence: not only is life short but all declines. The third Buddhist element is karmic causality: evil actions are appropriately punished. Here impermanence is linked to sin and retribution. The fourth Buddhist element, which is not stated in the opening but is implicit in the narrative, is that, having faced the impermanence of all things, one should devote oneself to being reborn in the Pure Land, the paradise of the Amida Buddha, who saves all who utter his name. Rebirth in the Pure Land based on faith in the Amida Buddha was advocated by Hōnen, who appears in *Tales of the Heike* and who was one of the founders of Pure Land Buddhism, which came to the fore in medieval Japan.

Copyright © 2009 Pearson Education, Inc. Publishing as Longman.

"The Death of Kiyomori"

Kiyomori, the leader of the Heike clan, is cast as an evil but fascinating character in *Tales of the Heike*. Kiyomori is not an ideal aristocrat. Instead, he is a man of extreme will and action—a characteristic of warriors in the medieval period. He represents a new medieval type, the man who lives at the limits all the time, with ferocity. "The Death of Kiyomori" brings this extended narrative to a close.

In the story of Kiyomori, which occupies the first half of *Tales of the Heike*, the Buddhist law that "all that flourishes must decline" is combined with a kingly law that takes the form of the Confucian ideal of the Heavenly Mandate. An individual or group is given the mandate to rule by heaven, but if the rulers turn their backs on virtue and sink into negligence, heaven will withdraw its blessing and bestow it on another. In other words, virtuous rule is rewarded by heaven, while unjust rule is punished. Kiyomori commits sins against the throne, burns temples, disregards the wishes of the people, and acts arrogantly. In "The Death of Kiyomori," Kiyomori's last words reveal a man who has violated both the Buddhist law and the kingly way.

> When I have ceased to be, erect no temples or pagodas in my honor, conduct no memorial rites for me! But dispatch forces at once to strike at Yoritomo [his enemy], cut off his head and hang it before my grave—that is all the ceremony that I ask! (p. 355)

This statement reveals a man of deep attachments (the worst of attachments being resentment), which in the Buddhist context form a strong barrier to salvation. Instead of concerning himself with salvation (and freeing himself from this world), he continues to cling to his secular objectives. Rather than being repentant, he is proud of his worldly accomplishments.

The Buddhist notion of karmic causality is also apparent in the manner of Kiyomori's death: he dies of fever and a burning body. The fever is not just a fever; it is retribution for the burning of temples and the killing of monks, particularly the destruction of the great statue of the Buddha at the Tōdaiji temple, in Nara. In a dream, the wife of Kiyomori, the Nun of Second Rank, sees Kiyomori in the most painful realm of hell, the hell of unending fire. Kiyomori's "burning" body thus anticipates his fate after his life.

"The Six Paths of Existence" and "The Death of the Imperial Lady"

The story of Kenreimon'in as told in "The Six Paths of Existence" and "The Death of the Imperial Lady" brings *Tales of the Heike* to an end. Kenreimon'in, the daughter of Kiyomori and the Nun of the Second Rank, became the first consort of Emperor Takakura and the mother of Emperor Antoku, who drowned in the last great battle at Dannoura, in "The Drowning of the Emperor." At the beginning of "The Six Paths of Existence" Kenreimon'in has become a nun and has retreated to

Copyright © 2009 Pearson Education, Inc. Publishing as Longman.

the Jakkō-in at Ōhara, outside the capital of Kyoto. The Retired Emperor Go-Shirakawa visits the Jakkō-in, where Kenreimon'in tells him of her past. Kiyomori's actions against Go-Shirakawa (during the Shishinotani conspiracy) started him on the path of war, and the Retired Emperor Go-Shirakawa ordered the destruction of the Heike. The meeting between Kenreimon'in, who represents the defeated Heike clan, and the Retired Emperor thus marks a final conciliation and reflects Kenreimon'in's understanding not only of the Buddhist way but of the kingly way (represented by the retired emperor). In "The Six Paths of Existence," Kenreimon'in looks back on the past, recounting her own life and the rise and the fall of the Heike. The speech represents a summation of the long epic tale in a Buddhist context of sin and retribution, darkness and enlightenment, with Kenreimon'in coming to a profound realization of the impermanence of the world and the sins of her clan.

The bell at Jakkō-in, which opens "The Death of the Imperial Lady," echoes the bell in the opening chapter of *Tales of the Heike*. The narrative starts and ends with the bells, one of impermanence and the other of religious retirement. Here Kenreimon'in offers prayers as means to pacify the spirit of the dead Heike, especially that of the former emperor (her son), who is beneath the sea as a dragon king. Some of the themes stated in the opening passage are reiterated here: impermanence, the notion that all that flourishes must fall, and karmic causality. More importantly, the final chapter implicitly contrasts Kenreimon'in with her father, Kiyomori. In the narrative of Kiyomori, his evil actions resulted in the destruction of his entire clan. Toward the end of "The Death of the Imperial Lady," the narrative notes:

> And all of this came about because the Lay Priest and Chancellor Minister Taira no Kiyomori, holding the entire realm within the four seas in the palm of his hand, showed no awe for the ruler above, nor the slightest concern for the masses of common people below. . . . [I]t was the evil deeds of the father, the patriarch, that caused the heirs and offspring to suffer this retribution! (p. 367)

By contrast, the good deeds of the imperial lady Kenreimon'in, particularly her deep awareness of the impermanence of all things, free her from the ties to this world.

The death of Kiyomori, which comes at the end of the sixth volume, stands in contrast to the death of his daughter Kenreimon'in, in the last and thirteenth volume. Unlike Kiyomori, who dies a fiery, tortured death and goes to hell, Kenreimon'in dies peacefully and is rewarded for her devotion to Buddhist law by being reborn in the Pure Land. In the last passage of "The Death of the Imperial Lady," the sound of music, the incense, and the purplish clouds from the West reflect the Pure Land belief that she will be reborn in the Pure Land, the Buddhist heaven in the West presided over by the Amida Buddha.

There are no examples in the Heian-period literature of women being directly reborn in the Pure Land. In the *Lotus Sutra*, a Buddhist sutra that had a large

Copyright © 2009 Pearson Education, Inc. Publishing as Longman.

impact in Japan, the daughter of the dragon is reborn, but only after being reborn as a man. The direct rebirth of a woman into the Pure Land, which *Tales of the Heike* presents here at the end, is a reflection of new medieval Buddhist beliefs, particularly those of Hōnen, one of the founders of Pure Land Buddhism in Japan, who argued for salvation for all, regardless of sex or social background. Hōnen argued that even the lowest sinner could be saved if he or she intoned the name of the Amida Buddha. So the fact that a woman is chosen as an example of direct rebirth in the Pure Land symbolizes the benevolence of the Amida Buddha, who is ready to save all living beings.

It is interesting to compare Chōmei's *Account of a Ten-Foot-Square Hut* with "The Death of the Imperial Lady" at the end of *Tales of the Heike*. Both occur at about the same time, describing the turmoil at the end of the twelfth century, and both are about two major recurrent themes in Japanese medieval literature: impermanence and reclusion. In both, the recluse hut is a transitional state between this world and the Pure Land. In *Tales of the Heike*, impermanence is revealed not through natural disasters, which devastate houses and the city (as in *An Account of a Ten-Foot-Square Hut*), but through the horrors of war and through episodes such as that of Giō, in which success and glory are short-lived. Both texts are Buddhistic in the sense that the confrontation with impermanence (death, destruction, and so forth) causes the protagonist/author to become a recluse and leave the secular world. The horrors of war or of natural disasters awaken the protagonist/author to the need to seek salvation in the Pure Land. Impermanence is thus not simply decline but a sign that we must look to the next world. In Chōmei's *Account of a Ten-Foot-Square Hut*, the ability to achieve salvation and rebirth in the Pure Land is called into question, while in "The Death of the Imperial Lady" it is clearly achieved. Both texts were written under the influence of Pure Land Buddhism, which came to the fore in the medieval period, from the twelfth century onward.

"The Death of Lord Kiso"

"The Death of Lord Kiso" is a good example of a warrior narrative, revealing the values and attitudes of the new samurai class that emerged at this time. The episode describes the death of Kiso no Yoshinaka and the relationship between the master and retainer. (Tomoe, who appears briefly in the beginning, is a rare example of a woman warrior; she is fearless, brave.) Both Kiso and Imai Kanehira, his retainer, are concerned with the manner of death. They desire to die an honorable death, to die attacking and killing the enemy. As Kanehira says, "No matter how fine a name a warrior may make for himself, if he should slip up at the end, it could mean an everlasting blot on his honor" (p. 273). In other words, it is better to commit suicide than to die in a dishonorable way, by letting a lesser soldier take one's head. But Lord Kiso fails at the end. He allows himself to be killed by an unknown warrior. Kanehira, by contrast, succeeds. He lives for his master, and when his master dies, he dies a brave death. Kanehira embodies three heroic qualities: (1) complete devotion to his master, placing devotion before personal gain;

Copyright © 2009 Pearson Education, Inc. Publishing as Longman.

(2) readiness to choose death rather than surrender, with no hesitation in action; and (3) no fear of death.

"The Death of Atsumori"

Kumagae, the protagonist of "The Death of Atsumori," first served the Heike but later switched to the Genji. His son becomes a warrior and is killed at the famous battle of Ichi-no-tani, at the age of sixteen. Kumagae captures an enemy soldier, Atsumori, a beautiful youth who reminds him of his own son. Kumagae decides to save the young man, but suddenly, with other Genji approaching, he is not able to. Atsumori does not fight back and tells Kumagae to take his head. The realization of the sin of killing leads to renunciation. The story is important because it becomes the source for a number of subsequent retellings, the most famous of which is the Noh play *Atsumori*, which is included in the *Anthology* (Vol. B, p. 285).

We have here a dramatic conflict between the warrior spirit, which must kill without hesitation, and the Buddhist spirit, which abhors killing and wants to turn to the next world. Kiyomori's fiery death is to be expected, a retribution for excessive pride and past sins. But Atsumori dies for no apparent reason, while still in his youth. Kumagae is also caught between implicit sexual attraction (young boys were often partners for adult warriors during periods of war), the emotional feelings of a father, and the duty to kill (the warrior who must suppress all feelings).

The story of Atsumori has as much to do with the fall of aristocratic society, with a courtly ideal represented by the Heike, as with warrior values. The Heike, who were defeated by a new class of warriors, were the last of the aristocracy (or at least portrayed that way), and this lends poignancy to their defeat in *Tales of the Heike*. Kumagae's discovery of the flute makes him realize how noble and beautiful the youth was. Atsumori represents a courtly ideal, with blackened teeth, the ability to play the flute, a beautiful face. His courtly qualities are represented by the flute Saeda, which Kumagae takes with him.

NOH: DRAMA OF GHOSTS, MEMORIES, AND SALVATION[1]

Noh is the oldest form of Japanese drama still practiced today. Noh performances consist of dance, song, and dialogue, which are traditionally performed by an all-male cast. Little is known for certain about how Noh came into existence, but it is generally accepted that in the late Kamakura period (1192–1333) sarugaku, a performance art that combined comic mimicry and short comic skits, emerged as a serious drama form and that Noh developed out of sarugaku soon after. Sarugaku troupes also served at temples, taking part in religious rituals, which helped to develop the complex dramatic form that became Noh drama. The oldest and most ritualistic piece in the current Noh repertoire, *Okina* (Old Man), in which the

[1]This entry was written by Akiko Takeuchi.

Copyright © 2009 Pearson Education, Inc. Publishing as Longman.

dances of deities celebrated and purified a world at peace, is believed to derive from a sarugaku-performed purification ritual.

By the mid-fourteenth century, Noh had gained wide popularity and was performed not only by sarugaku but also by dengaku troupes. Dengaku had originally been a type of musical accompaniment to the planting of rice, but its troupes came to specialize also in acrobatics and dance. In Kyoto, throughout the fourteenth century, Noh performances by dengaku troupes were in fact favored over those by sarugaku troupes.

In order to enhance the genre's popular appeal, both dengaku and sarugaku troupes made formal changes to the structure of Noh drama and added new plays to their respective repertoires. In the late fourteenth century, during a period of intense competition (both between individual troupes and between sarugaku and dengaku), a sarugaku troupe (called the Kanze-za) emerged to prominence from Yamato Province (present-day Nara Prefecture), led first by Kan'ami (1333–1384) and later by his son Zeami (1363?–1443?). The innovations and plays by Kan'ami and his son shaped the genre as it is seen today on stage.

Kan'ami attracted audiences with his unusual talent not only as a performer but also as a playwright. Among his innovations was the introduction of the *kuse-mai*, a popular genre that combined song and dance, in which the dancing performer rhythmically chants a long narrative. By incorporating the rhythms of *kuse-mai* singing into his troupe's performances, Kan'ami transformed the relatively monotonous Noh chanting into a more dramatic form, one that gained great popularity and was soon emulated by other sarugaku and dengaku troupes. From Kan'ami's time onward, Noh plays customarily included a special chanting section called the *kuse*, which was very similar to the song found in the *kusemai*.

In 1374, Kan'ami's growing popularity finally inspired the seventeen-year-old shōgun Yoshimitsu (1358–1408) to attend a performance by Kan'ami's troupe in Imagumano, in the eastern part of Kyoto, transforming the young shōgun into a fervent patron of the troupe. Yoshimitsu was also charmed by a beautiful boy who appeared on stage, the twelve-year-old Zeami. Zeami soon began serving the shōgun as his favorite page, mixing with court nobles and attending cultural events such as *renga* (linked poetry) parties attended by the intellectual elite. Although Zeami had already received solid training in linked verse and other such cultural pursuits, his experiences at the palace later helped him to lead Noh in a new direction.

After Kan'ami's death, however, Yoshimitsu's patronage shifted from Zeami, now a mature Noh performer and the head of his own troupe, to Inuō (also known as Dōami, d. 1413), a performer with a sarugaku troupe from Ōmi Province (present-day Shiga Prefecture). Inuō had gained a reputation for his "heavenly maiden dance" (*tennyo-no-mai*), an elegant dance that was said to epitomize *yūgen*—a term signifying profound and refined beauty, the dominant aesthetic among the upper circles of society.

Powerful patronage was crucial to the survival of Zeami's Kanze troupe. In order to maintain the shōgun's favor, Zeami kept creating new plays and changing his troupe's performing style in accordance with shifting aesthetic trends. The

Copyright © 2009 Pearson Education, Inc. Publishing as Longman.

number of plays he wrote is conservatively estimated at nearly forty (over fifty if plays he revised are included). They are marked by exquisite phrasing and learned allusions to Japanese classical texts such as *The Tale of Genji* and *The Tales of Ise*. In addition, he introduced Inuō's elegant dance into his own plays, even though his troupe, like other sarugaku troupes from Yamato Province, had originally specialized in wild demon plays and realistic mimicry. In an effort to incorporate the aesthetic of *yūgen* into his troupe's repertoire, Zeami created plays centered on elegant dance and refined versification, poetically representing elegant characters often drawn from classic tales. In his twenty or so theoretical treatises on Noh, he also emphasized the importance of embodying *yūgen* in every aspect of Noh.

Another of Zeami's innovations was the *mugen-nō* ("dream play") structure found in many of the Noh plays that are most popular today. The typical *mugen-nō* consists of two acts. In the first act, a traveler (often a traveling monk) meets a ghost, a plant spirit, or an incarnated deity, who, in the guise of a local commoner, recalls a famous episode that took place at that location. In the second act, this supernatural being reappears in its true form in the monk's dream. When the supernatural being is a ghost, the recalled event is usually the most crucial incident in its former life, the one responsible for its current state of attachment to the world, which obstructs its path to Buddhahood. By reenacting that incident, the ghost seeks to gain enlightenment through the prayer of the monk. In other words, in *mugen-nō*, the main incident occurs not in present time, the time in which the traveler and the supernatural protagonist meet, but in a scene from the past recalled by the protagonist, often through the haze of memory. Thus the focus of these plays is less on the interaction between characters than on the emotional state of the protagonist.

In his later years, Zeami suffered one misfortune after another. Yoshinori, who became the shōgun in 1428, favored Zeami's nephew On'ami, eventually placing him at the head of the Kanze-za. With the loss of the shōgun's patronage, Zeami's second son took the tonsure and left the theater altogether, and his elder son, Motomasa, who was the author of *Sumida River* and whose talent was Zeami's last hope, died in 1432, in his early thirties. In 1435 Zeami was exiled to Sado, a remote island in northeastern Japan. The year of his death is not certain, nor is it known whether he died on Sado or had been pardoned and permitted to return to Kyoto.

After Zeami

After his death, Zeami's renown as a playwright became almost legendary, and his plays were made part of the Noh canon, which was followed especially faithfully by Zeami's son-in-law Zenchiku (1405?–1470?), the author of *Nonomiya* (Shrine in the Fields). In the late Muromachi period, following the Ōnin War (1467–1477) that had devastated the capital, audiences began to exhibit a taste for different types of Noh, spurring the creation of more spectacular plays, such as those depicting dramatic events occurring in the present (e.g., *Ataka*), and often featuring realistic bat-

Copyright © 2009 Pearson Education, Inc. Publishing as Longman.

tle scenes. However, Zeami's plays, as well as those that followed his model, have always been at the core of the Noh repertoire.

During the late medieval period, Noh became especially popular among the warrior class, and many generals even came to enjoy performing in plays themselves. When Tokugawa Ieyasu established his shōgunate in Edo (present-day Tokyo) in 1603, he bestowed official patronage upon four sarugaku troupes, Kanze, Hōshō, Komparu, and Kongō, all from Yamato (later the Kita troupe was added, due to the next two shōguns' admiration for the exceptionally talented performer Kita Shichidayū). As a result, only performers affiliated with these four (or five) troupes were officially allowed to perform Noh. This tradition of official patronage continued until the end of the Tokugawa shōgunate in 1868. Following the shōgun's lead, feudal lords (*daimyō*) throughout Japan employed performers of these official Noh troupes, who performed Noh on ceremonial occasions.

One of the direct results of this ceremonialization of Noh was a lengthening of performance times to more than twice the original time, since the plays were now performed with much more rigorous precision. Noh drama was not brought into line with the latest trends, as it had been earlier, but instead it became a classic form, with the repertoires and performance styles left almost untouched.

At the same time that Noh was developing into a ceremonial art for the warrior class, it also continued to function as entertainment for commoners. The general public was rarely allowed to see a performance by an official Noh troupe in Edo, but nonofficial troupes (*te-sarugaku*) provided opportunities to see Noh plays in more casual settings. The practice of chanting Noh plays had been a popular form of entertainment since the sixteenth century, and it gained new momentum in the seventeenth with the development of wood-block printing and publishing of Noh chantbooks (*utai-bon*). The popularity of Noh among commoners is evident in kabuki and bunraku plays, which frequently draw on popular Noh plays.

The collapse of the Tokugawa shōgunate meant a loss of patrons for Noh performers and thus a radical diminution of their means of livelihood. Nevertheless, the genre survived, supported by the vigorous efforts of certain performers and of new patrons, including the Meiji government. Today, at least one Noh drama is performed somewhere in Japan virtually every day of the year. While there are around 2,000 extant Noh plays, the current repertoire consists of only about 240 plays, most of which were written between the fourteenth and sixteenth centuries. Even today, many of the plays most often performed were written by Zeami.

Role Types

The leading character in a Noh play is called the *shite* (literally "main hand"). *Shite* are often supernatural beings, such as ghosts, plant spirits, deities, and demons. Most Noh plays center around the words and deeds of the *shite*—that is, his or her telling of a story, usually of his or her own past, through monologue and dance. (In plays created from the mid-fifteenth century onward, this *shite*-centered structure becomes less dominant.) Characters subordinate to the *shite*, such as spouses,

Copyright © 2009 Pearson Education, Inc. Publishing as Longman.

siblings, and retainers, are called *shite-tsure* ("companions to the *shite*") or simply *tsure*. In two-act plays, the *shite* in the first act is called *mae-shite* (or *mae-jite*, meaning "the *shite* before"), and the *shite* in the second act is referred to as *nochi-shite* (or *nochi-jite*, "the *shite* after"). The *nochi-shite* usually appears in a different costume, signifying the revelation of his or her true identity, and sometimes even as a different character altogether. However, the *nochi-shite* is always played by the same actor who plays the *mae-shite*.

The *waki* (literally "side") is the character opposite—though not necessarily antagonistic to—the *shite*. When the *shite* is a supernatural being, the *waki* is usually a traveling monk who listens to the *shite*'s retelling of the past. When the *shite* is a living warrior, the *waki* is most often a warrior of the opposing camp. In any case, unlike the *shite*, the *waki* are always living men. Characters subordinate to the *waki*, often their retainers or traveling companions, are called *waki-tsure* (or *waki-zure*).

The *ai* (or *ai-kyōgen*) is a minor character in a Noh play, such as a local villager who, usually during an interlude in the Noh play, might provide the *waki* (and thus the audience) with a relatively colloquial, prose recapitulation of what the *shite* recounts in poetry during the first or second act. The *ai*'s speech is thought to have been much shorter when the plays were originally performed; it became longer only after the late sixteenth century, when the *shite*'s more elaborate costume changes between acts necessitated longer interludes. In some plays, especially those written in the late Muromachi period, comical characters (also called *ai*) appear *during* the Noh play (as, for example, in *Ataka*).

When a role in Noh is played by a child actor, both the role and the actor are called *kokata*. However, when the protagonist is a child, the character is always played by a mature performer wearing a child's mask. On the other hand, *kokata*, who never wear masks, sometimes play the roles of mature men and women (as in Yoshitsune in *Ataka*).

The chorus consists of six to ten members, who sit motionless throughout the play on the right side of the stage (to the audience's right). Unlike the chorus of a Greek tragedy, the Noh chorus does not assume a specific role in the play. At times it chants the words of one or another of the characters, and at other times it narrates the scene, chanting in homophony. Because the grammatical subject of a sentence chanted by the chorus, and even by the *shite* or *waki* performer, is not always clear, the lines being recited are often ambiguous and at times seem not to correspond to the character who is chanting them.

Noh performers are identified according to the types of roles they specialize in; there are *shite* actors, *waki* actors, *kyōgen* actors, and musicians. *Shite* actors may also play *shite-tsure*, perform in the chorus, and act as stage assistants (*kōken*). *Waki* actors play *waki-tsure* as well, and their chanting style is clearer and more prosaic than that of *shite* actors. *Kyōgen* actors, in addition to performing in comic plays known as *kyōgen*, also play the part of the *ai* in Noh plays. Musicians, too, are categorized according to their respective instruments: the flute (*nōkan*), shoulder drum (*kotsuzumi*), hip drum (*ōtsuzumi* or *ōkawa*), or stick drum (*taiko*). Within each specialty, there are several "schools," and each actor or musician is affiliated with

Copyright © 2009 Pearson Education, Inc. Publishing as Longman.

only one school. Each school has its own performing style, libretto, and interpretation of plays. The five schools of *shite*, for instance, descend from the five official troupes of the Tokugawa shōgunate.

The Noh Stage

The main Noh stage is a square space, about nineteen by nineteen feet, with additional areas on the right side and in the rear that serve as seating areas for, respectively, the chorus and the musicians. The stage is made of solid Japanese cypress (*hinoki*). Pillars at the four corners of the main stage support the roof. From the far left corner a bridgeway (*hashigakari*) leads to the dressing room (*kagami-no-ma*). Three small pine trees stand alongside the bridgeway. Originally, Noh was performed outdoors, and the bridgeway connected to the middle of the stage at the back. There was no rear wall, and audiences sat around the stage on all sides. In the late Muromachi period, the bridgeway was shifted to its present position and a rear wall was introduced, blocking the view from behind. Soon thereafter, it became customary to paint an ancient pine tree on this back panel. From the Meiji period onward, most performances have been indoors, and the audience sits in front or to the left of the stage.

During a performance, the actors usually enter and exit the main stage via the bridgeway. There is also a tiny, sliding side door at the back right of the main stage, which is used by the chorus and stage attendants, as well as by any characters who must exit the stage inconspicuously (such as characters killed during a battle scene). In some plays, the bridgeway serves as a second stage, signifying a separate space distinct from the main setting.

While a curtain hangs between the bridgeway and the dressing room, nothing conceals the stage from the audience's view; there is no main curtain, and the stage remains exposed before, during, and after the performance. When the performance is about to begin, the sound of tuning instruments is heard from the dressing room, and the musicians and chorus enter and quietly take their seats on stage.

Noh never uses painted scenery or backdrops; the pine tree painted on the back wall does not function as scenery in any of the plays. The setting is created verbally, and in many plays there are no stage props at all. In some plays a symbolic prop is used to represent the most significant element of the setting; when placed on the bare stage, this prop attracts the audience's attention and becomes the play's focal point. In fact, the play's climax is often reached when the *shite* approaches this prop. In *Pining Wind* (*Matsukaze*), for example, the climax occurs when the *shite* snuggles against a pine tree, set at center stage, and sees a vision of her long-awaited lover in the figure of the tree.

Small props held in the hands of characters include warriors' swords, monks' rosaries, and willow boughs, which signify that the holder is crazed (as with the mother in *Sumida River*). All performers, however, carry fans. The type of fan (its material, shape, color, and the design painted on it) serves as an indicator of a character's nature. In a dance, the character uses the fan to add variation to his or her

Copyright © 2009 Pearson Education, Inc. Publishing as Longman.

movements and to enhance the stage effect. Fans are also used as substitutes for things such as a brush pen, a saké bottle, or a knife.

Costumes and Masks

Most actors wear masks, although child actors and actors portraying living male characters in their prime (that is, in neither juvenile nor elderly roles) do not. Thus the *waki* and *waki-tsure*, who always portray living male characters, never wear masks, nor does a ghost appearing in the guise of a living adult male, such as the *mae-shite* in *Atsumori*. A performer not wearing a mask must never show any facial expression, nor may he use makeup; he is expected to use his own face as if it were a mask.

There are approximately eighty categories of Noh masks. Except for some that are exclusively made for and used by specific characters (for example, the *shite*'s mask in *Kagekiyo*), most masks represent generic character types, and the same mask may be worn by different characters and used in various plays. For example, *waka-onna* masks, which show a young female face, are used both for a female salt-maker in *Pining Wind* and for Lady Rokujō in *Shrine in the Fields*. However, even masks of the same category may differ subtly from one another, and a *shite* actor's choice of mask reflects or determines his interpretation of a character. It is customary for a *shite* actor to sit alone for awhile in the dressing room and gaze at his masked self in the mirror in order to enter into the character.

Demon masks, with their ferocious faces and large, protruding eyes, express fierce supernatural power, while masks of human characters (including ghosts), whose feelings and emotions are often the focus of a play, usually display not a specific emotion but a static and rather neutral expression. These masks are said to be either "nonexpressive" or, rather, "limitlessly expressive." In fact, the expression appears to change according to the angle of a performer's face: when he lets his head droop slightly, the mask tends to look sad; when he subtly tilts his head upward, the same mask may appear joyful. In addition, the actor's unchanging "face" encourages audience members to project onto his mask the emotional content they glean from the chanting. In *Sumida River*, for example, while listening to a boatman casually mention the death of a boy the previous year, the crazed mother barely moves upon realizing that the boy was her son. She bends slightly forward at the waist, and only at the end of the dialogue does she slowly raise a hand to her eyes to brush away the tears. Members of the audience who are following the chanting, however, will see in the static mask such emotions as shock, disbelief, or despair.

Another interesting feature of Noh masks is that, because they are slightly smaller than the human faces they cover and thus always reveal the tip of the performer's lower jaw projecting out from underneath, their artificiality is constantly laid bare. This creates a tension between theatricality and realism on stage and disrupts the audience's immersion in dramatic illusion.

Noh costumes are famous for their splendor and exquisite beauty. Most of them are made of stiff, heavy materials, which are folded around the performer's

Copyright © 2009 Pearson Education, Inc. Publishing as Longman.

body like origami. A lighter kimono, made from a translucent fabric and with long, wide sleeves, is sometimes worn over these costumes. Thus, just as masks conceal the facial individuality of the actor, so do costumes conceal his physical individuality; the beauty and expressiveness of his performance are sought not in the particular features of his own face and body but in the grace and expressiveness of his movements.

Costumes also signify the social status, age, and even mental state of the character. If red is used in a female character's costume, for example, this means that she is a youth; if the character wears an outer garment that exposes one shoulder (which actually remains wrapped by an inner garment), this means that the character is crazed, is in battle, or is engaged in physical labor.

Gesture, Movement, and Dance

Movements on the Noh stage are strictly choreographed and, in general, very slow and highly stylized; weeping, for example, is expressed merely by slowly lifting the right hand toward the eyes and then lowering it again. This strict economy of movement infuses each gesture with meaning. One step forward can express joy, resolution, or any other feelings that seem to fit the context.

The fundamental basis for the dances and gestures of Noh is the standing posture (kamae) and a stylized manner of walking called hakobi. Bending at the knees while maintaining a straight spine and neck, the performer's body is pulled both upward and downward, as well as both backward and forward. His upper arms are held slightly away from his chest, while his lower arms are pulled in toward his abdomen; thus he is poised between outwardness and inwardness. In order to stand still, he needs to concentrate on maintaining a subtle balance between opposing tensions. When walking, he shifts his balance laterally with meticulous care by a technique called suriashi, literally, "feet that rub the floor."

Unlike kabuki, where female roles are played by male actors who have mastered specific gestures connoting femininity, there are no explicitly feminine gestures in Noh. Nor are performers categorized according to the sex of the characters they play. Shite actors play characters of both sexes; gender is expressed by subtle variations of the angles of the performer's limbs and, above all, by the way he stands and walks. Differences in age, social status, and mental state are expressed in similar fashion. In Stupa Komachi, for example, the shite has to enact the life of a one-hundred-year-old character, including her past glories and her present miserable penury, all without words or distinctive gestures, but merely by the way she walks to the stage along the bridgeway. Komachi's entrance is considered the most difficult part of the play for the performer and thus the most interesting for the audience. Because so much emphasis is placed on such a simple movement as walking, Noh has often been characterized as "the art of walking." As a famous actor once put it, "Without arms, you could perform Noh; without legs, you could not."

Dance in Noh is performed to musical accompaniment, either by the musicians or by the musicians and chorus together. In many plays, dances set to the

Copyright © 2009 Pearson Education, Inc. Publishing as Longman.

chanting of the chorus appear in the *kuse* section and at the end of the play. The dance in the *kuse* section consists mostly of abstract movements. Because they do not have any fixed meanings, the *kuse* dance can be interpreted according to context or the accompanying lines, in much the same way that a single Noh mask can project a broad range of emotions. The dance at the end of the play, by contrast, usually includes many specifically representational movements that mimetically render the words of the text.

Dances set to instrumental music are also generally abstract and are usually quite similar to one another in both movement and music. The same series of movements can appear in a rapid, exuberant "deity dance" (*kami-mai*), an elegant and gentle dance (*chū-no-mai*), or a tranquil and meditative dance (*jo-no-mai*), depending on the tempo and mood of otherwise very similar music. As with the masks, these dances, too, are generic. The same *chū-no-mai*, for example, is performed by a noble youth in *Atsumori* and by a female saltmaker in *Pining Wind*.

Chanting Styles and Subsections

The chanting styles of Noh are divided into speech (*kotoba*) and song (*fushi*), although the speaking parts are actually intoned and thus not "spoken" in the usual sense of the word. Song can be further subdivided into congruent song (*hyōshi ai*), which is chanted in a steady rhythm, keeping precise time with the drums, and noncongruent song (*hyōshi awazu*), which incorporates prolonged grace notes on important phrases and thus is not chanted in measured time. In fact, the distinction between the speech style and the noncongruent song style is not always clear, and often the two styles alternate with one another in a single passage.

There are also two modes of singing: a dynamic mode (*tsuyogin* or *gōgin*) and a melodic mode (*yowagin* or *wagin*). The dynamic mode is generally used for the roles of warriors and demons, whereas the melodic mode is reserved for female and elderly roles. In many plays, however, the same character will employ both modes; for example, in *Kiyotsune*, though the *shite* chants for the most part in the dynamic mode, he frequently switches to the melodic mode (in segments indicated, for example, as *ge-no-ei*, *kakeai*, *jō-no-ei*, or *uta*) in order to convey two different aspects of the same character: warrior and loving husband.

Except for modes, which were introduced only after the Edo period, the distinctions in chanting styles, as well as the rhythmic patterns and the degree of regularity of the syllabic meter, are essential for distinguishing subsections of plays (*shōdan*). In the plays in the *Anthology*, the names of subsections are indicated, in parentheses, to the left of the text. These subsections represent musical and textual units, and together they add up to a whole Noh play. Each subsection has its own specific pattern of musical structure and/or content, which remains consistent from play to play. For example, the section called the *nanori* is a character's self-introduction and is chanted mostly in the speech style, while a *kuse* is a congruent song with narrative elements, often quite long, which starts in a lower register and

Copyright © 2009 Pearson Education, Inc. Publishing as Longman.

then moves to a higher one. On the next page, the list of the subsections that appear in the selected plays is categorized by chanting style.

List of Subsections

Subsections mostly in the speech style:
> mondō, nanori, tsuki-zerifu

Subsections mostly in the noncongruent song style:
> ge-no-ei, issei, jō-no-ei, kakeai, kudoki, kudoki-guri, kuri, sashi, waka

Subsections in the congruent song style:
> age-uta, chū-noriji, kiri, kuse, noriji, rongi, sage-uta, shidai, uta

Passages that do not fit into any specific subsection type are indicated in the
Anthology as "unnamed."

The order of the subsections varies according to the play, although there are certain fixed patterns that recur in many plays, such as the succession of *kuri*, *sashi*, and *kuse*. In addition, in every play there are repeated transitions from speech to noncongruent song to congruent song. Thus what begins as a relatively realistic conversation (or self-introduction) in the speech style always ends up as a more poetic, and often monologic, congruent song, with one or more noncongruent songs inserted between the two, facilitating a smooth transition.

Instrumental Music

Instrumental music accompanies the dances and some of the chanting, as well as the entrance and exit of the characters. The instrumental music is provided by one flute and three different types of drums, each played by a different musician. The shoulder drum, whose moistened skin produces mellifluous sounds, and the hip drum, whose hard, crisp sounds, by contrast, derive from its dry skin, are always played together. The stick drum is characterized by its bright, startling sound and the variety of its rhythms; it is employed in the latter half of a limited number of plays, usually from the moment a deity or demon appears onstage in its true form. The sudden sound of a stick drum signifies a transition to the supernatural world.

Three of the four instruments are percussion instruments, and the music of Noh consists more of silence than of sound. In fact, silence (*ma*, meaning "interval" or "gap") is traditionally regarded as the most essential element of Noh music. The sounds of the instruments, as well as the intermittent cries of the drummers, are introduced in order to interrupt the flow of time in Noh plays and to make the silence between sounds all the more taut and meaningful.

Categories of Plays

Among the several ways in which Noh plays are categorized, the one most widely used today is *gobandate*, which divides plays into five groups, generally based on the type of *shite*. The first of the five categories is deity plays (*waki-n⁻*

Copyright © 2009 Pearson Education, Inc. Publishing as Longman.

o or *kami-nō*), in which a deity explains the origin of a shrine or a related legend and celebrates the peaceful reign of an emperor. The second is warrior plays (*shura-nō*), in which the ghost of a warrior, now tormented in the hellish realm of constant battle known as the *shura* realm, reenacts a battle scene from his previous life. The third is woman plays (*kazura-mono*), whose protagonists are mostly elegant female figures, including the ghosts of women or female plant spirits. The fourth category is called simply fourth-category plays (*yobamme-mono*) and includes all plays that do not fit into any of the other four categories. As a result, this group includes a great variety of plays, which can then be divided into subcategories, such as plays about people driven mad, about living warriors, or about spirits perversely clinging to life in this world. The fifth category is demon plays (*oni-nō*), also called ending plays (*kiri-nō*); such plays' protagonists are mainly demons.

This categorization scheme originated in the late seventeenth century. Until recently, a formal program for a Noh play performance usually included one play from each of the five categories, performed in the above order, with a *kyōgen* play between each pair of Noh plays, so that four *kyōgen* plays were incorporated as well. Today, however, performances in this formal configuration can be seen only on special occasions, such as New Year's Day; most contemporary programs consist of a smaller number of Noh plays and still fewer *kyōgen* plays.

Another common categorization scheme opposes *mugen-nō* ("dream plays") to *genzai-nō* ("plays in present time") in which the central action is set in the dramatic present. This categorization is also a recent invention. Interestingly, the term *mugen-nō* itself was coined only at the beginning of the twentieth century, when scholars were first faced with the need to define the characteristics of Noh for purposes of comparing it to Western drama.

Religion

Most Noh plays contain Buddhist or Shinto elements. Among the most popular themes are the reunion of a long-separated parent and child (or two lovers) through the merciful intervention of a bodhisattva or a Shinto deity, legends about the miraculous origins of temples and shrines, and the pacification of vengeful or unenlightened spirits (*chinkon*). This last theme is especially common in *mugen-nō* plays, in which the ghost typically attains religious salvation at the end of the play.

As Noh was popular among commoners, it was used as a means of attracting people to *kanjin*, events at which Buddhist monks solicited donations. Originally, monks had restricted themselves to delivering sermons on such occasions, but from around the early fourteenth century, in order to attract larger crowds, they began to introduce, before or after their sermons, entertainment pieces by professional performers—pieces such as recitations of *Tales of the Heike*, sarugaku and dengaku performances, and, later, Noh play performances. One scholarly hypothesis holds that Noh's close association with *kanjin* strongly af-

Copyright © 2009 Pearson Education, Inc. Publishing as Longman.

fected both the structure and content of its early repertoire, including Zeami's establishment of the *mugen-nō* form (Matsuoka Shimpei, *Utage no shintai; basara kara Zeami e*, 1991).

Intertextuality

Many Noh plays draw on pre-existing literary works (such as *The Tales of Ise* and *The Tale of Genji*) or on folk legends of such famous figures as Ono no Komachi. However, these plays are not merely three-dimensional stagings of pre-existing narratives. Because the classics were largely disseminated in medieval Japan through detailed but often imaginative commentaries, many plays also reflect popular contemporary interpretations of their source material. In addition, playwrights often introduced new twists to old story lines, making their plays at once familiar and fresh for their contemporary audiences. The *mugen-nō* structure provided playwrights with the perfect format for such reinterpretations; famous episodes in the classics could be staged in highly subjective reconstructions through the personal recollections of a ghost.

In addition to featuring story lines drawn from existing narratives, Noh plays are also sprinkled with citations from famous poems and classic tales. Layers of allusion are added on top of the main story. *Atsumori*, for example, offers an analogy between its eponymous hero, who is a character from *Tales of the Heike*, and the Shining Genji, the protagonist of *The Tale of Genji*; similarly, the crazed mother in *Sumida River* compares herself to the nobleman protagonist of *The Tales of Ise*.

Such heavy use of classical allusions and rhetorical language, which are especially noticeable in the plays of Zeami and Zenchiku, suggests a high level of literary erudition on the part of not only the playwrights but also their audiences. In fact, the most popular literary activity at the time in high society—also practiced to some extent even among commoners—was the composition of *renga* (linked verse), which required the participants to allude constantly to a wide range of earlier literary works. It was in such a cultural milieu, for audiences more or less familiar with the classics, that Noh developed.

Copyright © 2009 Pearson Education, Inc. Publishing as Longman.

Classical Arabic
and Islamic Literatures

This section of the *Anthology* demonstrates the richness of the long Arabic and Islamic literary traditions. The cultural context of literary production and reception of the Arabic, Persian, and later Turkish texts varies tremendously, and with this the need to approach and comprehend these texts. This is so not only because it is important to locate literary texts in their cultural contexts but also because the interpretation and reception of these texts would be impaired without it. Hence it is vital to have more knowledge about the authors and the era in which they were writing. This section of the manual suggests some approaches and offers suggestions to make these texts accessible to students who know little or nothing about their context.

PRE-ISLAMIC POETRY

The first selection of pre-Islamic poetry is one of several consecrated odes known as *mu'allaqat*, the greatest odes, which hung on the walls of the *Ka'ba* Shrine at Mecca. The *mu'allaqa* of Imru' al-Qays is the most famous of these great odes, widely loved and quoted. A remarkable poem that continues to fascinate Arab readers today, it appears in educational curricula throughout the Arab world. It shows the ethos of life in the desert and the centrality of the poet and his poetry in its culture. We need to read beneath the scenes of the desert, the description of its nature, the vitality of its animals, and the endurance of its people to reveal a worldview that gives human interaction a central place over everything else.

The poems of al-Khansa' are a clear testimony that women played a significant role in their traditional society, had access to the symbolic order, and were widely recognized for their achievements. It is important to teach this remarkable early woman poet against the prevailing misperception of the role of women in Arabic and Islamic culture. It is equally important to emphasize the early feminist textual strategies employed by al-Khansa' in her poems. She selected the form of the elegy as her poetic genre, in which the man is always dead and the women are very much alive, full of vitality, sensitivity, and emotions. On the surface of these texts the

Copyright © 2009 Pearson Education, Inc. Publishing as Longman.

man is praised for his deeds and valor, but beneath this surface it is clear that he is dependent on women, not only in his mundane quotidian life but even in his quest for immortality and a record of his achievements.

The selections of the brigand poets are a good example of the prevalence of the spirit of individualism and rebellion in early Arab history. They are a clear expression of the free spirit of the Bedouins and their ability to challenge the tribal norms, violate taboos, and transgress established customs. These poets challenge even death itself, despite their clear awareness of its inevitability and their acknowledgment of the frailty of humans. There is also a clear element of subverting established codes in their work; rather than aspiring to be the pride of the tribe, despite their mastery of poetry, they became the critical voice challenging its supremacy. The brigand poets provide us with clear evidence of the pertinence of one of the perennial themes in Arabic literature, the conflict between the individual and the collective.

The Qur'an

The study of the Qur'an as a literary text needs to free itself from centuries of Western scholarly bias, both religious and literary. Westerners have often judged its verses by inappropriate standards derived from European poetry, while theological commentators have often distinguished polemically between the truth claims of the Bible and the Qur'an read as theologically false. The Qur'an is meant to be read as a divine text, for it is perceived as the sole miracle of Muhammad and is highly revered by Muslims. The Qur'an confirms but also supersedes former scriptures such as the Torah and the New Testament, and we need to take this claim seriously if we want to understand the text's assumptions and ambitions. In order to help students appreciate the Qur'an properly, it is useful to begin by stressing its dialogic nature, which implies both respect for the reader and emphasis on the text's rational dimension as well as on its spiritual nature. At many points, the Qur'an distinguishes itself from the earlier Judeo-Christian scriptures by deemphasizing miracles and taking a relatively rationalist approach, even as divine-human interactions remain its central focus. Historical and theological in intent, the Qur'an is also highly literary in method. Much of its message is conveyed in its poetically heightened language: the Qur'an was and still remains the pinnacle of the Arabic word, the reservoir of its rhetorical, poetic, and stylistic devices.

The verses and some full suras included in the *Anthology* cover a wide range of the Qur'anic genres. The liturgical and sermonic verses of "The Opening," "The Cow," and "Read" give some feel for the liturgical dimension of the text. The sacramental nature and literary repetition of some of these verses inspire awe and reverence in the community of believers. The genre of signs of the presence of God and his many manifestations can be glimpsed in "Light," "The Most High," "The Morning Light," "Help," and "Ya Sin." The legislative power of the text and its detailed clarity are represented in "Women," "The Bee," "The Spoils," and "Victory."

Copyright © 2009 Pearson Education, Inc. Publishing as Longman.

Other suras included in the *Anthology*, such as "Noah," "The Table," "Joseph," "Mary," "The Prophets," and "The Story," relate some of the biblical narratives and demonstrate the Qur'anic recension of significant details. In addition to all these biblical characters, the Qur'an has many nonbiblical ones, such as Hud, Salih, Shu'ayb, Idris, and Luqman. In Sura 18, "The Cave," there are two interesting narratives with Greek and fantastic connotations. The story of Dhu 'l-Qarnayn (verses 83–98) is generally regarded as that of Alexander the Great, and the story of the Men of the Cave (verses 10–26) is usually treated as a recension of the legend of the Sleepers of Ephesus.

An excellent strategy when teaching the Qur'an is to introduce the students to these different Qur'anic genres and to emphasize the link with the other sacred texts of what Jacques Derrida calls the Ibrahamic tradition, which starts with Judaism and continues through Christianity. Generally the Qur'an goes back to Ibraham and emphasizes his importance, so many of the stories linked to the Ibrahamic tradition were adopted in their entirety. It also returns to the prescriptive tendencies of the Old Testament without abandoning the spiritual and more poetic nature of the Christian narrative.

A comparison of the Qur'anic rendering of the stories of Joseph and Jesus with the biblical versions demonstrates the Qur'an's closer link with the Judaic texts than the Christian ones. The Qur'an presents the story of Joseph in a narrative nearly identical to its biblical version, but without emphasizing the importance of Jacob beyond his role as a normal father suffering for his lost son. In the Qur'anic rendering of the story of Jesus there are vivid details of the virgin birth of Christ and his miraculous deeds. There is also the acceptance of his ascension to heaven but a strong denial of the concept of the Trinity and the crucifixion of Jesus. In the Qur'anic version, the real Christ ascended to heaven and the crowd crucified somebody else, a man they thought to be Jesus.

RESONANCES

Ibn Sa'ad

The Resonances section that follows the Qur'an provides you with valuable contextual material for teaching both the Qur'an and the life of the Prophet, Muhammad. A knowledge of his life, *sira*, and the lives of his companions is essential for a full appreciation of the Qur'an, Islam, and Muslim cultures. The source anthologized here is among the earliest and most reliable of the wealth of works on the subject.

Ibn Sa'ad (Abu 'Abdullah Muhammad ibn Mani' al-Basri) was one of the most outstanding scholars of his time. He was born in Basra in c. 784 and died in Baghdad in 845. He studied theology, tradition, *akhbar*, and genealogy under the most prominent scholars of his time, traveled widely in search of knowledge, and worked as a secretary (to be understood in present terms as a research assistant) to

Copyright © 2009 Pearson Education, Inc. Publishing as Longman.

the great scholar, al-Waqidi (d. 822). The student surpassed his master in knowledge and rigor of scholarship. His encyclopedic compilation, *al-Tabaqat al-Kubra* ("*Book of Classes*"), is the most reliable "Who's Who" of the early period of Islam, containing biographies of 4,250 persons, including about 600 women. It starts with a biography of the Prophet Muhammad and follows with his companions and all those persons down to Ibn Sa'ad's time; he played a role in narrating the tradition, the Prophet's sayings and doings. His *Classes* not only is the first biographical dictionary but also was methodically developed and ordered in a manner that was long ahead of its time.

Hafiz

The poems of Hafiz are part of the genre of *ghazal*, a well-established tradition in Arabic culture that succeeded in translations into other languages. *Ghazal* is a word originally derived from the verb *ghazala*, to spin wool, but it also means to be fond of talking about or with women, to spin maudlin talk. In the *ghazal* genre, the more original the variations and genuine imagery on the act of expressing love, the better the poem becomes. The *ghazal* also is related to lyrical love poetry, which is deeply rooted in pre-Islamic literature. It was transformed later into a richer tradition with the introduction of the concept of divine/carnal love by the Sufis. Hafiz excelled in this fascinating combination, raising the carnal to the level of the spiritual and endowing the spiritual with palpable pleasures and sensations. It is also important when teaching Hafiz to keep in mind the fact that he was a *hafiz*, someone who learned the Qur'an by heart and internalized its rhythm, stylistic beauty, and evocative power, all of which he used effectively.

The first poem of Hafiz in this selection, "The House of Hope," is a good example of this combination of *ghazal*, the evocative power of poetry, and wisdom. The three main foci of the poem are reflected in its structure. It starts with a condensed wise proverbial saying, then moves to the ghazal/Sufi part in which evocations of the beloved are blurred with those of the divine, and finally ends in the resolution of this ambiguity. The poem starts with a memorable, almost proverbial imagery: "The house of hope is built on sand" (line 1) evokes sand-castles and ephemeral existence, introducing fragility into the poem from the beginning. The fragility of hope and of life itself is the main reason for the return to the beloved, who dwells freely from all entanglements of soul beneath the "turquoise bowl" (line 6). But the next stanza typically confuses devotion for God with love for a beautiful woman. Intoxicated with this love, the poet was further intoxicated with drinks in the tavern and started to hear voices or receive messages, which gives the drinking its double significance as the literal drinking of wine and the spiritual union with heavenly angels. This makes the middle section of the poem on the falcon highly symbolic of the complexity of the inter-

Copyright © 2009 Pearson Education, Inc. Publishing as Longman.

action with the divine. The reference to fate is pregnant with many allusions and the promise of heavenly pleasure, but this is also mixed with the impending gloom on which the poem is highly philosophical. The poem warns that in the sweet songs of the nightingale there is lament and cause for weeping. The final twist is the self-referentiality of the poem to Hafiz and the power of poetry, which is a gift of God but also a way to him.

Poetry, Wine, and Love

This section should be taught as an antidote to the stern and conservative image of Arabic and Islamic culture. It is living proof that when a culture is confident of itself and its identity, rather than weak and defensive, it is free to express itself, celebrate difference, and respect others. Abu-Nuwas is a very good example of this, for his range of topics, imagery, and bold sensibility give a clearly different image of Arab culture from the one prevalent now in the Western media. It is an open-minded culture characterized by its tolerance, richness, and rationality. The Resonance section following Abu-Nuwas's poems in the *Anthology* provides a contemporary reflection on this and demonstrates that it is not just something of the past but is still influential in the present too.

Abu-Nuwas is one of many like-minded poets who mastered the art of poetry and attained fame and influence as a result. The panegyric poetry of Abu-Tammam raised him from poverty to riches and an eminent status in his society, and his nature poetry (of which the *Anthology* gives us a taste) creates verbal delights parallel to the ones he saw around him in nature. So each poem is not a mere expression of nature but a twin to it. Al-Buhturi was also famed for his powerful nature poetry; his poem in the *Anthology* gives the reader a clear indication of the dignity of the poet and his high status in society. Of course, each poet was dependent on patronage, but this dependence does not compromise the poets or devalue their poetry.

Of the same class is the poet Ibn al-Rumi, whose knowledge of Islamic philosophy and Shi'ite and Mutazalite doctrines provided his poetry with philosophical dimensions. Similarly, al-Mutanabbi's poetry has philosophical dimensions of another, more spontaneous order. He was a poet first and foremost, and his belief in himself as poet was so excessive it landed him in trouble more than once. For he perceived the poet in a higher place than the ruler, and when rulers did not treat him the way he expected, he turned his powerful poetry against them. His satire on Kāfūr, the ruler of Egypt at the time, still resonates with significance even in today's Arab political reality. Al-Mutanabbi wrote his poetry at a time of social and political adversity when the Carmathians, a group of early revolutionary socialists, rebelled against the central authority, and al-Mutanabbi himself had his share of subversive ideas and imprisonment.

Copyright © 2009 Pearson Education, Inc. Publishing as Longman.

This general context is the one in which we read the poems of this Perspectives section. The following discussion of two of the poems should help you develop your own reading and teaching accordingly.

The first poem is Abu-Nuwas's "Splendid young blades, like lamps in the darkness." It is a poem before its time, in which the poetic "I," closely associated with the bisexual poet himself, is developing a *ghazal* of the masculine and a celebration of wine drinking at the same time, both of which are forbidden. Hence the sense of violating norms permeates the whole poem. The poem starts with an intertextual reference to the most famous *mu'allaqa* of pre-Islamic poetry, that of Imru' al-Qays, in which he speaks about his beloved who lights up the darkness with her beauty (see Vol. B, p. 333). But the inversion of the reference from the first line to the young men sets the imagination ablaze, for even time itself "bend[s] its tender neck over them" (line 3). Then the poetic "I" indulges in drinking with these young blades the best wine from Takrit to create a libertine atmosphere in which everyone is merry. The wine of Takrit or Tikrit, the town that has been in the news recently during the Iraq war, should be read in today's terms as a reference to some of the best Bordeaux vintage wines. The poem also refers to some of the wine served with the old monasteries, which were famed for their vintages, and this leads to the poem's biblical intertextual reference to David and Goliath.

The quest for the best wine leads the gathering party to encounter a woman who is posited in the poem not as a rival for the young blades but as a demonstration of their centrality in the poem. This section also provides the reader with some of the advanced cultural practices associated with wine: aging it in the depth of the earth for its constant temperature, drinking it without disturbing it, appreciating its aroma and complex fragrance, and refraining from drinking it with food. The poem's references to various aromas ("myrtle, acacia, pomegranate and mulberry," line 28) are among the aromas associated with wine even today. Wine at that time was a much more special and more potent drink than our present wine, hence the reference to mixing it with rain-water (line 21). The detailed attention to the drink is but a mere introduction to its handsome waiter, who becomes at this junction of the poem the focus of its ghazal. The waiter is also a singer; his song brings the poetic "I" to its aging self and to the vicissitudes of life and fortune.

The second poem discussed here is al-Mutanabbi's "Satire on Kāfūr." This poem can be read almost as a contemporary poem on present-day Egypt and its ruler, not only because the poem has endured over time but also because it has been frequently quoted as a still valid testimony of contemporary Arab political reality. Its beginning with the festival day resonates with the many false festivals of the illegitimate rulers. Its lament of the inverted situation in which the slave presides and the free are enslaved is still valid. Many contemporary Arab readers read line 17, "The gardeners of Egypt are asleep to the tricks of its foxes," as a reference to the corruption in the Arab world. The reference to the slave in this poem should not be read in the light of our present aversion to slavery but in the context of the Mamluks, who ruled Egypt for years with a slave mentality,

Copyright © 2009 Pearson Education, Inc. Publishing as Longman.

mean and vengeful. The reference to detention and the imprisonment of poets should also be read as a reflection of the lack of freedom and the suppression of intellectuals.

The Thousand and One Nights

The Thousand and One Nights should be approached as one of the richest reservoirs of narrative genres in medieval times and one of the most fascinating works of collective imagination. E. M. Forster considers it, in his *Aspects of Fiction* (1927), the origin of the modern novel. The more our understanding of narrative theory develops, the more we appreciate the complexity of *The Thousand and One Nights'* structure and the profundity of its literary strategies.

The frame story of Shahrazad and Shahrayar provides an interpretative frame for all of the work. It is important to take what Edward Said in *Beginnings* (1975) calls the beginning condition into account in approaching this fascinating and enduring work. The implied author/narrator of all the stories is a woman, Shahrazad, who succeeds through the power of narrative to ward off tyranny and suspend patriarchal time. The stories have also their own generative power to maintain their life by leading to other stories. The narrative structure of the whole work is akin to an endless Russian doll: when you open it, you find another doll, and another, and so on. The difference is that unlike a Russian doll, each story is unique and different from the one that led to it, and in their entirety they all hark back to the frame story, the motivation of the narrative, and its beginning condition. The structural unity of *The Thousand and One Nights* is reflected in every tale through generative narrative discourse, in which tales generate within them other tales or kernels of tales.

"The Tale of the Porter and the Young Girls" is selected for its elaboration of the generative narrative of the work. The story opens up and leads to another story, which in turns opens up to lead to another. The main story contains, apart from the opening section included here, three different tales of the three kalanders (only one of which is included in the *Anthology*), and three tales of the three girls (one of which is included as well). This set of stories wonderfully presents Haroun al-Rashid as ruling a Baghdad of fantastic abundance, desire, and proliferating stories.

"The Tale of Sympathy the Learned" is an early example of feminist perspective in Arabic narrative. Since al-Khansa' in the pre-Islamic period, women wrote poetry and used it to subtly subvert the prevalent patriarchal order. But the whole text of the Arabian Nights is on one level a text written from the female point of view to, as the frame story suggests, re-educate the male. Sympathy is offered here as the counter character of Shahrayar's Queen, the woman that led him to complete distrust of women. The testing of Sympathy as it unfolds demonstrates the arrogance of men and the erudition and modesty of women. The men set many traps before her, and she not only avoids them but also often turns them against their perpetrators, particularly when the doctor tries to em-

Copyright © 2009 Pearson Education, Inc. Publishing as Longman.

barrass her by asking her about copulation, a masculine ploy that fails miserably. It shows the limits of knowledge and the ability of women to master knowledge as much as men. The very act of stripping the learned men of their gowns is an act of striptease of the male audience rather than of the female protagonist, all done for the edification of Sympathy. The end also demonstrates the blindness of men to the many virtues of women and the inability of Sympathy's own master to appreciate the jewel that he had. It is the Caliph who draws his attention to the value of the woman who saved him and whose performance provided him with his job, when he was ready to sell her. In other versions of this story there is a thread of love between Sympathy and Abu al-Husn. He first refuses and then reluctantly agrees to offer her to the Caliph, and when she is asked at the end to choose between staying in the Caliph's harem or returning to her master/lover, her choice is seen as a happy ending.

The shorter pieces—"An Adventure of the Poet Abū Nuwās" and the selections from "The Flowering Terrace of Wit and the Garden of Gallantry"—are selected for their wit, humor, and absurdity. They demonstrate that the shorter narrative forms also had some attention from Shahrazad, the mistress of Arabic narrative. The structure of these shorter narratives varies from one to the other, and there is a clear awareness of the content of the form in these pieces.

RESONANCE
Muhammad al-Tabari

The Resonance selection from Muhammad al-Tabari's *History of the Prophets and Kings* provides some historical background of the period that produced most of the stories selected in this *Anthology* from *The Thousand and One Nights*. The most recurring reference in the book to a Caliph is to Harun al-Rashid (r. 786–809) and his vizier, Ja'far al-Barmaki. The two brothers, Ja'far and Yahya, rose to wealth and influence at the peak of the Abbasid period, and their demise presented here in the annals of the most respected medieval historian, al-Tabari, reads as a tale from *The Thousand and One Nights*, and gives a basis for examining the *Nights'* fictional vision of Haroun al-Rashid's life and death.

Jalal al-Din Rumi

The selections from Jalal al-Din Rumi and the following section, "Perspectives: Asceticism, Sufism, and Wisdom," demonstrate the enduring power of Sufism in Arabic and Islamic cultures. For a discussion on Sufism and Sufi poetry, see the entry for the Perspectives section on the next page.

Copyright © 2009 Pearson Education, Inc. Publishing as Longman.

Here is a reading of one of Rumi's poems included in the *Anthology*, "The king has come, the king has come, adorn the palace-hall," as an example of how to read many of these Sufi poems. The poem starts with the tidings of the coming of the king, who stands in the poems for the one who has spiritually prevailed. Hence he is "the Soul of the soul of the soul" (line 2), and one can go on ad infinitum. In the presence of this king, love is the only way to his soul, and to the way, the *tariq* or *tariqah*, of the Sufis. And in the *tariqah*, which does not distinguish between a Turk and a Tajik, the slave is near to the king because the slave has surrendered his soul to the king. With the union with the king, Satan is deposed. The poem also refers to the myth of King Solomon and his hoopoe and to his power over the kingdom of birds, using it as an allusion to the ability of Sufism to achieve the desired union with God.

PERSPECTIVES

Asceticism, Sufism, and Wisdom

In these texts, the intimations of immortality go back far beyond the time of Wordsworth's ode—almost ten centuries before the idea first occurred to him. Intimations of immortality lie at the heart of the mystic quest for inner meaning and perfect love, the Infinite, and the ultimate union with God that is commonly known as Sufism. *Tasawwuf*, the Arabic word for Sufism, refers to the one who wears woolen clothes (from *suf*, the rough garb of the ascetics and mystics). The early Muslim ascetics were concerned with the inner religious life and tried to achieve a sensitive relation with God, but the seventh and eighth centuries C.E. brought increasing secularization and luxury contrary to the ideals of early Islam. Sufism made its appearance in about the ninth century. Sufis wore rough woolen clothing in reaction to the more luxurious dress that became common with the conquest of wealthy lands of advanced cultures and ancient civilizations. While the majority of Muslims were seduced by material luxuries, the Sufis led austere lives; the only luxury they allowed themselves was the lavish expression of their love for God in highly sensual poetry.

The Sufis carry the very meaning of the word Islam, true surrender of oneself to God, to its ultimate meaning by renouncing all worldly pleasures and leading purely spiritual lives. They articulate in their thought and practice the universal yearning of the human spirit for personal communion with God. But this communion requires a long journey toward him, a *tariqah*, a way or road, through which a Sufi travels to a realization of his or her union with and true knowledge of God. Along this road there are several stations (*manazil* or *mawaqif*), some of which may last for years before the bliss of *sama'*, hearing inner voices, is bestowed on the traveler and puts him or her in a state of *wajd*, ecstasy, brought about in particular by the dance that was connected with the hearing. This state of *wajd* can only be attained through

Copyright © 2009 Pearson Education, Inc. Publishing as Longman.

a long process of meditation and reflection and an enduring yearning for union with God.

It is traditionally said that the Sufi spiritual path is shown only to those able to discern it because it speaks of a world beyond the realm of sensuality. As a direct experience of the Divine, Sufism has a universal dimension, for all religions aspire to such an experience, and thus it transcends culture, history, and all other human contexts. Yet Sufism is purely Islamic and did not spring from Christianity, from philosophies of antiquity, or any other sources. Sufism is both an individual quest and a communal ritualistic practice, for the *tariqah* (the "way" or "road," i.e., the Sufi order in which individuals are brought together in a collective search for Truth) is an essential part of the concept of Sufism. For many Islamic thinkers, Sufism is an integral part of Islam. The most influential among them, Al-Ghazali (d. 1111), perceived Islam as a full-bodied organism, with Sufism as its heart, theology its head, philosophy its rationality binding the different parts together, and law its working limbs.

The rich Sufi devotional and mystical practices reflect the diversity of the Islamic world with its wide range of cultural domains: Arab, Persian, African, Turkish, Bosnian, Malay, Uzbek, and many others. The celebration of the sensuous in their tradition allows for fertile variations on the devotional theme. The mystical poets and writers anthologized in this Perspectives section are steeped in a rich philosophical tradition and deeply concerned about the gulf between rational investigation and an acknowledgment of the inadequacy of human reason. They wanted to bridge the gap between hidden truth and rationality. Many of the odes of Rumi and Ibn 'Arabi are still sung with the greatest reverence today by Sufis, and the work of al-Niffari continues to influence contemporary Arab poets. As a result, they need to be taught almost as contemporary texts about spirituality, wisdom, and love of God.

This Perspectives section culminates in the selection from Farid al-Din al-'Attar's *Mantiq al-Tayr* (*The Conference of the Birds*). Al-'Attar followed with great interest the ideas of the Sufis and was edified by the stories of their lives, but he himself did not attempt to be one of them. Yet his work reflects a deep and creative understanding of the concepts of Sufism and the philosophical nature of the *tariqah*, road, and the *rihla*, journey. In addition to *The Conference of the Birds*, he wrote *Ilahi-nama* (*The Divine Epic*), *Musibat-nama* (*The Tragic Epic*), and *Asrar-nama* (*The Epic of Secrets*), three works of the epic tradition marked by their clear and well-constructed main story interspersed with numerous subsidiary tales. He also wrote another group of works, such as *Mazhar al-'Aja'ib* (*The Manifestations of Miracles*), *Jawhar al-Dhat* (*The Essence of the Self*), and *Lisan al-Ghayb* (*Articulating the Unknown*), with a reduced number of subsidiary tales; their concern is much more focused on a limited number of ideas pursued with emotional intensity. But they are marred by repetition and lack the coherent structure of the first group of works, to the extent that some scholars think that another writer produced them. Al-'Attar also wrote a *Diwan* of love poetry and exposition of religious thought.

Copyright © 2009 Pearson Education, Inc. Publishing as Longman.

Firdawsi and The Epic of Son-Jara

The overarching section on classical Arabic and Islamic literature ends with what we might call the epic tradition, with extracts from the *Shah-nama* of Firdawsi and from *The Epic of Son-Jara*. The former is not the first epic work of its kind even in Persian, as there were three earlier *Shah-namas* by Balkhi, Mu'mari, and 'Abd al-Razzaq, yet Firdawsi's epic was rapidly recognized as the masterpiece of its genre in Persian. The Mali *Epic of Son-Jara* is a good example of the epic oral tradition in Islamic literatures which develops the form of the *rihla* or journey for pilgrimage into a full-fledged epic narrative, and so together these works show something of the extraordinary poetic and thematic range, as well as the geographical reach, of these epic traditions.

The *Shah-nama* was modeled on *The Book of Rulers* compiled at the end of the Samanid period. Firdawsi's vast and powerful epic was compiled at a time of great political turmoil and upheaval, and Firdawsi completed his first version of *Shah-nama* by 981. But he continued to revise it until he produced the final version in 1010. During this long period in which Firdawsi was occupied with the composition and refinement of his epic, he traveled widely in Persia and the Muslim world, particularly to Baghdad, which was at the time a vibrant center of culture and learning. In Baghdad he offered its Amir his famous poem *Yusuf and Zulaykhah* in 994.

Among many of Firdawsi's heroes of superhuman proportions and strength, the famous Rostám (the subject of the selection in the *Anthology*) stands out. In addition to the main theme of war and heroism, the epic is rich in its splendid love stories and variations on human emotions. One of the most interesting aspects of the *Shah-nama* is its ability to establish plausible representations of social life. It is a work strongly linked to the Persian desire to revive Persian pre-Islamic history and Persian language and provide the country with a unique sense of national identity.

The Epic of Son-Jara is a different work altogether, for it succeeds in marrying Islamic epic tradition with genuine African folk narrative genres. Unlike the *Shah-nama*, the story of Son-Jara mixes epic, devotional, folkloric, and Sufi genres in a unique combination of narrative and poetic genres. Its hero is not the warrior but the wise magician whose insight and wisdom inspire the group and provide them with a sense of harmony and serenity. The very structure of the epic requires the active participation of the approving, surprised, amazed, or even disapproving collective audience as a parallel voice to that of the narrator. This provides the epic with a dialogic dimension, which is further enriched by the change in narrative perspective in a manner that accommodates many of the contradictory views and visions at work in the epic. Here we have a clear case of the content of form in literary epic structure, and you can point out to students how the oral nature of this African work manifests itself in its form and narrative strategies.

Copyright © 2009 Pearson Education, Inc. Publishing as Longman.

Ibn Battuta

Because Ibn Battuta teaches especially well in conjunction with Marco Polo, we discuss them together on page 235.

Copyright © 2009 Pearson Education, Inc. Publishing as Longman.

Medieval Europe

Medieval Europe holds a fundamental but equivocal place in the history of the West, for since the Renaissance it has been defined as everything that is not modern Europe. Much of recent criticism has been devoted to exploring the limitations of this division and the paradox of what we mean by *medieval*. Scholars have discerned traces of modern ways of thinking—secular, analytical, self-conscious—in historical moments such as what are known as the Carolingian Renaissance and the Twelfth-Century Renaissance, while others have uncovered the presence of conventionally medieval modes of thought—faith-based, analogical, intuitive—in postmedieval Europe. Much energy and research have been devoted toward reconstructing the heterogeneity of medieval culture (e.g., the experience of marginal groups such as women, Jews, Arabs, and heretics) and finding ways to document what everyday life might have been like for the vast population of ordinary peasants and serfs whose lives seldom found their way undistorted into the major documents of the Middle Ages.

What has emerged over the past couple of decades is a sprawling and unruly thousand-year epoch in which nearly every element of modern European culture can be found already in existence, but in strange forms and used for alien purposes. The traditional canon of vernacular medieval literature—*Beowulf*, *Gawain*, Chaucer in England; the romances, epics, and courtly poetry of Anglo-Norman England, France, and Germany; Dante in Italy—offers enthralling reading and a creative imagination that has seldom been matched. Combined with the brilliant literature of Iberia and the fascinating traditions of theology, mysticism, and popular piety, the study of medieval Europe can also spark insight and discussion on the great schisms of the world that came after it: between local, national, and international identity, between faith and science, between individual desire and social duty.

The familiarity students will have with the Middle Ages will be based primarily on nineteenth-century medievalism, which rediscovered the period and redefined it as a bastion of pastoral values, individual freedom, honor, virtue, and romance as a reaction against the modernization ushered in by the Industrial Revolution. They will enjoy recognizing these enduring notions in the readings here. Indeed, those familiar with C. S. Lewis's Narnia books or J. R. R. Tolkien's *Lord of the Rings* will feel quite at home; after all, both men were prominent scholars of medieval literature in their day. Fans of Monty Python may have a more irreverent form of recognition, but no less pertinent, for the creators of *Monty*

Copyright © 2009 Pearson Education, Inc. Publishing as Longman.

Python and the Holy Grail and *Jabberwocky* were well versed in medieval history. Umberto Eco's mystery novel, *The Name of the Rose*, includes a crash course in Scholasticism and the monastic life by an authority on hermeneutics. And then there are the myths of chivalry, notably the indefatigable industry of Arthuriana and the no less omnipresent Wagnerian adaptations of the Germanic epics. It behooves you as an instructor to take advantage of students' pleasure in this familiarity, especially if it can be made to serve as the basis of a comparative discussion, allowing the strangeness of the sources to emerge, to see how they are dark when the adaptations are light, and light when their descendants are dark, to get a sense both of what life was like in the Middle Ages and of what uses we are making of that world in our own today.

An important component of the selections in this section of the *Anthology* and another source of familiarity is the medieval lyric. Its themes of love and loss, its reliance on ostensibly simple effects of rhyme and rhythm, and its basis in sung performance make the medieval lyric familiar to students raised on the format of pop singles. In her brilliant book, *Shards of Love* (1994), María Rosa Menocal traces the lines of inspiration linking the lyrics of medieval Iberia with Eric Clapton's classic album, *Layla and Other Assorted Love Songs*, suggesting some of the ways in which lyric gains from a different approach than the more highly contextualized genres of epic or romance. Listening to these songs (many excellent recordings are now available) can provide an introduction to the material that will reach a place of critical analysis via the paths of listening pleasure. And, too, the troubadour lyrics are in many ways the original version of what we think of as the modern love song, with its seductive combination of high drama with beautiful sound and imagery.

Lyric is a poetic mode for expressing discursively what is in the end inexpressible discursively. This can either be an experience that is taken for granted, sufficient unto itself as action—dance, revelry, celebration, lovemaking—or it can be intentionally invoked—mysticism, religious experience, philosophy, love. In a lyric from his treatise on love, *The Dove's Neckring*, Ibn Ḥazm writes, "[I am] like the sound of a dove over a woody copse, cooing with its voice in every way, / Our ears delight in its melody, while its meaning remains obscure and unexplained" (p. 869, F.4-5). In both love lyric and devotional literature, the most straightforward and universal aspects of experience, such as nature, the senses, the emotions, are invoked to describe the most paradoxical and individual. Love and the divine (and in most of these lyrics it is impossible to distinguish one from the other, the literal meaning from the allegory) are presented as intimately familiar yet infinitely fleeting and intolerably difficult to pin down in words. Just as the aural effect of a song is derived from the combination of music, lyrics, and performance, so the thematic effect derives from a perfect melding of the natural and the supernatural. A gospel-based soul tune such as Al Green's "Take Me to the River" may have fewer philosophical pretensions, but its effect is similar. It is impossible to separate the singer's love and desire for God from his or her love and desire for a physical partner; one and the same sentiment binds them together. Moreover, the simple but enigmatic imagery of Green's lyrics ("Take me to the river / drop me in the water")

Copyright © 2009 Pearson Education, Inc. Publishing as Longman.

in no way hinders our comprehension of the song's overall meaning. We sense the relation to baptism and cleansing, but we are unclear exactly how this expresses the sexual meaning that is nonetheless unmistakable in the singer's delivery. Christian writers in particular were similarly adept at rendering the basics of life—bread, wine—into vehicles for expressing the essential mysteries of their religion.

This section of *Teaching World Literature* has been written so as not overly to duplicate material in the introductions and annotations in the *Anthology* itself. Consequently, where biographical material or fundamental aspects of a particular text, such as its prosody, are covered elsewhere, they are not repeated here. Similarly, while specific critical sources are singled out where relevant, no attempt has been made to cover again what is contained in the bibliographies at the end of each volume.

Beowulf

Criticism and Context

Beowulf is a product of the same sweeping migrations that brought down the Roman empire (see the section, "Rome and the Roman Empire" in Volume A), and the poem is the fruit of a transition from paganism to Christianity as profound as the one that had transformed Rome. Nevertheless, it is a vertiginous thought to consider that *Beowulf* is set during the same period that Augustine wrote his *Confessions* and Jerome undertook his translation of the Bible and that it was composed in a land just a few centuries removed from Roman occupation. Although recent scholarship has been directed primarily at uncovering traces of the monastic culture and residual Romanism of the Early Middle Ages in the poem and reconstructing some manner of precise historical context, its primary impact for readers has long been its absolute strangeness: the distance of its language from modern English; the lack of familiarity with the places, names, and customs depicted in it; and even the mystery of its date, its provenance, its author, and its original audience. These issues are well and thoroughly presented in *A Beowulf Handbook* (eds. Robert Bjork and John D. Niles, 1997); *Approaches to Teaching Beowulf* (eds. Jess B. Bessinger, Jr., and Robert F. Yeager, 1984) provides a less up-to-date but more succinct introduction. The single most influential figure in both the study and the popular reception of *Beowulf* remains J. R. R. Tolkien, whose 1936 essay, "*Beowulf*: The Monster and Its Critics," treated the poem for the first time as a work of imaginative literature rather than a historical document suitable only for philological inquiry. Moreover, because Tolkien incorporated many words and names out of the poem, as well as various minor characters and situations, into the fantasy world of his Middle Earth, he succeeded in creating a cultural currency for the poem where none had existed before.

Five sets of texts provide either source material or important parallels to *Beowulf*. Most significant perhaps are those from Scandinavia; indeed, it has been argued that the poem originated as a translation from a Scandinavian original.

Copyright © 2009 Pearson Education, Inc. Publishing as Longman.

Several Icelandic sagas provide evidence of a common source, including *Grettir's Saga* and *The Saga of King Hrolf Kraki* (the latter of which is included as a Resonance selection in Vol. B, p. 653), which tells of Bodvar, son of the were-bear Bjorn, and his adventures at the court of Hrolf, King of the Danes, among them the slaying of a marauding beast. Various scholars have argued for the *Beowulf*-poet's knowledge of classical literature, but no immediate connection has been conclusively demonstrated, although there remain interesting parallels to works such as Virgil's *Aeneid*. There are vague resonances with Irish legend, especially the lore of Cain's descendants. Some relation to ecclesiastical literature must exist, but the Christianity evident in *Beowulf* is of a received rather than a studied nature; as *A Beowulf Handbook* has it, the influence is more conceptual than textual. Finally, there is the corpus of other Old English poetry, including works such as *Exodus* and *Genesis B*; however, there is no narrative overlap, and *Beowulf* is unusual in being primarily secular in scope.

Situational Ethics

The opening of *Beowulf* plunges the reader directly into the world of the heathen-Germanic warrior, a world that was already a thing of the past but whose figures, customs, and history would have remained quite familiar to the poem's audience. Teaching the poem today requires both a reconstruction of this familiarity and a sensitivity to what the *Beowulf*-poet has done to recast that tradition in the poem. It is not necessary to resolve the decades-old dispute over whether the poem was composed orally or simply used the conventions of oral composition as an element of its poetic diction; recent scholarship on orality has gone a long way toward demonstrating that formulaic composition allows for a flexibility and subtlety in meaning comparable to those of written composition. Whether actual or imitated, however, oral composition does interpellate its audience in different ways than the written word. This distinction is equally relevant to *The Poem of the Cid* (Vol. B, p. 662) and, to a certain degree, the *Lais* of Marie de France (p. 785); it also inflects the lion's share of medieval vernacular literature, intimate as its authors and audience continued to be with the conventions of orality.

    Beowulf, like much of medieval literature, is about negotiating such transitions between past and future. Consequently—and this is a feature the poem also shares with much of medieval epic and romance—it never strives for the effect of presence so prominent in a poem such as Homer's *Iliad*; the meanings of *Beowulf* emerge instead from the interplay between the situational ethics of oral narrative and paganism and the temporal concerns of written narrative and Christianity. The pagan world depicted in *Beowulf*, as also the worldly aspects of *Sir Gawain and the Green Knight*, Marie's *Lais*, or *The Poem of the Cid*, is a world defined by action, in particular action that takes on meaning in comparison with other actions, in the context of one's situation in society, and as the member of a certain clan, as someone's child, someone's parent, someone's niece or nephew, someone's lord or vassal. The Christian world, by contrast, is a world defined by one's place in a temporal structure of beginnings and ends,

Copyright © 2009 Pearson Education, Inc. Publishing as Longman.

with one's every action evaluated not by its effect within one's society, in the present, but on its end, its role in determining one's salvation or damnation.

Some of the key aspects of the warrior ethic were *treow* or trust; a fatalistic belief in *wyrd*, or fate; the physical forces of weapons and treasure; the blood-feud and the need for revenge; and the sense that life is transitory, something to be lost or sacrificed rather than preserved. As a tenth-century Viking maxim put it: "Cattle die, kinsfolk die, we ourselves must die. But one thing I know will never die: the dead man's reputation." We discover this ethic situationally, through observing, weighing, and comparing the actions of the characters, rather than discursively. Beowulf, to be sure, is the center and focus of our knowledge, but his actions take on meaning only in the context of those around him. Why, for example, is the epic's hero not introduced until 170 lines into the poem? Rather than begin with Beowulf and introduce the Spear-Danes in the context of a tale about Beowulf's fight with Grendel, the poem opens on the Spear-Danes as if they were the primary subject. Moreover, it opens not on the glorious generation of Hrothgar but on the funeral of his great-grandfather, Scyld Scefing. The episode has a structural function, mirroring the funeral of Beowulf that concludes the poem. Comparison with that conclusion also introduces a contrast between the two peoples that grows out of this comparison, for Scyld's death gives a rising people their name, while Beowulf's slaying signals the decline of his own—nor, for that matter, have the Geats been blessed with the straightforward descent of leaders (Scyld to Beow to Healfdene to Hrothgar) stressed by the opening lines as having been responsible for the Scyldings' success and its physical embodiment in their great hall.

There are many such episodes in *Beowulf*. They used to be referred to in the criticism as "digressions," and much ink has been spilt to determine what, if anything, they are doing there. Oral composition tends to favor such apparently spliced-in pieces as what is known as "The Finnsburg Episode" (lines 933–1018); part of the singer's skill lay in his ability to assemble the many pieces of his repertoire of songs into a cohesive whole suitable for a particular audience. This does not have to imply digression or filler. Rather, the shared memory of singer and audience encouraged a lateral reading that would automatically work through thematic connections where a causal chain was not in evidence. First of all, narrative context: the saga of the Frisian king Finn and his followers is sung for Beowulf at the feast celebrating his victory over Grendel. At first glance, such a dark tale of blood-feud, defeat, truce, and truce-breaking vengeance seems ill-suited for the occasion. It tells of the leaderless Danes forced to winter in the hall of their king's slayer. They take their vengeance before sailing home, but the *scop*'s song is mournful, its own center the funeral pyre for the Danish King Hnaef. Finn's queen Hildeburh lays her own son on the same flames. The song captures the intricate threads of the warrior code—battle and truce, cooperation against nature, the inescapable force of the blood-feud. It underlines the grace of Beowulf's aid but also suggests how easily the alliance could be shaken. It recalls the loss of life in the battle just past, and its theme and mood look forward to the blood-feud about to be savagely but justly waged by Grendel's Mother.

Copyright © 2009 Pearson Education, Inc. Publishing as Longman.

Beowulf's Women

The Finnsburg Episode begins and concludes with the key figure in the blood-feud, Finn's wife Hildeburh; for the son she has laid on the pyre was Hnaef's nephew, and the song concludes with the lady returned to the land of her birth, having lost her husband, son, and brother. Like Hildeburh's son, Beowulf is sister's son to his lord, King Hygelac; such a relationship was fraught with the tension between the ties of kinship and the inheritance of power. The second part of the poem begins with a possible allusion to the fate of Hrothgar himself, soon to be usurped by his sister's son, Hrothulf, a fact of which the audience would have been keenly aware. This section of the poem, as recent feminist criticism has brought to the fore, is centrally concerned with the role of women in a male-dominated society. The Finnsburg Episode is followed by Hrothgar's queen, Wealhtheow, offering a cup to her husband, with worried words to Hrothulf to protect her young sons, and favors to Beowulf, seated between them, to request his protection as well. Introducing the episode, the poet reminds the audience of the futility of her efforts: "each still believing the other was loyal" (line 1026). As an added touch, he reminds us of the ambiguous Unferth, "Everyone thought him honest and trustworthy, / blameless and brave, though his blade had unjustly / stricken a kinsman" (lines 1029–1031).

Ringing Grendel's Mother at the other end of part 2 is Hygelac's queen, the generous Hygd, whom the poet in a long aside compares to the murderously fierce Modthryth, her temper tamed by marriage. When he recounts his deeds to his uncle, Beowulf recalls another woman at court, Hrothgar's daughter Freawaru, betrothed to Ingeld, lord of the Heathobards, in an attempt to assuage an old blood-feud. Beowulf doubts it will succeed. The first and last parts of the poem both treat of an elemental battle between hero and monster with no history between them; the central section intimates the daunting complexity of feudalism more familiar to the listeners than those mythic encounters. This complexity hinges on the women, both in the many digressions and in the main action: the blood-feud of Grendel's Mother, "maddened by grief . . . / a fearsome female bitterly brooding / alone in her lair" (lines 1110–1112). Her appearance and behavior may be monstrous, but the mourning and worrying women surrounding her emphasize the transgressive nature of her violent revenge while the violent revenge surrounding her emphasizes the utter familiarity of her situation.

Verbal and Physical Contests

Grendel's Mother has a pressing reason for the vengeance she takes. Her son's motivation is more tenuous: he doesn't like the nightly songs of the *scop* that echo from the mead hall to his dark den. The poem provides a metaphysical ground to this aesthetic reaction, blaming the hatred by the kindred of Cain for the songs of the Lord's Creation. But this, too, is a type of blood-feud, the creature hearing in the songs a reminder of an ancient injustice, just as the warrior culture would have

Copyright © 2009 Pearson Education, Inc. Publishing as Longman.

found in Cain and Abel biblical precedence for their own customs of the blood-feud. The challenge that is finally answered by Beowulf (who hears about it from "sad songs"), like the central contests of parts 2 and 3, is brutally physical in nature. But just as the origin of the feud is verbal, so too are the physical contests mirrored and framed by all manner of verbal sparring. The Anglo-Saxon words themselves have power, especially the names, and knowing how to wield them is as important to the poem as wielding a weapon. Arriving in the land of the Danes, Beowulf must negotiate a series of verbal challenges that seek through his bearing and speech to determine his motives. The first shore guard presumes a pillaging force, but even here, he tempers his words with appreciation of Beowulf's appearance of prowess. The second guard challenges them as they enter the hall, again praising their appearance, and giving (phrased negatively) the other possible reason for coming to strange shores—banishment. Allowed entry to the hall, they are informed, "wudu, wæl-sceaftas, worda geþinges"—"Your weapons can wait for words to be spoken" (line 355). The translation well captures the alliterative balance of weapons and words, responding to each other in the original just across the line break.

Beowulf proves himself in both forms, besting the exile Unferth in a *flyting* or verbal duel that simultaneously establishes his extraordinary prowess and demonstrates his control over that prowess, poise in words equaling poise in deeds. In his second great speech, Beowulf recounts for his uncle Hygelac more deeds of prowess, the same ones the reader has already witnessed firsthand. By repeating himself, the poet suggests that the recounting of deeds is as important as their initial performance, and in the differences between his own and Beowulf's versions shows the important social function of such storytelling. Beowulf's final speech tells us the biography that these days we would expect to find at the beginning of a story, another tale of kindred murdered and warring tribes. He ends with a boast, that in old age he can defend his people as well as he did in his youth. It is a boast he will back up with his life, and that was an essential component of the power of words: in this poetic world, he who could speak them best was he who could best back them up with deeds.

Monsters and Hells

The monsters of *Beowulf* appear human in their motivations—spite, revenge, greed—but animal in their lack of speech. The poet wisely holds in abeyance the question of their humanity, never placing them in a situation requiring speech. The lack of speech is also a mark of their disdain for the intricate codes of the *comitatus*; as the poet informs us of Grendel, "The monster craved no kinship with any, / no end to the evil with wergeld owed; / nor might a king's council have reckoned / on quittance come from the killer's hand" (lines 135-138). The combination of human cunning and malevolence with an utter disregard for the human conventions that might keep them in check is what makes these monsters so chilling and so compelling. It is also what distinguishes them from the devil figures they otherwise resemble; the devil, for all his wiles, still follows

Copyright © 2009 Pearson Education, Inc. Publishing as Longman.

the rules in the end. And unlike the warfare that lurks at the margins of the poem, the monsters are internal threats, emerging from the darkness beneath the light of the hall.

It is because they are internal threats that they can be dispelled only by traveling to the underworlds where they dwell and rooting them out. The descent to the underworld is a feature of many classical epics and fundamental to the mythology of the Christian Middle Ages, which held that Christ had harrowed hell between the time of his crucifixion and his resurrection. In the pagan mythology of northern Europe, these underworlds most often took the form of physical subterranea: pits, caves, barrows and burial mounds, the bottom of a body of water. Travel through such thresholds led in Celtic myth to an Other World both marvelous and horrible, full of adventure. The space where Beowulf encounters Grendel shares these qualities; for Grendel's curse has transformed the idyllic mead hall into an inferno, and the Danes themselves are something like an Other World for the traveling Beowulf, who returns home with wealth, fame, and wisdom. The pursuit of Grendel's Mother takes the hero deep into a sinister pool, surrounded by "mere-beasts," and into her lair— an underworld replete with associations to an alien, feminine space, where standard rules do not apply and his "famous blade faltered" (line 1353). Out of this strange space and after a hand-to-hand wrestling match, Beowulf discovers a new blade and emerges with a sword hilt covered with new truths. The only example of writing in the poem, the hilt recasts the battle in biblical terms, although heavily influenced by Nordic myths. Forged by giants, the hilt's runes tell the story of the giants' demise in the Flood. Beowulf reclaims the relic for the Danes, a holy token of divine revenge to memorialize their wresting of their kingdom from the race of Cain.

Grendel and his Mother are humanoid monsters, embodying rage and envy; the dragon, or *wyrm*, of part 3 is an equally internal demon, but this time in bestial form, an utter repudiation of the key custom of gift-giving, a single-minded gold-hoarder. This is the curse in Beowulf's own land, long dormant only to be awakened in his old age, after decades of peace. The lesson here is a lesson of wisdom, that "gold could not gladden a man in mourning" (line 1974). The poet delves in time to a race prior to the Geats, a dying race whose ringkeeper consigns its riches to a deep barrow, returning to the earth what they had taken from it. The *wyrm*, too, is a creature of earth and flames, burrowing its curse deep beneath the Geats' land and torching their houses in revenge for a theft. Unlike in his youth with the Danes, Beowulf requires the help of a kinsman, Wiglaf, to whom falls the last word. The slow winding down of the poem contrasts the lost support of the lord with the dead wealth of the gold, which while he was alive could have bought off their enemies but once he is dead will only summon them faster. Still, Beowulf, too, shared with the dragon a fascination with gold, for his dying wish is that Wiglaf bring him the treasure he had died for. By the time Wiglaf returns, Beowulf has died, his victory over this monster of greed not so complete as his defeat of those in Denmark.

Copyright © 2009 Pearson Education, Inc. Publishing as Longman.

The Poem of the Cid

Less well known perhaps than the classic medieval epics of France, England, and Germany, *The Poem of the Cid* is probably the most accessible of them all to the modern reader. The poem's accessibility is due primarily to the realism of its protagonist, who bears as close a resemblance to an embattled middle-class father as he does to an iconically epic medieval hero. The combination can set off fireworks, as we follow a character we identify with closely thrust into an appalling situation and consequently performing deeds with an equanimity of which few contemporary readers would find themselves approving. *The Poem of the Cid* elicits deep pathos, extreme shock, and great pleasure; picking apart the ways it does so is one of the fascinations of reading it.

Criticism

As with much of medieval literature, especially epics with a pretense to foundational status, such as *Beowulf* and the *Chanson de Roland*, criticism of the *Poema de mio Cid* was for a long time primarily philological in nature, aimed at establishing a noncorrupt text and resolving its linguistic cruces. This approach was epitomized by Ramón Menéndez Pidal, the doyen of *Cid* studies. Menéndez Pidal argued that in spite of its distortions and omissions, the poem essentially could be accepted as a valid historical source. As with *Beowulf* studies, the biggest critical dispute came with the importation of the thesis of oral composition from its origins in Homeric studies; Edmund de Chasca's *The Poem of the Cid* (1976) presents the case as made by one of the main proponents of an origin in oral performance. More recent studies generally accept at least some degree of oral composition and aim to read the poem in light of its social and economic contexts, both in the eleventh-century world of Rodrigo Díaz de Vivar and in the late-twelfth- to early-thirteenth-century milieu of the poem's composition. The gist of these studies is to ground the peculiarities of the *Cid* compared with other medieval epics within the unique situation of eleventh- through thirteenth-century Spain. The best of them, such as Joseph J. Duggan's *The 'Cantar de Mio Cid': Poetic Creation in Economic and Social Contexts* (1989), use that context to elucidate the complex assumptions underlying the characters' motivations and ask us to balance our modern evaluation of their actions with a nuanced knowledge of Castilian customs and exigencies.

Cantares de gesta

The medieval Spanish *Cantares de gesta* (literally "songs of deeds") are, like most epics, an exemplary genre. We are meant to assume the hero's deeds are correct; our task is to figure out why. We are seldom directly told the Cid's motivation and are certainly not privy to his thoughts, which must be gleaned through his dialogue and his actions, and the way they compare to those of others. The poem establishes patterns of behavior; when there is any deviation, even of the slightest de-

Copyright © 2009 Pearson Education, Inc. Publishing as Longman.

gree, we can expect serious consequences. Take, for example, Rodrigo Díaz's private discussion of the offer of marriage by the Carrión brothers: "They have a great name, these Heirs of Carrión; / they are swollen with pride and have a place in the court, / and this marriage would not be to my liking. / But since he wishes it who is worth more than we, / let us talk of the matter but do it in secret." This is the only time in the poem that the Cid voices even a murmur of hesitation to obey a king who has long afflicted him, and, sure enough, the marriage will prove disastrous. A modern reader might want to know how the Cid feels about the bind he is in; a medieval reader would have been more likely to sense the ominous weight of the decision he has already taken, to assume it is the only decision to have taken (because the Cid has taken it), and to evaluate the different external factors that have caused him to behave in this fashion.

Rather than a narrative of a character's development, the *Poem of the Cid* documents the exemplary ways in which the Cid responds to an adventure, an unforeseen occurrence—in this case the aggression of a weak and suspicious lord and an unwanted marriage to inferiors who also happen to be his enemies. Along the way, it shows the ways in which he behaves in the customarily epic settings of battle, but the poem is more concerned with how he negotiates his difficult feudal situation. Even the descriptions of battle tend to devote more time to his behavior in victory (how he deals with his captives, how much booty he captures, how he distributes the booty) than to his prowess as a strategist or as a fighter. It is through his behavior, also, that the Cid manages to educate the only character who does change in the course of the poem: King Alfonso VI. The poet does not bother to detail the complicated history between the two that would have given Alfonso cause to be both resentful and suspicious of his most powerful vassal (see the introduction to this selection in the *Anthology*, pp. 662–664); the only thing that matters now is the current situation. We know Alfonso has made the turn toward being a proper ruler when his epithets begin to change—we find *"el buen rrey don Alfonso"* almost exclusively in the later stages of the poem. An exemplary vassal behaves correctly for himself and his family; he also improves the character of his ruler.

Some epic heroes—Achilles and Roland would be good examples—are defined by their tragic lack of proportion. Others are heroes precisely for their quality of *mesura*: the Cid's first words in the poem are spoken with tears streaming from his eyes at the destruction of his property and his exile from Castile, words spoken *"bien e tan mesurado,"* "well, and with great moderation" (First Cantar, line 19). It is not that the Cid is a cold man (he is, in fact, touchingly emotional when it comes to his estates and to his family) but, rather, that he does not let his emotions cloud his actions. If revenge is the proper course, as with the Infantes of Carrión, he will plot it carefully and take it in full; if flight is the solution, he will take that decision as well. *Mesura* is an essentially Christian virtue. It is also a factor of maturity, betokened throughout the poem by the Cid's fabulous beard, which binds *mesura* and virility together in a single attribute. We witness a similar quality in Beowulf in his prime, as he recounts his past exploits in a swimming contest as youthful and foolhardy, a pointless test of strength. We see it somewhat lacking in Gawain's

Copyright © 2009 Pearson Education, Inc. Publishing as Longman.

inability wholly to resist the seductions of the Green Knight's lady; the Green Knight himself is a pagan picture of immoderation. *Mesure* (the Anglo-Norman equivalent of the Castilian *mesura*) is a key term for Marie de France and the courtly romance as well, for her knights equally require moderation to survive the *aventures* that arise out of courtly politics.

Booty

The spoils of victory are never wholly disregarded in any epic or romance; however, only in the *Poem of the Cid* do they play a primary role. The poem is perhaps unique in its focus on the financing and economics of the military campaign over the battles; far more than *Beowulf*, for example, it is punctuated throughout by the giving of gifts. From the opening *laisse*, the Cid's status is defined in terms of his goods (or loss thereof): "He saw doors standing open and gates without fastenings, / the porches empty without cloaks or coverings / and without falcons and without molten hawks" (First Cantar, lines 15–17). Without these things, the Cid remains a hero, but he is not a lord. Compare to the lovingly detailed description of the Cid dressing for his day of revenge in court, and it is clear already that he will win the day–his status is restored:

> he covered his legs   in stockings of fine cloth
> and over them he put shoes   of elaborate work.
> He put on a woven shirt   as white as the sun,
> and all the fastenings   were of silver and gold;
> the cuffs fitted neatly   for he had ordered it thus.
> Over this he put a tunic   of fine brocade
> worked with gold shining   in every place.
> Over these a crimson skin   with buckles of gold,
> which My Cid the Campeador   wears on all occasions.
> Over the furs he put   a hood of fine cloth
> worked with gold   and set there
> so that none might tear the hair   of My Cid the Campeador;
> his beard was long   and tied with a cord,
> for he wished to guard all his person   against insult.
> On top of it all he wore   a cloak of great value;
> all admired it,   as many as were there to see. (Third Cantar, lines 812–827)

There is, to be sure, an ideological impulsion to this glorification of wealth; for the majority of it was coming in these centuries from the stores of the defeated Moors (when it was not being stripped from local Jews, as in the fictional episode where the Cid cons the greedy merchants Raquel and Vidas)–after all, it was only through contact with the Arab and Byzantine worlds that the impoverished and backwards Europeans were able to obtain such delicate fabrics and valuable metals and gems to start with. And there is, as in *laisse* 74, a strong equivocation between

Copyright © 2009 Pearson Education, Inc. Publishing as Longman.

the dual motivation for battling the Moors: is it "*el sabor de la ganançia*" ("the odor of riches") or "*la buena cristiandad*" ("good Christendom") that draws men to join the Cid at the siege of Valencia (Second Cantar, lines 114–115)? As in the Crusades, the promise of riches went hand-in-hand with dutiful piety. According to the authorities, at least, there was no conflict of interest or hypocrisy in enriching body and soul simultaneously if the victim were an infidel. At the same time, there is also a deep feeling of reality to this theme, since the need for money and goods was indeed a driving force behind the myriad campaigns and skirmishes of feudalism, and there were plenty of legal grounds to be found for sacking the castles and towns of fellow Christians as well.

There emerges from the motif of booty an appreciation of its utility in smoothing over social conflict, easing the pain of defeat, and keeping one's men contented. Compare, for example, the Cid's munificence, both toward Alfonso and toward his men, with the stinginess of the Infantes, whose social status would equally have entailed gift-giving. The exchange of money and goods was an essential component of the long *Convivencia* between Christians and Muslims on the peninsula. And, indeed, the eleventh century was something of a "golden age of booty" for the kingdom of Castile, as Duggan puts it in his detailed study of the phenomenon; before and afterwards, the flow would be reversed. There is also a genuine feeling of pleasure and satisfaction in the texture of the description. The detail of the language mirrors the Cid's care in dressing himself, the way in which he seems to be taking a careful inventory of how far he has come back from the abyss. There is clearly nothing unheroic about the moment, for the poet has taken great care to weave into the dressing scene a reminder of the long beard, the risk the Cid takes of having it pulled, and his ability to avoid that risk through his prowess.

Domesticity

The interest the poem evinces in the economics of warfare and the very texture of the booty achieved thereby reflects the unusually domestic quality of this epic. It is not accidental that the rare hero with an ability to appreciate fine clothing is also the rare hero able to express genuine love for his wife, and whose principal trial in the narrative is to deal with the humiliation of his beloved daughters. Even the metaphor used several times to describe separation from Doña Jimena, "*commo la uña de la carne*," "as the nail from the flesh," is almost distressingly intimate. A parallel can be drawn here to Homer's *Odyssey*, which is also essentially domestic in sphere, although epic in scope. The difference is that the home and the wife to which Odysseus returns and for which he must fight are resoundingly permanent—hence the central symbol of the wedding bed-tree—whereas the goods, the estate, and the family in the Cid's world are all distressingly portable and transitory. To be sure, there is a good Christian moral here, as there is in the doom-knell of Beowulf's kingdom after his death, but there is also a straightforward depiction of an unstable reality.

Copyright © 2009 Pearson Education, Inc. Publishing as Longman.

The political maneuverings that motivate the Cid's banishment and the Infantes' betrayal are also surprisingly domestic and intimate in their depiction. Although the Cid is married to Alfonso's daughter, the Infantes consider themselves his social superior because of accusations that he was the bastard son of a peasant girl, descended from a miller. The strange insult regarding a mill on the river Ubierna in Vivar that gives rise to the third duel in *laisse* 148 derives from this legend, which appears in a ballad concerning the Cid. The interpolated episode of the lions that opens the Third Cantar with the humiliation of the Infantes works on an equally domestic level, as the Cid is napping on his couch. Their mode of vengeance for the perceived slight reminds us of the status of the daughters as chattels of their father, however well beloved; the Infantes' abuse of this greatest gift of the Cid in the forest of Corpes is further evidence of their villainy. The Cid is characterized by his ability to perform admirably both in battle and in the domestic sphere. The Infantes, by contrast, take inappropriate revenge, humiliating themselves by their very inappropriateness.

The ease with which the Cid wages his military campaign in exile thus compares strikingly with the initial disaster of his intimate doings with the court in the second part of the poem, a clear sign as to which aspect of Castilian life was the more complicated. The latter episode tests the Cid far more as a hero than the first part and helps to develop a far more situated definition of heroism than that of the conventional epic hero. The Cid attains satisfaction in the Toledo court through careful planning, loyal vassals, and the maturity of Alfonso rather than simply through prowess. It is the powerful display he stages that, in the end, wins the day. It is a theme that recurs in epic, romance, and lyric. Away from the court and the courtiers, all is well; the true tests always come when one world comes into conflict with the other. The Cid is blessed in being able to reconcile the two worlds and to remarry his daughters; in real life, needless to say, it was seldom so easy, even for a good Christian and loyal vassal such as he.

PERSPECTIVES

Iberia, the Meeting of Three Worlds

This section is organized around poetry (the most prominent literary form in medieval Iberia) and, in particular, the love lyric. As elsewhere in medieval Europe, the lyric was closely intertwined with religion and philosophy, as is evident from the work of Yehuda ha-Levi and others in both fields. Indeed, in the case of Ibn Ḥazm and Ibn al-'Arabi, as with Dante after them in Italy, it is impossible to distinguish where love lyric ends and religious mysticism begins. In medieval poetry in general, the language and imagery of love were essential in giving literary form to the experience of the divine; nowhere more so was this the case than in al-Andalus, whence, many scholars today believe, the medieval language of love originated. The thirteenth-century *cantigas de Santa Maria* are another prime example

Copyright © 2009 Pearson Education, Inc. Publishing as Longman.

of such a conjoined genre, and the stunning manuscript from the court of Alfonso X the Wise is a wonderful source of Christian images of the period.

The major linguistic traditions of Iberian literature are represented in this section—Arabic, Mozarabic, Hebrew, Galician-Portuguese, Castilian, and Catalan—but it is impossible to capture in translation and in the Latin alphabet the incredible linguistic, religious, and literary mix that saw different languages occurring in the same poem, hybrid tongues, one language written in another alphabet, and, of course, one poet able to converse and write in a multitude of languages and literary traditions. A recording such as the two-CD collection *Iberian Garden* (Dorian DIS-80151) can help provide students with a sense of the immense variety of Iberian poetry and song. The recent *Literature of Al-Andalus* (eds. María Rosa Menocal, Raymond Scheindlin, and Michael Sells, 2000) provides an excellent general introduction to the study of medieval Iberia, with individual essays and bibliographies on nearly every figure included in this section. That volume is exemplary of the ways in which contemporary scholarship has encouraged a collective and collaborative criticism of this complex place and time to supplement and revise the traditional academic approach, fragmented between distinct and relatively uncommunicative fields and disciplines.

——— ⚜ ———

Castilian Ballads and Traditional Songs

Simple in form, these traditional songs nevertheless bore a heavy ideological burden when they were assembled at the behest of Ferdinand and Isabella to provide a Spanish national identity for the Iberian peninsula. Saturated with the conventionally seasonal nature imagery of fertility and love—the midsummer's festival of St. John's Day, the wild herbs associated with medicine and lovemaking—they are set in a landscape equally saturated with the memories and scars of the many centuries of the *Reconquista*.

Love songs are traditionally concerned with the margins or thresholds between lover and beloved, between nature and society, between youth and adulthood, between the different seasons of the year, all of which help evoke the powerful ambivalence of desire. These lyrics equally occupy the boundaries between peoples and nations, especially the "Ballad of Juliana" and the hauntingly brief "Three Moorish Girls," set on the site of a famous battle, yet equally compelling as a bittersweet depiction of the loss of innocence on a purely personal level. The beautiful melody makes this a particularly rewarding song for classroom listening, especially the exemplary version on *El Cancionero de Palacio 1474–1516* (Astrée E8762); the extended interpretation on *Mudejar* (M.A. MO42A) amply demonstrates the potential of the apparently simple tune for instrumental improvisation. "Abenámar" turns the analogy in the other direction, using the language of love and marriage to personify the beauty of Granada and the political manipulations surrounding its control. The conventional tropes of attraction and repulsion, pas-

Copyright © 2009 Pearson Education, Inc. Publishing as Longman.

sion and violence between the sexes well befit the relationship between Christian and Muslim in Iberia, the sexual identity of each partner fluctuating as the balance of power shifts.

◆━━◄◆≥━ ◆━◆

Mozarabic Kharjas

What in the ballads and songs of Castile was expressed through the timeworn tropes of nature, the *kharjas* formalized in a complex play of language and structure. What the Arabic *muwashshah* (see p. 758) phrased in the conventionally refined phrases of the male lover's voice was given a Mozarabic *kharja* or exit spoken in the earthy and direct words of a woman speaking the Romance vernacular that was the lingua franca of al-Andalus. In this poetic coupling we find the intricate web of cultural relations negotiated through the familiar, if uneven and unstable, power dynamics of heterosexual lovemaking. "I'll give you such love!—but only / if you'll bend / my anklets right over to my / earrings!" ("*Tan t'amaray, illa con / al-šarti / an taǧma' halhali ma' / qurti*") bargains one prospective lover. Although the *kharjas* tend to be more direct in their language and desires, the resemblance to the Castilian songs remains; in their near total exclusion of the outside world from the private sphere of longing, however, these brief lines are also close to the Galician-Portuguese *cantigas de amigo* and the lyrics of the *trobairitz*, both also composed in a woman's voice.

Because the *kharjas* constitute the earliest known body of lyric in the Romance vernacular, they have been subject to a high degree of critical scrutiny since first recovered by Samuel Stern in 1948 as a philological curiosity. Peter Dronke argues in his insightful study, *The Medieval Lyric* (1996), that regardless of their brevity, these lyrics possess a "poetic self-sufficiency" and intensity that bespeak independent composition—and, indeed, the *kharjas* appear to have been adapted from orally transmitted folk songs and dances. On the other hand, as María Rosa Menocal maintains in *Shards of Love* (1994), it is the new context given them, the interplay with the Arabic of the *muwashshah* proper, that makes them so significant, their role in a hybrid poetic genre that exemplifies the heterogeneous unity of Andalusia.

◆━━◄◆≥━ ◆━◆

Ibn Ḥazm

Like Dante's *Vita nuova* two and a half centuries later, *The Dove's Neckring* combines prose with illustrative verse; it also contains a fair number of autobiographical details, although nowhere as many as Dante's. Ibn Ḥazm divided his treatise into thirty chapters: the first ten "concerned with the root-principles of Love," the second section comprising "twelve chapters on the accidents of Love, and its

Copyright © 2009 Pearson Education, Inc. Publishing as Longman.

praiseworthy attributes," the third part "six chapters on the misfortunes which enter into Love," and concluding chapters on "the Vileness of Sinning" and "the Virtue of Continence." The excerpts included in the *Anthology* come from the second part, the chapter on "Concealing the Secret"; for, according to the author, "One of the attributes of love is holding the tongue . . . [but] for all that the subtle secret will out." Ibn Ḥazm's primary source was the concrete and precise nature imagery of the pre-Islamic poetry of the Bedouin tribes, devoted to wine and love and based on the flora, fauna, and flowing water of the pleasure garden. In *The Dove's Neckring*, he adapted that language to a vision of Islam as seen through the lens of the same Neoplatonic philosophy that had so influenced Christian writers such as Augustine.

According to Neoplatonism, the soul has been imprisoned in the body, exiled from a higher place to which it strives to elevate itself and return. The ideal, personified here as the beloved, can never be phenomenal or visible: "I see a human shape, yet if I use my mind, then the body is a celestial one." Yet Neoplatonism tended to be logical in the relationship it established between soul and body, image and ideal. What is fascinating about the controversial mysticism of Ibn Ḥazm, and what makes this spiritual autobiography so compelling, is the way in which it accumulates concrete images that are utterly baffling and yet feel strangely right: "And if you say: 'It is possible to reach the sky,' I reply: 'Yes, and I know where the stairs may be found.'" The stairs that allow Ibn Ḥazm to bridge the ineffable gap between man and God, between lover and beloved, are the words on his page and the simple images out of which he builds his conundrums. The Qur'an, after all, is not the revealed word of God, as Christian and Jewish scriptures purport to be, but his literal words, things of beauty and artistry in themselves, whose meaning must be experienced, felt, and intuited directly rather than translated: "[I am] like a handwriting whose trace is clear, but which, if they seek to interpret it, cannot be explained."

Ibn Rushd (Averroës)

When Dante placed Averroës, "of the great commentary," and his predecessor, Avicenna (Ibn Sina), in Limbo among the virtuous pagans (*Inferno* 4.143–144), he was signaling his debt to their enormously influential translations and commentaries of Aristotle. He was also being highly heterodox; for as the origins of the proclaimed heresy of Averroism, these Andalusian philosophers should by all rights have been anathemized with Muhammed and Ali among the sowers of discord in the eighth circle or entombed with the heretics in the sixth. It was one thing to acknowledge the theologically lacking but intellectually compelling writings of the ancient Greeks and Romans, born before the coming of Christ; it was quite another to canonize the illicit allure of a near-contemporary thinker who maintained, among other heresies, that there was a measure of eternity to the world, a collec-

Copyright © 2009 Pearson Education, Inc. Publishing as Longman.

tive immortal soul, and a "Possible Intellect," or set of eternal truths accessible to that soul. Islam may have been a peril to the body and soul of Christendom (and Dante did, after all, place Muslim philosophers somewhere in his Hell), but it was also a precious conduit of sought-after and otherwise inaccessible knowledge. Moreover, no less a pillar of the Church than Saint Thomas Aquinas had based his entire philosophy of Scholasticism on Averroës's Aristotle. And, although Aquinas's writings were eventually accepted as a successful distanglement of Averroist heresies from Aristotelian verities, some of his own theses were condemned as heretical by Church authorities directly following his death.

The goal of Scholasticism was to find a place for the powerful philosophical tools of logic and rhetoric in a medieval epistemology based primarily on the power of revealed knowledge. It is difficult to determine which Scholastics paid lip service to the overarching authority of the divine in order to apply the principles of rational inquiry wherever they could get away with it and which of them truly desired to find a way to combine the materialist analysis of reality with belief in the existence of an authority beyond that reality and inaccessible to that analysis. What is clear, though, is that while the mystics held that the essential truths of experience lay beyond the reach of rational thought and analytical language, the philosophers believed that rigorous dialectic could satisfactorily explain just about every mystery of the universe worth explaining.

Although Averroës's solutions to the problems of first causes, of absolute truth, and of the nature of the soul diverged from those promulgated by mainstream Christian doctrine, his insistence on the necessity of a proper hierarchy between religion and philosophy, the subject of the *Decisive Treatise*, was identical to that of Christian Scholastics such as Aquinas. The Law commands the study of the phenomenal world, and the proper method for studying that world was what Averroës terms "intellectual reasoning": the Aristotelian method. The sticking point, as with all medieval rationalists, was where, if anywhere, to limit the purview of intellectual reasoning. At what point, as Bernard of Clairvaux chided Peter Abelard, did you reach the mysteries that could not be proven but must be accepted as articles of faith? It was a problem that haunted Christian thinkers throughout the High Middle Ages, and an intellectual turf war that has never really disappeared since. The controversy aroused by Averroës in Muslim as well as Christian Europe testifies to the intellectual fecundity of cultural boundaries and to a medieval thirst for knowledge so powerful as to push at the limits of acceptability.

Ibn 'Arabi

For a fuller treatment of the Andalusian mystic poet, see his selections in the Perspectives section, "Asceticism, Sufism, and Wisdom," earlier in Volume B of the *Anthology* (pp. 494–497). The translator, Michael Sells, has written illuminatingly about Ibn 'Arabi in several essays, as has María Rosa Menocal in *Shards of Love*

Copyright © 2009 Pearson Education, Inc. Publishing as Longman.

(1994). While *The Dove's Neckring* expands the mystical congruence of love and divine vision into an autobiographical narrative punctuated with lyric paradoxes, "Gentle now, doves" condenses the moments of vision and desire into an intense lyric. While replete with esoteric significance, the precise meanings of which scholars have debated for years, the powerful love-longing transcends those meanings without thereby negating their existence. Because love is portrayed as an incomprehensible and yet instantly recognizable phenomenon, just as doves and gazelles are conventional images of Arabic poetry, the poet can move freely between learned allusions ("In a grove of [tamarisks] / spirits wrestled"), the stations of the pilgrimage to Mecca, and fragments of passionate love. Like many mystics (and many love poets), Ibn 'Arabi also favors images of impressive violence as a means of imparting the depth of his experience: the gazelle that pastures "between breastbones / and innards," the "garden among the flames."

The final stanzas tie the diverse images together. First, the metaphorical equation of faith and desire—"I profess the religion of love"—is amplified into a definition of the poet-mystic-lover's role as one of nomadic wandering: "wherever its caravan turns along the way"; then comes the concluding turn into the pantheon of Arabic poets and lovers. The essence of the mystic—and of the lover—is adamantly to refuse the splintering of the world given perfect unity by his or her vision. Where the philosopher endeavors to parse the world into a model of rational coherence able to be assembled and disassembled piece by piece at will, the mystic confutes the proper boundaries, using the power of the divine to illuminate the experience of love and using the power of love to illuminate the experience of the divine.

Solomon Ibn Gabirol and Yehuda ha-Levi

The courtier-rabbis of Andalusia learned much from the lyrical writings of their Arab fellows. In particular, they cultivated the theme of loss and separation in creating a hybrid poetry able to express their own experience of the divine and their deeply rooted sense of exile from Israel and loss of a culture once unified by the Temple of Jerusalem. Raymond Scheindlin's seminal twin volumes of translations, *Wine, Women, and Death* (1986) and *The Gazelle* (1991), provide a strong context for the poetic output of Solomon Ibn Gabirol and Yehuda ha-Levi. Peter Cole's recent translation of Ibn Gabirol gives more of an introduction as well as a broader selection (2001). Ross Brann's study, *The Compunctious Poet* (1991), is the most comprehensive treatment of their works.

Of all the peoples of medieval Iberia, the Sephardim were probably the most hybrid in their culture, and in many ways they epitomize medieval Andalusia. While they achieved positions of power—the great poet Schmuel ha-Nagid was vizier in eleventh-century Granada—they never forgot the tenuousness of their position, and the stories of their lives are punctuated by abrupt shifts of status, trans-

Copyright © 2009 Pearson Education, Inc. Publishing as Longman.

formations, and loss. The poet Moses Ibn Ezra, member of a prominent family in Granada, had his world shattered by the fall of the city-states to the Almoravids in 1090. He spent the rest of his life in the cities of northern Spain, mourning his isolation and the loss of the world he had known and loved. Ibn Gabirol never adjusted to the intricate negotiations required of the courtier and remained a social misfit all his life. His very identity as a writer was split: only in the nineteenth century was it discovered that the well-known "Arab philosopher" Avicebron was none other than the Jewish religious and lyric poet Solomon Ibn Gabirol. The story of Yehuda ha-Levi is the most romantic of all, rejecting his worldly life and making a pilgrimage to the Western Wall, where, purportedly, he died. The lives of the Sephardic poets are the stuff of legend, but their poetry has stood the test of time equally well.

The Andalusian Jews could draw on the poetry of lament and exile in which the later books of the Hebrew Bible are steeped; they combined this with the Arabic imagery of nature and the garden. Of course, in the Song of Songs, they already had a perfect example of a sensual poem of love that had long been applied to the relationship between man and God. In both Hebrew and Arabic love poetry, the gender of the beloved often remains unclear, and this aids the ambiguity between physical and divine love. In the examples selected in the *Anthology*, we find love lyrics, poems of exile, and philosophical lyrics. Even the simplest of them—"Ofra does her laundry with my tears"—concludes its elegant lover's conceit with an image of divine presence straight out of the book of Exodus: "Nor sun needs she: Her face provides the blaze." In *Wine, Women, and Death*, Scheindlin notes of this poem, like many others, that it includes wordplay; here, the Hebrew word *'ayin* is used for "eye" and also for "well." He also recounts an anecdote recalling an eleventh-century prince of Seville being inspired to a poetic competition with his minister by the sight of a laundress while they were walking along the Guadalquivir River; he later made her his princess. Ha-Levi was adept at play with the conventions of his culture, as is also evident in the imitation of the Arabic original, "Once when I fondled him upon my thighs," where the clever play of reflections equally hints at the play on the image of divinity within the created world.

Ibn Gabirol's verse tends more explicitly to invoke philosophy and religion in its imagery, eschewing some of ha-Levi's concern with the good life and the courtier's wit. Compare the startling opening of "She looked at me and her eyelids burned" with the similar image that closes "Ofra does her laundry with my tears," where the mystical emerges lightly out of a simple description. Ibn Gabirol begins dramatically and, while we never lose sight of the exchange of gazes and the blush that answers the tears in the final lines, he expands his poetic lexicon into an economic metaphor of creditor and debtor that itself appears to allegorize an exchange between man and God. The good life goes on around the poet—the cup of wine continues to make the rounds—but he has been severed irrevocably from his beloved: "she will not return." Elsewhere, Ibn Gabirol is more explicitly philosophical, using a finely wrought description of nature to meditate on the relation between poetry and reality, imitation and nature, in "Winter wrote . . ." or enu-

Copyright © 2009 Pearson Education, Inc. Publishing as Longman.

merating the prison that is earthly life in "The mind is flawed. . . ." In the short poem written on the occasion of his patron's death, "Behold the sun at evening," nature again is made to mirror the occasion of the verse.

Ha-Levi's poems of exile beautifully capture the ambivalence of a relationship to the glories of al-Andalus that also motivated the legend of renunciation. "It will be nothing to me to leave all the goodness of Spain," he writes in "My heart is in the East," "So rich will it be to see the dust of the ruined sanctuary" (p. 774). In "Your breeze, Western shore, is perfumed," he gives the antithesis a basis in nature, showing how the sweet breeze of Andalusia is what drives the ship of the pilgrim back to the holy East. *The Book of the Khazars*, too, is a work of exile, reconstructing in the uncertainty of life in Andalusia a legend of far-flung conversion, a strange Caucasian sanctuary for the Jews. The structure of the book as a series of disputations followed by a dialogue of teachings was common enough in the Middle Ages; Abelard's *Dialogue of a Philosopher with a Jew and a Christian* (1135) and Boccaccio's story of the Three Rings in the *Decameron* (Vol. C, p. 155) are two of the best-known examples. Sorting through the multiple claims to truth of various creeds and religious doctrines would have had a powerful currency in al-Andalus, where ideas and doctrines were exchanged and disputed with great frequency. The framing tale of *The Book of the Khazars* recognizes the difference between scholarly and intellectual exchange, where a number of different positions could be maintained simultaneously, and a poet or philosopher could test a variety of stances, and the courtier's lot before his lord, where a decision was law and could brook no dispute. The victory of the lowly Jew is simultaneously a declaration of faith, a fantasy of wish fulfillment, and an ironic commentary on ha-Levi's own position as courtier. Ideas and allegiances might be freely exchanged, but not the religion of the leaders; such conversions were the stuff of distant legend, not of the Mediterranean.

<hr />

Ramón Llull

Like Ibn Ḥazm, Ramón Llull was a prolific polymath mystic, and also like Ibn Ḥazm, he retreated from the life of the court to devote himself to study. And, just as Ibn Ḥazm's lyrics were placed in the context of a treatise on love, so the *Book of the Lover and the Beloved* from which these aphoristic phrases are taken formed the ninety-ninth chapter of Llull's sprawling Catalan novel, *Blanquerna*. This allegorical romance treats of the place of religion and spirituality in the medieval world, as Blanquerna chooses to leave his parents and his fiancée to wander the world as a hermit. Following an episode in an enchanted forest, he settles in a monastery and begins moving up the church hierarchy. He becomes abbot, then bishop, and finally pope. Retiring to a hermitage, he receives divine illumination through meditation. The *Book of the Lover and the Beloved* and another treatise, *The Art of Contemplation*, are the fruits of this meditation.

Copyright © 2009 Pearson Education, Inc. Publishing as Longman.

Love makes the Lover his Fool; this is both a convention of love poetry and an allegory of mystical experience. "'My Beloved,' he answered, 'has taken my will, and I myself have yielded up to Him my understanding; so that there is left in me naught but memory, wherewith I remember my Beloved." The existence of God in memory was a motif of Neoplatonism, which held that the soul remembered the place of its origin in the heavens. In his *Confessions*, Augustine described seeking God everywhere and finding him finally in his memory, after abandoning everything else. The Book of Memory, too, plays a key role in Dante's *Vita nuova*, where the poet presents his love for Beatrice as if it were the incarnation of Christ. Dante also paints himself in courtly convention as a fool, dumbfounded by the effects of love. Where the Islamic mystics tend to focus on the lyrical moment of illumination, Christian mysticism (and love poetry) tends to be more narrative in its portrayal of illumination; the meaning of Christianity was revealed in the sequence of historical events culminating in the crucifixion and resurrection. The doctrine of the Trinity introduces a trio of potential characters (in addition to the poet/lover), with Love, the Beloved, and the Lover seeming sometimes to mirror the tri-fold God, sometimes to depict the relationship between man and God. The refusal to resolve this equivocal allegory and the refusal to resolve the paradoxes of his aphorisms distinguish the mysticism of Llull from that of Dante, and his conception of love (along with those of the Andalusian poets mentioned earlier) from those of the troubadours and the northern European poets who appear otherwise to derive so much from Iberian lyric.

Dom Dinis and Martin Codax

According to Peter Dronke in *The Medieval Lyric* (1996), thirteenth-century Portugal was the site of the "greatest flowering of women's songs in medieval Europe": the *cantigas de amigo*. It is not clear why the predominantly male poets of the northwest corner of the Iberian peninsula chose to compose so many of their songs in the voice of a young woman; one explanation may be the evident debt to the folk tradition of the Castilian *cancioneros* and *romanceros*. The conventions of the *cantiga de amigo* were highly restrictive in subject matter, limited to a single image of a young woman yearning for a lover, with none of the potential to unfold the drama of the situation into a narrative that characterizes the songs of the troubadours and other poets elsewhere in Europe. Where the Galician-Portuguese tradition shone, as Dronke demonstrates, was in the ability to hold the dramatic possibilities of the situation in tension through the highly patterned use of repetition in the refrain, in the slight variation on the same situation in each verse and in the rhyme schemes, and in a musical setting that was highly melismatic—syllables stretched out for intensity through many notes of music.

We are fortunate in being able to appreciate the relation between words and music firsthand because musical notation has survived in two manuscripts:

Copyright © 2009 Pearson Education, Inc. Publishing as Longman.

a single leaf of the Vindel Manuscript now at the Pierpont Morgan Library in New York, which contains music for seven *cantigas de amigo* of Martin Codax, who flourished under the patronage of Ferdinand III (1198–1252), king of Castile (from 1217) and Léon (from 1230), the father of Alfonso X; and the Sharrer Manuscript in Lisbon, which includes seven of the seventy-three *cantigas de amor* composed by Dom Dinis, king of Portugal from 1279 to 1325. The latter can be heard on *Music from the Court of Dom Dinis* (Harmonia Mundi 907129). There are many recordings of the beautiful *marinha*, or sea-songs, of Martin Codax, which give an excellent sense of the complex simplicity of the form. Barbara Fowler's recent translation, *Songs of a Friend: Love Lyrics of Medieval Portugal* (1996), provides a representative selection of the 1,680 *cantigas de amigo* that have survived.

The melodic rhythms of this poetry rely heavily on the musical setting for their dramatic intensity, but even on their own, the emotional impulse and the contrast between the speaker's enforced state of passive waiting and her distant lover's mobility are strikingly evoked by the insistent variation within the formal confines. The limitations of the form perfectly correspond to the limitations of the content: in the shortest of Martin Codax's lyrics, "O waves that I've come to see," as well as in "My beautiful sister, come hurry with me," the rhythm of the ocean, standing in for the absent friend, motivates the rhythms and the repetition of the song. In other poems, such as the selections by Dom Dinis, we find such interlocutors as a mother, a flowering pine, and a river. "O blossoms of the verdant pine" is the closest in form and tone to Martin Codax's earlier lyrics, its eight stanzas following a two-line variation on the query to the pine regarding the lover's whereabouts with the plaintive refrain, "O God, where is he?" In "The lovely girl arose at earliest dawn" (where the sexual motif is displaced onto the petticoats and camisoles the girl is washing and the resonance of dawn in the popular dawn-song of lovers' partings, and the drama arises from the girl's anger at the wind for scattering the clothes), the playful variation on the pathos of many of the *cantigas de amigo* reminds us that the emotional intensity of the other songs is equally conventional, yet not less moving for being so. The simple equation of nature and sexuality also recalls the folk tradition.

The Galician-Portuguese poets were by no means unaware of the flourishing schools of lyric north of the Pyrenees either. The pilgrimage route to Santiago de Compostela on the Galician coast kept them current with the rest of Europe; moreover, by the thirteenth century, the Albigensian Crusade had pretty much eliminated sources of patronage in Languedoc, and Spain was one of the refuges of the out-of-work troubadours. Dinis's "Of what are you dying, daughter" and Codax's "Ah God, if only my love could know" exhibit various motifs of Occitan lyric, the former in the dawn-parting, and especially the latter in its reference to "spies," but both songs place those motifs firmly within the genre of the *cantiga de amigo*. In his *cantiga de amor*, "Provençals right well may versify," Dinis does more than demonstrate familiarity with the Occitan troubadours; he plays their own game of poetic and amorous one-upmanship.

Copyright © 2009 Pearson Education, Inc. Publishing as Longman.

Marie de France

It should not surprise us that the *Lais* of Marie de France display many of the same interests and concerns as the poetry of the troubadours and *trobairitz*, or female troubadours; Marie most likely was attached to the court of Eleanor of Aquitaine, granddaughter of Guillem de Peiteus, one of the first Occitan poets. Eleanor had been married to the Capetian monarch, Louis VII of France, from 1137 until 1152, when their marriage was annulled on grounds of consanguinity. When she was married to Henry II Plantagenet, control of Aquitaine, Limousin, Poitou, and Berry was transferred to England. The court followed, and it was in Norman England that Marie de France composed the three works attributed to her: the *Fables*, the *Espurgatoire Seint Patriz*, and the *Lais*. The intricate web of political conflict and intermarriage that characterizes the relationship between England and France during this period and led, among other things, to Eleanor being imprisoned by Henry II for the fifteen years from 1174 to 1189 for conspiracy imbues Marie's mythical narratives of Arthur's court in the same way that the intrigues among the petty lords and nobles of Aquitaine imbue the poetry of the troubadours and *trobairitz*.

Where formal virtuosity in the Occitan lyric is based on verbal and thematic inventiveness, Marie's is primarily narrative in focus. Her virtuosity appears in symbolic density, wordplay, and variations on a theme. In her "Prologue," she shows herself acutely aware of her audience: a court enamored of the *matière de Bretagne*, the Celtic legends at the origin of the Arthurian cycle. In good medieval fashion, she is concerned with establishing her authority. This was customarily done with reference to the works of the ancients—Marie cites the Latin grammarian Priscian in particular—but Marie also includes the oral, folk tradition of the legends she is translating here into the Anglo-Norman dialect of her court. The "Prologue" stresses the moral good of her undertaking, both for herself and for her audience. This was equally a rhetorical convention, and students may wonder what is particularly morally uplifting about a series of Arthurian legends. Marie is quite serious about entertaining and edifying at the same time. In her *Fables*, each brief story ends in a moral, just as her Aesopian models did. The morals of the *Lais*, by contrast, are exemplary rather than explicit, to be worked out by the audience from the behavior and fate of the characters, and cumulative, each *lai* gaining in significance by comparison with its companions.

The central premise of each *lai* is to recount an *aventure* ("Prologue," line 38) that occurs to one or more of the characters. *Aventure* in Anglo-Norman means not only the fantastic events implied by its modern descendant, *adventure*, but also chance or fate. The essence of a knight or a lady's *curteisie* is called out or tested by the unforeseen things that happen to him or her, rather than in the day-to-day life of the court. The *Lais* are full of tellings and retellings of *aventures*, each time permitting a new or revised ethical judgment. The first *aventure* could be said to be staged by Marie in her "Prologue," as she challenges the king to whom she dedicates the work, Henry II, "so brave and courteous" to be worthy of appreciating

Copyright © 2009 Pearson Education, Inc. Publishing as Longman.

the *aventures* she had determined in her heart to present to him. The *Lais* are full of such symbolic exchanges, different forms of language and communication: the coded messages of "*Chevrefoil*" ("The Honeysuckle"); the beast's behavior in "*Bisclavret*" ("The Werewolf"). To be able to interpret correctly an unforeseen symbol or a strange communication is to be able to respond ethically to a modern *aventure*, to be able to read correctly one of Marie's *lais*.

Her characters are simultaneously figures of the legendary past and stand-ins for the courtly present, and the *aventures* are both the marvelous events of that past and the intricate codes of the present into which they have been translated. So, the original *aventure* of "*Bisclavret*" is the figure of the werewolf, the title of the *lai*; translated by Marie, it becomes an object lesson in ways of losing or preserving one's humanity—the wolf is *francs* (noble) and *deboneire* (well behaved) toward everyone except his treacherous wife and her lover, to whom he reacts with bestial fury; it addresses the king with due deference and protocol. The members of the court react properly to the miracle of a beast acting in this manner, assuming "that he wouldn't act that way without a reason" (line 208). Even the brutal punishment he inflicts on his wife—ripping off her nose—was a common punishment for adultery, and thus fits her crime. The wife, too, has had her test, her *aventure*, in the revelation by her husband of his terrible secret, but she failed. "Terrified of the whole adventure" (line 99), repulsed by him and plotting his downfall, she reveals her true character as well in the face of this wonder. It is fascinating to compare the treatment of the werewolf here with the man-bear in *The Saga of King Hrolf Kraki* (Vol. B, p. 653), where the supernatural remains a matter-of-fact element of everyday life and the beast-form the immediate result of human actions, the physical manifestation of a curse.

In Marie's retellings, by contrast, supernatural events and individual desires are intensely private affairs, relegated to spaces beyond the court—to nature and to the Other World of Breton myth. The crises they give rise to can usually be resolved only in the public sphere of the court itself, where they can be incorporated into its fabric and made whole. As often as not, this resolution fails, due, for example, to an unworthy ruler. This is the situation behind the episode from the Tristan and Yseult legend recounted in "*Chevrefoil*": the absent lord, Mark, unworthy of his nephew, Tristan. Here, there is no chance of reconciliation, only the secret satisfaction of private desire. The *aventure* is not so much the exile of Tristan (that is a matter of the legend as a whole) but the specific chance of the queen's passing. It is instructive to compare this episode with the slightly later romance of Gottfried von Strassburg, itself adapted from the *Tristan* of Thomas of Britain, a contemporary of Marie's at the Norman court. Marie's story is more realistic in its fleeting nature and spontaneous decision-making. Rather than the discovery of the lovers and the loss of their idyll seen in Gottfried's version, "*Chevrefoil*" permits their brief tryst and then extends it eternally through the vehicle of Tristan's harp. Marie claims that Tristan himself composed in Breton the *lai* she has just retold in Anglo-Norman, and that he, not she, originated the title metaphor of the honeysuckle, which entwines

Copyright © 2009 Pearson Education, Inc. Publishing as Longman.

around the hazel tree, binding the plants as the two exemplary lovers are bound together, "*ne vus sanz mei, ne jeo sanz vus*," "You cannot live without me, nor I without you" (line 78).

Amor, love, is the only real subject of the *Lais*, but it is examined from many different perspectives. As narrator, Marie defines it in the opening *lai* of the collection, "Guigemar":

> *Amur est plaie dedenz cors*
> *E si ne piert nïent defors;*
> *Ceo est un mal ki lunges tient,*
> *Pur ceo que de Nature vient.*
> *Plusur le tienent a gabeis,*
> *Si cume cil vilain curteis*
> *Ki jolivent par tut le mund,*
> *Puis s'avantent de ceo que funt.*
> *N'est pas amur, einz est folie,*
> *E mauvestié e lecherie!*
> *Ki un en peot leal trover*
> *Mut le deit server e amer*
> *E estre a sun comandement.* (lines 483–495, ed. Jean Rychner)

> Love is a wound in the body,
> and yet nothing appears on the outside.
> It's a sickness that lasts a long time,
> because it comes from nature.
> Many people treat it lightly,
> like these false courtiers
> who have affairs everywhere they go,
> then boast about their conquests;
> that's not love but folly,
> evil and lechery.
> If you can find a loyal love,
> you should love and serve it faithfully,
> be at its command. (trans. Joan Ferrante and Robert Hanning)

The key word here is *plaie*, originally the physical wound inflicted on Guigemar's thigh by a doe he was hunting, able to be cured only by the distant woman, "*franche, curteise, bele e sage*" ("noble, courteous, beautiful, intelligent") for whose unconsummated love he now suffers far more. As token of her love, she places *un plait* ("a knot") in his shirt, which only she can untie. Just as honeysuckle and hazel are knotted together for life, unable to survive if separated, so the knot that binds Guigemar and his beloved is equally a wound. This tale is reconciled happily, however, for the lady is justified: her aged husband is jealous and intemperate and has locked her in a castle. She escapes and unbinds

Copyright © 2009 Pearson Education, Inc. Publishing as Longman.

the knot, thus communicating her identity to her beloved, and they live happily ever after: "all his pain was now at an end." Such love is the central theme of the *Lais*, but in Marie's definition of "service" above, she equally includes love between lord and vassal and between God and man under the same rubric. Bisclavret loves his lord and is loved by all his neighbors in turn—both turn out, unlike his wife, to merit the love.

Although Marie's ethics of love is no more identical with Christian doctrine than most medieval doctrines of courtly love (she selectively condones adultery, for one thing), her stress on the way in which love elevates the lover is compatible with Christian mysticism and a familiar tenet of medieval allegory and lyric. Similarly, the way in which she epitomizes life as a series of tests, or *aventures*, brought on by chance or fate is equally compatible with a Christian conception of divine providence. Nevertheless, we should hesitate to read a Christian allegory directly into these stories any more than into any other medieval writing. Love brings the lover closer to God because it ennobles and because its pleasures are the closest one can experience to divine inspiration, but love also remains a resolutely earthly and physical experience. What it permits here, and in much of medieval romance—*Sir Gawain and the Green Knight* being a good example—is to bridge the distance between the oral and pre-Christian world of Celtic Europe and the literate Christian courts of the High Middle Ages without reducing one to the other. For there were many concerns, primarily those of the individual and of the passions, that could be addressed positively only from within a pagan framework. In Marie's *Lais*, as in *Gawain*, the romance provides an Other World where Christian and pagan ethics can be compared, played with, and tested, without risk of heresy, to see what could be translated from one to the other as well as to worry about what might be lost in that translation.

Sir Gawain and the Green Knight

Written some two centuries after Marie's *Lais*, the world of *Sir Gawain and the Green Knight* stands out by continuing to be concerned with translating the gap between oral and literate cultures and between paganism and Christianity that was also evident in the earlier *Beowulf*. The temporal and cultural gap provided by the Arthurian legends and the codes of courtly love associated with them continued to constitute the fault line of meaning in the text of romance. For many scholars, the poem is characterized by its very isolation in place and time, written in a now-obscure regional dialect of northwest England in a unique stanzaic form and an archaic nonrhyming alliterative meter based on oral performance, and surpassingly strange. Still, as Ad Putter notes in *An Introduction to the "Gawain"-Poet* (1996), it could as easily have been composed in London for a Cheshire patron at the sophisticated court of Richard II. In either case, the poem makes a powerful case for a quintessentially English language and culture, a case wholly different than the poet's contemporary, Chaucer, and his translation of continental material to a cosmopolitan London English in his writings.

Copyright © 2009 Pearson Education, Inc. Publishing as Longman.

The Text, Its Sources, and Its Critics

Gawain survives with three other poems in a single manuscript that found its way to a private library in Yorkshire sometime in the late sixteenth or early seventeenth century. It nearly burned in a fire in 1731 and now resides in the British Library (Cotton Nero A.x.). It is a luxury manuscript, with twelve illuminations and colored initial capitals; scribal errors have led scholars to assume it is not the original. The three other poems are written in the same dialect and also in alliterative verse. One, *Pearl*, has long been assumed to be of the same authorship as *Gawain*; the other two, *Patience* and *Cleanness*, are now also commonly attributed to the *Gawain*-poet. The manuscript first came to light in the nineteenth century, and the first printed edition was published in 1839. The standard edition was edited in 1925 by J. R. R. Tolkien and E. V. Gordon, updated in 1967 by Norman Davis.

Not surprisingly, a large portion of the considerable scholarly attention received by the poem has focused on establishing solid facts about the author, as well as the date and place of composition of the poem. The date of Cotton Nero A.x., circa 1400, provides a *terminus ante quem* for the composition of the poem; time of composition is usually set in the last quarter of the fourteenth century, but critical agreement does not extend much beyond that. The language is a regional dialect of northwest England. Its form appears to be intentionally archaic, for alliterative poetry had been fairly dormant since the tenth century. Critics hypothesize an alliterative revival in the second half of the fourteenth century, a national phenomenon but one rooted in the north. The only substantial manuscript evidence of this revival belongs to the widely disseminated *Piers Plowman*; it is not clear whether this was due to a limited audience or a loss of interest in preserving a poetic form that would have felt passé to a fifteenth-century readership accustomed to the now-standard London English and rhyming couplets.

Source studies are another major tradition in *Gawain* criticism. The most important influence is probably Scandinavian, in particular Old Norse. The Danes had occupied northern England during the eighth and ninth centuries (whence *Beowulf*), and their language and customs had been assimilated into the regional dialects. As J. A. Burrow puts it in *A Reading of "Sir Gawain and the Green Knight"* (1966), this was a local movement, but not a provincial one. The poet was by no means ignorant of continental culture; however, unlike Chaucer, as James Winny points out in his recent edition of *Gawain* (1992), the poet frames Old French words as if they were foreign rather than incorporating them into the fabric of the language and milieu. The *Gawain*-poet knew the *Roman de la rose*, Mandeville's *Travels*, and Old French Arthurian romances. *Pearl* evidences a familiarity of Boccaccio and of Dante's *Commedia*. The *Gawain*-poet also knew the Vulgate Bible quite well. As Putter observes, this was a nonspecialist's knowledge, and it is used actively by a poet who had assimilated what he or she had read. Putter also notes the broader influence of Geoffrey of Monmouth's *History of the Kings of Britain* (c. 1150), which treated King Arthur as a historical figure rather than a figure of legend.

Copyright © 2009 Pearson Education, Inc. Publishing as Longman.

The Court

Another major focus of *Gawain* criticism has been on its relation to the Arthurian cycle, its portrayal of the court, and, more recently, the various sorts of ideological work being done through the representations of Arthur and his knights as images of Englishness. Interest in the matter of Britain was a product of the Norman conquest, and Arthur's court was replete with Christian imagery and morality. The *Gawain*-poet quickly establishes the continental origin of Arthur's reign, opening the poem with a conventional romance topos of *translatio imperii*, tracing the foundation of Britain back through Felix Brutus to Aeneas and the scattered seed of Troy. Courtly manners are seamed with the lexicon of courtly love and verse romance: Arthur will sit for his New Year's feast until someone tells, "Of sum aventurus thing an uncouthe tale, / Of sum mayn mervayl that he might trowe" (lines 93–94). A marvel and an adventure: the two key terms that set a romance narrative in motion, here demanded by Arthur as if he knows the conventions by heart. Still, the Anglo-Saxon words that stand out in each line, "uncouthe" ("strange") and "trowe" ("believe in") hint that Arthur's courtly wishes may not precisely coincide with his local reactions to them. When the Green Knight appears, the knights let Arthur speak first, "for cortaysye" (line 247); Arthur addresses him as "Sir cortays knight" (line 276). The Green Knight's use of the term is almost mocking, bracketed in pure dialect: "And here is kyd cortaysye, as I have herd carp"— "and here is knighthood renowned, as is noised in my ears" as Tolkien's translation has it (line 263), capturing the diction and the alliterative interplay between "kyd" ("renowned"), "cortaysye" and "carp" ("noised"), but losing the sharp aural difference between the blunt and harsh local pair and the long, sonorous imported term sandwiched between them.

The encounters between Gawain and the lady of the knight who shelters him on his quest are similarly punctuated by courtly vocabulary. Trysting with Gawain in his bed, the lady taunts his refusal of her favors: "So good as Gawayn gaynly is holden, / And cortaysye is closed so clene in himselven, / Couth not lightly have lenged so long with a lady / Bot he had craved a cosse by his cortaysye" (lines 1298–1301). When Gawain and the lord exchange their winnings, Gawain kisses him, saying, "'Tas yow there my chevisaunce, I cheved no more" (line 1391); alliterating the multisyllabic courtly term for winnings or merchandise, "chevisaunce," with the monosyllabic verb from which it derives, "cheved," meaning "acquire or bring about." At the lady's second visit, she tempts the knight with recourse to the discourse of courtly love, wondering rhetorically how someone "So cortays, so knightyly, as ye are knowen oute" could be ignorant of the signs of love, the true essence of knighthood. And at the third tryst, when the lady persuades him to accept her green silk belt, that it might preserve him from harm, "He wolde it prayse at more pris, paraventure" (line 1851), the poet uses a triple alliteration of Romance words: two forms of "prize," the courtly term for the value of one's love, and "peradventure," reminding the audience of the test Gawain has just failed.

Copyright © 2009 Pearson Education, Inc. Publishing as Longman.

The Green Knight

When teaching a poem in translation, even a translation that attempts to capture the alliterative meter as Tolkien's does, there is only so much weight you can place on specific words and linguistic choice. The deliberate interplay between courtly and uncouth, Christian and pagan, continental and English comes into play at least as much on a thematic level, however, for the figure of the Green Knight bursts onto the scene as an indigenous and atavistic challenge to the imported culture. Putter stresses the poem's concern with "trawþe," the Anglo-Saxon term for truthfulness and faithfulness familiar from the warrior code of *Beowulf*, and relates it to the Peasants' Revolt of 1381, which challenged pre-ordained hierarchies and pushed society toward a contractual basis. It does not seem too far-fetched to see in the Green Knight's bursting onto the scene of Arthur's court a reflection of the disruptive force of the Peasants' Revolt. Neither is there any need to limit his meaning to such a historical reference, however; what is so compelling about this figure is the way he embodies excess as a principle, in all its diverse forms. Still, there is little doubt that these forms are united in their identification within the poem with indigenously English, pagan, and natural qualities.

The Green Knight has been identified by Brian Stone in his translation of the poem (1972) with "the jovial demon of old popular tradition," or with Job's Satan, and by others with the disruptive force of carnival, refusing to be serious; with the rural pagan deity, the Green Man, who personified spring and life resurgent; or with related figures from village festivals such as Jack in the Green or the Wild Man (and here he can be usefully compared with the less expansive figure of Bisclavret in Marie de France's *lai*, a pagan force that threatens to disrupt another Christian court). Some critics stress the Green Knight's pagan qualities; others note how conversant he is with the customs of courtly life and Christianity, and the ways in which the poem in the end assimilates him to a Christian model as some form of avatar of Christ. What all agree on is his originality as a literary invention and his poetic force as a character—there is nothing else quite like him, and like all great villains he threatens to outshine the hero of the poem.

One way to include all of these possibilities within his expansive frame is to recall the medieval propensity to conceive of character in conjunction with ideas in a structural setting, to compose narrative as a place of social testing rather than a sequence of cause and effect that exists in order to be followed out to its inevitable conclusion. Just as Arthur's court provides a narrative space for outlining ideas that conform to current social norms through a conventional set of situations and settings, so the Green Knight vividly personifies a set of ideas, values, and traditions with no self-evident place in that court. The various disjunctions in theme and tone that many have noted—realism and moral seriousness on the one hand and marvel and fantasy on the other; the straightforwardness of the courtly code versus the trickster behavior of the Green Knight—can be accounted for as a rendering into narrative of the disjunctions in cultural life between the demands

Copyright © 2009 Pearson Education, Inc. Publishing as Longman.

and constraints of Christianity and continental ethics on the one hand and folk beliefs and traditions on the other.

The Green Knight's ambiguity and moral equivocalness—he sets up Gawain for death, leads him into temptation, and then saves him—are consistent with representations of the Christian devil in his more popular incarnations (rather than in his later Jesuitical identity as the prince of darkness). The devil has consistently embodied temptation, power, and autonomy in such a way that they seduce even as they are meant to repel (compare, for instance, the way Satan steals the show in Scene 1 of *The Play of Adam*, Vol. B, p. 875). One reason for this ambivalent portrayal is that the figure of Satan was a key repository for preserving the memory of pagan deities for whom no other place could be found in the restrictive Christian pantheon. The Green Knight's alienness is perhaps strongest in his first appearance, to the description of which the poet devotes a full 85 lines, in language that is composed equally of horror and of admiration. "For many marvels had they seen, but to match this nothing," translates Tolkien (line 239); the word for "marvel" is not the Old French cognate but the English "sellyes"—a local apparition.

The Green Knight is closest to a Satanic figure in the concluding encounter, where he will requite the blow Gawain had given him, in "a worn barrow on a brae by the brink of a water" (line 2173). This is a traditional entrance to the Celtic Other World, but for Gawain an entrance to Hell: "Here the Devil might say, I ween, / his matins about midnight!" (lines 2188–2189). The poem makes it clear, however, that Gawain misrecognizes as evil a site that is far more ambiguous, for the surprise sprung by the poem at its climax forces the knight and the readers who have identified with him somehow to reconcile the monstrous Green Knight with the courtly lord and lady who had housed him so hospitably, the test of the beheading game with the test of the lady's temptations, and the lady with Merlin's erstwhile lover, the sorceress Morgan le Fay, Arthur's half-sister. Just as the Knight, now no longer a monstrous apparition, but naming himself Bertilak de Hautdesert, greets Gawain's weakness with a dismissive laugh, so the infernal opposition to the court appears rather something like a supernatural mirror-image, its customs both nobler and stranger than those of Arthur's round table.

Theme and Structure

Sir Gawain and the Green Knight is intricately and elegantly structured around a series of mirrorings and balancings. Structural and formal symmetry are characteristic both of the ring composition of oral epic and of medieval romance, where they also reflect a belief in the beauty of God's design of nature. The two poles of the poem are Arthur's court and the Grene Chapel. The two courts also happen to be, as Burrow (*A Reading*, 1966) has noted, carefully situated by the physical details of Gawain's journey in south England and Cheshire, respectively. So, while the Green Knight's domain may exist in the realm of the Other World where all quests

Copyright © 2009 Pearson Education, Inc. Publishing as Longman.

are resolved, it also is located in a far more physically real way than the eternal present of Arthur's Britain. Not only does the Green Knight appear as if in response to Arthur's demand for a wonder, but his bizarre Beheading Game is reciprocal both in its demand for a blow to the neck to be given and then received and in its demand that Gawain journey from one court to the other to fulfill his part of the bargain, one New Year to the next. The entire poem is thus structured around a single exchange.

The first *fitt*, or part, concludes with the Knight leaving, bleeding head held high; the second *fitt* recounts Gawain's departure on All-Souls' Day (November 2), his journey, and his arrival at the knight's castle, which appears as if in response to his prayers, in time to hear Christmas Mass. The third *fitt* tells of what scholars call "The Exchange of Winnings," the three days of hunting that lead up to the New Year's beheading. Much has been written detailing the strict parallelism of the lord's hunting and Gawain's play with his lady, and the possible meanings of the three quarries of deer, boar, and fox; the poem fairly demands such an analysis by the way the two men themselves label it. Moreover, hunting and lovemaking were the two activities sanctioned for the courtly knight, and their metaphorical equality was a commonplace of love lyric and romance. In Gottfried von Strassburg's *Tristan*, for example, the young man first proves his nobility by his intimate knowledge of how to butcher a deer and dress the remains for best effect at court. A similar realism of detail is in evidence in *Gawain* in the lengthy description of the rituals of butchering and presentation (lines 1324–1362).

There is, to be sure, a contrast between this violence in nature and the intimate interaction within Gawain's bedroom—"Thus laykes the lord by lyndewodes eves, / And Gawayn the good mon in gay bed lyes" (lines 1179–1180)—but the contrast serves more to stress Gawain's uncomfortable position as the prey than to distinguish the two events. His eventual sin, after all, is one of passive acceptance rather than active commission, and here, as elsewhere, the poem's symmetry causes jarring moments to stand out. For all his perfection as a knight in Arthur's court, and for all his bravery, Gawain is caught by the lady and then by the lord. He is sent home shamefaced to his own king to be comforted for the "token of untrauthe" (line 2511) he has brought with him and which the court adopts to keep him company. The parallelism leads to a paradoxical comparison of the two courts that is quite difficult to resolve one way or another, except perhaps to say, as with similar comparisons in Marie's *Lais*, that one court reflects the fantastic extremes while the other is meant to stand in for the real one.

In an example of ring composition, the middle two *fitts* balance each other in relating Gawain's arrival at and rest in the castle and then his game there with the lady; they also relate the quest narrative and an interlude in that narrative, taking Gawain from one court to the Grene Chapel. The first and fourth *fitts* provide the poem's adventure and its resolution, the two halves of the Beheading Game. While the formal symmetry of the poem is striking, what is

Copyright © 2009 Pearson Education, Inc. Publishing as Longman.

even more noteworthy is the way this symmetry heightens the mystery of its themes and ambiguities rather than resolving them. In what way can we regard Gawain's behavior as exemplary? Has he achieved or failed in his quest, or both at once? Are Bertilak de Hautdesert and Morgan le Fay villainous or chivalrous, friend or foe, pagan or Christian? The *Gawain*-poet found an ideal style and theme for bringing together the antinomies of the society the poet inhabited and the audience for whom he or she composed. Rather than seek a full resolution of those antinomies, however, he or she seems to have preferred the more resonant form of the New Year's mystery, able to be parsed, analyzed, and appreciated but not fully explained.

Peter Abelard and Heloïse

The twelfth-century correspondence between Peter Abelard and his erstwhile lover, the abbess Heloïse, is both a document of one of the most extraordinary and sensational affairs of medieval Europe and a fascinating demonstration of the medieval art of letter writing. Originally composed in Latin, the letters were not published until the 1270s, when they were translated by Jean de Meun, who also included the first account of the affair in his continuation of the *Roman de la rose* (lines 8729– 8802; his description of Abelard's castration was one of the instances in which his language was accused of obscenity); however, it is likely that the letters circulated privately before that time. The literary interest of the letters, coupled with the refusal to accept that a woman was capable of such a high level of rhetorical skill in Latin, has led over the years to suspicions of forgery, but most scholars today accept their authenticity. The correspondence is a virtuoso exercise in multilevel argument through citation and allusion around an emotionally charged past.

The style of the correspondence, seamed with citations, exempla, and commentary, demonstrates the degree to which what are now purely academic tropes were in the Middle Ages a vital means of making meaning. The subtlety of the call and response of allusion is noteworthy, although not unprecedented. Nor was it entirely anodyne, for much of the give-and-take between the pair concerns the propriety of the classical allusions that they interweave with the biblical as well as the particular biblical moments chosen. After all, this is an abbot and an abbess who are corresponding, and the appropriateness or inappropriateness of a particular allusion was a fraught subject. In his *Historia Calamitatum*, Abelard recalled that at the moment she unwillingly took up the veil in obedience to his wishes, Heloïse had quoted the famous lament of Cornelia at the defeat in battle of her husband Pompey: "What prompted me to marry you and bring about your fall? / Now claim your due, and see me gladly pay" (Lucan, *Pharsalia*, 8.94)—a singularly inappropriate outburst at the moment she is being wedded to Christ. In her second letter, Heloïse cited an earlier passage from the same Roman epic about desiring blindness in the future. In the final of so-called "Personal Letters," Abelard rebukes Heloïse in frustration at her persistence: "I beg you, beware lest Pompey's reproach

Copyright © 2009 Pearson Education, Inc. Publishing as Longman.

to weeping Cornelia is applied to you, to your shame: 'The battle ended, Pompey the Great / Lives, but his fortune died. It is this you now mourn / And loved'" (*Pharsalia* 8.84–85). For Abelard, the past is cut off as irrevocably as the organ that embodied its excesses; for Heloïse, there is a necessary continuity of past with the present, including the classical texts that would have been a primary teaching material when he was her tutor and lover.

The argument is simultaneously personal, rhetorical, philosophical, and theological. Rather than engage Abelard in his specialty, the *disputatio*, where reason is set against reason in a dialectic, Heloïse counters his recourse to reason with the discourse of passion. "For nothing is less under our control than the heart–having no power to command it we are forced to obey": these are the words with which she concedes to Abelard's demands in order to be allowed to continue corresponding (Letter 5, p. 1014). As her heart maintains a passionate link with the past he has severed himself from, so she will allow him to overrule that heart only because he commands it, not because he has persuaded her with his logic. To her expressive rhetoric, he responds with a flat, factual tone of argument; to her insistence on the continuing presence of the past, he insists that it has been converted into a Christian narrative of sin overcome by Providence; to her continuing love, he counters his vanished lust. This is no simple battle of the sexes, however; both of them are arguing in the highly polished written Latin of the educated elite.

Heloïse quite consciously framed her arguments as a repudiation of Abelard's theology. In *Sic et Non* (*Yes and No*), Abelard had argued that the Church fathers could be demonstrated to contradict one another on any doctrinal issue; consequently, the only rational answers were to be found through the tools of reason and logic. Their dispute rehearses the debate between Realism and Nominalism (see the discussion of the *Roman de la rose* above). For the Nominalists, words were based in the reality of individual phenomena and thus corresponded to the things they signified, even to the articles of Christian faith; for Abelard, the Trinity expressed God's power, wisdom, and benignity in such a way as could be understood by any intelligent individual. For the Realists, words referred to an external, ideal reality in comparison to which they were wholly inadequate; for Bernard of Clairvaux (whence his doctrinal difference with Abelard) the Trinity was an expression of the essential mystery of faith and in itself had no intelligible meaning. Where Abelard applies the principles of Nominalism to love, making his current lack of feeling contingent upon a situation brought about and remedied through purely physical means, Heloïse is a Realist, refusing to reduce the mystery of love to rational categories or to the constraints of temporality.

In her application of a religious doctrine to the profane phenomenon of love, however, Heloïse was consciously and radically heterodox, for her passion led not to a realization of the divine but toward a lost unity with her lover. When she begs him to respond to her first letter–"I beg you to restore your presence to me in the way you can–by writing to me some word of comfort, so that in this at least I may find increased strength and readiness to serve God"–she is in a way setting him up as a mystery in himself. Abelard responds with the standard rhetoric of the con-

Copyright © 2009 Pearson Education, Inc. Publishing as Longman.

verted Christian, dead to whatever he had known before. The contradiction, which Heloïse subtly but pointedly draws out, is that his insistence on her foregoing the past is refusing her request for Christian charity, leaving her in a sense unconfessed and thus damned for her sins of intention. Heloïse's religion is derived from Abelard's ethics of intentions, which held that actions can be judged only by the intentions with which they were carried out, not by their results. Abelard's ascetic credo seeks to negate the intention of their past love and refuses to believe that that love could persist in a new context. Instead, he recasts that love in material terms as an Ovidian seduction.

While their respective attitudes are easily recognizable in myriad contemporary "she said/he said" arguments, the conventional gender roles are also readily adaptable to the task of working through the dilemmas presented by their new positions as abbot and abbess, just as their prior carnal relations were equally imbued with the pleasures of *lectio* and *disputatio*, commentary and argument. How can the emotions of passion and love be expressed in the context of Christian chastity? Where the lyric tradition found itself addressing this question through the compression of metaphor, and the mystical tradition through the medium of paradox and ecstatic vision, for Abelard and Heloïse, their very lives enacted the dilemma. Heloïse pointedly recalls Abelard's talents as a Goliard, or wandering cleric and love poet and pleads with him to carry over those gifts into the sacred sphere. The lament of David for Jonathan included in the *Anthology* can be interpreted as his response to this dilemma, fruit of the compromise he and Heloïse reached in their letters.

As a twelfth-century woman, there were limited options for Heloïse if she desired to participate in the intellectual fervor of her time, something her mind and character had clearly prepared her to do. It is evident throughout her letters that the dependence on Abelard was not only emotional but also intellectual—his success as a philosopher and theologian had allowed her to participate vicariously in the heart of the twelfth-century renaissance. The selection from *Yes and No* gives some of the flavor of Abelard's dialectic; the letters of Bernard of Clairvaux included in the Resonance section demonstrate the degree to which that method was perceived as a threat by many Church authorities. After all, as M. T. Clanchy has observed in *Abelard: A Medieval Life* (1997), Abelard was the first "theologian" in the modern sense, using the term *theology* to mean the reconciliation of human reason with Christian revelation. The issues dealt with by Abelard and Heloïse through the medium of their tragic relationship can provide an instructive lens through which to view the interrelationship between love lyric, classical literature, Scholasticism, the Goliards, monasticism, and theology in two exemplary twelfth-century lives.

The Play of Adam

Contemporary with the lives of Abelard and Heloïse, *The Play of Adam* (*Le Jeu d'Adam*) provides quite a different perspective on the popular perception of religion. Composed in the same Anglo-Norman dialect that Marie de France would

Copyright © 2009 Pearson Education, Inc. Publishing as Longman.

use later in the century, the play would have been performed outside a church for a lay audience, with lessons and chanted responses in Latin (as are the stage directions). Medieval scholars have devoted much attention recently to the theater, in particular for the glimpse it provides into the popular culture and society that are less immediately evident in medieval narrative. The Latin title given the play in the sole surviving thirteenth-century paper manuscript, *Order for the Representation of Adam* (*Ordo representacionis Ade*), should remind us that there was not yet any conception of theater in the modern sense of the word. The performance combined verse, miming, and music and would have been elaborately staged. As Wolfgang von Emden discusses in the introduction to his edition (1996), the play borrows from liturgical sources. Scene 1 ("Adam and Eve," included in the *Anthology*) and Scene 2 ("Cain and Abel") borrow the *lectio*, or reading, and responsories of Matins for Septuagesima, or seventy days, the third Sunday before Lent and ninth before Easter; Scene 3, the procession of Prophets, derives from a *lectio* for the end of Advent, the Sunday before Christmas, or for Christmas itself. Combining material from two wholly different seasons suggests that the author conceived of the play as a free-standing work, independent of a particular occasion. And, although it has at times been labeled a "Mystery," there is no evidence that the three scenes as we have them once comprised part of a full-fledged cycle, as later in the Middle Ages.

First-time readers of the play are often struck by the combination of high moral seriousness—the drama of the Genesis stories, the Latin of the lessons and responsories—with the colloquial tone and popular characterizations of the characters of Adam, Eve, God, and the Devil. As Erich Auerbach put it in his still-instructive chapter on the play in *Mimesis* (1946), "Adam calls his wife to account as a French farmer or burgher might have done when, upon returning home, he saw something that he did not like." Adam admonishes her in the rhyming octosyllabic couplets typical of Old French verse:

> *Nel laisser mais venir sor toi*
> *Car il est mult de pute foi.*
> *Il volt traïr ja son seignor,*
> *E soi pose al des halzor.* (lines 289–292)

> Don't let him come near you again!
> He's not a person one can trust;
> He wanted to betray his master,
> And put himself in high command.

Indicative of the colloquial tone is the adjective *pute*, which means "stinking, dirty, or infected," and, by extension, "evil"; during the early twelfth century it had also taken on the meaning of "whore," which persists in the modern French *putain*. Indicative of the popular characterization is the adaptation of the temptation scene to a feudal context. Adam labels Satan a disloyal vassal and wants nothing to

Copyright © 2009 Pearson Education, Inc. Publishing as Longman.

do with him. Eve, by contrast, is shown to be susceptible to the courtly tones of the flatterer's tongue.

Such contrasts rendered arcane material accessible to a popular and unlettered audience, cloaking, as medieval writers would have it, bitter kernels of wisdom in the honey of fable. Spectacle played its part, too, in the costumes and in the setting, with the hellmouth the apogee of the scenarist's art, and Satan and the devils playing the fools and stealing the show. The awesome splendor of the Church in all its glory could not be forgotten, either—and this is the context that students may need to be reminded of. The interior of the church or cathedral itself, tallest building in the town, would serve as Paradise, with God entering and exiting by the porch on its western end. The words of the chanted Latin responsories would not have been understood by most of the audience, but their beauty and the association with services heard within the church would powerfully recall the divine backdrop of the play. The Play of Adam thus enacts in its various apparent clashes of register a negotiation between the demands and pleasures of everyday life and the demands and pleasures of the Church. The physical location on the threshold between these two places stages this negotiation. In this sense, Satan offers the temptation of a wide and easily comprehensible bridge between low and high; the salvation offered by God, by contrast, is narrow, harsh, and sublime, grounded in the theme of obedience but voiced in beautiful laments by Adam and Eve.

It is not difficult to see the author of the play striving for a dramatic form able to encompass both aspects of medieval life. It would be too simple to say that the play translates the social relations in Genesis into a feudal arrangement. Rather, the feudal system provides a space midway between the twelfth-century Anglo-Norman world and the Garden of Eden. The bond of fealty would grant the vassal a fief in return for service to his lord; God grants Adam and Eve the custodianship of Paradise in return for their promise not to eat of the forbidden tree. Like the lord's castle, the Church is a space into which the populace is invited periodically in order to observe a ritualized ceremony. Like most medieval allegories, however, one scheme does not quite fit the other. The events of Genesis retain a mythic distance in spite of the feudal analogy. This is not accidental: the allegorical intention is generally more to make comprehensible and accessible an otherwise distant mystery than to reduce it to something mundane. So, The Play of Adam works as a didactic morality play, presenting biblical doctrine as a fable with contemporary strokes and lots of spectacle, but it is also a sophisticated negotiation of popular and doctrinal religion, French and Latin, sacred and profane, for a diverse audience ranging from members of the court to the local serfs.

Dante Alighieri

It has long been said of Dante's *Commedia* that it constitutes a *summa* of medieval culture. This is true, but what is startling about the poem, and what enthralls readers to this day, is that it did not simply summarize the world around it but also

Copyright © 2009 Pearson Education, Inc. Publishing as Longman.

placed diverse and often contradictory disciplines in dialogue with each other, as if the enormous tension generated by the clashing modes of thought and styles of writing could achieve what nothing else could: reproduce the perfection of divine truth in the fallen medium of the written word. The physical and metaphysical worship of the courtly lyric, the obscenity of the *fabliaux*, the irreverence of the Goliards, the piety of the hymnist, the dramatic staging of the theater, the syllogisms of the Scholastics, the pagan wisdom of the ancients, the popular piety of the otherworld vision, the spiritual autobiography of Augustine, the narrative drive and situational ethics of the romance, the investigative curiosity of the natural philosopher, the vituperative warnings of the prophet, the invective of the satirist, the visionary intensity of the mystic—these and many other forms are all given their proper place in Dante's afterlife.

Criticism and Reception

Perhaps even more than Shakespeare studies in English, Dante studies, by virtue of the man's utter dominance of Italian literature, are a world of their own. *The Cambridge Companion to Dante* (ed. Rachel Jacoff, 1993; 2nd ed., 2008) provides a reasonably current introduction to the major categories of the field. The eight volumes of *Dante: The Critical Complex* (ed. Richard Lansing, 2003) cull the best of many years of critical writing. Particularly noteworthy volumes in the American tradition of Dante studies are the essays collected in John Freccero's *Dante: The Poetics of Conversion* (1986) and Teodolinda Barolini's *The Undivine Comedy* (1992), among other things a rejoinder to Freccero's reading. Both the University of California Press and the University of Pennsylvania Press have published a series of volumes devoted each to a single canto of the *Inferno*. Multiple commentaries also exist. Particularly useful are Charles Singleton's volumes, less for their fairly sparse (and often tendentious) interpretation than for their generous selections of sources for particular passages, both in the original language and in translation. The Dartmouth Dante Database provides a line-by-line searchable database of the full-text *Commedia* and some 60 commentaries dating from ca. 1322 to the present: http://dante.dartmouth.edu/. To give students a sense of the degree to which Dante remains a seminal source for writers, *The Poet's Dante* (eds. Peter S. Hawkins and Rachel Jacoff, 2001), a collection of essays of poets from modernists to the present day, is especially illuminating. Also noteworthy is *Dante's Inferno: Translations by Twenty Contemporary Poets* (ed. Daniel Halperin, 1993).

Dante's imagination has inspired many artists; some of these are represented on the Digital Dante website (http://dante.ilt.columbia.edu/) and Peter Chou and Prof. John Freccero's Dante Resources on the Internet (http://www.wisdomportal.com/Dante/DanteResources.html). Students may be familiar with the celebrated late-fifteenth-century drawings by the Florentine artist Sandro Botticelli, the iconic nineteenth-century illustrations by Gustave Doré, or the marvelously idiosyncratic ones of William Blake. Of more recent artists, Robert Rauschenberg

Copyright © 2009 Pearson Education, Inc. Publishing as Longman.

and Tom Phillips have produced especially memorable contributions to the visual tradition of the *Inferno*.

Dante's Lexicon

Perhaps the greatest difficulty—which is also the greatest pleasure—in teaching the *Inferno* (and, to a lesser degree, the other two canticles of the poem) is distracting students from their sheer engagement with the poem's gripping details to examine what exactly is going on and why. One way to link these two aspects of reading the poem is to lay out the various aspects of Dante's lexicon. Like many medieval writers, but to a far greater degree, Dante weaves together a tissue of keywords, issues, images, places, events, allusions, citations, and autobiography that accrue meaning as the poem progresses. A good place to start from are those works the students may already have read in Volume A of the *Anthology*: the hero of Homer's *Odyssey* (although Dante knew the poem only at second-hand) makes a startling and seminal appearance in Canto 26 of the *Inferno*; Virgil and his *Aeneid* are a key intertext on many different levels; the role of Ovid's *Metamorphoses* is more implicit but nearly as important to Dante's poetics as Virgil's epic. Limbo (*Inferno* 4), where Dante puts the virtuous pagans (including several medieval figures), includes many familiar authorities: the Old Testament patriarchs; the poets Homer, Horace, and Ovid; the heroes Hector, Aeneas, Caesar, and Latinus; the Greek philosophers; the more recent Avicenna and Averroës. The fifth canto, describing the circle of the Lustful, includes Dido, Cleopatra, Helen, Achilles, Paris, and the Briton Tristan. Muhammed and Ali are punished in the eighth circle among the Schismatics; there too is the troubadour Bertran de Born. And in *Paradiso* 31, students will encounter the twelfth-century abbot and mystic Bernard de Clairvaux.

As this partial list makes evident, Dante's use of the past is highly syncretic: he mixes together pagan and Christian, classical and medieval, mythic and historical figures. Moreover, he often conflates authors with their works. There is no simple system here, but neither is there a simple mishmash; rather, Dante's allegorical framework allows him to consider these different categories on a single plane without eliding all differences between them—patterns may not be immediately in evidence but can nearly always be found. Odysseus in *Inferno* 26 is a good example: he is consciously paired with the shade who dominates the following canto, the thirteenth-century Ghibelline leader Guido da Montefeltro, setting up a series of parallels and contrasts between the two. The comparison is made explicit only in the structural sense that the two figures are juxtaposed as being punished for the same sin, appearing in adjacent cantos with a comparable amount of time "on stage," as it were. There are many formal and thematic parallels to be drawn out as well—almost infinite, in fact, for Dante's poem in many ways aspires to the status of a divine work, susceptible to endless exegesis.

Certain formative events, historical figures, and political issues recur throughout the poem as Dante wrestles with their meaning in different contexts and through

Copyright © 2009 Pearson Education, Inc. Publishing as Longman.

different actors: the arch-villain of the poem, Pope Boniface VIII; the battle of Montaperti; the Hohenstaufen dynasty; the corruption of Florence; the conflict between Church and Empire; the role of pagan authorities in Christian culture. The poem is by no means inert on questions of doctrine, either; for nearly every section of each part of the afterlife includes at least one heterodox move by Dante, some of them flagrantly so, like the special "no-place" reserved for the neutral shades or the eternal damnation of particularly heinous sinners before they are yet dead.

The poem signals these issues situationally rather than discursively, relying both on the reader's prior knowledge and on the particular skills accrued through the experience of reading the poem. The ideal reader would possess (as we assume Dante and his more educated contemporaries did), among other things, an intimate and encyclopedic knowledge of the Latin classics, of Scripture, and of the Church fathers; a detailed familiarity with every aspect of medieval knowledge and literature, from science and philosophy to theology and mysticism to lyric and romance to popular fable and folklore; a personal investment in the intricate politics of Florence, Italy, and Western Europe; a passing knowledge of Arabic literature and philosophy (as much as was available in translation); and an awareness of Dante's prior writings. All that was lacking was Greek, which was known only through citations in the Latin corpus, although any self-respecting medieval scholar was highly conscious of this lack. Dante's readers are expected to do more, too, for the poem transmutes its sources into active participants in the poem; indeed, even without the requisite knowledge listed above, attentive readers (with the help at times of plentiful annotation and commentary) will quickly become familiar with the inner dynamics of the poem, with the lexicon that the *Commedia*'s structure actively instructs them in how to read.

Form and Structure

Like any literary artifact, the *Commedia* reinforces, deepens, and complicates its meanings by structural mirroring and play between its elements. Like any medieval artifact, that structural mirroring and play take the place usually reserved in modern literature for the psychological depth and chain of cause and effect associated with realism. In the *Commedia*, the explicit framework guides and refines this effect further, urging the reader to seek similarities and differences between the three canticles of *Inferno*, *Purgatorio*, and *Paradiso*; between identical cantos of each canticle; between cantos within each canticle; within cantos; and through the language and rhyme scheme. Moreover, the physical structure of the worlds Dante has invented also encourages comparison between the broad similarities of circles (and then terraces and heavens) and the specific differences within each one. The use of an overall principle of punishment, the *contrapasso*, creates an interpretive system (subsequently refined for the punishments in Purgatory and the rewards in Paradise), while the endless variation within the overall system encourages distinction.

As Barolini has formulated it, the poem oscillates between the two poles of a Platonic (or Augustinian) unity and an Aristotelian (or Aquinian) differentiation.

Copyright © 2009 Pearson Education, Inc. Publishing as Longman.

The same tension also governs the theological play between a divine cosmos unified in its expression of God's omnipotence, omniscience, and benevolence—a world purportedly glimpsed in a moment's ecstatic vision—and a temporal, fallen, and fragmented world—the way things look from the flawed perspective of humanity and the earthly representational form of language.

The poem's time scheme reinforces this tension between temporality, linearity, history, and narrative on the one hand and eternity, circularity, repetition, and non-narrative on the other. On the one hand, the poem is dynamic and dramatic, narrating the journey of the character Dante through Hell, Purgatory, and Paradise to God, and back to earth. The journey through Hell, we are told, occurs in real time, occupying the seventy-two hours between Thursday and Sunday morning of Easter weekend in the year 1300, when the poet would have been thirty-five years old. On the other hand, the matter of the poem, the vision it relates, is eternal; by definition there is no change in the afterlife. There is a tension inherent to this dialectic, a tension that makes palpable in narrative terms a key theological crux familiar from Augustine's *Confessions* between free will (the doctrine that held each person responsible for his or her actions) and predestination (the doctrine that held God to have foreknowledge of all that was to pass in the world he had created). That same tension also helps render into narrative the poetic crux of the work: how to unpack temporally the inspiration of a moment's glimpse of truth. Put another way, Dante divides the work of his poem between its human and its divine aspects. One effect of this division, as Barolini has explained, is to make it appear as if God is the author of a major part of what Dante himself created (or, if we credit him with a mystical vision, what he, like Hildegard, took on himself to give intelligible form to).

A further consequence of this structure is that whenever there is a clash between the two systems of representation, that clash will be perceived by the reader in narrative rather than in theological or poetic terms. We wonder if Dante is in any peril from the shades or the monsters of Hell; we get incensed at the treatment of certain shades (classically, Francesca, Brunetto Latini, Ulysses, and Ugolino); we debate whether certain shades belong where they are put rather than elsewhere and whether certain sins are really worse than others from a circle higher up; we are outraged that Virgil must be damned, and we search for clues as to his eventual salvation. Dante makes his authorial choices into dramatic plot points, pulling us further and further into the world of a poem that seems more real the more we argue with it. Our own reactions are *intended*, incorporated into the design of the poem; the more we incorporate those reactions into our interpretation, the more the artistry and complexity of the poem reveal themselves to us.

Conversion

The goal of Dante's labor is conversion: of the reader into a good Christian, learning what to embrace and what to shun, as Freccero put it, and of an earthly artifact into a divine creation, as Barolini has it. In both cases, Dante conceived of conver-

Copyright © 2009 Pearson Education, Inc. Publishing as Longman.

sion as a dynamic rather than a static process. In his theology, only a person who had thoroughly grasped the allure of sin and comprehended the full range and capacity of evil in the world would be in a proper state of mind to appreciate the greater good of the divine plan that incorporated them within itself. The character of Dante within the poem duplicates the tension discussed earlier, for the author borrowed from Augustine the temporal structure of the narrative of conversion—the saved soul recounts in retrospect the steps whereby he found his way back to God, while recording at each stage exactly how his state of ignorance felt at the time.

It can be helpful in discussing the poem to distinguish between Dante-pilgrim, the benighted soul who loses his way in a dark wood, and Dante-poet, recounting how he was saved from the vantage point of a safe return from danger. The point of view of Dante-pilgrim allows the unconverted reader to experience the process of conversion firsthand; the point of view of Dante-poet allows a safety net of reassurance and a didactic voice able to interpret the meaning of what he had blundered into first time around. What complicates the scheme further is that both points of view are dynamic rather than discursive. When Dante-pilgrim faints upon hearing Francesca's moving story of her plight, Dante-poet does not simply tell us this is bad; rather, he allows the textual dynamics of the poem to do so—if Francesca is damned, what she describes must have been sinful, and it is up to us to use the clues given to uncover the precise contours of that damnation, including the resonant concluding verse of the canto: "*E caddi come corpo morto cade.*" It may also be useful to keep in mind (although not always necessary for students to consider) two other "Dantes" to distinguish from the two stages of the character Dante: the historical Dante who had a vision of the otherworld (or the poetic inspiration to invent such a vision) and the Dante-author who set about giving poetic form to that vision.

The doubleness of conversion does not stop with Dante himself, however; each character encountered, especially in Hell, should also be regarded doubly. On the one hand, we have the personality and history as presented by each character in his or her dramatic monologue or dialogue with Dante-pilgrim. On the other hand, we have our foreknowledge of that character's historical identity and/or prior literary depictions, as well as the way in which he or she is framed and presented within the narrative by Dante-poet. Within the conversionary dynamic of the poem, damned souls are not to be trusted, however pitiful or seductive they may appear, and even though Dante may go out of his way to make them appear so. It can be assumed that these dramatic moments identify the sins Dante considers to be most dangerous and/or pernicious; at other times, his poem appears to settle for rank dismissal. In either case, there is no question that the *Inferno* in particular is structured around moments of high drama. These are also the episodes on which instructors with a limited allotment of time will probably choose to focus (see the section on "Selections and Strategies" below).

Besides Dante, the only other character in the *Inferno* with the ability to move through Hell is Virgil, who is in many ways the dramatic highlight of the poem even more than Dante, the focal point of the feelings of injustice aroused by

Copyright © 2009 Pearson Education, Inc. Publishing as Longman.

Dante's portrayal of the difficult topic of divine justice, unfathomable within the categories of human thought. Virgil is double in character like the other shades in Hell; indeed, he could be said to form an elaboration of the general model. Like the other personifications in Dante's complex allegory, Virgil is a conglomeration of diverse and incommensurate aspects. At various times, and often simultaneously, the character Virgil incorporates the historical Roman poet, the texts of his poems (especially the *Aeneid*), the legendary figure of Virgil the magician and philosopher-sage, the particular Virgil as Dante had read and emulated him, and the exemplum of the virtuous pagan and dutiful citizen of the Roman empire. A damned soul who nevertheless leads Dante to paradise; a trustworthy and reasonable person who inhabits a land where no one is supposed to possess either quality—Virgil's character, to whom the reader becomes more attached the further the poem proceeds, encapsulates the paradoxes essential to Dante's conception of the Christian faith and the meaning of conversion to that faith.

Allegory

That the *Commedia* is allegorical to its very core has never been in doubt; however, the precise nature of that allegory has for many decades been the subject of a heated debate that shows no sign of lessening in the new millennium. Fortunately, teaching the *Commedia* does not require entering any further into this debate than one wishes. Like medieval allegory in general, Dante's poem uses the form not as a symbolic template but as a representational tool to dramatize abstract debate in terms of narrative drama. At the core of the poem's allegory are its primary actors: Dante, Virgil, and Beatrice. The conventional reading would call Dante "Everyman," Beatrice "Faith," and Virgil "Reason" in a dramatization of conversion. This convention is not inaccurate, although when provided with such a simple scheme some students will prefer not to search any further for meaning in the poem. The key is to draw out the diverse qualities with which Dante has chosen to associate these three terms in his poem. Beatrice was a contemporary Florentine woman whom Dante knew and with whom he claims to have been profoundly in love, despite scarcely even having spoken to her. She is a figure refined out of the courtly lyric, especially in the metaphysical form given that lyric by Dante and the other Italian practitioners of the *dolce stil novo*, the "sweet new style" as he coined it in *Purgatorio* 24.57. As is made abundantly clear by the symbolic structure of the *Vita nuova*, Beatrice is also an avatar of Christ, the incarnation of a heavenly spirit come down to earth with the express purpose of Dante's salvation. The fact that her blessed path intersects with that of the damned Virgil only in the brief meeting described by the latter in *Inferno* 2 helps to delineate their proper roles within the allegory. Virgil is an ancient, a pagan, a poet, and a damned soul; he is also learned, virtuous, and, in his poetry, an unknowing prophet of the coming of Christ. His character explores the limits and uses of human reason just as Beatrice dramatizes the role of faith in conversion. Thus, all of their dramatic interactions should be susceptible to interpretation in these terms in addition to their narrative import.

Copyright © 2009 Pearson Education, Inc. Publishing as Longman.

The other principal aspect of allegory worth exploring with students is the temporal component of the four-fold method of allegorical interpretation, the standard mode for expounding the meaning of scripture. There were, of course, many variations, just as there are many issues and debates associated with Dante's combination of personification allegory (which he terms in the letter to Can Grande della Scala the "allegory of poets") and figural allegory (which he terms in the same letter the "allegory of theologians"), but these are the key aspects. In figural interpretation, as Erich Auerbach established in his seminal 1944 essay "Figura" (rpt. in *Scenes from the Drama of European Literature*, 1959), an Old Testament figure or event is revealed to have prefigured an aspect of Christ or the Christian church in the New Testament. The example Dante used in his letter, which is also the scene at the opening of *Purgatorio* where the angel brings the saved souls to the shore of the mountain, is the movement of exodus as recounted in Psalm 105:

> for if we inspect the letter alone the departure of the children of Israel from Egypt in the time of Moses is presented to us; if the allegory, our redemption wrought by Christ; if the moral sense, the conversion of the soul from the grief and misery of sin to the state of grace is presented to us; if the anagogical, the departure of the holy soul from the slavery of this corruption to the liberty of eternal glory is presented to us.

The events of the Old Testament are regarded as literally true but also as having been invested by God with hidden meaning that was revealed only through the mystery of Christ. The event referred to in the psalm is the "literal" meaning; the hidden Christian sense of it is the "allegorical"; together they form a "figure." For those living after Christ, each figure can be shown also to be imbued with a "moral" meaning, applying to life in the world redeemed by Christ, and an "anagogical" meaning, applying to the life to come after death. The four-fold method of interpretation regarded world history as a cosmic allegory of conversion of mankind from sin into redemption through the coming of Christ. Each individual conversion was viewed consequently as following this cosmic model in what was known as the *imitatio Christi*, the imitation of Christ. The *Inferno* rehearses this model when it shows Dante-pilgrim following in the footsteps of Christ's passion—medieval belief held that between the crucifixion and the resurrection, Jesus had descended into hell and "harrowed" it, removing to heaven the Old Testament worthies, physically enacting the process of converting historical characters into allegorical figures.

Autobiography and the *Vita nuova*

"Dante" is the most vexed of the personifications that move through the figural allegory of God's afterlife. On one level, the character is patently anything but universal because, rather than modeling his life after Christ, he is literally following

Copyright © 2009 Pearson Education, Inc. Publishing as Longman.

in his footsteps, the only other person to take this physical journey through the afterlife. Moreover, the accomplishment of this difficult journey authorizes Dante to fulfill a specific task: to record and reveal to the world what he has seen—to be, in other words, a prophet. At the same time, the details of the spiritual autobiography that he provides—a profound, perhaps suicidal despair leading to a vision that gives new meaning to his life—closely follow the contours of the classic conversion narrative, and in this sense, his story can be said to be exemplary, an *imitatio Christi*. On the moral level, which would make Hell a state of mind and the vision of Hell a comprehensive experience of the moral state of the material world, his journey can indeed apply to any Christian, and the dangers he is said to run would represent the risks of mortal sin undergone by a Christian amid the temptations of the world. Similarly, the moral experience of Purgatory would constitute a lesson on how to live in the present world as if one were already headed toward the next, suffering equivalent punishment but always with one's spirit already in Paradise—the fulfillment of the anagogical level of the allegory.

In addition to the allegorical aspect of Dante's autobiography, the poem is also constructed around two key events in his life: the encounter with Beatrice and the exile from Florence. As with other aspects of his work, Dante took a common medieval convention—the genre of the palinode, a work of retrospection, retraction, and reinterpretation of one's past life and writings (see Augustine in Vol. A of the *Anthology* and Abelard and Heloïse in Vol. B for other examples)—and expanded it enormously. The *Vita nuova* was the first step in this process, assembling a corpus of his early lyric work that fit within a seamless narrative of the transformation of a profane impulse into a spiritual one, excluding from that corpus whatever did not fit the new conception. In the form Dante gives it through the metaphor of the Book of Memory, the facts of the past are irrevocably fixed, but just as the events of the Old Testament are transformed by what came after them, so is the past subject to transformation by a new context or new events. The *Vita nuova* is autobiographical to a point, but its scope does not include family, work, duties, most of the urban setting of Florence, and all of its politics, radically delimiting Dante's "life" to ladies and love in a pastoral setting.

Like two of the poets Dante references—the Florentine Guido Cavalcanti and the Bolognese Guido Guinizelli, both of whom play significant roles in the *Commedia* (note the presence of Guinizelli in Francesca's speeches in *Inferno* 5 and the over-determined misunderstanding around Cavalcanti in *Inferno* 10)—the *Vita nuova* is concerned with developing an incarnational poetics, a poetic language that could truthfully describe the transformative effect of love. There is little sense in this work of the social perspective of the *Commedia*. Here, Dante appropriates the language and imagery of the incarnation to represent the Christ-like effect on him of Beatrice; in the *Commedia*, conversely, he reconceived that incarnational poetics to describe the effect of religious conversion. Students may be puzzled by the highly technical way in which Dante glosses or explicates his poems here. The Scholastic approach to the analysis of poetry seems to argue in its pure formality that only through the language of poetry itself can meaning emerge. The conclud-

Copyright © 2009 Pearson Education, Inc. Publishing as Longman.

ing paragraph of the book seems to revise itself yet again, signaling an artistic dead end and the need for a more expansive poetics (a need many readers assume was eventually answered by the *Commedia*).

Before that moment, however, Dante met with the personal tragedy of a lifetime's exile from his native and beloved home of Florence. It is not difficult to see how such a debilitating encounter with hard-nosed politics and intrigue would have been responsible for the conception of a poetic work reaching beyond the proscribed world of the lyric into society at large. It is certainly true that Dante encouraged this reading of his life and work by means of the fundamental role he gives the exile in the *Commedia*, dotting the poem with references to it that grow in explicitness until his ancestor Cacciaguida finally tells him the whole story in the Heaven of Mars:

> Tu lascerai ogne cosa diletta
> più caramente; e questo è quello strale
> che l'arco de lo essilio pria saetta.
> Tu proverai sì come sa di sale
> lo pane altrui, e come è duro calle
> lo scendere e 'l salir per l'altrui scale.
>
> (*Paradiso* 17.55–60)

> You shall leave everything you love most dearly:
> this is the arrow that the bow of exile
> shoots first. You are to know the bitter taste
> of others' bread, how salt it is, and know
> how hard a path it is for one who goes
> descending and ascending others' stairs.
>
> (trans. Allen Mandelbaum)

Indeed, many of the most fascinating moments of the poem involve Dante working through the relationship between the form of the lyric and the individual desires to which its worldview is restricted, and other genres of writing, especially epic, that treat the great movements of history but to the detriment of the individual.

Selections and Strategies

Various strategies can be adopted to solve the problem of teaching the *Inferno* in a limited period of class time. Most common is probably to focus on the framing cantos and the most dramatic encounters: the opening cantos, which set up the entire poem, Cantos 4 and 5 (Limbo and the circle of the Lustful); Canto 10, with the political tragedy of Farinata and Cavalcanti; Canto 15 with Dante's mentor, Brunetto Latini; Cantos 26–27 with Ulysses and Guido da Montefeltro; Cantos 32–33, with the tale of Ugolino (reproduced in a couple of alternate versions in

Copyright © 2009 Pearson Education, Inc. Publishing as Longman.

the Resonances in the *Anthology*), and Canto 34, with the anticlimactic appearance of Satan and the escape from Hell. These cantos allow many of the key themes to be raised; still, it can be fruitful to consider the cantos around them and other episodes as well: the shocking contrast of the sodden gluttons of Canto 6 with the courtly rhetoric of Francesca; Virgil's failure to move the rebel angels in Cantos 8-9; the low comedy of the demons of Malebolge in Cantos 21-23—Dante's version of a *fabliau*; and, certainly, Guido's contrast to Ulysses. Or discussion can follow the poem's urging to reread and revisit, tracing a particular theme or motif. Virgil's character in particular works well thematically.

The extent of Dante's *Nachleben* is scarcely calculable. Chaucer's inclusion of Ugolino's story in "The Monk's Tale" is an early example. The *Inferno* in particular has provided so much of the iconography of Christian hell that the two often feel inseparable, notwithstanding the Jesuits' later attempt to create a hell that was pure fire and brimstone. In particular, Dante's conception of a satirical Hell, full of identifiable figures given punishments suitable to their crimes, has been influential. The English Romantics were particularly enamored of Dante. In addition to his collaborative translation of the Ugolino episode included in the *Anthology*, Shelley's satire of London as Hell in *Peter Bell the Third* may be mentioned. The twentieth century was replete with infernal calques and allusions. All of the modernists made use of Dante; of more recent encounters, Amiri Baraka's *The System of Dante's Hell* (included in the *Anthology*) is an especially radical reworking, while Seamus Heaney and Derek Walcott have made strong use of the poem as a way to think about their own postcolonial contexts in Ireland and Santa Lucia, respectively.

Purgatorio and *Paradiso*

Whenever he wrote or lectured about Dante's *Commedia*, Jorge Luis Borges never failed to cite his favorite lines, the tercet where the poet first describes the shores of Purgatory on "that incredible morning" when the pilgrim "has left the filth, the sadness, and the horror of Hell" (*Seven Nights* 11): "*dolce color d'oriental zaffiro / che s'accoglieva nel sereno aspetto / del mezzo puro infino al primo giro*" (1.13-15). While there will be no way to deal in any comprehensive manner with the concluding canticles of the *Commedia*, a glimpse at them can give students a taste of the longing beauty of *Purgatorio* and the diamond-hard brilliance of *Paradiso*. The selections in the *Anthology* include the framing cantos as well as a representative encounter—enough to allow a general comparison of the three canticles and to suggest some of the ways Dante contrived different pairings between them, giving both unity and difference to the whole.

The opening cantos from *Purgatorio* introduce the new geography, rules, and mood of the mountain purgatory, while the appearance of Cato as the mountain's custodian inexplicably offers a pagan suicide at the gateway to the realm of the blessed. Cantos 29-30 present the dramatic and emotional climax of the entire poem: Beatrice's arrival and Virgil's departure make for a chiasmatic exchange of

Copyright © 2009 Pearson Education, Inc. Publishing as Longman.

guides. Both episodes raise as many questions as they answer. *Purgatorio* 22 provides in a nutshell the scheme of the mountain; it also introduces the minor Latin epic poet Statius, saved while his better Virgil was damned, and through a misreading of the *Aeneid* (22.40–41) no less.

The opening and closing cantos of *Paradiso* likewise frame Dante's mystical ascent to the Heavens, with both Cantos 1 and 33 sparkling with allusions to Ovid, of all people. Canto 3 introduces the idea of the different Heavens and of difference in Heaven; Canto 31 provides a vision of the unity of the celestial rose, the final guide, Bernard of Clairvaux, and the final, transfigured smile of Beatrice. Lest students believe that the two canticles of salvation are any less fraught and heterodox than the *Inferno* and the egregious examples of Cato's precedence over Virgil or Beatrice's arrival in an allegorical procession in the place of Christ be not sufficient to persuade them, there is always the marvelous case of the Italian noblewoman, Cunizza da Romano, who had several husbands and counted among her various lovers the poet Sordello. Her brother, Ezzelino, is damned among the Violent against their Neighbors (*Inferno* 12.109–110), but the apparently unrepentant Cunizza explains to Dante from the Heaven of Venus that ". . . I shine here / because this planet's radiance conquered me. / But in myself I pardon happily / the reason for my fate; I do not grieve— / and vulgar minds may find this hard to see" (*Paradiso* 9.32–36). Dante's Heaven is full of mysteries that serve the cause simultaneously of demonstrating the inscrutability of the divine will and of establishing the validity of Dante's representation of that will.

Marco Polo and Ibn Battuta

Finally and most extensively in this Crosscurrents section, *The Travels of Marco Polo* and *The Travels of Ibn Battuta* work especially well when taught together as they both blend the pleasures of distant adventure with religious, political, and economic concerns. The selections from these works have been chosen to provide direct opportunities for comparison and contrast. You can ask students to compare Polo's and Ibn Battuta's accounts of Kublai Khan's capitol ("Kin-sai" in Polo's account, pp. 1078–1079, "El Khansa" to Ibn Battuta, pp. 530–531), and their versions of the vast mythic bird the rukh or rokh (pp. 531 and 1082). Working outward from these parallel passages, students can discuss the ways in which both Polo and Ibn Battuta find East Asia to be a place of magic and extraordinary adventures, even as both authors pay close attention to detail and seek rational explanations for the things they observe. Students can also compare the sorts of details that each writer finds noteworthy, with Polo's commercial interests more pronounced versus Ibn Battuta's eye for providential patterns seen in his own encounters and in the stories he hears of magical trees and of demons quelled by the Qur'an. These are elements of the sort that we find in the more fanciful tales of *The Thousand and One Nights* (Vol. B, p. 406), but here they are found side by side with Ibn Battuta's sober reports on the storage of rice and on Hindu religious practices such as *suttee* or the self-immolation of widows (p. 523).

Copyright © 2009 Pearson Education, Inc. Publishing as Longman.

Both authors have an uneasy fascination with "idolatrous" practices. Students can debate whether Polo is accurately conveying the Khan's wish to have evidence justifying a conversion to Christianity or whether the Khan is putting him off with a challenge he doesn't expect the Christians to be able to fulfill—to perform miracles that can trump those of the "idolaters" around him (pp. 1076-1078). The Khan, indeed, is shown covering his bases by invoking all major deities, so as to receive the favor of "whichever among them is in truth supreme in heaven" (p. 1077). Polo is firm in his own Christian beliefs, yet believes that the pagan demons and their adepts have great powers of sorcery, able to raise storms or calm the sea at will (p. 1081).

For both Marco Polo and Ibn Battuta, the East is a place of sexual abundance and license. Polo tells of remarkable, gender-specific islands and describes people's scanty clothing in south India; Ibn Battuta goes so far as to describe his own aphrodisiacally enhanced sexual exploits in the same region (p. 528). This erotic Orientalism, common to both the Arab and the Christian writer, can be further discussed in Coleridge's "Kubla Khan" (p. 1082). You can ask students to see how many of the images in the poem have analogs in Polo's (and indeed in Ibn Battuta's) accounts: as for them, for Coleridge the East is a place of danger and erotic attraction, antiquity and timeless allure. At the same time, Coleridge adapts Xanadu in specific ways, turning what was in fact a major metropolis into a dramatic Romantic landscape, itself presented in distinctly sexualized terms.

Coleridge's poem is in part a hymn to the power of poetry itself, and Marco Polo and Ibn Battuta already emphasize poetry and storytelling as powerful forces. Students can look at the various points at which writing plays an important role, as when Ibn Battuta gets himself out of serious trouble over debts by writing a poem of praise to the sultan who has failed to deliver on a promised supply of funds (p. 524). Both works also begin by speaking of their own process of composition, and both narratives were clearly intended to have practical effects: Polo dictated his life story—to a writer of romance, no less—in hopes of restoring his fortunes after he gets out of prison, while Ibn Battuta's stories bolstered his position in Fez at the end of his life, as the narrative's opening and closing passages indicate.

Storytelling is a major theme in the other Resonance to Marco Polo's *Travels*, the selections from Italo Calvino's *Invisible Cities* (p. 1084). Picking up on the erotic theme just mentioned, it can be pointed out that all of Calvino's cities have feminine names; many of the cities Polo describes in Calvino's book are sites of erotic encounter, often dangerous or uncanny in nature, as in the case of Valdrada in these selections (p. 1085). Calvino's Marco Polo is a kind of Symbolist poet, who communicates in songs without words, with striking, ambiguous images that tell the Khan more than literal descriptions could do (p. 1084), even as they secretly express his longing for his home city, Venice, the one city of which Polo never—or always—speaks (pp. 1086-1087).

Taken together, the readings in this Crosscurrents section introduce a wealth of issues and literary techniques that can be traced throughout Volume B, from the hidden paradise of the Chinese "Peach Blossom Spring" (p. 70) and the mystical journey to (and by) Cold Mountain (p. 79), to Genji's exilic sojourn at Suma

Copyright © 2009 Pearson Education, Inc. Publishing as Longman.

(p. 184), to the magical adventures of *The Thousand and One Nights* (p. 406) and the mystical journey in search of the Simorgh in Farid al-Din al-'Attar's *Conference of the Birds* (p. 498), to the adventures of Sir Gawain (p. 798) and of Chaucer's pilgrims (p. 1089). Everywhere these adventurers find pleasure mixed with danger, radical cultural differences side by side with unexpected recognitions; home never looks the same again, to these authors or to their readers.

Geoffrey Chaucer

Chaucer's *Canterbury Tales* are in many ways an anti-*Commedia*, and they make a striking comparison when taught one after the other. Testifying to an equally strong authorial persona and an equally impressive survey of medieval society and culture, Chaucer's work nevertheless eschews completely the impossibly tight structure that binds everything in Dante's *Commedia* into a single vision, choosing instead the loose framework of a collection of tales unified only by the shared pilgrimage of their tellers. Rather than the foregrounded autobiographical first person of Dante-pilgrim, the narrator "Chaucer" masks himself behind the persona of each storyteller. The two works share the Christian topos of life as a journey; they share a collection of characters fully realized through the words they choose to speak; they share much of the same background material. Where Dante chose to depict the world through its crystallization in the afterlife, however, Chaucer's tales are resolutely wedded to this world. The pilgrimage that motivates the collection of representatives of every estate of life provides a Christian context, but Chaucer treats that context just as his characters treat their pilgrimage: an occasion for everything but an exclusive regard for the next world, even while never quite deviating from the letter of its rigorous demands. Even the textual status of the work reflects its openness. Composed in different parts between 1388 and 1400, some of it was composed expressly for the *Tales*, some of it incorporated from earlier work; apparently, but not certifiably incomplete, the book is customarily edited in ten groups, or fragments, of stories.

Criticism and Translations

As with other major English authors, Chaucer's writings have been subjected to extensive scrutiny by every critical movement of the past few decades, from deconstruction to new historicism to gender studies, queer studies, and cultural geography. Particularly useful for teaching Chaucer in the context of medieval Europe are several of the volumes listed in the Chaucer bibliography in the back of Volume B of the *Anthology*, notably the works by Boitano, Fyler, Ginsberg, Lynch, Miller, Minnis, Muscatine, and Neuse. There are also individual bibliographical volumes devoted to each of the selections included in the *Anthology*. You will want to bring to bear whichever particular critical viewpoint especially interests you; *The Canterbury Tales* provides ample material for them all.

Copyright © 2009 Pearson Education, Inc. Publishing as Longman.

A useful starting point might be the timeworn talking points that continue to structure contemporary discussion (including this one), however informed by current theory. Does Chaucer imply a moral standpoint or judgment on his characters? Do *The Canterbury Tales* have an overall plan and order to them, an ordered disorder, or no order whatsoever? Are the characters intended as realistic individuals or social types? To what degree do the stories reflect the character of the storyteller? Many instructors (and a fair number of students) will be familiar with the work in the original Middle English, but few will have time in the survey format of a World Literature course to work through it. The classic translation by J. U. Nicolson used in the *Anthology* is extremely faithful to the original, reproduces its rhyming couplets, and is just archaic enough in its language to give the flavor of Chaucer's English without sacrificing the easy flow of ready comprehension.

Chaucer and Continental Europe

Whereas twelfth-century England was characterized by the fluidity of its linguistic identity with France (Marie de France and the author of *The Play of Adam*, among others, were associated with the Anglo-Norman court), Chaucer's literary identity—not to mention his livelihood—was based on translation. This is not to say that his contemporary, the *Gawain*-poet, was not equally involved in translation, but where the latter poem is centrally concerned with conjunctures between past and present, Chaucer's conjunctures are primarily lateral, shifting between the different languages and cultures of his own time, just as his *Canterbury Tales* are resolutely present-minded in their outlook. The use of French as the language of statecraft and civil record keeping (and in some of the literature of the court) did connect Chaucer's world to that of Henry II and Eleanor of Aquitaine, but his piecemeal appropriation of French into English bears little relation to Marie's self-conscious translation of Breton words such as *bisclavret* into an Anglo-Norman context. In forging a new literary language, Chaucer was probably quite aware of his debt to Dante's similar endeavor in the *Commedia*, but he surely also knew that his pragmatic borrowings were quite different from the way Dante marked every intrusion into his native Tuscan with the poetic equivalent of quotation marks.

The earliest known tribute to Chaucer came from the continent: the French poet Eustache Deschamps addressed him in a ballad composed in the mid-1380s as "*O Socratès plains de philosophie / Seneque en meurs et Auglus en pratique / Ovide grans en ta poëterie.*" The enumerative praise continues for over 30 lines, summed up in the refrain, "*Grant translateur, noble Geoffroy Chaucier.*" Deschamps' ballad predates *The Canterbury Tales*, but it suggests the foundation of learning from which it emerged. Chaucer had translated both the *Roman de la rose* and Boethius's influential sixth-century allegory, *The Consolation of Philosophy* (see Vol. A of the *Anthology*); his dream-visions dealt with fame, poetry, and love in the manner of the French tradition; he used Boccaccio more than he did any other writer. As David Wallace observes in his essay in the *Cambridge Chaucer Companion* (eds. Piero Boitano and Jill Mann, 1986), Chaucer twice parodied his continental borrowings

Copyright © 2009 Pearson Education, Inc. Publishing as Longman.

in *The Canterbury Tales*: in Chaucer-pilgrim's tale of Sir Thopas, a romance so poorly told that the Host protests "Thy drasty rymyng is nat worth a toord!" (line 2120); and in the subsequent prose "Tale of Melibee," a translation of sources on the subject of Dame Prudence with which the Host is equally exasperated, although this time he lets it run its interminable course before saying so. Like the languages it translates from, the sources used in *The Canterbury Tales* are subordinated to the characters and the task at hand rather than a primary reason for their presence. The tales of the Miller and the Wife of Bath are a case in point: both are highly indebted to a long tradition of continental sources, but the speakers and the story are such as to cause that tradition to recede well into the background.

The General Prologue

The prologues are the only parts of *The Canterbury Tales* where the narrator speaks to us in his own voice. They thus provide what framework the work has, and "The General Prologue," with its setup of the pilgrimage and detailed description of the pilgrims, has always been granted a privileged status. Chaucer's celebrated opening takes the courtly topos of love's season and turns it on its head: "Thanne longen folk to goon on pilgrimages" (line 12). The immediate source Chaucer is playing with is probably Guillaume de Lorris's conventional opening to the twelfth-century romance *Roman de la rose*, which runs (in Chaucer's own translation): "That it was May, thus dremed me, / In tyme of love and jolite, / That al thing gynneth waxen gay, / For ther is neither busk nor hay / In May that it nyl shrouded ben / And it with newe leves wren" (lines 49-56). The twist of Chaucer's version, of course, is that pilgrimage does not provide the all-consuming passion of courtly love, but instead provides the participants with an unwonted leisure that gives rise to a series of tales on all manner of activities, a large number of them in fact concerned with love. There is a strong parallel to be drawn also with the framing narrative of Boccaccio's *Decameron* (Vol. C, p. 148), which takes the plague in Florence as the occasion of enforced leisure that allows the ten young noblemen and noblewomen to pass their time in storytelling. Boccaccio's characters are wholly worldly—moral rather than overtly pious—and the variations of tone and subject matter in their tales may range as widely as Chaucer's, but their bawdy is a reflection of an innate virtue unafraid of earthly matters and humor rather than an extension of the social estate of a particular character. Chaucer's characters are pious in the medieval way, as a matter of second nature; Boccaccio's more modern characters must actively recover some manner of ethics in a society shaken to its core by the plague.

"The General Prologue," along with the tales of the Knight, the Miller, the Reeve, and the Cook, belongs to Fragment I, generally dated with the earliest of the work, around 1388-1392. In her influential book, *Chaucer and Medieval Estates Satire* (1973), Jill Mann first made a sustained argument that the work originated out of the established literary genre of the estates satire, a qualitative rather than strictly hierarchical representation of the diverse strata of society and the ways they conditioned character. In the words of Chaucer-pilgrim, "Me thynketh it acor-

Copyright © 2009 Pearson Education, Inc. Publishing as Longman.

daunt to resoun / To telle yow al the condicioun / Of ech of hem, so as it semed me, / And whiche they weren, and of what degree, / And eek in what array that they were inne" ("General Prologue," lines 37–41). This need not imply a static set of conventional types any more than an allegory is composed of an inert set of fixed symbols. The descriptions of the characters seem poised midway between familiar types and quirky individuals, often the latter following after the former, and associated with the tail end of the promise of the lines above, "And eek in what array that they were inne." The tokens of their positions are so finely etched as to take on individuality: the way, for example, the Prioress "Hir over-lippe wyped she so clene / That in hir coppe ther was no ferthyng sene / Of grece, whan she dronken hadde hir draughte" (lines 133–135).

Some manner of order has been discerned among the assemblage of portraits in the "General Prologue," which roughly descends in order of status and ideality. Some critics find that it falls loosely into three groups, each fronted by an evidently emblematic figure: the Knight leads the Squire, the Yeoman, the Prioress with her Nun and Nun's Priest (the text gives three of these, but only one tells a tale), the Monk, the Friar, and the Merchant; the Clerk leads the Man of Law, the Franklin, the five Guildsmen, the Cook, the Shipman, the Physician, and the Wife of Bath; the Parson and Plowman lead the Miller, Manciple, Reeve, Summoner, and Pardoner; and the Host is described last. It has been noted that there are only three women among the twenty-nine pilgrims, and only two portraits (the Nun is dismissed in a line)—consistent with the existence of two major roles for women in fourteenth-century England. Still, as Jodi-Anne George notes in her edition of the "General Prologue" (2000), neither woman perfectly fits her role, and the same can be said for each of Chaucer's characters. Even Chaucer-pilgrim is uneasy in his role as poet and narrator. They know what is expected of them, but they also know that that expectation does not adequately sum up their identities. Much can be gleaned of everyday life in fourteenth-century London, although much of it may need to be unpacked for students who no longer know even what half of the professions represented might be.

The other task of the "General Prologue" is to frame the storytelling itself, both in terms of the realism of the situation, narrating the Host's proposal for passing the time between London and Canterbury (with the earthly prize of a free supper the reward), and poetically. The latter comes in the narrator's disclaimer, derived from Jean de Meun's continuation of the *Roman de la Rose* by way of Boccaccio, regarding the content of the stories he will retell. He asks "curteisye" of his readers not to find "vileynye" in his plain speaking in reproducing in the name of "truth" the tales as he heard them. In fact, Chaucer's poetics negates the very distinction between courtesy and villainy, for his text depicts both with equal equanimity and no conclusive evidence that would privilege one or the other. Chaucer does not simply elaborate on the legacy of medieval materialism evident in Abelard; like the cross-section of society his conceit of pilgrimage brings together, his "General Prologue" asserts that the courtly and the *vilain* co-exist, if, as we shall see, rather uneasily. It should re-

Copyright © 2009 Pearson Education, Inc. Publishing as Longman.

mind us of the distinction between Chaucer the narrator and Chaucer the author that the former remains unaware of this fact.

The Miller's Prologue and Tale

"The Miller's Tale" appears as a programmatic disruption of the order of introduction in "The General Prologue" from high to low. Drunkenly ignoring the Host's instructions that the Monk "quite" the Knight's long and courtly opening Tale, the Miller provides a brief but potent fable that "requites" (p. 1110, line 19) the Knight's seemly words in such a memorable fashion that even the 1960s English rock band Procol Harum saw fit to include the moment as the chorus to "A Whiter Shade of Pale." The Miller gives a version of Chaucer-pilgrim's disclaimer, blaming any misspoken words or phrases on the Southwark ale he has drunk (lines 30-32). Moreover, rather than the Knight's idealized and ostensibly disinterested tale, the thrust of the Miller's bile is inspired directly by the Reeve's none-too-gentle attempts at quieting him (the Reeve will take immediate revenge in kind with his own Tale about a miller). Situational ethics bleed between prologue and story, for the climactic gag is born of Absolon's (Absalom's) desire to "requite" his tormentors, Alison and Nicholas.

Chaucer's version of the *fabliau* retains the genre's crudity and vitality but unmistakably heightens the formal complexity and thematic density. As Derek Pearsall notes in his essay on comedy in the *Cambridge Chaucer Companion*, there are six comic tales in *The Canterbury Tales*—the Miller's, Reeve's, Shipman's, Merchant's, Friar's, and Summoner's—of which the first four are *fabliaux*. Comedy, Pearsall stresses, is not more realistic per se than romance or religious tales, but it comes with a different set of rules and assumptions. The settings of these tales are present day and homely; the values represented are survival and the satisfaction of the appetites above all else—values equally embodied in the Miller's own behavior. "The Miller's Tale" includes comic representatives of the other genres within its basic structure: Absalom's efforts to play the courtly lover make him even more the fool, while Nicholas tricks John the carpenter with a religious fable demanding pious obedience to achieve a miracle. Still, although the fable is physically hard on all the characters but Alison, it makes no moral judgments. The lover is punished not for adultery but by accident; the simple reeve never has his faith shaken, and the forsaken buffoon Absalom gets some measure of revenge.

Chaucer opens up the basic *fabliau* triangle by doubling it into an elaborately intertwined gag, the climax of one setting off the punch line of the other. And this, after all, is the hallmark of popular genres: pleasure in the pyrotechnic performance of a series of demanding stunts, not an edifying exercise in thematic depth. The paradox is that Chaucer accomplished the latter, too, interweaving a series of allusions to the mystery plays that have primed John to believe Nicholas's cock and bull story. It is interesting to compare it, on the one hand, to the bare-bones treatment of animal fables by Juan Ruiz in *The Book of Good Love*, thrown like epigrams between the Archpriest and his would-be lover; and, on the other hand, to the

Copyright © 2009 Pearson Education, Inc. Publishing as Longman.

episode with the demons of Malebolgia in *Inferno* 21–23, a low comic setup wholly reworked for its new role within the divine plan of Dante's afterlife.

The Wife of Bath's Prologue and Tale

The Wife of Bath's Prologue and Tale come from Fragment III, often known as the "Marriage Group," and is usually dated with the majority of the collection, around 1392–1395. It can be quite illuminating to compare the Wife of Bath's version of a Breton *lai* with those of Marie de France. While Marie restricts herself to the milieu and tone of her oral sources, "The Wife of Bath's Tale" is built around a question, "What thing is it that wommen moost desiren?" that in the context of the Prologue to her Tale reads like a joke. Alison's knight promptly fails the first adventure with which he is presented: coming across a "mayde" along a river, he takes her "maydenhed" by force. Attempting to resolve the second adventure to requite the first, he is discoursed by a foul old woman who quotes Dante, Seneca, and Boethius at him before her requisite transformation into the woman of his dreams, both beautiful and true—the combination that in her prior worldly rhetoric she had expressly denied existed. And this, after the narrating Wife of Bath has made her own digression with the Ovidian tale of Midas. We are left to debate whether Chaucer is making fun of his storyteller, or praising her, or revealing her character through the ways she distorts her material, or crediting her with the invention herself.

The Prologue is no less equivocal in its standpoint: the Wife of Bath, born under the sign of Venus, is, as Helen Cooper puts it in the *Oxford Guides to Chaucer: The Canterbury Tales* (1989), a "professional wife." The primary site of debate over Alison comes from the fact that she is Chaucer's creation, not her own. We do not know if she travesties her authorities as a rhetorical strategy or to demonstrate her ignorance, if her infectious exuberance is criticism or praise or a nuanced sketch of individual character. But that is the way of Chaucer and the openness that distinguishes *The Canterbury Tales* among the great medieval works.

Copyright © 2009 Pearson Education, Inc. Publishing as Longman.

Volume C
The Early Modern Period

◆ ═◆═ ◆

The Vernacular Revolution

Vernacular Writing in South Asia

Many of the vernacular language traditions in South Asian literature of the early centuries C.E. had their origins in courtly circles. This is comparable to the situation in contemporaneous Europe, where the troubadour tradition offers a good example of how literate, learned, and privileged were the authors and audiences, or in Japan, where the pioneers in using Japanese in place of Chinese for expressive writing (as in *The Tale of Genji*) were aristocratic women. (See Volume B of the *Anthology* for more information on early European and Japanese literature.) Very little of the courtly vernacular literature from South Asia has been successfully translated into English, in part precisely because of its courtliness, which catered to the very refined concerns and tastes of a narrow and highly educated sector of the population.

Far more successful have been translations from the religious poetry that in most parts of South Asia historically succeeded the courtly literature in a kind of second vernacular revolution, again not unlike the religious and cultural upheavals in Europe at around the same period that led to the Reformation. These texts spoke to more popular and in many ways more fundamental concerns of human existence. Yet that does not mean the works are straightforward. However much the authors may claim to be uneducated, simple people, mere empty vessels to be filled with the divine spirit that would speak through them, much of their vernacular religious poetry is as artistically complex as that of their courtly predecessors.

Basavanna

Nothing illustrates so well the anticourtly form and content of South Asian vernacular religious poetry, and also the complexity behind its apparent simplicity, as the *vacanas*, the "plain-speaking" poems of the Kannada-language religious writers of the twelfth century. The words "poems" and "writers" should not be taken too literally because the *vacanas* were not conventional poems in form, and so far as we know, they were not even written to begin with, though there is no reason to assume that any of the prominent *vacana* authors were actually illiterate. (The

Copyright © 2009 Pearson Education, Inc. Publishing as Longman.

works were apparently collected and committed to writing, along with biographical information on the authors, first in the fifteenth century in a work called the *Shunyasampadane*, or *The Attainment of Emptiness*; Karnataka University Press published an English translation, 1965-1972, in five volumes.) To this day, the texts are read and sung and revered by people in Karnataka, especially among the Lingayats, the members of the south Indian community that are the descendents of the Militant Devotees of Shiva.

Although the *vacanas* are not conventional poems, they remain stylized language nonetheless. Here is the original Kannada version of Basavanna's poem "The rich will make temples for Śiva" the way we find it printed in modern editions:

> *Ullavaru Sivalayava madiharu*
> *Nanena maduve badavanayya,*
> *Enna kale kambha, dehave degulavayya,*
> *sira honna kalasavayya.*
> *Kudala Sangamadeva kelayya,*
> *sthavarakkalivuntu jangamakkalivilla.*

There is no obvious metrical organization to the lines—it is not even clear they should be printed as lines—but it is impossible to believe that such stylistic effects as the rhymes *badavanayya/degulavayya* and so on were not sought by the author.

Basavanna's *vacanas* are some of the most accessible and compelling in the entire corpus, which comprises thousands of texts from hundreds of authors. Students should find immediately intelligible and appealing such texts that speak of the difficulty of mindful devotion to spiritual matters ("Like a monkey on a tree") or the unwisdom of procrastination ("Before the grey reaches the cheek"). "You can make them talk" is another such text, one of several of Basavanna's included here that denounce the stolid arrogance of the wealthy, a common theme among *vacana* authors.

More deeply rooted in the specific religious practices and theology of the Militant Devotees of Shiva is "The rich will make temples for Śiva." For the Militant Devotees, the Hindu temple, however ubiquitous and grand, was a sign of all that was wrong in the social and religious order. These vast, splendid edifices were the conspicuous consumption of the wealthy landowners, and entrance to them was restricted to members of the higher castes. The often low-caste artisans who filled the ranks of the Militant Devotees responded by turning their very own bodies into temples—they wore around their necks miniature icons of the deity, which would normally be installed in the inner sanctum of the temple—and to this body-temple no one could ever restrict their entrance. The paradox of all this was one they not only did not refuse but actually celebrated. As Basavanna powerfully phrases it, the motionless grand temple seemingly rooted to the ground for eternity will eventually fall, whereas the moving temple that holds the devotee's spirit, however impermanent to all appearances, will last forever.

Copyright © 2009 Pearson Education, Inc. Publishing as Longman.

RESONANCE

Palkuriki Somanatha

In its early phase, the movement of the Militant Devotees of Shiva was profoundly countercultural. Nothing shows this better than the legends that grew up around Basavanna's role in the regicide that ended the rule of the Kalachuri dynasty in northern Karnataka. Basavanna had been appointed finance minister of King Bijjala and thus held a position of authority in support of established norms and powers. But the movement he led, which challenged all social convention, eventually escaped his control. A political crisis was precipitated by an event, remembered to this day, that stood as a metaphor of the magnitude of the challenge: The children of two families of Devotees were to be joined in marriage. The bride was from a Brahman family, the highest caste, the groom from a family known today as Dalits (formerly, Untouchables), traditionally viewed as the lowest group on the social hierarchy. When the king, whose customary duty was to preserve the order and separation of castes, learned of this marriage, he executed the bride and groom by having them dragged through the streets of his capital, Kalyana. This led to a revolt and to the assassination of the king.

The countercultural aspect of the Militant Devotees movement is powerfully expressed in Somanatha's biography of Basavanna. What is uncertain is just how literally we are to take some of the narrative. Clearly Somanatha had no interest in mimetic realism: Eight-year-old Basavanna's refusal to participate in the Brahmanical rite of passage is couched in the language and argument of a mature theologian. But are we to extend such metaphorical interpretation to other narratives of the collection, for instance, "The Story of Kakkayya," the devotee who, on encountering a reciter of traditional lore of the God Vishnu who refuses to mention the superior power of Shiva, beheads and dismembers him; or the story of King Nidumara, who impales members of the Jain faith for their refusal to convert to Shaivism? Other more or less contemporary south Indian narratives suggest strongly that such stories are not always to be taken at face value. But the capacity of religious conviction to induce acts of violence against those who do not share such convictions is something with which we are all too familiar. And thematizing this problem, and the limits of "hermeneutical charity" for the interpretation of such texts, can make for a rewarding classroom discussion.

Mahadeviyakka

Although women authors were not unknown in the courtly vernacular traditions, they are especially prominent in the vernacular religious movements. Poets like Lalla Devi, or Lal Deb (who composed in Kashmiri), Janabai (Marathi), or Mirabai

Copyright © 2009 Pearson Education, Inc. Publishing as Longman.

(Hindi) have been central to these literary traditions for centuries (see *Women Writing in India*, ed. S. Tharu and K. Lalitha, 1991, Vol. 1). And while legends have grown up around all of them, none is more dramatic than those associated with Mahadevi, the "elder sister" (*akka*, an honorific term). She is said to have abandoned her husband when a young woman and wandered off naked, covered only by her long hair. She joined the other Virashaiva devotees in Basavanna's Kalyana but took to wandering again. She died on the holy mountain of Shri Shaila in Andhra Pradesh.

Mahadevi's poems typically are addressed to Cennamallikarjuna ("my lord white as jasmine," in the translator's poetic rendering), the name of a local manifestation of the great god Shiva. And the fervor of her love for this being is a powerful flood, at times overwhelming to the reader: Mahadevi cannot touch other men, who pierce her like thorns; her body means nothing to her once it has been embraced in love by her lord; because the pleasure of lovemaking after long absence is so intense though the absence is so painful, she wants to be at once with her lord and not with him.

Critics typically think of such utterances as "metaphors for the phases of mystic ascent" (A. K. Ramanujan, *Speaking of Shiva*, 1973, p. 113). But there is no obvious reason to believe the author is speaking metaphorically. Spiritual and sexual ecstasy have many features in common, after all. If we can't ever know what the author really intended here, if we can't even assume the author herself knew, it is at least worth asking why she might have needed or wanted to be understood allegorically rather than literally—or why we modern readers should feel so compelled to argue that she did.

Kabir

The remarkable Kabir, a weaver by profession, is in many ways the epitome of the devotional vernacular poet (the best recent work on the poet is by Charlotte Vaudeville, *A Weaver Named Kabir*, 1993). He self-consciously avoided the use of the high-culture language of Sanskrit, preferring to its stagnant "well water" the "live water of the brook" of his eastern Hindi dialect (Avadhi). The voice he developed in the demotic idiom and the kind of immediacy he achieved are uniquely his own, though his combination of simplicity and power will remind readers of other poets, though a very small class, including Catullus, Li Bo, Villon, Mir, and Heine (all represented in Vols. A–C of the *Anthology*).

Concentrating on this question of the poetic effects of directness and simplicity might be one way to enter pedagogically into this section, instead of taking the more obvious route of Kabir's piercing social commentary. How striking in this regard is the poem "Saints, I see the world is mad." Devoid of poetic figure, indeed of any literary artifice, the poem moves at a no-nonsense pace through its catalog of stupidities of religious prejudice. It is only at the very end that we get the rich rhetorical paradox: "Whatever I say, nobody gets it. / It's too simple." A comparable force is generated by the very simple metaphor in the lyric that ends the se-

Copyright © 2009 Pearson Education, Inc. Publishing as Longman.

lection: The true path of wisdom is untraveled, it is high and difficult and lonely;
"Kabir keeps climbing."

But Kabir's social critique is of course the core of his poetry, and here one has to be struck by the extraordinary immediacy, even modernity, of his views, even if he sometimes draws on archaic imagery ("so many ornaments, all one gold" echoes the fifth-century B.C.E. *Chandogya Upanishad*). It is not only caste distinctions that he denounces (very like the Militant Devotees of Shiva, of whom he was almost certainly ignorant), but even more strikingly religious distinctions drawn between Hindu and Muslim (or "Turk" in Kabir's parlance). It is arresting to think about the salience of this critique in the contemporary world. South Asia witnessed some of the bloodiest spasms of communal violence in the annals of a very bloody twentieth century, when in 1947 the two independent nation-states of India and Pakistan were created from the unified British colonial entity. It has been calculated that some 2 million people died, nearly 15 million were forced to flee their homes permanently, and some 75,000 women were raped. Religious exclusivism on both sides—Pakistan being demanded as homeland for the Muslims, India as homeland for the Hindus—was in large part responsible for this monumental tragedy. And the passions drawn on then have hardly been tempered in the following decades, as the three wars, the threats, and, on a smaller but even more worrisome scale, the events in 1992 in the north Indian town of Ayodhya show (see "Public Address, Benares," in Ramayana Resonances, Vol. A). Kabir stares into the face of this monstrous problem and does not blink. He demands that we understand that ultimately there is "No Hindu. No Turk"; "all belong to earth."

As noted in the introduction to this section, Kabir's poems have been on the lips and in the hearts of everyday people, both Hindu and Muslim, across India for centuries. This fact should give us pause about the capacity of poetry to instruct. Instead, it sometimes seems to have only the capacity to console: "Yes, Kabir told us all these things hundreds of years ago. He understood. We couldn't. It was too simple."

Tukaram

If the relationship between devotee and deity can sometimes be represented and experienced as a sexual one—as in the case of the Kannada poet Mahadevi—so it can sometimes be not only metaphorically represented but indeed experienced as a predominantly aesthetic one. The work of the great Marathi poet Tukaram exemplifies this perhaps better than any other Indian vernacular religious poetry.

It is often thought that the devotional poetries of premodern India were the spontaneous outpourings of simple, illiterate, untutored low-caste singers, whose works were transmitted orally until the modern methods of textual scholarship turned them into the stable artifacts we find today in printed books. While this picture is no doubt true in some cases—Kabir says explicitly, "Ink or paper, I have

Copyright © 2009 Pearson Education, Inc. Publishing as Longman.

never touched, nor did I take a pen in hand. / The greatness of the four ages I have described by word of mouth" (trans. Vaudeville)—it decidedly does not apply to Tukaram. Indeed, we will seriously misunderstand the true cultural challenge of the new vernacular poets if we fail to grasp the place of literacy and literariness as well as the intensity of their aesthetic claims against the high tradition of Sanskrit and Persian. This is well illustrated in an eighteenth-century account, whose general message there is no reason to disbelieve, concerning the poems of Tukaram:

> One night Tukaram had a divine vision, and thereafter lovingly worshipped Vishnu, and performed hymns of praise to the god. The people were enraptured as they heard the pleasing and inspired poems. As Tuka's reputation increased, some evil-minded Brahmans were burning inwardly with rage. They entered Tuka's house and said, "You teach principles contrary to religion and lead people to accept devotion. That language of yours is Marathi and therefore impure. It should never be heard." Saying this they took away by force the manuscripts of his *abhangs*. They made them into a bundle and put stones into it, and taking it to the riverbank, they sank it in the river. The Brahmans said, "If within thirteen days Vishnu takes them out dry, only then we shall honor them." Tuka went into the temple and cried, "O Lord, you appeared to me in a dream and ordered and inspired me, ignorant as I was, to write. Why have you brought this calamity on me?" In this way thirteen days passed, and lo and behold, the revilers saw the manuscripts of Tuka floating on the water and the water had not touched the writing.
>
> (adapted from Justin E. Abbott and N. R. Godbole,
> *Stories of Indian Saints: An English Translation of Mahipati's
> Marathi Bhaktavijaya*, 1934, pp. 289–291)

Tukaram's challenge to convention was not just that he was composing in the Marathi language; he was composing *literature* in Marathi and *writing* it down. On both counts the defenders of tradition were outraged because literature was a Sanskrit practice, and writing was reserved for Sanskrit.

In keeping with the thrust of this history, a core feature of Tukaram's poetry, in addition to the powerful autobiographical impulse that is a peculiarly new and evident feature of much seventeenth-century Indian writing ("When my father died," "Born a *Shudra* . . ."; compare Banarasidasa's "Half a Tale" in Vol. D), is that it concerns the creation of poetry itself. Poetry about poetry is certainly known the world over, in the West beginning at least as early as Horace's *Epistles* (2.3) and it became something of an obsession to twentieth-century poets (see "Poetry about Poetry" in Vol. F).

One strategy for teaching Tukaram could be to explore the dimensions of poetry that are salient for him and thereby to chart how far the concerns of an in-

Copyright © 2009 Pearson Education, Inc. Publishing as Longman.

surgent low-caste poet of seventeenth-century India—the divine compulsion to write ("I was only dreaming"), the self-doubt of the poet in his talents and training ("Have I utterly lost my hold on reality"), the sense that some other force is writing, not the poet ("Some of you may say / I am the author")—may depart from or intersect with those of the modern West.

Kshetrayya

Few works of late-medieval India produce so systematic and multilevel a blurring of the boundaries of genre—between spiritual and secular literature, or between religious devotion and ecstatic sexuality—as well as of the boundaries of gender as the songs of Kshetrayya. A dizzying gender confusion inhabits the very performance history of the lyrics: They were composed by a male poet, using the literary voice of the female courtesan (or the ingénue, or the adulterous married woman), and have traditionally been sung by male dancers (of the *kucipudi* tradition in Andhra Pradesh) who take on female roles in the dance-drama. (The form of the poems, the *padam*, consists of short stanzas followed by a refrain, printed in italics in the *Anthology*. Additional information on the traditions of Telugu poetry in which Kshetrayya may be situated is now available in V. Narayana Rao and David Shulman, trans., *Classical Telugu Poetry*, 2002; the general historical situation is reviewed in the same authors' *Symbols of Substance*, 1992.)

Equally confused, and charmingly so, is the genre of the narratives themselves. We may think we know that the courtesan is really a devotee and the customer really the Lord, but we are quickly bewildered by the stories told in the poems, which typically present the most erotic of encounters and are not readily transposed into any kind of theology. The Lord has been unfaithful, another woman has left nail marks on his chest and love bites on his lips during their lovemaking ("'Your body is my body'"); the Lord dresses up as a woman to find an innocent (or perhaps not so innocent) way to sleep with the resistant beloved ("Those women, they deceived me"); one courtesan doesn't care what price the Lord is ready to pay, she still won't have him ("Pour gold as high as I stand, I still won't sleep with you"); and another woman becomes pregnant by the Lord and demands that he find a way to help her have an abortion ("Go find a root or something"). Not your normal religious hymns.

One thing we try to teach students when they first encounter works of literature from very distant times and places—to them, often very confusing works—is to strive to enter into the thought-world of the poets and their primary audiences by acquiring historical (and perhaps one day even linguistic) knowledge, suspending prejudgments, and learning to cultivate a certain sympathy for difference. Students also need to be shown, as Kshetrayya can show them, that the confusion sometimes does not yield and that it is intentional and irreducible, indeed, an index of the very sophistication of a tradition that knew how to reproduce in literature the true complexity and mystery of love and spirit.

Copyright © 2009 Pearson Education, Inc. Publishing as Longman.

Wu Cheng'en

It should not be surprising that the best-known abridged translation of this novel into English, published by Arthur Waley in 1942, is known as *Monkey*, rather than by its Chinese title, *Xi you ji*, which translates as *Journey to the West*. The book's opening chapters focus exclusively on the exploits of a supernaturally gifted simian, and the actual pilgrimage that is the heart of the novel does not get under way until much more background has been provided. This leisurely entry into the narrative is typical of the vernacular novel in premodern China, which appears to be less anxious than its Western counterparts to "get to the point."

Much ink has been spilled regarding the origins of the genre, of which four significant examples—including *Journey*—were published in the seventeenth century. The typical division into chapters that often end on a suspenseful note inviting readers to "stay tuned" for the next installment led many scholars to assume that the novels derived directly from the popular storytelling tradition, perhaps traceable to prompt-books that urban raconteurs may have relied on as scripts. Early twentieth-century scholars like Hu Shi and Lu Xun (see Vol. F of the *Anthology*) seeking to reform China by, among other means, the promotion of a new written language ostensibly closer to popular speech were eager to locate its roots in these great "masterworks." Often based on the adventures of well-known historical figures, these novels displayed stylistic features that appeared to offer alternative models to classical language and forms and, potentially, messages subversive of the dominant social and political order as well. Subsequent research, however, has demonstrated that these novels cannot be traced directly to "the people" but were rather the products of a literate elite happy to draw upon successful stylistic practices from the oral and popular tradition. This mixed heritage produces the novels' characteristic features. As Wai-yee Li writes:

> The copresence of or tension between high and low diction—between literati culture and popular culture—is but one token of the intrinsic hybridity of vernacular fiction. Lyric poetry, songs, descriptive verses, poetic exposition, parallel prose, dramatic arias, doggerels, quotations from and summaries of historical texts and other fictional works, and the rhetoric of oral performance are often woven into the fabric of narrative. The best examples of the genre almost never fail self-consciously to exploit the interplay of different generic traits and stylistic levels to achieve ironic disjunctions or visions of totality based on complementary opposites and balanced juxtapositions. ("Full-length Vernacular Fiction," in *The Columbia History of Chinese Literature*, ed. Victor Mair, 2001, p. 620)

In teaching any traditional Chinese novel, then, it is important to set aside expectations about narrative shape that are based on nineteenth-century European models. In addition to the variety of literary forms, and especially the substantial number of poems, students should be prepared to deal with an ex-

Copyright © 2009 Pearson Education, Inc. Publishing as Longman.

tensive cast of characters and an apparently meandering course of events that may seem to be more repetitive and cyclical than teleological. The organization by chapters will be familiar, at least, as well as the tendency to leave the reader dangling at the end of each section, a common strategy of serialized fiction. The headnote couplets provide an elliptical glimpse of the events to come and a clue to the principle of parallel structure that is fundamental to most novels in the Chinese tradition.

One important reason for selecting Anthony Yu's translation of the novel is his commitment to including all of its poetry. Waley's *Monkey* leaves it out, but Yu argues persuasively for its importance on many grounds. Not only does it play a bigger role in *Journey to the West* than in other traditional novels (perhaps because the author was so eager to display his talents), but it is also unusually exuberant, characterized by greater than usual formal variety, and carries a larger share of responsibility for advancing the narrative and commenting on it. Its significance is especially notable in landscape scenes. As Anthony Yu writes:

> Not unlike some of the great landscape paintings of the Sung and the Yuan periods, in which a thousand details subsist in a delicate union of concreteness and ideality, the poetry here at once heightens and elevates by pointing simultaneously to the peculiar quality of a certain site and to its mysterious and elemental character. Most important of all, the lyric impulse is always placed at the service of the epic: the descriptions do not invite attention to themselves as poetic entities in their own right but, rather, are called upon constantly to strengthen the élan and verve of the story itself. ("Introduction," *Journey to the West*, vol. 1, 1977, p. 30)

Needless to say, the profusion of characters and leisurely pace of *Journey to the West* disappear in the face of radical excision: less than ten percent of the novel is included in this selection. All you have are the search for and introductions to the group of pilgrims who will be charged with traveling to India to bring the Buddhist scriptures back to China, excerpts from two of the eighty-one ordeals to which they are subjected, their arrival at their destination, and their swift and successful return to the Tang capital. This is sufficient, nevertheless, to provide a sense of the author's narrative techniques, the traits of his main characters, and the outlines of his most important themes.

Although the figure of a gifted monkey, known as Sun Wukong (here Wuk'ung or Pilgrim), had already appeared in earlier literary versions of the pilgrimage of the monk Xuanzang, referred to as Tripitaka, Wu Cheng'en's account of Pilgrim's own history is a distinctive contribution to the tale. His cunning and physical gifts are crucial to the narrative, but equally important is his pride. The opening chapters to the novel show him attempting to prove himself by challenging and disturbing the peace of various deities, most of whom he easily bests, until he confronts the all-powerful Buddha (Tathagata). His insolence is duly punished, and he can be acquitted only by agreeing to accompany Tripitaka on his journey:

Copyright © 2009 Pearson Education, Inc. Publishing as Longman.

this is the supreme example of the Buddha's mercy. As Andrew Plaks notes, many critics have seen in the eight-chapter prologue "in effect a structural model for the rest of the book: a mini-quest for salvation complete with many of the motifs later developed, in a kind of parody of the enlightenment process." This is existing popular material being treated humorously, but, as Plaks continues,

> at the same time it also lays much of the terminological groundwork for the allegory, and ultimately begins to outline such weighty problems as the constraints of mortality, the impossibility of self-contained perfection, even questions of social order and chaos, which cast a shadow over the otherwise amusing career of the "Great Sage Equal to Heaven" . . . and the story of his ultimate submission to the all-encompassing power of the Buddha nature. (*The Four Masterworks of the Ming Novel*, 1987, p. 209)

Readers will be reminded of details of Sun Wukong's historical exploits throughout the novel, and students should be advised to pay attention to both his traits and his tricks.

Tripitaka's three other companions are, as the story tells us, like Pilgrim immortal beings blessed with magical powers, but they are equally delinquent and need to expiate their wrongdoings. This is the doctrine of karma at work. Thus, as Anthony Yu writes,

> the meaning of the journey, as it is developed in the narrative, is not confined to the benefits of acquiring sacred scriptures for the people of T'ang China. On a more personal and profound level, the journey signifies for the pilgrims a new beginning, a freely given opportunity for self-rectification. It is in this way that the theme of the journey as a protracted process of merit-making complements and magnifies the theme of Buddha's mercy. ("Introduction," *Journey to the West*, p. 55)

Compared with his companions, the actual historical pilgrim-monk Tripitaka (Xuanzang) is at best unimpressive. He is as conventional in his piety and as helpless in his timorousness and gullibility as his sidekicks are excessive in their appetites and willfulness. You may wish to consider, as some critics have, the extent to which the band as a whole might be viewed as embodiments of archetypical human emotions and, perhaps, facets of the human psyche viewed as a whole. Such discussions will lead inevitably to consideration of the allegorical message of the novel as a whole.

Traditional critics have discerned allegorical structures of many different sorts at work in *Journey to the West*. For some it enacts, in multiple overlay, movements toward perfection from various philosophical and religious perspectives. These are generally embedded in sustained narrative puns that are difficult to capture in translation. Ancient cosmological theories, for example, viewed natural and historical processes as moving through cycles dominated by each of Five

Copyright © 2009 Pearson Education, Inc. Publishing as Longman.

Phases (earth, fire, water, metal, and wood), and the principal characters, it has been argued, may each correspond to one of these elements. Daoist processes of self-perfection involving alchemy and sexual practices may similarly be encoded in the novel's figures and events. Given the fact that the novel is framed as a quest for the scriptures of India, however, the Buddhist layer of meaning ought to be considered paramount.

Is *Journey to the West* an allegory of spiritual enlightenment? Can it be compared fruitfully with a work like Bunyan's *Pilgrim's Progress?* Putting aside the comic and ribald dimensions of the novel, to which we should return, we might still wonder if the narrative conventions observed by the novel are commensurate with a plot of structured or unilinear directionality. Critics have pointed out that on the literal level the pilgrims' "progress" in *Journey* seems to retrace its steps if not go in circles, with identical landscapes reappearing, and the promised land looking suspiciously like the Tang capital from which they departed. There is no clear rationale for the sequence of the episodes, whose ultimate number (81) is simply mandated by the Buddha's wish to have their total be a multiple of the ideal number 9. The sample episodes taken from the journey itself are typical in that they could have appeared at almost any point in the narrative and appear to be excuses for amusing or thrilling storytelling, rather than instruments for moving the group closer to its goal. The visit to the Nation of Women of Western Liang (Chapter 53; see Vol. C, p. 66), for example, offers an opportunity to invert conventional hierarchies, poke fun at the clueless heroes, and indulge in some scatological description as well. And the rescue of the king's wife recounted in Chapters 69–72, included in the *Anthology* (see p. 73) because of its resemblance to an episode in the *Ramayana*, is primarily a vehicle for a display of Pilgrim's pyrotechnics and guile. From this perspective, at least, it could be argued that excerpting the novel inflicts less damage than it might to a tightly organized and teleological whole, although there is an obvious diminishment of the sheer power of the massive repetition.

We might well ask why the journey—or its simulacrum—needed to be undertaken at all. Given his supernatural powers, why could the monkey not simply have somersaulted his way over the mountains to fetch the scriptures? And what are we to make of the "wordless scriptures" given to the pilgrims by Ananda and Kaspaya? Is it simply a joke played by corrupt and venal guardians of the Buddha's treasures? Or are empty scriptures more real, either because they are—in Buddhist thought—more reflective of the ultimate emptiness, i.e., the contingent and transitory nature of all beings, or because any truth worth knowing transcends language? In that case, what is the value of the "real" scriptures with which the pilgrims eventually return? Andrew Plaks notes that this eleventh-hour substitution is an innovation of the novel that clearly undermines the fulfillment of the mission and develops suggestions made by the novel's first critics about how to interpret the journey allegorically. The "quest narrative" should be read not as a literal pilgrim's progress, he argues, "but rather as an internal pilgrimage of the mind," in which "all the demons who threaten the life and limb of the travelers are essentially manifestations of the unenlightened state of the mind in its process of cultivation."

Copyright © 2009 Pearson Education, Inc. Publishing as Longman.

(See Plaks, *The Four Masterworks*, pp. 243ff, in which he provides several examples supporting this point.) If the trek seems to go nowhere, it's because it's depicting an internal struggle to unify discordant elements of the self and liberate oneself from desire, attachments, and the impediments they create to the liberation of Buddhist enlightenment. The journey, then, is both internal and also doesn't need to go anywhere, as "a *psychomachia* of the cultivation of the mind" (Plaks, p. 258).

We could take this line of interpretation further and note that according to Chan or Zen Buddhism, to regard enlightenment as a goal to be actively pursued is to fail to realize that it is always already there within one, to be realized in an instant of sudden illumination. Han-shan's poems (see Vol. B, p. 78) provide good expressions of this position, which would make even the process or struggle that Plaks describes unnecessary. Quite apart from the obvious point—that without it we would not have a story—"the question remains as to how allegorical meanings are connected to comic surface," as Wai-yee Li observes ("Full-length Vernacular Fiction," p. 250). As Li points out, interpretations of *Journey to the West* have clearly gone through cycles of their own. Its early readers were quick to argue for an allegorical structure, among other reasons to validate it as a work of literature worth taking seriously. By the early twentieth century these impulses had yielded such strained readings that critics were happy to discard them all. In his preface to Waley's 1942 abridged translation, for example, Hu Shi claims that "Freed from all kinds of allegorical interpretations by Buddhist, Taoist, and Confucianist commentators, *Monkey* is simply a book of good humor, profound nonsense, good-natured satire and delightful entertainment" ("Introduction to the American Edition," *Monkey*, 1942, p. 5). Waley himself, and later scholars writing from a humanist tradition, staked a greater claim for the novel as a moral drama of human possibilities, whereas Marxist critics saw it enacting the sociopolitical resistance of a rebel monkey against entrenched celestial authority. If contemporary critics have succeeded in reminding us of the philosophical and religious depth of the novel, they have not lost sight of the fact that its characters and events are also deeply engaging. (Sun Wukong's battles with heavenly deities are still some of the most popular performances in the Peking opera repertoire.) And neither, of course, should we.

The Rise of the Vernacular in Europe

For most students, and probably for most instructors as well, this introduction to the vernaculars of early modern Europe will contain wholly new material, which may appear to be only peripheral to the subsequent literary works in the volume. Yet the reflections on and examples of the vernacular writings of Europe can provide an excellent introduction to a number of issues relevant to early modern literature.

Several points can be quickly clarified before launching into a more detailed discussion of the texts at hand. First, as a lover of Norse epic or a student fresh from the *Chanson de Roland* will no doubt protest, European vernaculars existed

Copyright © 2009 Pearson Education, Inc. Publishing as Longman.

and were beautifully utilized long before the Renaissance. This is, of course, true and worth pressing: There were vernaculars before Dante, and the second point might involve recourse to that favorite pastime of literary scholars, indulging in etymologies. The word *vernacular* comes from the Latin (and probably Etruscan) *verna*, meaning a slave born in one's home. It gradually acquired the broader meaning of anything related to the domestic space. Vernacular languages—so-called originally to distinguish them from Latin—have their roots in the household: among women, children, lower-class members whose rank in society prevented them from taking part in the broader culture of Latinity that, after the fall of Rome, was increasingly restricted to an elite few. Yet the vernacular literary languages that developed in the course of early modernity would quickly lose their connections with "mere" households and go on to define not only national literatures but also nations. In the revolutionary period of state-building that marks early modernity, there could be no new nations without new languages.

Another relevant term is the word *vulgar*, which now has a largely derogatory meaning but is also used to specify a vernacular language; its roots are in the *vulgus* or crowd. Especially confusing at this point but worth mention is that the Bible translated into Latin by Jerome in the fourth century was (and still is) referred to as the *Vulgate*. Latin was the official language of the Roman empire when Jerome was writing, whereas the Greek and Hebrew from which he was translating were the languages of small, learned elites. The so-called Romance languages spun off from Latin at some point. Linguists do not wholly agree on when this began to happen, but over time, as the various governmental and bureaucratic systems of Rome's vast empire fell into disuse, the Latin language did the same. The influence of northern peoples—Lombards, Angles, Saxons, Franks—markedly changed the oral discourses of the day in areas where Rome had once ruled.

This is a far from systematic explanation for the complex and massive shifts in European languages from roughly the fifth century through the fifteenth. But it gives a broad outline as to the scope of the problem, and some basic observations emerge that are particularly relevant to a discussion of the "canon" and how it has been constituted in a course on world literature. First, the Latin inheritance was a tremendously forceful one in the emergence of modern European literatures, as Ernst Robert Curtius convincingly argued in his *European Literature and the Latin Middle Ages* (1953). In Italy, where that inheritance was strongest, the mature vernacular style was the first to emerge. While fourteenth-century English, French, and German look very different from their contemporary manifestations, fourteenth-century Italian is still the Italian largely spoken today, and some of the greatest works of Italian literature were written during those hundred years when the vernacular came into its own: not only Dante's *Divine Comedy* but Boccaccio's *Decameron*, Petrarch's sonnets, and the letters of Saint Catherine of Siena.

Second, the literary languages that emerged in late medieval and early modern Europe were informed by everyday usage as well as more poetic influences that sprang in part from renewed contact with the literary works from antiquity, increasingly Greek and Hebrew as well as Latin. Interestingly, some authors

Copyright © 2009 Pearson Education, Inc. Publishing as Longman.

chose to write exclusively in Latin. Erasmus, whose native Dutch he is said to have spoken as an adult only once, on his deathbed ("Liefe Godt"), is a case in point. The smattering of Latin that Shakespeare is famously said to have had perhaps helped him unleash an inspired English. But no doubt more influential was his attentiveness to his contemporary Englishmen and the way they spoke. One could add Boccaccio's affection for the speech of his native Florentines, Rabelais's ear for the cadences of conversations in Paris (and his humorous juxtaposition of French with the mangled and meaningless Latin of Renaissance clerics), and the attentiveness of Cervantes—who, unlike the other three writers just mentioned, probably knew no Latin at all—to Catalan and Basque. All produced in their works a highly fluid, highly realistic prose style that marks them with an incipient modernity.

The Soviet critic Mikhail Bakhtin has been the most provocative theorist of the confrontation of Latin and the vernacular in the early modern period, seeing in this clash the birth of modern literature. And while his discussion of the rise of the vernacular's multileveled meanings over the far more constrained "monologism" of Latin culture may be oversimplistic, it can provide an interesting and accessible glimpse into the origin of early modern writings. Bakhtin suggests in *Rabelais and His World* (English translation, 1968) that European vernacular literature arose from the great meeting places of late medieval and early modern life, particularly the marketplace, where different classes and tradespeople came together in the absence of clerical or governmental authorities. In fact, as Bakhtin clarifies in his essays collected in *The Dialogic Imagination* (1981), the inability of the *vulgus* to understand the "official" language of Latin contributed greatly to the acceleration of vernacular languages in ways that simultaneously undermined Latin's supposed pretensions to truth. Thus the word *hocus-pocus*, which has come to mean "sleight of hand," derives from a vernacular and arguably irreverent rendition of the line spoken by the priest at the high point of the Mass, "*Hoc est corpus meum*" ("This is my body"), as he elevates the Eucharist before God.

The section on early modern vernaculars in the *Anthology* consists of two parts plus a translation feature. The first part of this section of the *Anthology* contains some condemnations of biblical translation as well as some spirited defenses, for debate over vernacular Bibles was fierce. As Terence Cave points out in his insightful *The Cornucopian Text* (1979), the driving force behind modern biblical translations was the idea first articulated by Augustine in his *De doctrina christiana*, of "discovering the thoughts and intentions of those by whom it was written, and through these the will of God" (*On Christian Doctrine*, Book I, Chapter 5). As Cave goes on to argue, one difference between the moderns and the medievals was the desire to initiate such discovery without the aid of intermediaries. Erasmus, the first to produce a New Testament based on the original Greek texts, uses striking metaphors to make the point: "the sage rightly warns that you should drink water from your own cistern; that it is not necessary to seek help from elsewhere. . . . Make your own heart the library of Christ himself" (quoted in Cave, p. 85). But others before Erasmus had drunk water from their own cistern—often at their peril. Thus one has both the sour

Copyright © 2009 Pearson Education, Inc. Publishing as Longman.

complaints of the English Church against Wyclif, who dared to sow pearls among swine in the 1380s, and Luther's sarcastic response 150 years later to those Catholics who rebuked his godless translations into German, the language of the "common people." Students should be interested in reading the excerpted letter that prefaced the King James Bible; in it, the translators, who spent several years virtually sequestered at Oxford in order to complete the mammoth task, justify the creation of a sacred text worthy of the sanctity of England's new religion, Anglicanism.

The second Translations feature illustrates the important role played by biblical translations in facilitating vernacular development and, in turn, accelerating the religious differences that would become the hallmark of the early modern era. The passage from Luke of Gabriel's visit to Mary allows us to see a writer such as Martin Luther at his most polemical—he makes Mary a "gracious lady" rather than "full of grace," the traditional understanding of *gratia plena*. And the Italian Lucrezia Tornabuoni in turn makes Mary the agent of her own desire ("I / have not yet desired to know any man"), while Luther says more straightforwardly, "I do not know of any man." William Tyndale, who paid for his biblical translation with his life, translates the line similar to Luther: "I know not a man."

Finally, keeping in mind the vernacular's origins in the household, the third part turns to the ways in which the vernacular's development was associated with children, the lower classes, and especially women, as Dante was fond of saying in several of his works. Women's writing has not been overwhelmingly represented in the curricula of early modern courses; Marguerite de Navarre has tended to be the lone voice with her tales inspired in part—but only in part—by Boccaccio. But Marguerite was far from alone. In the selections included in the *Anthology* of two of the period's most remarkable women—the Tuscan Catherine of Siena and the Mexican Sor Juana Inés de la Cruz—one can see the struggles that accompanied women's entrance into the world of writing. Catherine must justify her initiation into a skill possessed largely by male clerics and notaries in fourteenth-century Italy by claiming that God graced her with a miraculous gift, teaching her to write as she slept. Placed alongside Sor Juana's more detailed "Response to Sor Filotea," one of the most articulate defenses ever composed of women's right to learn, Catherine's letter must seem naïve. While we will never know the extent of Catherine's literacy, that of Sor Juana is well documented and evident in her complex sentence structures as well as in the sophisticated nature of her response. Yet Sor Juana also justifies her "inclination" to letters as divine, showing that she too has recourse to an argument that portrays God as all-powerful and herself as passive recipient—although, cannily, she suggests that the "sacred translator" Jerome and the Psalmist who wrote in verse were also gifted. Thus does she place herself in a long, distinguished line of writers and poets that has included women only on rare occasions. But Sor Juana's own choice to write in Spanish (she could easily have written in Latin and probably even Greek) marks her as thoroughly modern as well as domestic—not a surprising thing for a woman who praised the science that one can learn while in the kitchen, cooking eggs. (For more on Sor Juana, see the entry dedicated to her on page 327.)

Copyright © 2009 Pearson Education, Inc. Publishing as Longman.

Acquaintance with these selections will hopefully alert students to the range of vernacular literatures that claimed distinction in early modern Europe, as well as to the advantages and limitations of a traditional canon that has tended to focus largely on English, Italian, and French literature, most of it secular. Yet the national literatures of those countries—or of Germany, Poland, or Portugal—did not emerge, like Athene from Zeus's head, full-grown. They were the products of contact with other cultures, including both ancient and late medieval Latinity, and the entrance of the vernacular onto the literary scene was in many ways a contested one. This contest was considerably aggravated by the fact that late medieval and early modern spirituality was profoundly rooted in that problematic and dynamic text, the Bible. Ongoing attempts from those of Erasmus and Luther to Sor Juana to make the Bible one's "own" and their own hearts "Christ's library" helped to define much literary production until the eighteenth century. They also helped establish the parameters within which the validity of early modern vernaculars would be debated. Perhaps the debate officially ended only with Vatican II in the early 1960s, when Catholic priests were no longer required to say the Mass in Latin. At the same time, as English has risen to the position once occupied by Latin and as television, radio, and the Internet transmit "official" national languages to places where local dialects have long held sway, other debates—such as the desirability of bilingual education in U.S. schools or the value of preserving regional variations—have taken over.

Copyright © 2009 Pearson Education, Inc. Publishing as Longman.

Early Modern Europe

Students may not be familiar with the term "Early Modern," but they will undoubtedly have heard of the Renaissance: that supposedly glorious awakening after dark ages to the light of secularism and reassuring rationalizations. Such a view, while not wholly unfounded, is also not entirely correct (for starters, the term *dark ages* has to go). For one thing, if students have read the selections in Volume B of the *Anthology*, they will be well positioned to see the continuities between Chaucer and Boccaccio, or the troubadours and the lyric tradition. For another, it's important to point out that the "Renaissance" as commonly understood owes its characterization not so much to Renaissance figures themselves as to more recent historical interpretations. The most notable is *The Civilization of the Renaissance in Italy* by the nineteenth-century Swiss historian, Jacob Burckhardt, who argued that the Florentines in particular rejected medieval superstitions and embraced the true dignity of man. Thanks in large part to Burckhardt's secular reading as well as the tendencies by pre-Raphaelites such as Walter Pater to promote a narrowly aesthetic definition of the Renaissance, one tends to think of Botticelli's or Raphael's works as definitive of the period—works in which serene and stylized Madonnas or Venuses seem to exist in a realm untouched by mundane earthly concerns.

But Botticelli and Raphael represent only a single moment—a single renaissance among many—in a historical sweep that a number of recent scholars of the period between roughly 1350 and 1650 have taken to calling *early modernity*. Asking students how these different nomenclatures might skew our understanding of the period can generate more than simply pedantic discussions. *Renaissance* is typically used to refer to an awakening to or renewed appreciation for ancient Greece and Rome. Yet European men and women of all social classes were increasingly interested in the "rebirth" of a purer form of Christianity than the Catholic Church had been able to accommodate over the centuries. A number of them, like the northerner Erasmus, sought to bring together both pagan and early Christian cultures. The term *early modernity* looks ahead rather than back, assuming that there is something incipiently but not quite modern in the works written over roughly three centuries. To be sure, Rabelais looks to Joyce, Petrarch to the Romantic lyric. By bringing both terms together in your discussions, you will enable students to see these several key centuries in European literature as a point on a continuum rather than too radical a break with either what came before or what followed.

Finally, however, perhaps the most useful aspect of *early modernity* is that it works well as a comparative term, designating in as inclusive a way as possible an

Copyright © 2009 Pearson Education, Inc. Publishing as Longman.

entire era that encompasses not only Europe but European colonies across the
ocean. "Renaissances" must rather be understood within their local contexts:
Luther's impatience with the Church, Elizabeth I's extensive patronage network,
the arrival of Greek scholars in Italy. Encourage students to see "early modernity"
as the sum total of multiple renaissances and to chart a geography of various regional and national awakenings that took place in Europe and eventually the
Americas. The centers of medieval Europe had been Castile and Paris. The former
boasted a mixture of Arabic and Christian cultures that produced love lyrics influential for all of Europe. Paris offered a rich university culture that spawned the
writings of Peter Abelard, Andreas Capellanus, and Thomas Aquinas, as well as sophisticated courts where the troubadour poets flourished and the *Romance of the
Rose* was born. But the Italian *comune* or city-state, increasingly led by hard-nosed,
unsentimental businessmen who had made their names and, at times, their fortunes because they lived either on the populated pilgrimage routes to Rome or on
rivers flush with trade, became the new cultural capital in the century after Dante's
Commedia. In small Italian towns such as Florence and Siena, the term *rinascimento*
("renaissance") was in fact first used to describe a conscious return to the past (and
an implicit rejection of much, though certainly not all, of medieval culture). The
awakening of both pagan and Christian antiquity was soon vividly imagined in the
Netherlands and Germany, France, Poland, Portugal, England, and Spain, and
eventually in the New World. Clearly it took different forms as it "moved," and
even its origins are hardly of a piece, as evident in the radically diverse works of
Petrarch and Boccaccio or, in France, Rabelais and Montaigne.

Montaigne's legendary sedateness aside (in fact, he had an active career as a
political figure in mid-sixteenth-century France, which his own *Essays* attempt to
dismiss), many early modern writers were themselves itinerant, taking after the figure often called the consummate Renaissance man, Francis Petrarch. If the centers
of medieval culture had been the university and the court, many writers from
Dante on spurned—or were spurned by—these largely conservative institutions. It
might be helpful to point out to students how many of these writers were exiles,
some literally, others metaphorically, anticipating in many ways the condition of
the modern writer. Rabelais was shunned by the Sorbonne. Machiavelli never really succeeded in winning the Medicis' attentions. Cervantes and Camões failed to
get the civil posts that would have given their lives some economic stability.
(Women, of course, had no access to the university, and only a few, like Marguerite
de Navarre, were centered in courts, but even the at-times impolitic Marguerite
wasn't on good terms with her brother's extended household. In Mexico a century
later, Sor Juana Inés de la Cruz fled from the busy court of the vice-regent to the
convent—which had always served women as a space apart in which they might pursue activities other than the strictly domestic ones that preoccupied women like
Anne Bradstreet.) One could say that the city emerged in the period as the new
lifeblood, and indeed, the growth of Madrid and London enabled new institutions
like theater and playwrights like Lope de Vega and Shakespeare to flourish. But for
the vast majority of authors in this section, it was difficult to make a go of writing

Copyright © 2009 Pearson Education, Inc. Publishing as Longman.

and scholarship unless one had courtly patrons or a university post; we are not yet in the eighteenth century when Addison could live off of his essays. Just as artists had to travel to fulfill commissions—even Michelangelo, the greatest artist of his time, went back and forth from Florence to Rome—so did writers need to pursue opportunities that would provide them space, and time, for their solitary work.

Several threads worth pursuing emphasize the itinerant nature of early modernity, one of which is the literary exploration of what can be called "alternate worlds." Clearly these explorations were vastly enhanced by the discovery of worlds far different from any previously conceived, and it is helpful to read the works in the section on Europe against those in the section on Mesoamerica in Volume C. Rabelais's *Fourth Book*, Montaigne's "Of Cannibals," and Shakespeare's *Tempest* were in no small way inspired by the encounters with new world peoples. There were also "discoveries" to the east as well, as Camões's *Lusiads* attests. Such works, read in concert with Columbus's tortured letters or "Songs of the Aztec Nobility," suggest that exploration as such had its darker side, and not only for the newly colonized. The Europeans who were involved in confrontations with the other—whether it be the Tupi of Brazil described in Jean de Léry's *History of a Voyage to the Land of Brazil* or the Muslims Cervantes fought in the Battle of Lepanto—had difficulties coming to terms with the questions, doubts, and struggles that the confrontation provoked. (That otherness, in fact, can also signify the works of the ancients, which Petrarch sees as "friends" but which Louise Labé or Sor Juana might read as hostile to women.) There were risks involved in the exploration of difference, and many of the texts found in the *Anthology* interrogate those risks.

Another thread to pursue is the creation of new audiences and new authors, thanks largely to the diffusion of vernacular literatures and the invention of movable type that made written texts far more itinerant than their medieval precursors, those laboriously generated manuscripts, could have been. The vernacular revolution that was as formative in Asia as it was in Europe will help students recognize the importance of this diffusion: but it is then worth turning to the individual selections in the "Early Modern Europe" section and asking what works wouldn't have been read—or even written—without the vernacular and the possibilities it offered. Antiquity could boast the inimitable Sappho, and medieval northern Europe gave us Hildegard of Bingen; but women's writing as such only takes off with the introduction of the vernacular. Read the mystics Catherine of Siena and Saint Teresa alongside the medieval Mechthild of Magdeburg, one of the first to write in Flemish. Chiara Matraini, Louise Labé, and Vittoria Colonna challenged the Petrarchan tradition, and Sor Juana's works are crucial for understanding the American response to tired European conventions. (You might also compare the works in this section with those in the "Courtly Women" section about medieval Japan in Volume B.) Without the invention of the printing press, we would probably not have had the second book of *Don Quixote*, a response to a false sequel to Book 1 (we may not have had *Don Quixote* at all, inspired by a mad knight's obsession with books of chivalry). Luther's angry prose and German Bible would not have reached a population eager to define itself against a Mediterranean Rome,

Copyright © 2009 Pearson Education, Inc. Publishing as Longman.

and the Puritan Revolution in England, animated in large part by the increasingly outraged pamphlets that flooded London and the countryside, many written by John Milton, may never have taken place.

Early modernity is not only (and not principally) a discrete chronological period but a stepping stone to and from somewhere else. The works in this section adapt themselves quite wonderfully to this project in that many of them are very self-conscious in their backward glances. Especially if one is focusing on different genres, these texts provide terrific examples of epic (Milton, Camões), lyric (Petrarch and his many followers), the novel (from Boccaccio's and Marguerite's "novelle" to *Don Quixote*), autobiography (Montaigne, Santa Teresa, Bradstreet's "To My Dear Children"), the letter (Saint Catherine, Petrarch, Laura Cereta), the dialogue (Castiglione, More), and the romance (Shakespeare's *Tempest*). Some of the works represented in the *Anthology*, on the other hand, are virtually *sui generis*: Where to put Lope's *Fuenteovejuna*, that odd crossover between medieval chronicle and peasant play? How to classify Sor Juana's *Response to "Sor Filotea"*: autobiography, passionate defense and catalog of women's learning, or apologia? As Rabelais's exuberant prose attests, early modern literature is marked by an at times ungainly capaciousness that can border on the encyclopedic (and it's worth helping students come to terms with the sprawling nature of many of these works: Why are there so many references to literary traditions long gone?). It is thus often very different from the most memorable examples of Italian Renaissance art: Botticelli's Venus, Raphael's self-possessed courtiers, Leonardo da Vinci's serene Madonnas. Even that most Florentine of early modern works, Machiavelli's *Prince*, defies description; unpublished in the author's lifetime, what exactly should we call it? (No doubt Machiavelli would be upset to find that his treatise is being read as literature, even if it does end with a rousing echo of one of Petrarch's lyrics.)

The image of Machiavelli turning over in his grave leads to one last observation: early modernity seems to everywhere raise the question, what *is* literature? How self-consciously must a text mark its status as fictional in order to become part of a "canon"—and how are old canons challenged and new ones reconstituted between 1350 and 1650? (Further reflections would lead to more far-reaching questions. How has the "Renaissance" canon been altered by "early modern" additions of women and Latin American writers and works drawn from popular culture? How can and will the canon continue to change?) While there are abundant treatises written during early modernity that would certainly be classified as literary criticism, most of them are belabored and dry; one must look to the creative texts themselves for the most inspired musings on literature's status and meaning. Critical to early modern minds is the insistence that the imaginary serve as a vehicle for other things: for political or religious complaint, for the inspiring of national sentiment. Often the presence of alternate worlds or voices within a work such as Thomas More's *Utopia* served to cushion the overly critical, potentially hostile perspectives articulated by its author. Even at their most critical, however, early modern authors generally tried to think within

Copyright © 2009 Pearson Education, Inc. Publishing as Longman.

several registers at once, not so much ignoring the contradictions among them as seeking grounds for accommodation. Accommodation didn't always work—the Reformation and its bloody aftermath are ample evidence of that. But in ways that human lives or religious doctrine do not, artistic works enable the coexistence of opposites, the cohabitation of characters as diverse as Petrarch and his brother, Panurge and Pantagruel, Sancho Panza and Don Quixote. Last but not least, and undoubtedly more conducive to modern sensibilities, is the sentiment that one writes in order to define or identify the self, to grasp onto, or "*mettre en rolle*"—as Montaigne says in his essay on "Idleness"—the fleeting "I." Noticing the markers that create these texts as imaginary spaces (or as in Machiavelli's case, the attempt to move from beyond the purely imaginary creation of an ideal prince to a *real* principate) will help to give these works a theoretical dimension that will connect them with ongoing discussions in the other volumes of the *Anthology* about literature's place in the world.

Giovanni Boccaccio

Boccaccio provides a bracing introduction to the Renaissance, with his racy stories and unflinching look at human greed, wit, stupidity, and—as in his final tale about the patient Griselda—cruelty. Much of this will at the same time not be wholly new to students who have read Chaucer. The palpable mixture of characters and classes in the tales told and the apparent tolerance of the narrative audience for the wide range of issues addressed bring Chaucer's and Boccaccio's masterpieces together in fruitful ways. And Boccaccio did, in fact, influence Chaucer, although it is not clear exactly what works of his the English poet read.

That Boccaccio predated Chaucer by some thirty years might argue for including Chaucer in Volume C of the *Anthology* (or moving Boccaccio back to Volume B). It is certainly the case that the *Decameron*'s status has been much debated, and there has in fact been much discussion in recent years of a "medieval" *Decameron*. Inevitably, all attempts at periodization are somewhat arbitrary. You don't need to spend too much time on the relevant historical differences between a fourteenth-century court culture in London still deeply tied to aristocratic and clerical cultures and the culture of bustling, mercantile Florence. (Vittore Branca, author of *Boccaccio: The Man and His Works* [1976], has in fact called the *Decameron* a "mercantile epic.") But you might ask students to try to identify what, if anything, strikes them as particularly novel. One thing worth noting is that Boccaccio wrote in vibrant, muscular prose: not the poetry of Dante or Chaucer, but a uniform prose style that, as Alberto Asor Rosa has characterized it, elevates the low and liberates the "refined" from any falsely sophisticated tones. As Asor Rosa goes on to say, Boccaccio makes his subject "human reality," for which he sought a realistic style, free from stale conventions and reflective of common parlance despite its reliance on a Latinate structure ("'*Decameron*' di Giovanni Boccaccio," in *Letteratura Italiana: Le Opere*, Volume 1).

Copyright © 2009 Pearson Education, Inc. Publishing as Longman.

Certainly one dimension of Chaucer not present in Boccaccio is the way tales are "bound to the teller," as Lee Patterson has said of the "Merchant's Tale" (*Chaucer and the Subject of History*, 1991). The tale-tellers in Boccaccio are not distinguished by class or occupation but are rather generic young people of elevated social status (only Dioneo genuinely stands out as craving a different kind of story from his cohorts). But there are other riches to be gained by addressing the various dynamics between the stories' frame and the tales themselves. Is the *Decameron* demarcating a separate space, and if so, of what kind? Is it pastoral, or play—a playfulness on which Giuseppe Mazzotta focuses in his difficult but rewarding book on the *Decameron* (*The World at Play in Boccaccio's "Decameron,"* 1986)? What might the relationship be between the characters in the tales, constantly confronted with problems of all shapes and sizes, and those outside who must eventually return to Florence in the wake of the massive death and destruction the narrator so pitilessly describes? How does human ingenuity transcend the boundaries of gender and class, not to mention ethnicities and religion, since some of the stories—such as Tale 3 from Day 1—happen in far-off places, not in nearby Italian locales? Consideration of the stories' settings and the traveling that many of the characters do (in ways both geographical and metaphorical) reveals to what extent the *Decameron* is a book about circulation of all kinds. Like the plague itself, people are not bound to a single place (the wandering Alibech) or class (Griselda) or partner (Tofano's wife). And interestingly, like the plague, which had its origins in the Orient, many of these stories, especially the more exotic ones, came from the East, carried westward to "infect" their listeners with, one hopes, more delight than dread.

Such reflections may suggest that the characters in the stories are not, perhaps, so different from the tale-tellers, despite variations in age or class; they too have experienced hardships firsthand and are relying on their wit to survive. The complete breakdown of the categories that define social order is clear from passages describing mass communal graves in the work's opening, as well as the rampant theft that ensues in the breakdown of law and order. (One is reminded of the scenes from *Monty Python and the Holy Grail* in which charitable neighbors walk through the streets carrying stretchers and calling "Bring out your dead!" while not-so-charitable townsfolk use the occasion to do away with querulous but otherwise healthy elderly relatives.) Do the tales attempt to restore order in the same way that the tales' narrators are looking for therapeutic solutions? Or do the tales occupy some midway point between the lack of regulation in plague-ridden Florence and the perhaps excessively orchestrated rituals of the ten in Fiesole, who, since they have no garrulous innkeeper to reign them in, play at being kings and queens for a day?

The four *Decameron* tales represented in the *Anthology* might be fruitfully presented as two pairs. Melchizedek, an actual historical figure later celebrated by the German dramatist Gotthold Lessing as Nathan the Wise, outwits a ruler just as the young Alibech will outwit—at least physically—the monk who takes advantage of her refreshing young naiveté. The story of Tofano and his adulterous wife could be

Copyright © 2009 Pearson Education, Inc. Publishing as Longman.

said to invert the stark story of Griselda; in the first tale, the wife establishes control over her possessive husband, while the arguably sadistic Gualtieri seeks to have and, indeed, maintain absolute control over his wife. At the same time, all the stories, particularly the last one, are more complex than brief plot summaries can show. The tale of the three rings is a story of (and argument for) religious tolerance. That of Alibech and Rustico reveals, on the other hand, the vocabulary shared by religious and sexual discourses, and it is one of many stories lambasting the religious orders for their failure to observe their professed vows—although Boccaccio shows sympathy for the tempted, eventually exhausted, hermit. Tofano's public shaming shows us the dynamics of a small Italian town in which everyone knew what everyone else was up to, while Gualtieri's secrecy and high social standing prevent the general populace (the reader included) from fully knowing his intentions. Here students might reflect on questions of class thrown into relief by the last story (is the upper class exploiting the lower, and for what reason?) or on the possible connections between Boccaccio and Gualtieri (do they both "use" characters for whatever purpose they deem necessary?).

As the final tale, Griselda's story has special status with regard to the whole collection; on the other hand, the clever, rule-breaking Dioneo has been the teller of this particular story, and all of his tales must be taken with a grain of salt. Finally, the figure of Griselda herself is worthy of considerable attention. In some ways, she is similar to the patient saints who were at the center of medieval hagiographies, suffering stoically whatever tortures and trials happen to befall them. Set alongside Tofano's wife (or Chaucer's wife of Bath, a striking contrast with Chaucer's own version of "patient Grisele," the subject of the "Clerk's Tale"), Griselda comes across as almost unearthly. In a book specifically dedicated to (elite) women who spend too much time cooped up in narrow rooms, as Boccaccio informs us in his preface, it is striking that Boccaccio has chosen to end with this story. Is he perhaps warning women *against* the very submission to which Griselda succumbs?

While each tale presents its own narrative crux, it is best to read the tales in concert with one another, as well as against the frame. Or frames—one surely being that of the life of the author himself, who reacted to disorder with the order of his book. Against the devastation of massive death, one must set the productivity of all the tales, a productivity reflected in their utility if not always in their ethics. Melchizedek and Tofano's wife use stories to get out of sticky situations; Rustico employs a devilish tale to get himself *into* one. Again, Gualtieri's apparently gratuitous tale-telling—murdered children, a new bride—seems to go against the grain. What ends do his stories ultimately serve? Perhaps by putting Griselda's tale last and sending the ten tale-tellers off to Florence with her bizarre example ringing in their ears, Boccaccio is forcing them, and us, to confront the fact that the desire to impose *absolute* order over life represents an extreme to which only the most egocentric will go; and only a foolish "saint" like Griselda (whom Petrarch, in his own reading of the last novella, compared to Job) can withstand such efforts without protesting too much.

Copyright © 2009 Pearson Education, Inc. Publishing as Longman.

Marguerite de Navarre

The life of Marguerite de Navarre in many ways runs like a thread throughout this volume of the *Anthology*. She had a lively correspondence with the Italian poet Vittoria Colonna, who was widowed when her husband died in a battle opposing Marguerite's brother, Francis I. Rabelais dedicated the third book of his adventures of Gargantua and Pantagruel to Marguerite, which also happened to be the first book for which he did not use a ridiculous pseudonym. And Gerard Défaux has argued in his recent edition of the works of Clément Marot that Marot was asked by Marguerite herself to translate what would be one of the best sellers of sixteenth-century France, the Psalms (*Oeuvres poétiques complètes*, 1990). She was central to the cultural and religious conflicts that shaped her day, tending to take sides with the more heterodox elements of France and at times paying the price for her reformist ideas.

These ideas are reflected throughout her *Heptameron*, both in its criticism of religious orders and its advocacy of personal interpretation. But the figure with whom Marguerite should probably be compared is Giovanni Boccaccio. Even the title (not, by the way, Marguerite's choice) demands that we consider the two works side by side. And yet the contrasts are easily more prominent than the similarities. The discussants are far more individualized, the tales take place closer to home—one in which a wicked prior is finally brought to task for trying to seduce a virtuous nun even involves the Queen of Navarre, Marguerite herself—and the stories become the topic of at-times prolonged and often heated discussions. Finally, the world of the tale-tellers in the *Heptameron* is only temporarily disrupted; they are threatened not with earth-shattering events like the plague but with a bridge that has been flooded out, and the world to which they will return will be virtually identical to the one they ever so briefly left. Such immediate differences force us to wonder as to the nature of the aesthetic space the tales and tale-tellers alike inhabit. There seems to be more fluidity between the stories and the outlying frame in Marguerite's tales than in Boccaccio's, less insistence on seeing the tales as discrete, narrative events—especially when the interlocutors argue so insistently about their significance and relevance for their lives. But in many ways, we can see Marguerite as having taken Boccaccio to the logical next step. Her characters' discussions reveal that the tales do not present simple narrative examples but moral conundrums, opening up rather than closing down questions about their applicability. Like so many other early modern texts—and arguably, like the *Decameron* before it—the *Heptameron* stages problems of reading and interpretation, relishing process rather than product.

As for the stories themselves, the four tales presented in the *Anthology* touch on a number of the main thematic interests that preoccupied Marguerite: the corruptness of friars (Story 5); the importance of defending honor, even when taken to extreme measures as in Story 32; husbands'—and wives'—infidelity. Almost all of the stories focus on love, or lust, or some aspect of early modern sexuality. But

Copyright © 2009 Pearson Education, Inc. Publishing as Longman.

when placed alongside the Boccaccian stories of Tofano's wife or the tireless Alibech, it is clear that sexual activity is not, generally, cause for great pleasure. Marguerite's stories are instead haunted by what might be called the sad aftermath of sexual practices, whether they are frustrated, as in the case of the friars left on deserted islands, or fulfilled, as with the adulterous wife forced to drink out of her lover's skull (the sadistic dimensions of which may prompt students to return to Boccaccio's problematic tale of Griselda). Tales such as Story 32 reflect what Robert Cottrell has called Marguerite's preoccupation "with the problematic of penance"—a penance of which, he argues, women's bodies frequently bear the signs ("Inmost Cravings: The Logic of Desire in the *Heptameron*," in *Critical Tales: New Studies of the Heptameron and Early Modern Culture*, ed. John D. Lyons and Mary B. McKinley, 1993). The shifting interpretations offered for the stories by their lively audience suggest that Marguerite probably saw her stories as conveying ethical and moral problems through the lively banter and clever turns of phrase of a sophisticated but hardly homogeneous group, diverse in sex, station, and age. These problems include the extent to which the tales can be treated as "examples" from which one might learn. Insofar as they purportedly derive from contemporary history rather than the work of art crafted by a narrator for edifying effect (Aristotle's distinction in the *Poetics* between history and poetry comes to mind here), perhaps their staying power is limited. At the same time, the immediacy of so many of the tales suggests that they precipitated urgent reflection on the issues at hand.

Finally, it is worth pointing out to students that like so many early modern works, such as the plays and sonnets of Shakespeare, the *Heptameron* has no authoritative edition. Unpublished during Marguerite's lifetime, the tales exist in 17 different manuscripts. To incorporate this knowledge of the text's instability into classroom discussion, you might call attention to several bracketed excerpts in the stories, where the translator has included variants from an alternative manuscript of the *Heptameron* (as in Story 5, for example, where the addition spells out the retribution paid out to the friars). This might in turn lead to a discussion about the reasons why some early modern literature did *not* get printed. Death seems to have undone Marguerite before she completed her hundred tales (although this fact is itself in dispute). But you could also ask what one of France's most prominent figures, who had already run into trouble from conservative religious authorities despite her royal connections, might have faced had she published some undeniably scandalous tales. Other contemporary women writers chose not to seek publication, such as Vittoria Colonna—like Marguerite, a sympathizer with Protestant "heresies." The mid- to late 1540s when Marguerite was writing were marked by considerable suspicion of reformers. Her criticisms of monks, friars, and the platitudes of Catholic orthodoxy at large were none too subtle, and she may have simply deemed it best to circulate her tales among a circle of likeminded friends similar to the little group gathered for a time at the Abbey of Our Lady at Sarrance. Finally, in a provocative article, Edwin Duval has suggested that Marguerite's "*nouvelles*" should be seen not as "short stories" at all but as "news":

Copyright © 2009 Pearson Education, Inc. Publishing as Longman.

reports of anything new and true, and therefore to be distinguished from the "merely" literary ("'Et Puis, quelles nouvelles?': The Project of Marguerite's Unfinished *Decameron*," in Lyons and McKinley, 1993). Such veracity contrasted with Boccaccio's false stories, Duval argues, as well as with the "*bonne nouvelle*" or good news of the Gospels. But the stories' references to purportedly true events may also have been an argument against their publication, at least in Marguerite's own lifetime.

Francis Petrarch

"Although I much doubt whether my obscure little name can have reached you at such a distance of time and space, it is possible that you have some inkling of me, and it may be that you would rather like to know what sort of man I was, and what became of my works, especially those which you know only by repute" (*My Secret Book*, trans. J. G. Nichols, 2002; p. 95). Thus wrote Petrarch in his "A Draft of a Letter to Posterity" when the poet was in his early fifties (and not, as one has been led to think, on his deathbed). The fact that his "obscure little name" has indeed reached us—and is he being falsely modest to imagine that it might not have?—is a testament to his apparently ceaseless energy as a scholar, humanist, and writer who did what he had to do in order to devote himself full-time to his craft. In her foreword to J. G. Nichols' recent translation of Petrarch's *Secretum* and the letter cited above, Germaine Greer offers us an arresting image of this life: "Condemned to lifelong bachelorhood [through having entered minor orders], he flitted restlessly from place to place, back and forth across Italy, France, Flanders, and Provence, lugging with him an immense weight of manuscripts both of his own works and the works of others, terrified that they would be lost or damaged in transit" (p. ix). Or as Petrarch puts it more succinctly at the end of his autobiographical letter, "I was never able to stay still; and I went not so much from the desire to see once more what I had already seen a thousand times, but, as sick men do, endeavoring to cope with tedium by a change of scene" (*My Secret Book*, p. 103).

Petrarch wrote this letter, like hundreds of others and much else besides, in Latin. Yet despite his avowed preference for what was still in the fourteenth century the undeniably universal language, he is best remembered for his work in Italian, particularly his lyric poetry (which goes unmentioned in the "Letter to Posterity"). Gathered together in the volume Petrarch christened with the Latin title *Rerum vulgarum fragmenti* ("Fragments of vernacular poetry"), the poems are more popularly known as the *Canzoniere* or the "rime sparse" (scattered rhymes) to which Petrarch alludes in his opening sonnet. The fact that Petrarch devoted so many years to writing, revising, and ordering the 366-poem sequence belies his attempts to trivialize his work in Italian. The chronology he constructs from these "fragments" allows us to participate in the unfolding not simply of an unrequited passion but also of a life, albeit told in highly selective moments. That this life speaks to us with such directness, despite the formality of the metrical and verse constraints within which

Copyright © 2009 Pearson Education, Inc. Publishing as Longman.

Petrarch worked—the fourteen-line sonnet that he perfected, the sestina, the more flexible canzone that occasionally rises, as Robert Durling has suggested in *Petrarch's Lyric Poems* (1976), like a "structural pillar" in the midst of the collection—is one of the paradoxes of the sequence, one that poets after him struggled to repeat with varying degrees of success. Students may initially find the artificiality of the poems' formal structures off-putting, and it's easy to accuse Petrarch of whining. Yet it's worth it (imperative, actually), to read closely and to use the contrast between style and content to your advantage. Playing on the literal meaning of "*stanza*" (room), you might ask students how Petrarch enables that Shakespearean sleight of hand, great reckonings in little rooms. (Durling's edition of the poems, cited earlier, provides both the Italian text and a literal, prose translation that may be useful to have on hand if it is possible to introduce some Italian into the classroom.)

Once students have begun to be intrigued by the mysteries of form, you might turn to the difficulties presented by classical citations, many of which students may be familiar with from Volume A of the *Anthology*. (Given that Petrarch is famously said to straddle medieval and modern, he's a good person to use in glimpses both forward and back.) These allusions in turn can help unravel the tensions between the sacred and the secular that are everywhere felt in the *Canzoniere*, as well as in Petrarch's other works. (His *Secretum* or *My Secret Book*, a dialogue between himself and St. Augustine, simply refuses to resolve the struggle between carnal love and commitment to God; a clearly exhausted Augustine closes the third and final book of the dialogue admitting, "Let things carry on like this, since they cannot be otherwise. I pray God that He will accompany you on your way and permit you, however far you wander off, eventually to reach safety"; *My Secret Book*, p. 93). But is this struggle only about the inability of Petrarch to restrain his desires? Laura, first glimpsed in a church on Good Friday, is introduced with explicitly devotional imagery, as in Sonnet 3; and there is the danger that there might be something potentially idolatrous about this earthly passion, as suggested by Durling in his introduction to Petrarch's lyrics, and by John Freccero in "The Fig Tree and the Laurel," *Diacritics* 5 (1975): 34–40. This is the theme not only of Petrarch's imaginary dialogue with Augustine and of his letter written on Mount Ventoux but also of sonnets such as Sonnet 16, where the "little white-haired pale old man" traveling to Rome to see Veronica's veil doubles for the pilgrim Petrarch who is searching for the "longed-for true form" of his lady.

Petrarch's supposed inability to choose between Christian salvation and the idolatrous love that might bring him the fame associated with classical poets is adumbrated throughout the *Canzoniere*, especially in those sonnets where he mourns the fact that life is swiftly overtaking him and that he has nothing to show for his gray locks but a handful of poems. And yet one also wonders if lurking within Petrarca's "dilemma" is a forceful contrast with Dante, whose supremely divine Beatrice of Dante's own poetry book, the *Vita nuova*, had functioned as the medium for the poet's salvation. More than a contrast: Petrarch may be furnishing a *critique* of the beloved's genuine ability to send one to Paradise—and hence a challenge to the veracity of Dante's poems.

Copyright © 2009 Pearson Education, Inc. Publishing as Longman.

Canzoniere 126 imagines an encounter with the woman of "divine bearing" who seems as though she *should* be able to lead the poet to paradise. But as Nancy Vickers has argued in "Re-membering Dante: Petrarch's 'Chiare, fresche et dolci acque'" (*Modern Language Notes* 96 [1981]), in this echo of *Purgatorio* 30, where Matelda invites Dante to walk through Eden and meet the resplendent Beatrice, Petrarch resists such a crossing—a crossing that, in Dante's case, forced him to leave his guide Virgil behind. If we read the poems as a sustained narrative on Petrarch's emotional and spiritual life, Petrarch forsakes neither Virgil nor, until the closing hymn to the virgin, his earthly vision of Laura. This suggests, to be sure, allegiance to the classical texts that Augustine warns Petrarch to jettison. But it also emphasizes the extent to which Dante's poetry is a *fiction*. Countering Dante's own attempts to convince his readers that he wrote the truth, Petrarch asks whether it is even remotely possible that Dante's fiction is real: How could Dante have traveled to Purgatory and met both Matelda and his beloved Beatrice? Isn't Petrarch's poetry more authentic, as it admits that mere words and mere humans can never bridge the chasm between the terrestrial and divine?

These issues are also central in the Latin letters Petrarch wrote throughout his lifetime, two of which are presented in the *Anthology*. The letters can serve as useful starting points to the *Canzoniere* for a number of reasons. The later letter, to Boccaccio, contains some of Petrarch's most provocative statements on the process of imitation, which can be said to be at the center of the *Canzoniere* as Petrarch navigates through the poetry of antiquity and medieval Europe to attempt to emerge with an authentic voice of his own. Particularly instructive is Petrarch's reference to the analogy of the "bee," which probably originated with the Roman poet Lucretius and found numerous echoes in later centuries, among them Seneca's insistence that the bee necessarily alters the substance of what it gathers, thereby attesting to the poet's maturity and individuality. Yet as Thomas Greene has observed in *The Light in Troy: Imitation and Discovery in Renaissance Poetry* (1982), the mark of Petrarch—and for Greene, of the Renaissance—is that he can no longer embrace the positive mastery that is implied in the metaphor of the bee, as perhaps Petrarch's own practice, if not his manifesto to Boccaccio, suggests. The nightingale allusion, found in numerous sonnets but particularly central in Sonnet 311, may elucidate such a practice, as reference to the original simile, from Virgil's *Georgics*, might suggest. Students could be asked to differentiate between Virgil's and Petrarch's two birds (one, female, mourning the loss of children; the other, male, mourning—but only perhaps!—that of a dear consort), as well as to comment on the distance between the nightingale and the suffering, Orphic singer. In Virgil, the nightingale is isolated from Orpheus, contained within the simile, while in Petrarch, as Greene has noted, there *is* no simile anymore, since both speaker and nightingale share the same space. What had appeared to be "objective externality" has "collapsed into a privacy on the verge of solipsism" (p. 123). Moreover, Petrarch will take a single Latin word, "*durus*" ("harsh," used in reference to the *arator* or ploughman who kills the nightingale's children in Virgil) and effectively divide it into two words: the "*dura sorte*" or "harsh fate" that he laments as his own in the

Copyright © 2009 Pearson Education, Inc. Publishing as Longman.

second stanza, and the inability of anything that is pleasing to "*dura*" or endure ("*come nulla qua giù diletta et dura*"). What one might characterize as the secure unity of the Latin language is doubled and fragmented, as the Italian in which the modern Petrarch writes is shown to possess a new openness of meaning.

The letter to the Augustinian monk Dionigi, published in full in Volume C, could introduce students to larger narrative issues that preoccupy the poet in the *Canzoniere*: the conflict between the earthly and the spiritual, Petrarch's passion for Laura, the relevance of the "ancients" for the moderns. What brings poet and epistolarist together? The similarities may not only be thematic ones, and here students can think about the role of narrative in Petrarch's work as a whole. What is in the Latin a single tormented sentence (broken up into several in the English translation) might furnish a good example of Petrarch's stylistic complexity and the extent to which it provides, or fails to provide, narrative and spiritual resolution. This is a moment in which Petrarch is reflecting on the nature of his penitence regarding his sinful love (students are well reminded that Petrarch was a minor cleric)—"What I used to love I no longer love" (p. 188, near top)—and culminating with "sorrowfully and mournfully." Statement followed by revision, followed by another revision, followed finally—perhaps—by the "truth": like many Renaissance writers, Petrarch values process over product, and indeed, much of the letter written on Mt. Ventoux is about the meandering routes that the poet takes to arrive at the mountain's summit. Does attaining the summit truly change him in any meaningful way? Dante's arrival on Mt. Purgatorio transformed him utterly, and so did Augustine's memorable experience in the garden in Book 8 of the *Confessions* (see Vol. A of the *Anthology*, pp. 1321–1322). What is Petrarch really telling us about the quasi-epic journey he travels with his brother Gherardo, a journey that indeed reaches back both to Christian and pagan antiquity in its supposed symbolism? This is a symbolism that Laura Cereta would seem to pointedly exclude from her own account of her voyage (presented as a Resonance selection in the *Anthology*, discussed next).

RESONANCE

Laura Cereta

In Laura Cereta's letter, she is more responsive to natural details than Petrarch is. Only her return affords her the opportunity for reflections that preclude her from making herself into an example for others. Unlike Petrarch, she is seized by no hubristic desire to equal or better the ancients; unlike him, she does not place herself within a lineage that includes Virgil, Ambrose, and Augustine. Yet the relative modesty of her claims and her refusal to situate her outing within the framework of Livy's *History of Rome* should not conceal from us her own accomplishments. Others spoke for this young Brescian woman of considerable talent who had been given an exemplary humanist education by her father, Silvestro; hence the

Copyright © 2009 Pearson Education, Inc. Publishing as Longman.

Dominican Fra Tommaso of Milan calls her a "new Penelope, weaving garments skillfully with her nightly work" and as skillful a depicter of battles as she is of women's cosmetics. Cereta spoke out, vigorously, against men who attacked women's right and ability to learn and women who shunned the life of reason and learning to deck themselves out in makeup and fancy clothes; for her part, as she writes in one letter, "Let Marc Antony be attracted by bejeweled Cleopatra; I shall imitate the innocence of Rebecca. Let Paris seek the wandering Helen; I choose to imitate the modesty of Rachel" (from *Laura Cereta: Collected Letters of a Renaissance Feminist*, trans. Diana Robin). And all this before she reached the age of twenty.

The letter (in Latin) about Cereta's climb up Mt. Isola is one of 82 left behind when Cereta died in 1499. It seems to start in the midst of an argument Cereta is having with her sister, who by 1487 was in a convent. Cereta is typically modest, even self-deprecating at the beginning ("I have acquired only a shadow of learning," p. 192) and is subdued in her description of the mountain climb, one from which any allegorical meaning seems to be deliberately absented. Yet in many ways the joy in the "small gardens" and her expressed "freedom from care" are a prelude to her later thoughts on Epicurus: the "banquet" on which they dine is sufficiently modest, they find contentment in the small pleasures of their climb and descent, the lovely, yet never overwhelming "nature" that she finds on the mountainside gently leads her to "incline her heart freely and deliberately toward the good." This urge to contentment in the here and now as a means of fixing the mind on God is in its own way a rousing criticism of the itinerant Petrarch's inability to dwell with delight in a single place: "Long enough have we wandered in all directions in an attempt to change places. But can this wandering through various pastures, this exchange of one forest for another, touch in any way the mind . . . ?" (p. 194). She has suffered, like Petrarch, from self-delusion—"I believed that I was crossing a threshold to greater tranquility by this running to and fro of mine"—but unlike him, she has found, she maintains, true serenity, aided perhaps in no small part by her sister, who even though she is locked in "solitude" is still a lively and consoling presence.

cᴏ❦ᴐ

RESONANCES

Petrarch and His Translators

A discussion of *Canzoniere* 190 and 209, along with Thomas Wyatt's and Chiara Matraini's "revisions," can introduce students to the comparative enterprise as a way of revealing the intricacies of poetic process. Both these revisers of Petrarch enable us to see what we missed the first time through. The two Petrarchan poems take up the familiar topos of the hunt, but the narrator occupies different subject positions in the sonnets. In Sonnet 190, he is the hunter, in Sonnet 209—as we learn only in line 8—he is the hunted, the *cervo*, or the hart or stag. Reading 190 next to Wyatt's haunting lyric, "Whoso List to Hunt," a poem more inspired by

Copyright © 2009 Pearson Education, Inc. Publishing as Longman.

Petrarch than a pretense to a literal translation, we realize that Petrarch gives us within fourteen lines a single, distinctive episode that ends as the *cerva* runs off. As Stephen Greenblatt has commented in *Renaissance Self-Fashioning* (1980), Wyatt's narrator is a lover as obsessed at the poem's end as at the beginning; disturbingly, he seeks to involve the reader in this obsession as he directs the poem toward us not once but twice ("Whoso list to hunt," line 1; "Who list," line 9). Once we read Wyatt, we recognize to what extent Petrarch's poem occupies a small protected space that we watch only from afar. Wyatt permits no such distance nor does he allow us (or himself) any temporal closure.

In shifting to Sonnet 209 you can ask what in this poem permits Chiara Matraini to respond in kind: Is Petrarch's narrator in any way feminized by turning himself into the hunted beast, reminiscent of Virgil's Dido in *Aenied* 4? (See Volume A of the *Anthology*, p. 1146, lines 91–98.) Whereas Petrarch turns to the *cervo* only halfway through the poem, using the first two quartets for a dazzling display of introspection, Matraini introduces her simile immediately, and it dominates the entire poem as a result. She focuses less on the linguistic self-reflexivity everywhere apparent in Petrarch's language and more on the paradox that flight from the powerful impulse of *eros* can only lead to destruction—a flight made real by the metamorphosis of hart into bird.

Lyric Sequences and Self-Definition

The poets represented here in the section on lyric sequences—to which should also be added the selections of John Donne and Anne Bradstreet—reflect only a small portion of the verses published in the sixteenth and seventeenth centuries. Petrarch's *rime sparse*, written in the vernacular and revelatory of love's losses and their natural corollary, poetic identity, were *the* poems to imitate in early modern Italy as well as France, England, Spain, and eventually Mexico. Numerous explanations have been offered for Petrarch's staying power, ranging from Anne Ferry's provocative suggestion in *The "Inward" Language* (1983) that he offered the first example of an early modern self, to Roland Greene's *Unrequited Conquests* (1999) arguing for Petrarch's adaptability to colonial contexts. More prosaically, Petrarch's poems were short and his vocabulary relatively circumscribed, encouraging imitation by the most mediocre of poets (and there were plenty of them). Even though many poems circulated in manuscript, the printing press facilitated publication and promised fame if not financial fortune to the more entrepreneurial writers. Publishers themselves were ready to make a quick buck by producing anthologies, as in the best-selling collection *Diverse rhymes of some of the most noble and most virtuous of women* printed in Venice in 1559.

Copyright © 2009 Pearson Education, Inc. Publishing as Longman.

The writers selected here are of interest not for their slavish reproduction of Petrarch but for their revisions of and challenges to Petrarchan models. As will be immediately clear, they were relatively uninterested in recreating the sequence of the *rime sparse*. Louise Labé and Jan Kochanowski alone were preoccupied with ordering the poems of their brief sequences for publication, and neither one followed the "in life/in death" division of Petrarch's lyrics: Labé's would-be lovers are very much alive, and Kochanowski spends nineteen poems mourning the death of his young daughter. For the other poets, the order is largely hypothetical. Vittoria Colonna had no role in putting together the slender volume called *Poems of the Divine Vittoria Colonna*, the first such published collection of poetry by an Italian woman, while Shakespeare was as careless in publishing his sonnets as he was his plays. Meanwhile, Michelangelo, many of whose poems were dashed off in the margins of architectural designs, wrote in a variety of meters and on a wide range of topics completely alien to Petrarch's corpus.

"The value of the object is clear: the way to approach it is not." This is the critic Harold Toliver in *Lyric Provinces in the English Renaissance* (1985) isolating one of the central dynamics of lyric poetry, a poetry that has tended since its inception in Greece and elsewhere to idealize its object, usually, but not always, a beloved. In introducing the lyrics of early modernity, you might bring in the poems of Anacreon or Sappho (whose name was invoked frequently in regard to Renaissance women writers such as Labé and Sor Juana). The other end of the spectrum—contemporary music—can also afford lively comparisons, as the innovative work of Nancy Vickers amply bears out (see "Lyric in the Video Decade," *Discourse* 16.1 [1993]). At the same time, you will want to ask students the same questions that Michelangelo and Shakespeare asked themselves: How could they make their poetry seem new, rather than a tired echo of past verses? How to find a different approach to the object? And most disturbingly, but from a poetic point of view perhaps most interesting: What if the value of the object is no longer clear—no longer a given, as in Shakespeare's poems to the dark lady? Or conversely, what if poetry is simply not up to the project of idealization, of valorizing the beloved as beyond value? Sor Juana, like Shakespeare, is a wonderful ironist. Her poem on her own portrait might be fruitfully read against Elizabeth Cropper's article, "The Beauty of Women: Problems in the Rhetoric of Portraiture," in *Rewriting the Renaissance* (eds. Margaret W. Ferguson et al., 1986), in which Cropper observes that like verses, paintings were frequently done to render the lady beautiful and in turn to reflect back on the talents of the artist. Sor Juana's poem, however, curtly dismisses art's ability to monumentalize: the portrait is "nada," as the Spanish makes painfully clear.

Sor Juana's interference with the long tradition of idealizing art is to a large extent shared by all the writers in this section. As Carol Thomas Neely notes in an excellent article in *English Literary History* on Petrarch and his English followers, idealization and consummation are "equally invalid alternatives" for the sixteenth-century writer of sonnets ("The Structure of English Renaissance Sonnet Sequences," *ELH* 45 [1978], pp. 359–389). But this is particularly the case with the

Copyright © 2009 Pearson Education, Inc. Publishing as Longman.

women poets, from Labé to Matriani to Bradstreet and Sor Juana herself. Petrarch's Laura had been mostly silent, the untouchable *cerva* of *Canzoniere* 190 (and the "wyld" hind of Wyatt's Petrarchan paraphrase), at least, that is, until her death, when her tongue is unfettered, as it were, to chide the poet from a safe distance. As William Kennedy has observed, the women writers "seek to evade the female role that Petrarchism forces upon [them]" ("Petrarchan Textuality: Commentaries and Gender Revisions," in *Discourses of Authority in Medieval and Renaissance Literature*, eds. Kevin Brownlee and Walter Stephens, 1987, p. 161), asking themselves, "What happens when Laura speaks?" The answers are surprising, especially if it turns out, as it does with Labé and Matriani, that Laura herself is the desiring subject. Vittoria Colonna's beloved, however, is dead, and arguably her husband's distance gives her the possibility of writing as she can admit to a desire that can no longer endanger her chaste identity. Sor Juana has her *own* Laura who dies, her erstwhile patroness the Marquise de Mancera, known as "Laura" in her works. The fact that she was also close to another patroness, the Condesa de Paredes, has led to some speculation as to an erotic love interest between the two women, mostly dismissed as unfounded. But the elegies open up an interesting window onto poetry between women, whether or not it has a lesbian dimension.

Taking the male as an object of desire was not limited to women poets. You could make the case that Michelangelo (who had a long correspondence with Vittoria Colonna) and, far more tentatively, Shakespeare were influenced by a body of women's poetry in which the beloved was a man. The homoeroticism of Michelangelo's unpublished verses was camouflaged by many of his first editors, who breezily altered pronouns; and Michelangelo seems to have engaged in some gender-bending scenarios himself, judging from multiple revisions of single poems. A comparison of Shakespeare's "young man" sonnets (also the victims of bowdlerized editions) and Michelangelo's poems to the aristocrat Tommaso Cavalieri makes for fascinating reading, not least because of their quirky print history. In particular, you can raise the question as to the effects of an idealizing tradition on the possibly autobiographical elements captured in the poems and thus point out how the Platonic love that Cavalieri inspires in Michelangelo could be a cover for a more physical passion (albeit one unconsummated between the sculptor, then in his seventies, and the young Roman). This playing with the real and the ideal is especially marked in Shakespeare. While the young man sonnets only occasionally let in the "real" world in the form of stinging words from rival poets, the dark lady poems, two of which appear in the *Anthology*, reveal the first 126 sonnets as a delicate construct that cannot withstand the pressures of reality. In sonnet 130, sonnet-making is thus declared bankrupt. The flesh and blood of a woman of unconventional beauty call into question the fragility of the narrator's relationship with the young man—much as the horrendous fact of the death of Kochanowski's daughter calls into question the fragility of Christian belief.

As almost all the poets' seemingly anguished questions about the nature of their art reveal, the Petrarchan model enables its most talented practitioners to question art's role in the world, particularly its ability to either enhance or disfig-

Copyright © 2009 Pearson Education, Inc. Publishing as Longman.

ure its subject. The model also forces poets to ask themselves what happens when they "go public" with their love: Doesn't this open them up to others' questions about the veracity of their verse (Michelangelo), to possible competition (Shakespeare), to criticism (Labé)? These questions in turn touch on some fascinating topics in literary criticism. The lyrics here can be cited as instances of an early modern inquiry into the nature of the literary, and how isolated it is—or is not—from the world beyond the written page.

Last but by no means least, there is much to be gained from a close reading of the Shakespearean poems, along with the later entries from Donne and Bradstreet, the only ones not in translation. In particular, you will want to note their constant punning, such as "eye" and "I," "will" and "Will"; these are only two of the most obvious examples. As for the other poets, it is rewarding to work in the original wherever possible. Bilingual editions exist for all of the poems included here, and reading them aloud in the original Italian, Spanish, or French is meaningful insofar as students can hear that the poems are also musical events; it is not surprising that much early modern lyric was set to music. In recognition of lyric's proximity to music, Labé likens her "companion," the lute, to her scribe (see Vol. C, p. 213), and several poets invoke the consummate singer Orpheus as their archetype. Like the typical Renaissance lyricist, Orpheus is at his best when the distance between himself and his beloved is insurmountable, having lost his bride Eurydice to Hades because the power of his song could not conquer his own human frailty. You might use the Orpheus story (in Ovid's *Metamorphoses*) to interrogate the role of all the "singers" represented here and to ask students: Without the great distances implicit in so many of the verses between lover and beloved, how would the poems have looked? Would there have been any occasion for poetry at all?

Niccolò Machiavelli

Machiavelli's *Prince* is the first of many works encountered in this volume that sets itself up as a book of good "counsel." Castiglione's *Courtier*, Rabelais's *Gargantua and Pantagruel*, even Montaigne's *Essays* fall into the category of advice literature for readers of Europe's elite classes. The trick with *The Prince*, however, is that the counsel offered has been judged as almost universally repugnant since Machiavelli addressed his little book to two different Medici princes. Much scholarship of the past few decades has attempted to understand why Machiavelli became associated with the devil or anti-Christ (Shakespeare's Richard III and Iago are just a few of the most famous Renaissance "Machiavels"). Other scholars have sought to reform this traditional image of Machiavelli's writings. Thus in some cases, such as J. G. A. Pocock's magisterial *The Machiavellian Moment* (1975), his work has been seen as the catalyst for a vibrant republican tradition that would culminate in the creation of the American republic. But Pocock's work is largely dependent on the treatise Machiavelli wrote on the heels of *The Prince*, his *Discourses on Livy*. The *Discourses* are very different in tone and intent

Copyright © 2009 Pearson Education, Inc. Publishing as Longman.

from the more scurrilous piece said to have been Mussolini's favorite book. Confronted with *The Prince* alone, how are we to read it?

One necessarily reductive way, although useful as a starting point, is to present *The Prince* as a document written for political scientists, thereby suggesting that we must take Machiavelli at his word. He is a struggling political strategist, the inside man of a party now out of power, trying to interest the new regime in his areas of expertise. Even if the Florentine republic for which Machiavelli slaved for many years did not have a prince, in his role as secretary Machiavelli came into contact with many such leaders, including the one placed on a pedestal for his ruthless ambition and ability to separate what *should* be from what *is*. Cesare Borgia, ruler of the large territories outside Rome and ideally poised at one point in his career to move into Tuscany as well, had managed to divorce whatever ethical inclinations he might have had from ideas about political expediency. While the concept of an immoral leader is hardly palatable to our Puritan-influenced sensibilities, to Borgia, and certainly to his shrewdest commentator, it seemed to be the only means of releasing Italy from the grip of foreign powers. Yet Machiavelli is also aware that princes need to invoke ethical platitudes in order to stay in power, even and especially if they don't observe them. Hence the unsettling corollary that follows, the one that has made Machiavelli most unsavory for his readers: The prince doesn't have to *be* good, he only has to *seem* to be good.

The consideration of such "advice" could easily be followed up with a classroom discussion of contemporary politics and the media's role in both unveiling our leaders' moral failings and defending the necessity of ethical veneers. But Machiavelli was more than the isolated, radical demystifier of political machinery. For one thing, his method of reading history should raise red flags as to whether he thinks his own advice can be taken as seriously as readers have thought. Like Montaigne, he is good at posing alternatives without pronouncing definitively on a necessary resolution; he wonders why opposing methods sometimes yield the same result, generating—as in Marguerite de Navarre's *Heptameron*, or Rabelais's *Gargantua and Pantagruel*—the possibility of multiple interpretations. And like many of his contemporaries, he is painfully aware of the role of "Fortune," which overturns the best-laid plans. (You might ask students whether or not the *machismo* of Chapter 25, where Machiavelli likens Fortune to a woman who must be beaten to be controlled, is a convincing solution to the problems laid out in the book. Hanna Fenichel Pitkin's *Fortune Is a Woman: Gender and Politics in the Thought of Niccolò Machiavelli* [1984] is a good introduction to that elusive quality of *virtù*, rooted in the Latin word *vir* or male, and mentioned many times in *The Prince*.) Borgia's failure to create an Italian state, detailed in Chapter 7 (not excerpted in the *Anthology*), is due to two events beyond his control: the death of his powerful father, Rodrigo, better known as Pope Alexander VI, in 1503 (Alexander fathered at least five children), and a sickness that laid Cesare low at a time when he should have moved forward with his conquest of Tuscany. We are thus faced with a gap, as it were, in the middle of *The Prince*. The Borgia model—one Borgia a pope, the other a ruthless "prince"—looks to be duplicated by the Medici, as Giovanni de'

Copyright © 2009 Pearson Education, Inc. Publishing as Longman.

Medici is elected Pope Leo X just as the family returns to dominate Florence and its many holdings in Tuscany. But the Borgia, like any family, ruthless or not, is helpless before the most severe blows of fortune's slings and arrows; and even Machiavelli's original dedicatee, Giuliano de' Medici, dies in 1516 shortly after *The Prince* is completed.

Such musings lead us to address *The Prince* as a literary work. In the introduction to their volume of essays, *Machiavelli and the Discourses of Literature* (1993), Albert Ascoli and Victoria Kahn ask to what extent Machiavelli's turn to writing in the wake of the Medici's return to power was conceived as a lesser, unworthy occupation for one who had been so gifted in political organization. This question is an important one, emerging in Machiavelli's embittered preface to *The Prince*. At the same time, it is also the case that he had a lifelong interest in writing plays and poetry (Ronald Martinez rightly calls his masterpiece, *Mandragola* or *The Mandrake*, "one of the funniest plays ever written"; see "The Pharmacy of Machiavelli" in *Renaissance Drama* 14 [1983], pp. 1–43), and his remarks in *The Prince* on the divorce between seeming and being hearken to a consummately theatrical sensibility. To a certain extent, this could be said to have been the product of Machiavelli's intense engagement with the small, vibrant town that was Renaissance Florence: a town dominated by over fifty piazzas and twenty private loggias where, as Machiavelli's contemporary Benedetto Dei suggested, "men of every class play at hazard and others hold discussions about the goings-on of the Comune." These boisterous images of give-and-take suggest the existence of a social and political culture dependent on both reasonable exchange and, at times, back-biting gossip, a world in which everyone knew everything about their neighbors. But for those who sought to dominate this world, the need for secrecy, for dissimulation, for the deliberate withholding of information from the men of the piazza, was paramount.

Yet *The Prince*'s literary preeminence can be conceived in other ways, as we consider the strong influence of vernacular writings on Machiavelli's work, as does Carlo Dionisotti in "Machiavelli, Man of Letters" in the Ascoli and Kahn volume. The closing chapter with its allusion to Petrarch's rousing *canzone*, "Italia mia" (see p. 239) is the most poignant example of what Ascoli (in "Machiavelli's Gift of Counsel," Ascoli and Kahn) has seen as the abyss in Machiavelli's writings between political reality and literary utopias: in the absence of a political savior, one can have recourse only to myth. The Bible, too, plays a prominent part in *The Prince*, not only with the frequent allusions to Moses as the triumphant Hebrew leader who brought his people out of slavery but also with the seemingly apocalyptic rhetoric of the last chapter—an odd note in a book that has tended to reduce Christianity to a political ploy. Even Dante, Machiavelli's Florentine compatriot, has a part, as Sebastiano de Grazia argues in his insightful *Machiavelli in Hell* (1989). The weight given by Machiavelli to literary texts should not lead us automatically to assume, however, that writing functioned for him as merely an escape from problematic junctures; rather, he no doubt saw himself as following a tradition of Italian writers committed to probing the issues of the age through imagi-

Copyright © 2009 Pearson Education, Inc. Publishing as Longman.

native constructions. And perhaps *The Prince* can be approached as such a construct. It sets up a hypothesis, an alternate world as in Thomas More's Utopia or Dante's afterlife, vigorously and realistically laid forth, but without finally procuring any commitment of authenticity from its troubled, and troubling, inventor.

c∞,

RESONANCE

Baldesar Castiglione

Castiglione has typically been seen as providing a striking contrast with the rough-and-tumble of Machiavelli's political manifesto. Product of the elegant court of Urbino, which Castiglione nostalgically commemorates in his preface, *The Book of the Courtier* indeed breathes forth a very different air. It is no accident that Raphael, a native of Urbino, is celebrated in its pages as the epitome of a painterly, at times ethereal beauty. His serene women exist in a world far from that of the tortured, sinuous bodies of Michelangelo—who hailed, like Machiavelli, from Florence.

In "The Flexibility of the Self in Renaissance Literature" (in *Disciplines of Criticism*, eds. Peter Demetz et al., 1968), Thomas Greene suggests that Castiglione's courtiers ultimately hold to the belief in a "vertical flexibility of man" that for Greene was one of the primary tenets of the Renaissance. Machiavelli summarily rejects the possibility of positive change: flexibility can lead only "downward to the brute, rather than upward to the angel." Greene's article is a succinct and insightful account of the loss of an early Renaissance optimism in self-fashioning and is highly recommended as an introduction to many of the authors in this volume. One must ask, however, whether Castiglione's courtier is as "flexible"—in either a vertical or horizontal sense—as Greene imagines him to be; and further, whether the supposed taint of Machiavelli's amorality really escapes Castiglione's dignified interlocutors. As the first chapter excerpted in the *Anthology* suggests, the courtier must excel at "concealing art" and the very practices by which he makes himself pleasing to his prince and those around him. We could say that much of *The Courtier* dissects the relationship Machiavelli appears to take for granted, one in which the prince will actually listen to what his advisors have to say.

For unlike Machiavelli, Castiglione, who spent many years as a diplomat and court secretary, focused on the means whereby one gains access to the prince and wins not only his confidence but also that of his other servants. At the same time, self-fashioning in Castiglione involves knowing about fashion, as well as music, dance, horseback-riding—activities that in fact bring the male courtier precariously close to being in a feminized position. And the chapter on female grace—as well as that on the Queen of Castile, Isabella, from the third book, dedicated to stories about women and the perfect "*donna di palazzo*" or court lady—does show how women are central to courtly practices. *The Courtier* could be seen as staging a crisis in masculinity provoked by a courtly system in which all power devolved from a single individual and all others had to compete for his attention (or hers: al-

Copyright © 2009 Pearson Education, Inc. Publishing as Longman.

though Elisabetta Gonzaga does not speak much, she is the presiding authority as the Duchess while her husband lies ill upstairs).

These concerns are expressed in the last book, devoted to the "ends of courtiership" (an excerpt from which appears as the final Castiglione selection in the Resonance section). Probably written over a decade after the first three books, the first section of Book 4 dramatically redirects the previous discussion as Castiglione demands that we take seriously the courtier's real job: to educate his prince and lead him to *virtù*—the same virtue Machiavelli said should guide the prince in his struggles against fortune. In *Courtly Performances: Masking and Festivity in Castiglione's Book of the Courtier* (1978), Wayne Rebhorn speaks of the "profound gulf" between Books 3 and 4, while suggesting that we should not privilege Ottaviano's and Gasparo's remarks simply because they were added belatedly to the text. Rebhorn argues that *The Courtier* should be read as a "symposium" that allows multiple perspectives to co-exist, and it is useful to think of Castiglione's work vis-à-vis not only Machiavelli but also Plato's *Symposium* and other literary dialogues such as Marguerite de Navarre's *Heptameron*. Yet for all of the grace in which Castiglione shrouds his interlocutors, there are still, as in Machiavelli, profound tensions that cannot easily be masked either by the framework of a game or the artful *sprezzatura* that Ottaviano alone seems to disdain.

François Rabelais

The Rabelaisian world is like no other and in its constant metamorphoses probably resembles to a large degree its author, frequently changing careers, frequently on the run from authorities hostile to and suspicious of his idea of "fun." And Rabelais is without doubt funny, even though, as Barbara Bowen has recently pointed out (*Enter Rabelais, Laughing*, 1998), his laughter is not infrequently tinged with cruelty. But he was born in bad times, at least for a parodist and free-thinker like himself. While France would eventually become one of the more tolerant of European countries, in the early years of the Reformation it was particularly repressive. The years 1532 and 1545 (dates coinciding, respectively, with the publication of *Pantagruel* and the *Third Book*) marked occasions of intensified hostility to "heretics," and publishers paid the price for spreading Protestant "lies." Etienne Dolet, Rabelais's first publisher, was burned at the stake, not for publishing *Gargantua* and *Pantagruel* but for disseminating Platonic dialogues that questioned the immortality of the soul.

Plato looms large in Rabelais too, particularly the idea of the symposium or "drunkards' feast" to which we are treated in *Gargantua*, when Friar John proclaims, "How good God is to give us this good drink!" and discourses on the size of his nose (pp. 272–273). The Silenus figure, described by Alcibiades in the *Symposium* as a figure for Socrates, was also a favorite for Rabelais. In the prologue

Copyright © 2009 Pearson Education, Inc. Publishing as Longman.

to *Gargantua*, Rabelais discusses the Silenus at some length: it is a little box found in apothecaries' shops, ugly, comical, and grotesque on the outside, full of rare drugs "and other precious things" (p. 250) on the inside. According to Rabelais, Socrates was always laughing and always drunk, but the "superhuman understanding" (p. 250) and virtue he possessed within were unmatchable. The tricky thing is to move from Silenus and Socrates to Rabelais and his books, likewise comical, arguably grotesque, reeking of wine rather than oil; and yet, perhaps—only perhaps—containing therein the precious drug or delicious marrow a dog sucks from the bone. Rabelais opens the possibility that his books about giants contain deep and abstruse meaning only to dissuade us from searching for it. He is arguably both parodying the extensive use of allegory in late medieval culture, still practiced in the conservative Parisian universities such as the Sorbonne which Rabelais detested, and minimizing the trenchant criticisms of that culture laid out in his text (criticisms that indeed got him into trouble, as the banning of his books by the Sorbonne attests). More interestingly, Rabelais may be putting less emphasis on finding meaning and more emphasis on the processes through which it is made—through laughter, the grotesque, hyperbole, and above all, constant dialogue and jovial conversations. In contrast to Augustine, for Rabelais the journey is arguably more useful than the arrival and certainly more fun than understanding life as a body of knowledge capable of being pinned down and taught altogether too dryly in school.

The four books known to be by Rabelais (Book 5 is universally admitted to be spurious, no doubt the work of an author anxious to make a buck by writing a sequel), written over a twenty-year period, are also reflective of a process, a writer trying not merely to hone his craft but to discover exactly what it is. The four books are indeed very different from one another. It is generally agreed that *Pantagruel*, the first written but second in the series, is more slapstick and "populist" as it treats in episodic, almost chaotic fashion, Pantagruel's birth, childhood, arrival in Paris, and war with the Dipsodes when he drowns the giants' camp with his urine, which the enemy interprets as a sign of the last judgment. The humor is relentlessly scatological and the geography, excepting Paris, a fantastic one; Pantagruel's mother, who dies in childbirth, "because Pantagruel was so amazingly large and so heavy" (*Pantagruel*, Chapter 1), is the daughter of the king of the Amaurots in Utopia, a blatant allusion to More's equally fantastic geography. Two of the most significant features of the book are the letter from Gargantua, touted as one of the period's most upbeat expressions of the benefits of a humanistic education, and Pantagruel's encounter with Panurge, who will go on to play a major role in Books 3 and 4.

The letter Gargantua writes to Pantagruel when the latter is off at school distinguishes between the shadowy and unhappy time of the Goths as a time of little learning and the current age when one can learn "parfaictment" the languages of antiquity: Greek, Latin, Hebrew, Chaldean, and Arabic. With them, one could study not only the liberal arts but also medicine (in which as a doctor Rabelais had a special interest) and holy letters: every man could become a theologian. Edwin

Copyright © 2009 Pearson Education, Inc. Publishing as Longman.

Duval has noted the sea changes marked by the letter of the wistful giant to his son. Pantagruel is indeed fortunate, because the study of barbaric Latin is now replaced by the three classical languages, and logic by history and geography, while theology—studied as ecclesiology and metaphysics—gives way to daily personal study of scripture ("The Medieval Curriculum, the Scholastic University, and Gargantua's Program of Studies (*Pantagruel 8*)" in *Rabelais's Incomparable Book: Essays on His Art*, ed. Raymond C. La Charité, 1986, pp. 30-44). Yet as uplifting as such a letter is, it seems slightly out of place in the otherwise irreverent text, and we must wonder if this "parfaicte" comprehension can only be a utopian dream.

This seems particularly so when the polyglot Panurge cannot make his hunger understood as he uses no fewer than thirteen languages in a vain attempt to communicate with the "scholar" Pantagruel in Chapter 9. Described as "a mischievous rogue and a cheat"—like the *picaro* Ginés de Pasamonte in *Don Quixote* (Book 1, Chapter 22)—Panurge will add a significant dose of unpredictable fun to Pantagruel's adventures, proposing, for example, in Chapter 15 that the best fortification for Paris's walls would be women's "thing o' my bobs": their vaginas. In Books 3 and 4 he and Pantagruel go off in search of someone who can tell Panurge definitively whether marriage (to an as-of-yet undetermined spouse) will turn him into a cuckold. In Book 3 they consult with a number of "authorities," drawing lots, for example, and seeking counsel from both judges and fools, while in Book 4 they go to sea in search of the oracle of Babut; the episode of the frozen words they encounter while on board is included in the *Anthology* (p. 284).

In these last two books, the giant status of Pantagruel is diminished, and the flight out in Book 4 from all things recognizably French to uncharted new worlds suggests that a fiercely divided country—or continent, for that matter—can no longer contain the answers to individual quests. Alternatively, given that Books 3 and 4 are anti-epics satirizing the works of Virgil, Homer, and their kin, Rabelais may be intimating that the individual quest no longer has any meaning in the world of the 1540s, Gargantua's earlier optimism notwithstanding. From this perspective, Book 1, or *Gargantua*, published in 1534, two years after *Pantagruel*, and from which most of the Rabelais selections in the *Anthology* are drawn, occupies an interesting and important place. It is firmly situated in France, with most of the book's events taking place in the Chinon valley, where Rabelais himself had a home. Gargantua leaves for Paris for his education, but his learning is interrupted by the ridiculous war begun by Picrochole's bakers, which escalates to such heights that he must return home to fight. Unlike the war with the Dipsodes, however, this one is won not with massive quantities of urine or giant-inspired feats but by the "expeditious assault" led by Gargantua and the inspirational talks his father gives to the troops. Too, Gargantua is helped to no little end by the magnificent monk, Friar John.

On the one hand, Book 1 partakes in the populist humor of Book 2, as well as its exhilarating claims to the generativity not only of the body in its many processes—digestion, defecation, pregnancy (Gargantua spends 11 months *in utero*)—but of language itself. Rabelais delights in lists, but he also takes great plea-

Copyright © 2009 Pearson Education, Inc. Publishing as Longman.

sure in multiplying what might be called the basic building blocks of communication itself: praise, the curse, the enigma, the proverb, the harangue. Mikhail Bakhtin's seminal *Rabelais and His World*, first translated into English from the Russian in 1968, has been especially formative in celebrating this Rabelaisian delight in bodily and linguistic fecundity, tying it to medieval *fablaiaux* and the strong presence of oral cultures in early modern Europe when some 90 percent of the population was still preliterate. Writing as he was in Soviet Russia (although frequently at odds with Soviet authorities), Bakhtin takes special interest in the material aspects of Rabelais's text, suggesting that Rabelais firmly resists any move beyond the material to the transcendent, just as Marx had protested Hegelian synthesis. Less informed by Bakhtin's political views and perhaps more germane to Rabelais's text is the notion of the dialogue as depriviliging a single, unique voice: even when Socrates himself speaks in the *Symposium*, it is to recount his exchange with the mysterious teacher Diotima, thereby revealing identity as both male/female, self/other. In this context, it is inadvisable to try to pin down a single authorizing voice in Rabelais. For Bakhtin, Rabelais is challenging the ecclesiastical and university authorities whose fixed and elitist worldview was ultimately indefensible (perhaps in some way identifiable for Bakhtin with the Soviet hierarchy itself). He celebrates rather the "heroicization of the functions of the life of the body" and by extension, that of the *people*, signified by a "grotesque body" which is ever growing and "ever-victorious."

In *Rabelais and Bakhtin: Popular Culture in Gargantua and Pantagruel* (1986), Richard Berrong notes some limitations of Bakhtin's work, one of which is surely its refusal to acknowledge that Rabelais was writing for the elite reader, the 10 percent of the population that could, in fact, read. He also suggests that *Gargantua* is notably *less* driven by "folk culture" than *Pantagruel*, and more populated by "official" figures. They include Friar John, denizen of that good old medieval institution, the abbey, as well as the teacher and tutor Ponocrates (whose name means "power") and Gargantua's father Grandgousier. The latter metamorphoses from the belching, fantastic giant who feeds on massive quantities of tripe to an enlightened ruler ultimately merciful to Picrochole and his bakers and open to rewarding his soldiers with such prizes as a radically new (and arguably unrealizable) version of the abbey in which men and women politely co-exist and "do as they will"—reminiscent of the civilized storytellers of the *Decameron*, but also of Augustine's mandate that you should "love and do what you will." After a rowdy battle and much feasting, the Abbey of Thélème brings us to a quiet, muted close. Yet throughout *Gargantua* there has been a movement to embrace the disciplined rituals of a thoughtful, educated life that involves both one's physical and intellectual development. In this light, Friar John's ceaseless activity may seem somewhat out of place, or at least hard to reconcile with a world in which the excess of giants has been, if not chastened, at least channeled to productive uses. His looming presence in the second half of *Gargantua* and his reward of the utopian (and perhaps for that very reason, impossible) abbey richly complicate an already complicated text that refuses to disclose any easy answers to problems such as the ubiq-

Copyright © 2009 Pearson Education, Inc. Publishing as Longman.

uity of war, religious intolerance, and the close-mindedness of Europe's most powerful figures (for whom the belligerent Picrochole is no doubt a mirror). At the same time, the combined energies of the good friar, the supple Gymnaste, and Gargantua himself argue for the necessity of collaborative strategies to address early modern complexities. Like that later (and very different) epic text, Camões's *Lusiads*, Rabelais's books single out no one hero in particular, and the "faicts" lauded on the title pages of his four works are deeds performed by a dazzling array of very different characters.

Luís Vaz de Camões

In Canto 8 of *The Lusiads*, after he has been greeted warily by the Hindu ruler of Calicut and proposed a treaty that will open up a new trade route for the Portuguese, the explorer Vasco da Gama is confronted with a plot devised by the leaders' Muslim subjects: "That none should return home was the sole / Purpose of the Muslims' strategy, / So Portugal's king should never know / Where the lands of the east lay." The prospect of the mariners' return is both absolutely necessary to the success of da Gama's voyage—unless he can report back to his king, the ocean route to India will remain unknown and Portugal will never become a maritime power—and an astonishing innovation in an epic genre that featured either exile from one's homeland (the *Aeneid*), the loss of all men but one (the *Odyssey*), or a bitter homecoming (*Argonautica*). But the Portuguese sailors do return happily to Lisbon, thwarting the plans of India's conniving Muslims and being rewarded en route by sensuous nymphs smitten with love, or lust, from Cupid's arrows. Thus does da Gama defy the oblivion that would otherwise have settled over his name, and so does Camões better the ancients, as his heroes wind up with everything epic heroes want: the bold new discovery, the girl, the return to their "homeland, the country long yearned for," where they give their king "still greater titles."

This is the payoff, summarily dispatched in the final two stanzas of the poem's narrative, after Venus has told da Gama and his men that they may leave the floating island that has been their tropical paradise for a far shorter time than Odysseus enjoyed the pleasures of Circes'—or Calypso's—isles. It is not surprising news, since the opening council of Jupiter and the other gods in Book 1 learns that Fate has mandated that Portugal will become an imperial power in the East (and, to a lesser extent, the West). But the loss, at least from a modern perspective, would seem to be that of an individual, personal drama, one we know from both an earlier work like the *Aeneid* and contemporary works such as the *Essays* of Montaigne or Shakespeare's plays. Vasco da Gama is not explicitly named until stanza 44 of the first canto, and Camões opens his poem with a resolute plural: unlike Virgil's "I sing of arms and a man," *The Lusiads* is launched with a paean to arms and "*os barões assinalados*"—the matchless heroes who journeyed on oceans not ventured on before. And the very name of the poem, of course, refers to "sons of Portugal"

Copyright © 2009 Pearson Education, Inc. Publishing as Longman.

rather than, as in the *Odyssey* or *Aeneid*, a single man. As Thomas Greene nicely puts it, in *The Lusiads*, "The traditional heroic awe for individual capacity is replaced by the impression of historical sweep, the living personality of a nation reincarnated in leader after leader, reaffirmed in crisis after crisis, and ultimately stamped upon the vast oriental world" (*Descent from Heaven*, 1963, p. 227). Da Gama's particular role is minimized even as Camões celebrates the uniqueness of what he has done, incorporated into a "historical sweep" that began before he was born and that will continue after his death. He may thus seem a mere instrument of "eternal Fate," pawn of a conflict played out in the heavens above where Jupiter and Bacchus do battle. Such an observation can lead to useful comparisons with the *Aeneid* or the *Odyssey*, as students reflect on the extent to which those heroes are portrayed as free agents or largely susceptible to the influence of outside forces.

But da Gama is also depicted as unfailingly generous in taking up his mandated role, and the one power that Camões does give him is that of rhetoric: in many ways, he can be said to be a mirror for Camões himself, who also sailed eastward, only in less revolutionary times. You might focus on the closing sections from Camões's lengthy narrative to the Muslim king of Malindi toward the end of Canto 5, in which he rhetorically asks, "Did you think, O King, the world contained / Men who would tackle such a journey? / Do you imagine that Aeneas and subtle / Ulysses ever ventured so far?" (p. 313, lines 393–396). The king's reaction was by no means reassured; but thanks to da Gama's performance, he acknowledges the captain and, more importantly, his men, as heroes from whom "none could take his eyes" (p. 314, line 435). In turn, Camões would like to claim da Gama's power as *racconteur* for himself, capable of unleashing memorable lines that are the only fitting commemoration for daring mariners. Indeed, much of *The Lusiads* seems concerned with the necessity of remembrance, whether it involves Portuguese kings of the past, Adamastor's haunting curse, or the young King Sebastião.

Such transparent praise for Portugal, along with the poem's condemnation of Muslims and patronizing of the Africans, make *The Lusiads* very unpolitically correct in the current age, and it has been criticized for, among other things, trying to impose a classical framework on a Christian narrative. But both da Gama's and Camões's era (and regrettably, perhaps our own) were obsessed with an ongoing crusade against Islam. The apocalyptic rhetoric of Columbus in his later letters was not out of place in a fifteenth century still intent on regaining Jerusalem from the "infidel" and driven by the belief that finding easier routes to the East would undermine Muslim dominance. Closer to Camões's day, October 1571 would see the famous Battle of Lepanto, in which the Christian Holy League won a decisive victory against Turks who had sought to expand into the rest of the Mediterranean from their base in Cyprus. (Portugal was uninvolved in this particular battle but had other turf on which to fight, as it tried desperately to maintain its expansive overseas holdings and to regain Morocco.) An active Inquisition in Portugal increasingly suppressed much of the humanistic learning that had shaped Camões's own career, and Dom Sebastião, the young, unstable king to whom Camões dedi-

Copyright © 2009 Pearson Education, Inc. Publishing as Longman.

cated his poem, was nurtured in an environment marked by what Helder Macedo has called "hysterical religious fervour accompanied by an anachronistic revival of chivalrous ideals" (quoted in John de Oliveira e Silva, "Moving the Monarch: The Rhetoric of Persuasion in Camões' *Lusíads*" in *Renaissance Quarterly* 53 [2000], p. 743). This was a Sebastião, too, who had resolutely refused to consider marriage, despite the fact that he was the only member of what had once been the plentiful Avis royal line. (Camões's praise at the end of his poem of the female body and chastisement of the hunter Actaeon who disdained women—"to pursue ugly, ferocious beasts, he shunned the lovely female form"—may be an implicit critique of his hunt-loving king, on whose generativity the future of Portugal rested.)

The existence of such lines (the stanza ends with the warning "Take care, Actaeon, you are not supper for / The very dogs you now so much adore!") suggests that Camões is never simply caving in to a reigning ideology, no matter how desperate he may have been for patronage, for he was probably as idiosyncratic a writer as he was an individual. John de Oliveira e Silva notes that Camões was exiled from Portugal twice, the second time for murder, and hence was a persona non grata at home: his "stormy personality and brilliant wit would have made it difficult for him to survive in any European court of the time, even those more tolerant than the increasingly dogmatic and bellicose royal course of Lisbon" (p. 737n). The fact that he satirized Portugal's beloved Renaissance king Dom Manuel in a play suggests that even the opening verses of *The Lusíads*, which praise the current king as easily victorious over "the fearful Moor" and "unbroken Indian," cannot be taken wholly at face value (indeed, in stanza 16 he talks undiplomatically about offering Tethys, Neptune's bride and the lover of da Gama, to the bachelor king).

But some readers have gone further. In *The English Epic and its Background* (1954), the famous scholar E. M. W. Tillyard suggested that Camões had an extraordinary ability, like Homer, to see both sides at once; and it is worth pursuing with students what, exactly, those sides might be. Not all of Camões's non-Christians are wicked. The Muslim king of Malindi offers assistance to the sailors, and the navigator Musayeed helps da Gama escape from Calicut (and in Canto 8, Camões alludes to Moors whose help was sought by the Portuguese to defeat the greatest enemy of all, Spain). But is it possible that Camões might have identified with what David Quint has called in *Epic and Empire* (1993) epic's "losers," those defeated by forces that have been chosen as history's victors? One of them might be the old man who warns against the extension of Portugal's greatness into the world; better to remain an isolationist at home than court danger abroad. While he sounds at the time like a spoilsport, given the decline of that empire during Camões's lifetime, his words would not have come across as simply hollow. Adamastor's curse in Canto 5 is more problematic. On the one hand, as many scholars have commented, the giant become promontory utters a curse that echoes the prophetic utterances of the Cyclops to Odysseus and Dido to Aeneas; and their words will, in fact, outlast their respective epic poems. But as Quint suggests, Adamastor has been turned to stone in punishment for his "atrevimento" or dar-

Copyright © 2009 Pearson Education, Inc. Publishing as Longman.

ing transgression, a transgressiveness also embodied by the daring Portuguese themselves. Far from being representative of the hapless natives of southern Africa and India who would suffer under Portuguese domination, Adamastor is an uncanny double for the Portuguese, and the episode provides what Quint calls an example of "remarkable self-consciousness," "in which the epic announces and points to its own act of creating a new myth out of the stuff of history" (p. 123)—an act in which history itself, along with the "losers," disappears.

Such mythic creation, Quint goes on to argue, enables Camões to make his own transgressive claim that he has bettered the ancients. Indeed, one must finally read the poem not only against the real histories that Camões worked with, such as the Journal of da Gama's voyage (not actually written by da Gama himself), but also against the epic poems to which plentiful allusions abound. That the poem is supposedly "true" is one measure of its superiority, according to its creator, who after all verified the details of the voyage east by observing them himself. (The map on p. 289 of Vol. C can be helpful to chart the voyage around the coast of Africa that da Gama recounts in Cantos 3-5, or the trip across the Indian Ocean to Calicut in Canto 6.) But it is not only the historic return to Portugal of da Gama's sailors, or Camões's empiricism, that makes *The Lusiads* supposedly the better poem. Camões everywhere competes with the claims of ancient myth and story, overgoing the Virgilian storm by having no one die, rather than the one sailor who drowns in the *Aeneid*. Phaethon's story, found in Ovid, is of special significance for a poem that focuses for so long on Africa: when Phaethon came too close to the lands of the southern hemisphere, the sun is said to have scorched the people immediately below, turning their skin permanently dark. But Camões suggests that the young man whose daring caused his death and that of others has no parallel in Portugal's epic "history"; and perhaps, one of the most interesting approaches to *The Lusiads* is to see it as a poem whose writer tries to cancel out the possibility not only of da Gama's "transgressions" but also his own.

Michel de Montaigne

The best guide to Montaigne is Montaigne himself; the more one reads, the better one feels one knows the man. And Montaigne cleverly seems to have planned things this way. *Montaigne in Motion* is the title of a 1985 study by Jean Starobinski, and it nicely captures the essence of the *Essays*. They are constituted by words that simply do not stop—both because Montaigne never really finished his project and because he finds it difficult, impossible, actually, to pin his project down. And it is helpful to come to the *Essays* thinking of them as open-ended—although not necessarily in the sense that we often think of Michelangelo's unfinished sculptures, for which the term "non finito" has been coined. Michelangelo was marked by a restlessness that drove him to move on to other things, sometimes—as in the case of the Rondanini Pietà, one of his last sculptures—attempting even to destroy the incomplete work. Montaigne's writing career can be said to be marked by the re-

Copyright © 2009 Pearson Education, Inc. Publishing as Longman.

fusal to bring closure, because to bring closure to a project like the *Essays* was arguably to bring closure to life.

To explore this sense of openness in Montaigne, you might first discuss with students the various layers that constitute the *Essays*, which went through numerous publications between 1580 and a posthumous 1595 edition that thanks to the sure hand of Montaigne's literary executor, Marie de Gornay, incorporates the many changes he made in the margins to his 1588 text. You might point to that briefest of essays, I.8, "Of Idleness," which tells why Montaigne began to write in the first place, as a way of calling attention to the archaeology of the text. The "A" (1580) version of the essay contained everything but the quotes of Virgil and Martial, which were added in the 1588 ("B") edition: Montaigne surely knew the *Aeneid* before 1588, but something in this passage, from Book 8, resonated with the essay he had already written, and the same could be said for the line from Martial. The longer essays are more complex, often containing additions from the last four years of Montaigne's life. Thus "Of the Power of the Imagination" started out in 1580 as a relatively short piece and concluded more than three paragraphs before the current close, with "I refer the stories that I borrow to the conscience of those from whom I take them" (Vol. C, p. 334). In the 1588 edition, Montaigne added the next sentence ("The reflections are my own"), but he was still unhappy with the essay's end and wrote what are now the essay's three final paragraphs in the margins. More significantly, the memorable incident about his friend, the count, and the medal that he needed to place over his kidneys to conquer impotence, is a post-1588 addition, as is the long defense of Montaigne's "honorable member"—his penis—at the very middle of the piece. Finally, "Of Repentance," like all of Book 3, was not even begun until at least the mid-1580s; it contains many additions incorporated into the 1595 text.

Such reflections enable students to see the text as almost a living, breathing thing. This surely does justice to Montaigne's conception of his life's work as well as to show how Montaigne moved away from textual exegesis and toward what Warren Boutcher has called something new: "the strong emphasis on the cultural production of the 'natural' person" ("Vernacular Humanism in the 16th Century," in *The Cambridge Companion to Renaissance Humanism*, ed. Jill Kraye, 1996). In particular, we get to see Montaigne talking to his book, as it were—or, as George Hoffmann has recently suggested in his fascinating *Montaigne's Career* (1998), to his secretary. Hoffman's careful study of the day-to-day details of book writing and publishing in sixteenth-century France provides strong evidence that Montaigne dictated many of the essays, nudging him "away from the controlled, smooth (Ciceronian) prose" he had used early in life, "and toward the distinctive stop-and-start style of the *Essays*" (p. 51). At the same time, the tendency to see the *Essays* as the extension of the man, a view clearly encouraged by Montaigne himself, represents only one, albeit very popular approach from the last century.

Beginning with Terence Cave's *The Cornucopian Text* in 1979, Montaigne criticism has focused increasingly on the discontinuities of the *Essays*, the extent to which the very practice of writing itself can threaten the subject's integrity.

Copyright © 2009 Pearson Education, Inc. Publishing as Longman.

Foremost in this kind of study is attentiveness to Montaigne's quotes (which, by the way, he cavalierly refused to reference, leading his first English translator, John Florio, to bitterly complain) and hence to the patterns of intertextuality that constitute the *Essays*. Even as Montaigne claims that "The life of Caesar has no more to show us than our own," he relentlessly cites from others' lives, and texts; and you could discuss the *dangers* of relying too much on what is not one's own. While they may constitute the Renaissance self, do the examples and interpolations from "outside" infect or contaminate a man, much as Montaigne worries in "Of the Power of the Imagination" that he became ill after sitting with a sick man to make him well? Is it possible that one of the effects of reading can even put one into a feminized position, bringing to mind the irritating statement Montaigne makes in "On Some Verses of Virgil" in his "B" text: he is "annoyed that [his] essays serve the ladies only as a public article of furniture, an article of the parlor"; he prefers, he claims, "the boudoir."

At the same time, the discontinuities that so many have noticed in the *Essays* may also have something to do with what might seem a surprising quality of Montaigne's: his reticence. As in the classic essay "Of Cannibals," Montaigne is fascinated with the limitations of knowledge, whether it be that of the ancients, so revered in the Renaissance, or of himself. The Tupi Indian from Brazil is as removed from Plato and Aristotle's grasp, despite the fact that his songs sound like Anacreontic verse (Greek lyrics), as from Montaigne's, who struggles with a "stupid" interpreter to understand the Brazilian who is feted by the king in Rouen. (However, Montaigne did have the discerning work of Jean de Léry at hand, a portion of which is included as a Resonance selection, p. 344. You might ask why he fails to mention this far more reliable source who had spent several years among the Tupi on the coast of Brazil. But Montaigne was undoubtedly influenced by Léry's work; a devout follower of Calvin, Léry had nonetheless experienced firsthand the difficulties of converting the heathen other, and his chapter on native religion reflects many of the kinds of ambivalence we find in Montaigne. If anything, for Léry, the rituals of the Tupi Indians had qualities vaguely reminiscent of Catholicism—assuredly an odd displacement of European practices to far-off lands.)

This professed inability to *know* either the other or the self has inspired historians of skepticism such as George Popkin to embrace Montaigne as one of the movement's founders; others, such as Lucien Lefebvre, label him an agnostic. But you might also suggest a more strategic posture. Montaigne uses a number of devices to illustrate that he can be held accountable only for the planting of ideas, rather than what is done with them. As Mireille Djenno has written in an unpublished paper, "he seeks to be held accountable neither for the reader's transformative process or the final outcome," going on to cite one of the most "exemplary" moments of the *Essays*, from "A Consideration upon Cicero": "Neither those tales nor my quotations are always intended merely as examples, as authorities or embellishments. I do not regard them solely for the use I make of them. They often bear, outside of my purpose, the seeds of a richer and bolder matter; and obliquely sound a more subtle note." Is Montaigne not seeking to avoid the

Copyright © 2009 Pearson Education, Inc. Publishing as Longman.

political climate cultivated by Luther's and Calvin's followers, who set themselves up as models to be followed even as they disowned other models, such as fifteen hundred years of Roman Catholicism? His celebrated "indirectness" rejects, that is, a contemporary movement that tried to persuade readers to a course of action based on individual revelations and experience alone—such as certain radical strains of Protestantism, which Catholic France long struggled, often brutally, to contain. Yet another possibility is Montaigne's acute sensitivity as to the changing nature of textuality in the early modern world. Given the new access to printed texts in the Renaissance and the inability of authors to control the dissemination (or plagiarism) of their works, how much of his work could Montaigne *really* call his own? In the end, perhaps Montaigne offers himself up as a model to be "appropriated" as we wish—cannibalized, perhaps—while clearly recognizing that he has already cannibalized others.

Miguel de Cervantes Saavedra

Ideally, students should read *Don Quixote* in its entirety (as of course in an ideal world they would read all of this *Anthology*'s works *in toto*), and it was difficult to select just a few adventures from the dozens in which Don Quixote is mixed up. The first part of *Don Quixote* is presented in the *Anthology* virtually in its entirety: the first nine chapters, that is, up until the narrator comes upon the manuscript by Cide Hamete. The noted Hispanist scholar Menéndez Pidal suggested that the first part, which consists of Don Quixote's first sally out, alone, into the wild and his return at nightfall with a sympathetic neighbor, represents the kernel of a story originally meant to be only a novella. It breaks off shortly after Don Quixote has taken off again, Sancho Panza at his side, both of them fresh from their infamous encounter with windmills. "Cide" inspired Cervantes to new heights, and his contributions include the encounter with real goatherds and literary shepherds, droll conversations between the Don and Sancho, and the ill-advised release of the captives that puts Don Quixote squarely in front of the picaresque tradition and Ginés de Pasamonte. The selections then turn to the last few chapters of Book 1, where Don Quixote is returned forcibly to La Mancha. From Book 2 of ten years later we have Don Quixote's discovery of the false sequel, the renewed encounter with Ginés in which the tables are reversed and the former galley slave suffers at his liberator's hands, the "disenchantment of Dulcinea," and the return, again, to La Mancha: this time to death, amidst dreams of pastoral paradises. It cannot be said too often that deprived of his madness, Don Quixote must die, and deprived of Don Quixote, Cervantes dies as well, a year after the publication of Book 2, his health severely compromised by years of prison, captivity, and indigence.

What is not included in the *Anthology*, regrettably, is a good deal: most notably, the (lengthy) intercalated tales, which in at least one case are largely autobiographical ("The Captive's Tale" from Book 1). Also regrettably missing are the extended plays with Don Quixote's sanity in Book 2 by the conniving Duke and

Copyright © 2009 Pearson Education, Inc. Publishing as Longman.

Duchess who end up giving Sancho Panza the island he has desired—a much distorted utopia—and arranging for Don Quixote's return home. Still, there is enough of Book 2 to have a fruitful discussion about how Don Quixote has changed in the intervening decade. It seems that almost everywhere in the second book, Don Quixote is confronted not only by the false shadow of the sequel by Avellaneda (which gives us a Quixote no longer in love with Dulcinea and a Sancho no longer as funny) but also by the legacy of Book 1, which almost all the characters have read. He is, that is to say, a man who must deal, often unwillingly, with newfound fame, much as Cervantes may have found it hard after years of obscurity to reconcile himself to popular acclaim. Strikingly, in this second book, Don Quixote is far less center stage; to a certain degree, he is also less confident about who he really is. This is in part because other "authors" have emerged in Book 2, including a Sancho Panza who must suffer a painful penance for having manipulated what Don Quixote believed to be his *own* chivalric fictions about Dulcinea.

What were those chivalric fictions, and where did they come from? One could spend a great while poring over the stories of the Arthurian knights as well as tales from Celtic folklore that found a receptive audience in France after the Norman Conquest. Some of the earliest romances bring Celtic and Arthurian material together—the lais of Marie de France, the narratives of Chrétien de Troye—and, particularly in the latter's works, direct a hero's life toward two supreme goals, as Edwin Williamson writes: "the winning of renown through feats of arms, and submission to the demands of courtly love" (*The Halfway House of Fiction: Don Quixote and Arthurian Romance*, 1984, p. 7). More problematically, as Williamson goes on to point out, the one goal is often in conflict with another: thus "the central concern of the romances is the striking of a lasting balance between the public duties of the knight and his private obligations to his lady" (p. 7). Yet rarely is this balance achieved; and perhaps one of the best (and most succinct) accounts of the fate of a knightly class that finds itself experiencing a double alienation common to the roots of Christianity itself—"estrangement from God and estrangement from the world"—is the article of Gerhard Ladner in *Speculum*, "*Homo Viator*: Medieval Ideas on Alienation and Order" (Volume 42 [1967]: 233-252; quote on p. 238). Ladner suggests that the knight-errant, desperately isolated within his personal vision of honor and perfection, was ripe for insanity, set on a pilgrimage without end and without any recourse to testing his faith in a "real world": he can be "absorbed by the world, or transcend it, or be destroyed by it" (p. 247). Such fates do indeed greet, for example, the eponymous character of Gottfried Von Strassburg's *Tristan*, as well as a host of other figures who would embark on adventures for their ladies over the next several centuries. (*Sir Gawain and the Green Knight* from Vol. B is a fine example of the genre, while Marie de France's *Chevrefoil* gives us only the end of the intriguing Tristan story.) Spain's and Italy's early-sixteenth-century writers such as the author of the adventures of Amadis de Gaul and Ariosto would render this poetry even more fantastic and the knights more isolated, adding magicians who deal in magic both good and evil, entire kingdoms dependent on a single knight's services and disappointed by his dalliances in love, and knights tortured

Copyright © 2009 Pearson Education, Inc. Publishing as Longman.

by penances for imperfect love and madness. Don Quixote clearly becomes the be-lated heir to these hyper-chivalric characters, and you can point out the exagger-ated egocentricity he manifests in his desire to imitate Amadis, Orlando, and the other great knights of romance through an occasional "acto posesivo"—an act of possession—with respect to what he sees as the most salient details of chivalric tra-dition, such as sleeping under the open sky. But he doesn't always get the details right. He chooses his armor and his horse before selecting a lady with whom to fall in love, rather than being inspired by a lady to set off on an adventure.

Don Quixote is not the only character infected with the love of chivalric ro-mance, and that is one of the central ironies of the novel. Montaigne's contem-porary, the French Jesuit François de la Noue, warned against the dangerous in-fluence of chivalry books on the general population, suggesting they were as harmful to the young as Machiavelli was to the old. Plus, he added, by the late six-teenth century, the chivalric ethos was dead—everything in books like *Amadis* was utterly passé. De la Noue notwithstanding, it is clear that as the book-burning in Chapter 6 of *Don Quixote* suggests, *Amadis* and other works like it still had plenty of fans in Cervantes' time, and they occupied a niche in oral culture as well thanks to puppet shows and ballads sung in the plaza. Nor, of course, does Cervantes par-ody only the chivalric romance. Great fun is had at the expense of the pastoral novel with the episode of Marcela, who remains aloof from and unaffected by the would-be shepherds who fall in love with her and write misogynistic poems about her intransigence. The picaresque novel, which burst onto the literary scene with the anonymous *Lazarillo de Torme* about an orphan trying to make his way in a hos-tile world, shows up in the figure of Ginés de Pasamonte, already celebrated as au-thor of a story he candidly admits he can never finish: his own. But other forms of fiction are interrogated, too, and perhaps the question is not so much whether Don Quixote is mad but whether it is possible to imagine a world in which some level of fictive construction does *not* play a part. As Ariosto's narrator asks himself in his *Orlando furioso* or "Mad Orlando," *can* one "leave the dance" once it is begun? Can one escape from a world in which, as Erasmus's *Folly* insists, to act fool-ishly is to be human?

In this light, Maria Rosa Menocal's recent musings in *Ornament of the World: How Muslims, Jews and Christians Created a Culture of Tolerance in Medieval Spain* (2002) on the narrator's chance encounter with a Morisco in Toledo (Book I, Chapter 9) are especially pertinent. She remarks that in the heyday of the medieval era when Moors still controlled Andalusia, Toledo had been a thriving cultural center, a mecca for writers, artists, and translators who, among other things, trans-lated the great Greek philosophers into Arabic. Cervantes' Toledo is sadly reduced from what it once was. In its once-thriving Jewish quarter where no Jews have lived for a hundred years—"Or at least no Jews admitting to being Jews, a very different thing" (Menocal, p. 253)—"Cervantes" finds a pile of papers written in Arabic script and looks, as Menocal says, for "an Old Muslim who, like the Old Jews, go around saying they aren't that at all, that they are New Christians. But who is to believe that? Who in this world ever says that he is what he seems to be? And who

Copyright © 2009 Pearson Education, Inc. Publishing as Longman.

seems to be what he no doubt really is?" (p. 254). The intolerances of the early modern world strikingly contrast with the genuine catholicism of the medieval one, and in the new kingdom of Spain, identity itself demands constant sleights of hand. Hence the Morisco who can translate for Cervantes a dangerous Arabic text (that is not Arabic but a medieval version of Castilian transliterated into Arabic script) laughs at the allusion to Dulcinea as "the best hand at salting pork of any woman in all La Mancha." He laughs, Menocal suggests, because Dulcinea and her family are no doubt old Jews, trying too hard to look like new Christians at a time when Spanish "honor" lay in religion and race alone, when exhaustive genealogies were taken every time someone switched jobs, when—the final blow—four years after the publication of Cide Hamete's manuscript, all Moors, having already had their books burned and clothes prohibited, were expelled from Spain, with disastrous consequences for the country's economy and, of course, the Moriscos themselves. It has been standard to read *Don Quixote* as a fictional work about other fictions. And yet Menocal searchingly asks, "Do we use this great story to forget history or to remember it?" (p. 265)—a remembering that situates *Don Quixote* within a tragic moment of Spain's history and that sees "fictional" constructions not only as constitutive of reality but as protection against it. A remembering, too, one might add, that takes into account the fact that the chivalric romance was *born* in Christianity's fight against Islam, fought nowhere more doggedly than in the Spain of those most Catholic kings, Isabella and Ferdinand. (On the relevant historical details, see B. W. Ife's "The Historical and Social Context" in *The Cambridge Companion to Cervantes*, ed. Anthony J. Cascardi, 2000.)

In the classroom this might lead you, time permitting (and time is always a pressing matter in discussions of *Don Quixote*), to question the uses of fiction in early modernity. Were stories sheer entertainment or of particular moral value? What did that new genre, the novel, contribute to literature's "uses"? Dante's *Vita nuova* had supposedly opened a path to God; Boccaccio's *Decameron* provided relief from plague and the debilitating isolation experienced by upper-class women; Rabelais noisily began *Gargantua* questioning to what extent "deep" meanings should be forced onto literary texts, and what the price. Unlike the vast majority of authors encountered in this section, Cervantes did not receive an extensive, formal, humanistic education (although he did briefly study in Madrid with the Spanish humanist Juan Lopez de Hoyos). Cervantes was in some sense too late to be humanism's beneficiary, born in the wrong country and possibly of the wrong class (his father may have been a *hidalgo*, like Alonso Quixano, but he had no money to send his fourth child to school). Yet are we to take him at his word that the classical authorities meant little to him? As the prologue states, as far as books of chivalry go, "Aristotle never dreamed of [them], St. Basil never mentioned [them] and Cicero never came across [them]": ergo, all that Cervantes should do is to "try to ensure that the melancholy man is moved to laughter when he reads [this] history, the jovial man laughs even more, the simpleton is not discouraged, the judicious marvel at its inventiveness, the serious-minded do not scorn it nor the wise fail to praise it." Such lines seem to belittle the knowledge Cervantes did

Copyright © 2009 Pearson Education, Inc. Publishing as Longman.

have of the traditions that preceded him, while at the same time he was conscious, arguably proud, of the fact that he was doing something radically new. (And critics from Georg Lukacs to Michael McKeon have credited him with the birth of the modern novel; see Lukacs' *Theory of the Novel*, 1971, and McKeon's *Origins of the English Novel 1600–1740*, 1987.) But Cervantes also realized that he had the weight of neither time-honored tradition nor extensive classical learning on his side—and students will thankfully realize that *Don Quixote* necessitates far fewer footnotes than the average Renaissance text). You can thus ask, what profit do we gain in reading *Don Quixote*—the book that, as Lord Byron claimed, ruined Spanish feeling for chivalry, or as Menendez y Pelayo claimed, represented the *last* book of chivalry, the culmination and most perfect example of a long tradition?

Félix Lope de Vega y Carpio

Lope's *Fuenteovejuna* offers some convenient ways to think about a number of transitions in early modern Europe. Certainly one of the most interesting is that between feudalism and the emergence of the modern nation-state. That women— more particularly, a single, resistant woman—are at the center of this transition in Lope's play is a bit of an invention on Lope's part, but only in part: according to the historical *crónicas* or records of late-fifteenth-century Spain, peasant women were involved in the violent uprising against the dastardly *comendador*, Fernando Gómez de Guzmán, and one of their complaints was sexual exploitation. But as was the case with the American Revolution three hundred years later, the peasants were more concerned about the high rates of taxation to which they were subject by feudal overlords. Lope chose to ignore the more political and economic aspects of the peasants' exploitation, concentrating instead on the aristocrat's sexual license. (On the rigidly hierarchical society that characterized seventeenth-century Castile—and the resistance of Castilians to the so-called *droit du seigneur* that gave noblemen the first "right" to virgins about to be married—see Sheila Ackerlind, *Patterns of Conflict: The Individual and Society in Spanish Literature to 1700*, 1989.)

Such focus made for a tighter story and, perhaps, a more entertaining play. You might ask students what they think Lope gained by reducing the peasants' complaints to the stark, single issue of rape and female victimization (take note of the grueling scene where Jacinta is dragged into service as whore for the soldiers). This, however, opens up another question: *Was Laurencia actually raped?* Her appearance on stage after she has been abducted by Ferdinand—her hair loose, her clothing disheveled—certainly seems to suggest that she has been, while Frondoso's later lines indicate that she succeeded in fighting off her attacker. If the ambiguity is deliberate, what effect does it achieve? Victims of rape in early modern Europe, particularly those of the lower classes, seldom had recourse to justice, although aristocrats and upper-class women did; on the other hand, the dishonor associated with a raped noblewoman was such that she would rarely risk being seen in public again. It is striking that another well-known play of seventeenth-century Spain

Copyright © 2009 Pearson Education, Inc. Publishing as Longman.

takes women's violation as its central plot. In Tirso da Molina's *Trickster of Seville*, which introduced to the theatrical world the nefarious figure of Don Juan, the women are most definitely deflowered. They show up at play's end to participate in his overthrow, as though their loss of virginity under questionable circumstances does not prevent them from continuing to have a voice in the play.

Laurencia very much has a voice, and it is one of the strongest in Lope's play. It is worth mentioning to students that her role would have been performed by an actress rather than—as in Shakespeare's England—a young boy. (For details of the stage in the Spanish golden age, see Melveena McKendrick, *Women and Society in the Spanish Drama of the Golden Age*, 1974.) But it does admittedly take us a while to get to her. The first scene is hard going, full of historical background and allusions to Spain's vast network of rural villages and frictions between the community and the order of Calatrava, which claimed to bear ultimate allegiance to the pope. One also has here seeds of the conflict between Spain and Portugal, which would continue through Lope's lifetime. The consolidation of power in the 1470s under Ferdinand, King of Aragon, and Isabella of Castile, was a threat both to the fragile kingdom of Portugal and to the *grandes* or titled nobles who had been used to reigning over their vassals with a relatively free hand.

The allusion to the play's main characters occurs only toward the end of the long first scene, when Fuenteovejuna is mentioned as the place where the Commander's family lodges: the "humble folk" of the village are "not trained for war" but are "skilled in labor in the fields." With a sigh of relief, one arrives at the square in Fuenteovejuna, where we encounter two peasant women hoping that the Commander, who has just spoken so forcefully about his love for the village, will never return. In this early scene, Lope sets up the differences between city and country in the spirited discussion between Frondoso and Laurencia. But it is not the contrast one necessarily expects: The city "flatters," while the country is suspicious of any positive trait, calling the just man cruel, the generous intrusive, and beautiful women whores. This suggests that the contrasts to be delineated in the course of the play will not be the usual ones (wicked city versus virtuous country). It also suggests early on the complexity of Laurencia's character. Not only was she christened with something "stronger than water," in Mengo's memorable phrase, but her lively wit and passionate feelings compel her to argue forcefully and on behalf of others for what she believes is right.

When Flores arrives to announce the outcome of the battle in which the knights of Calatrava have been temporarily victorious, we get a graphic sense of the brutality both of Renaissance war and of the Commander. His effectiveness in battle would demonstrate itself in the village as well, and his pique when Laurencia refuses him—"proud virgin" that she is—plays out one of the central dynamics of the play, indeed, of the feudal code that persisted in Spain throughout the seventeenth century: the belief of the nobleman's right to exact his will over his subjects and to set himself up as absolute lord. Therein lies much of the play's drama, as well as the force of its critique. In hindsight, Lope is able to look back on the success of a centralized monarchy in quashing the aspirations of nobility. (Although

Copyright © 2009 Pearson Education, Inc. Publishing as Longman.

this success was not as straightforward as Lope would make it: Ferdinand and Isabella had not been involved in the goings-on in Fuenteovejuna, nor were they the target of the Commander's wrath. Moreover, ongoing frictions in Europe—such as the bloody uprising of the French nobility against the Crown in 1648, called the Fronde—suggest that the taming of Europe's aristocracy by increasingly absolutist monarchies had a lengthy history.) But Lope's own loyalties, like those of his peasants, are never in question: as Esteban puts it in Act 3, "Only the King is master under heaven, not Fernando Gómez."

One of the reasons for the play's enduring success is its remarkably varied portrait of village life. In particular, Lope conveys its deep conservatism, its need for stability and continuity. In Laurencia's first extended conversation with Frondoso, we can see the investment a village had in its young people: Everyone is "counting the days" until their wedding. (For a similarly lively portrait you might wish to show students the movie *The Return of Martin Guerre*, based on a true story about a village in mid-sixteenth-century France. Gérard Dépardieu plays a con man who tries to take on the role of a villager who never returned from war. As long as the Dépardieu character actively contributes to the life of the town—and fathers children for its future—he is accepted, but as soon as he begins to contest its time-honored customs, he is suspected as a fraud.) The gender dynamics of the play represent such a contesting of the mainstays of village life, particularly the patriarchy represented by its able body of aldermen. These dynamics come to a head in Act 3 when Laurencia incites the women to action: "Shall we stay at home when we were the greatest sufferers from [the Commander's] wrongs?" The women's refusal to name a captain suggests a desire for egalitarianism that opposes the men's hierarchical inclinations, manifest in their awe of the Commander's station, which the women do not share.

Women's revolts were rare in early modernity, but they did exist; Natalie Davis's fine articles called "Women on Top" and "City Women and Religious Change" in her collection *Society and Culture in Early Modern France* (1976) discuss uprisings on the other side of the Pyrenees. Allusions to the Amazons—the mythical women who kept men as slaves and used them only to father their children—would have called to mind the putative existence of such matriarchal groups in the New World (mentioned by Columbus in his letters). One can argue that the revolt incited by a woman does go to particular extremes, given the gruesome death of the Commander and the hacking of both his body and coat of arms to pieces. Is this excessive cruelty, or is it only Flores's telling, to an initially sympathetic King and Queen, that makes it so? That is, does Lope in any way condemn the peasants for their violence? Queen Isabel is asked to judge the villagers in a moment that would make it seem that women will continue to "rule" at the play's end, but she coyly refuses, and Ferdinand pronounces the lenient sentence: suggesting, perhaps, that Lope is firmly reestablishing the dominant social order at his conclusion. But this is, to be sure, something students will want to discuss. Anthony Cascardi in *History in the Spanish Golden Age* (1997) and Walter Cohen in *The Drama of a Nation* (1985) have very different ways of reading the revolutionary potential of the play and addressing Lope's sympathies

Copyright © 2009 Pearson Education, Inc. Publishing as Longman.

with his rebels. See too the general study by Dian Fox, *Refiguring the Hero: From Peasant to Noble in Lope de Vega and Calderón* (1991).

Finally, one last aspect of village life featured prominently in *Fuenteovejuna* and worth mentioning is its music. The musicians gather to celebrate the Commander's victory in battle; they play at Laurencia's and Frondoso's wedding with verses that hauntingly act as a summons to the Commander as they sing of the knight of Calatrava watching a lovely maiden walk through Fuenteovejuna's valleys. The poem recalls us to the medieval *pastorelle*, a popular, ballad-like poem that staged the confrontation between a knight and a shepherdess or peasant girl in a verdant landscape, often ending in seduction or violent rape. Oddly, in this wedding song, the musicians seem to reveal their sympathy for the Commander, unable in his passion to do anything but follow the girl whose beauty has captivated him; at the same time, it portrays the woman terrified and helpless before the knight's lust. Later, of course, they will sing praises to Ferdinand and Isabel and denounce tyrants. The inclusion of the musicians' songs is another indication of Lope's attempts to make his play as realistic a portrait of village life as possible— in part by including the villagers' own hapless attempts to align themselves, in the case of the musicians, with the figure in power. At the same time, the ominous wedding song not only foreshadows events to come but also links the play back to a poetic genre that can be said to resurface from time to time in early modern poets such as Petrarca, whose "pastorella" doing her wash in *Canzoniere* 52 (see Vol. C, p. 209) can recall us to the hunted maidens of medieval woods—and to the lurking knight here linked, however allusively, with the poet Petrarca.

William Shakespeare

The Tempest

The *Tempest* is a richly comparative text, one for which Shakespeare drew on a number of sources both classical and contemporary. Some of these sources were clearly literary, such as Virgil's *Aeneid*. Others, like Montaigne's essay "Of Cannibals" (see Vol. C, p. 335), translated into a lively English by James Florio in 1603, offered readers a glimpse of the New World's "savages" both at home and abroad. Shakespeare also incorporated into his play a variety of performative practices, ranging from his own experiences in tragedy, comedy, and the hybrid romance to the courtly masque that had become a favorite of King James I. The *Tempest* thus can play a pivotal role in the course, given the extent to which it intersects with so many texts the students might already have read. It asks that teachers and students alike reflect on a variety of influences literary and historical, as well as to talk about how Shakespeare moves beyond conventional dramatic genres to explore a more complex version of theatrical form. And once the "how" is ascertained—insofar as tragic scenarios are rehearsed again and again, only to be deflected, and Shakespeare mars the comic ending by giving us Antonio's hostile silence and newlyweds wrangling at chess in the "discovery space" (a small, secretive compartment separated

Copyright © 2009 Pearson Education, Inc. Publishing as Longman.

from the rest of the stage by a curtain)—the question as to why the playwright chose to engineer such a complicated new world can be addressed.

Recent criticism of the play has chosen to answer the "why" by pointing largely to contemporary contexts. One of them is the nature of kingship in James I's England, and indeed, in *The Tempest* as in so many of his works, from *Julius Caesar* to *King Lear*, Shakespeare is fascinated by the deeply flawed humanity of rulers. Prospero himself had been an inattentive duke, more in love with magic than his subjects, and it is not clear that he has much improved since being forced into exile. One of his several subjects continuously asks about his freedom, another stages an attempted mutiny. Even Miranda, far from being the innocent and obedient creature on which her father (and many productions of the play) insist, is notoriously hard-headed. She opens Act 1, Scene 2, questioning her father's art ("*If* by your Art, my dearest father, you have / Put the wild waters in this roar," lines 1–2, emphasis added) and then instructing him to cease the violence if he is responsible ("allay them"). Some of the harshest lines in the play are hers when she rebukes Caliban for his attempted rape, and she shows her independence when she becomes as forthright a wooer as her prototype Juliet ("Do you love me?"; "I am your wife if you will marry me"). Like Prospero, King James I, who ruled from 1603 until his death in 1624, dabbled in magic, and like him, he had a tendency to presume on his irrefutable authority; he is one of the first kings with whom the doctrine of absolutism is associated. James had his occasionally unruly subjects as well, but we would not necessarily want to read *The Tempest* as either complementary or critical of England's king. It is, however, worth reflecting on the extent to which the play muses on royal power and how that power can be likened to an art, to be used for better or worse and to varying successful effects.

A more fruitful avenue has been the play's relationship to England's colonial enterprises, which were still few and far between in the early seventeenth century. A consideration of documents related to the troublesome founding of the Virginia colony has yielded interesting readings of *The Tempest* as both a procolonial and an anticolonial play. The Council of Virginia's *True Declaration of the state of the colonie in Virginia*, of 1610, reveals how difficult it was for Englishmen to establish roots in the Americas, while the letter of William Strachey known as "True Reportory of the Wrack" is a lively account of the storm that threatened to devastate an English ship, as well as an attempt to portray what Ariel calls "the still-vex'd Bermuthas" as consummately habitable: "I hope to deliver the world from a foule and generall errour: it being counted of most, that they can be no habitation for Men, but rather given over to Devils and wicked Spirits; whereas indeed wee find them . . . to bee as habitable and commodious as most Countries of the same climate and situation."

Not surprisingly, the figure of Caliban and his relationship to Prospero are at the center of most criticism that focuses on the play's colonial contexts. In a line that has baffled scholars for centuries and that has proved difficult to present in the theater, Prospero tells the awestruck Italians when they inquire about Caliban, "This thing of darkness I / Acknowledge mine" (5.1.273–274). What does

Copyright © 2009 Pearson Education, Inc. Publishing as Longman.

Prospero mean by such a phrase? Is he claiming him as his subject—an odd claim, given that the Europeans are soon to leave the island, with Caliban perhaps still on it? Or is he acknowledging his awareness that he has demonized the man he calls "a lying slave" (1.2.345) in an attempt to name the island as his own? Whatever the case, as Prospero leans out over the stage in his epilogue to ask that we "release" him from his "bands"—another difficult moment that seems to imply that the audience has indulged in its own fantasy about subjecting theatrical slaves to their powerful "spell"—it is apparent that the colonial mission has been aborted. As dependent as he might have been on reports from the Bermudas or Virginia, Shakespeare has created a magical blueprint for colonialism only to undo it, never even bothering to name the island that rightfully belongs not to Prospero but to Sycorax, Caliban's mother. Similarly, eighty years earlier, in another formative text about an island, Thomas More had regretfully noted that Hythlodaeus omitted to tell his audience one crucial fact: where, exactly, Utopia was located.

Attentiveness to the play's more fantastic elements can only deepen an understanding of the way that it wrestles with contemporary political and social problems. Among them are the scenes with Ariel, where he helps to produce not only a masque but a banquet for Harpies and magical music, as well as the jests of Trinculo and Stephano and the seemingly inane dialogue about the "widow Dido" (the words rhyme; 2.1.86) while Gonzalo, like Strachey, is trying to be upbeat about the island on which the king and his courtiers have unceremoniously landed. The last plays of Shakespeare's career take place in remote, at times magical places; the stifling courts of his tragic period are left behind for the out-of-doors as encountered in *The Winter's Tale*'s pastoral scenes, the rugged climes of English deserts in *Cymbeline*, the islands in *Pericles*. (Northrop Frye's *A Natural Perspective*, 1965, remains one of the best discussions of the romances in general, but see more recently Constance Jordan's *Shakespeare's Monarchies: Ruler and Subject in the Romances*, 1997.) What effect does this generally unrecognizable, mysterious place where passages in Virgil and Ovid come to life actually have on the issues debated in the play? More importantly, how is Shakespeare trying to cast an imaginary spell over his audience, drawing them into a fiction that can convince for only three hours? Here the long-standing connection between the playwright and Prospero can be usefully addressed, as students ponder the deliberately theatrical strategies Prospero invokes. But the limitations of those strategies—the fact that they cannot be protected from Caliban's revolt, for example, or finally procure Antonio's repentance—are also apparent, vulnerable, just like Gonzalo's inherent goodness, to the rougher magic of the world with its contingencies brought on by human ambition, greed, and small-mindedness. At the same time, once Prospero himself is seen as a fallible "human" rather than a great artist who rises effortlessly above the fray (an interpretation put forward by Stephen Orgel in his masterful introduction to his Oxford *Tempest*, 1987, and one that usefully contrasts with Frank Kermode's more glowing account of Prospero in the Arden *Tempest*, 1958), readers are less inclined to contrast in absolute terms the superiorities of Art and the messiness of Life. Artists themselves are not immune from Life's contingencies, as perhaps

Copyright © 2009 Pearson Education, Inc. Publishing as Longman.

Shakespeare tries to show by making his superb playwright also the self-imposed governor of an island.

Nor is Art necessarily eternal. Last and certainly not least, reading *The Tempest* can offer students the possibility of thinking carefully about the process through which England's, and possibly the world's, greatest dramatist has been canonized. In *Puzzling Shakespeare* (1988), Leah Marcus has written of the extent to which such a process was paradoxically at odds with the genuine ephemerality of most early modern plays. (The masque was probably the most ephemeral of dramatic productions, designed, often at great expense, to be produced only once. The masque we witness in *The Tempest* is not even allowed to finish, as the spirits "heavily vanish" before Prospero's distemper.) Shakespeare was notoriously careless about seeing his works into print, and *The Tempest* was one of many plays that went unpublished in Shakespeare's lifetime. The first printed copy that we have, from the 1623 First Folio, is thus not necessarily only the poet's play but perhaps the result of a collaboration among surviving members of Shakespeare's company, the King's Men. The fact that *The Tempest* was placed first in the Folio might suggest that it has special status in Shakespeare's *oeuvre*, but this status was not of Shakespeare's own making.

One fascinating detail about the Folio's production can enable us to realize how, at times, the "canonizing" of Shakespeare's theaters depends on odd vagaries of technological history. For decades, scholars wrangled over the meaning of a phrase Ferdinand speaks during the wedding masque: "Let me live here ever; / So rare a wonder'd father and a wise / Makes this place Paradise" (4.1.123-124). It was only when Jean Addington Roberts went through the several hundred copies of the First Folio housed at the Folger Shakespeare Library in Washington, D.C., that "wise" was revealed to have started out its typographical life as "wife"; as Roberts demonstrates in her article in *University of Virginia Studies in Bibliography* 31 (1978; "'Wife' or 'Wise'—*The Tempest* l. 1786"), in the midst of the printing process, the cross-bar broke off from the "f", so that the letter came to look like an "s." Thus what had once looked like Shakespeare's mysterious poetry becomes the far more prosaic "So rare a wonder'd father and a wife / Makes this place Paradise." And while such accidents were no doubt as rare as wondered fathers, we are, perhaps, well warned against reading too much into lines that William Shakespeare never saw into print—unlike his contemporaries Ben Jonson and, across the Atlantic, Lope de Vega, who shepherded their plays into volumes of their collected works.

RESONANCE

Aimé Césaire

When discussing this selection in class, you might first note that this work is just "a" tempest and secondly, that Césaire uses the Shakespearean panoply of characters while carefully redefining two of them, Ariel and Caliban: the one a mulatto,

Copyright © 2009 Pearson Education, Inc. Publishing as Longman.

whose hybrid status points to his complicity in the colonial enterprise, the other an African black who refuses to compromise with his conquerors and insists on maintaining his own identity. While other Shakespearean characters appear in the play, the primary tensions are between Prospero, the European colonizer, and his two colonial subjects. What happens when the drama is pared down thus starkly, and when the origins of Caliban are located not in the diabolical witchcraft of Sycorax, the mother who we never see, but in African culture and a long history of exploitation? Does this completely reconfigure Shakespeare's play and conclusion? Or is *The Tempest* unsettled enough at its end to easily allow for the kinds of revisions Césaire incorporates?

At least two revisions will come as a surprise, in the wake of the 350 years that intervened between initial journeys to the New World in Shakespeare's time and the radical black liberation movements of Césaire's day. Ariel's song in Act 1, Scene 2, about the "sandy seashore" as the ideal place for lovers to "find contentment, find romance" surely emerges from the decades of tourism that have significantly altered the Caribbean, obliterating the real history and struggles of the islands to turn them into tropical paradises for wealthy Americans and Europeans. And at the end of the play, Prospero decides to stay rather than go back to Milan, arguably so that he can succeed in the "mission" defined bitterly by Caliban as imposing on the island's natives an image of themselves as "underdeveloped" and "incompetent." Refusing to abjure his magic, Césaire's Prospero rather chains himself to his "brutish monster" that he claims he has "made man"—an echo of the Shakespearean line, "This thing of darkness I / Acknowledge mine" (5.1.273-274) as well as of Frankenstein and the Hegelian dialectic of master and slave.

Othello

In coming to *Othello* from *Fuenteovejuna* and the Portuguese and Spanish literary traditions, one will note that Shakespeare's play offers a twisted version of the heroic, self-determining *caballero* who is problematized in Lope and Cervantes. Not so in Camões, whose *Lusiads* gave us a Vasco da Gama untarnished in action and reputation alike—the untarnished figure Othello aspires to be remembered as when, seconds before his suicide, he claims to be a man who has "done the state some service." At the same time, the Portuguese navigators and colonialists who are the subjects of Camões' poem can be said to have planted the seeds for the conditions underlying *Othello* and the life of an enslaved African: one who breaks free to wander the world and see its monstrous wonders, only to be enslaved anew by the wily, embittered Iago.

There is clearly much to be said of the work's colonial subtexts, even if those subtexts are more blatant in *The Tempest*, a play that transpires, like much of *Othello*, on a contested island. At the same time, the betrayal imagined so vividly by Iago—and subsequently by Othello—is part and parcel of the unusual couple that Desdemona and the Moor represent. One reason Iago can play on Brabantio's

Copyright © 2009 Pearson Education, Inc. Publishing as Longman.

as well as Othello's fears is that Othello is not only black but also significantly older than the "fair" Desdemona, and their marriage exemplifies the May/December mating that was subject to many a scurrilous treatment in European popular culture. In Venice, moreover, where every tenth woman was a courtesan, anxieties about women's infidelities ran high, and the Venetians tended to be more solicitous than most of their wives' propriety (with mixed results; one of the bawdiest plays of the Italian Renaissance, the anonymous *La venexiana*, has two women—one a widow, one a bored wife—openly seducing a handsome young-ster named Giulio). Iago's protest that it is his "nature's plague / To spy into abuses," like his brutal midnight awakening of Brabantio ("Even now, very now, an old black ram / Is tupping your white ewe") plays on both a society's fears that its chaste daughters could be confused with courtesans and a long-lasting assumption that young women married to "old rams" were sure to have a wandering eye. The rowdy *charivaris* in early modern France, of which Natalie Zemon Davis and oth-ers have written, were performed in part to remind couples that the community played an important role in ensuring "fruitful" marriages—and hence condemning marriages that would bear no fruit. In this context, Iago's "spying" and his subse-quent destruction of Othello's marriage can be seen as attempts to correct the im-balance that the wedding threatens to produce. Of course, the end of the play is far from balanced, unless we want to see Cassio's promotion to ruler of Cyprus as reinstating Venetian leadership—a Cassio who, were the play a comedy, would have been the obvious husband for Desdemona.

Surely you will want to focus on one of the most famous props of all time: the handkerchief. Mentioned over twenty-five times, this "spotted napkin" is in some ways a better index of the tragedy's pulse than any single character. As it is dropped by Desdemona, retrieved by Emilia, snatched by Iago, found by Cassio, and handed to Bianca (who calls it "some minx's trifle"), it literally weaves a narrative about the ways that meaning is constructed in the tragedy and theater's role in encouraging acts of misinterpretation as it ruthlessly plays with surfaces, with masks and roles and borrowed costumes. "I saw the hand-kerchief," Othello tells Desdemona, repeatedly, before he kills her. Yet the gulf between what the object *is* and what it is thought to *mean* can be as large as that between a comic ending and a tragic one. Even the handkerchief's own origins are in doubt. Othello initially claims it was woven by a sibyl who gave it to his mother as a charm to ensure her husband's love in perpetuity, but by play's end he says his father gave it to his mother as a gift; and in the meantime, it has be-come associated with Desdemona's very body, now considered fair, now foul. But like the bedclothes with which Othello presumably stifles his wife, the handkerchief is the product of women's handiwork, and this, paradoxically, is what undoes her. Such undoing, moreover, has the complicity of other women. Bianca flings the handkerchief at Cassio at a crucial moment in the play that delivers the "ocular proof" Othello has been waiting for. More problematically, Emilia picks up the dropped fabric to give it to Iago, "who has woo'd me to steal it," while neglecting to inform the desperate Desdemona several scenes later of

Copyright © 2009 Pearson Education, Inc. Publishing as Longman.

the handkerchief's whereabouts. Emilia will redeem herself by revealing Iago's insidious role at play's end, paying dearly for her insistence that she is "bound to speak" (on which see Peter Stallybrass's seminal article, "Patriarchal Territories: The Body Enclosed" in *Rewriting the Renaissance*, ed. Ferguson, Quilligan, and Vickers, 1986). Yet Iago's plot could not have been carried out single-handedly, and the handkerchief becomes a sort of accomplice as well, the material correlative of the "net" that Iago says he will construct out of Desdemona's goodness to capture not only her but also her husband.

This intense focus on psychological conflict and jealousy—seen also in Shakespeare's romance, *The Winter Tale*, where suffering will give way to redemption—suggests why *Othello* can be read profitably alongside the Greek tragedies in Vol. A of the *Anthology*, despite its Italian source. And if so done, Othello will inevitably loom larger than Iago or Desdemona or a mere fabric. He is the cursed Oedipus, forced to pay for a crime based on insufficient knowledge—although in Othello's case, there is also the burden of insufficient trust in his wife. And this becomes the play's starkest question: why Othello so blindly trusts the "honest" Iago rather than the innocent Desdemona. A man of the world, Iago undertakes Othello's education by introducing the dark subtexts that supposedly underlie an alien culture, destabilizing conventions such as Cassio's innocent petition to Desdemona by hinting at the erotic motives and potentials subtending them. Even Desdemona's professions of love to Othello—professions that leave him wistfully saying, as Mrs. Dalloway will in Virginia Woolf's novel of that name, "If it were now to die, / would be most happy"—become suspicious, evidence of some "unnatural" trait in a woman who should rightly have married a man of her own kind. In determining how Othello falls from this kind of grace, it is critical to examine the play's center, Act 3, Scene 3. It begins with Cassio departing from Desdemona as Iago utters a telling aside meant to be overheard—"Ha? I like not that"—and ends more than 400 unbearable lines later with Othello damning his "lewd minx." How Othello could go from calling his wife "Sweet Desdemona" to "fair devil" in a single scene is revealed in this tour-de-force of cunning, false flattery, and commonplaces, as the real devil of the play insinuates himself into Othello's psyche with a rhetoric as smooth as that of Milton's Satan. For finally, as Frank Kermode has noted (in his introduction in the *Riverside Shakespeare*, 1997), *Othello* rehearses that primal fall, as a blissful couple come under the poisonous influence of a serpent and death is introduced into the garden. Or as Emilia puts it in 4.2 to Othello, "If any wretch have put this [thought] in your head, / Let heaven requite it with the serpent's curse." At the same time, even if evil is localized in Iago, his words call up an entire cultural vocabulary of the West's anxieties about "strangers" and those strangers' fears about themselves.

Othello can occasion instructive textual comparisons in at least two ways. First, reading the story of "Disdemona" and the Moor in Giraldi Cinthio's *Ecatommithi* alongside *Othello* provides a fascinating glimpse of how Shakespeare worked and why; this is one of very few plays that depends largely on a single source, and thus a comparative analysis is easy to do (the bulk of Cinthio's story has been capably

Copyright © 2009 Pearson Education, Inc. Publishing as Longman.

translated for the Arden *Othello*). Note how Shakespeare sharpens the conflict—Cinthio's story spans years, not days—and the heightened complexity of his characters, including the minor ones of Cassio and Emilia (and Roderigo is wholly new). Secondly, attention to almost one thousand variants in the Quarto text—several of which are noted in the Longman edition—can demonstrate to students the textual uncertainties of Shakespearean plays in specific and of the theater in general; it is far from likely that we have a completely "authorized" version of *Othello* or, for that matter, any other of Shakespeare's plays. For like *Hamlet* and *Lear* (but unlike *The Tempest*), *Othello* exists in several different versions, including that found in the 1623 Folio, a collection put together by Shakespeare's fellow actors after his death that has tended to be used as the basis for most modern editions. Yet the version published a year earlier in a Quarto edition—possibly originating in a prompt-book used for the 1604 performance, possibly a transcript of Shakespeare's foul papers—has a number of what many editors consider to be superior readings, as well as stage directions far more explicit than what is offered in the Folio. At least one of these variants is worth considering in detail. In the Quarto, Othello refers to himself in his final speech as the "base Indian" who "threw a pearl away / Richer than all his tribe," like those natives who traded gold or pearls or other rare items in exchange for baubles offered by greedy colonists. The Folio gives us "Iudean," suggesting an Othello who sees himself as Judas, who betrayed an innocent Christ, or the jealous Jewish king, Herod, who had his wife beheaded when he thought she was unfaithful. These very different references are each in their own way telling, as they leave us asking whether Shakespeare conceived his Othello—and Othello conceived himself—as the deceived Indian, or the rash Herod, or, for that matter, the traitor Judas, thereby making of Desdemona the innocent Christ, the lamb led to the slaughter. What salvation is to be had from that death remains unclear, as does the intended interpretation, serving as a useful reminder that Shakespeare as author is always at some distance from the words that have remained.

John Donne

Donne criticism has been especially intense during the last two decades or so, accelerating and refining in many ways the rehabilitation of a snubbed poet begun by T. S. Eliot in the 1920s. Overlooked by the Romantics as needlessly complex, Donne has emerged as one of the most talented and original of English poets, and some knowledge of his life, compellingly told by John Carey in *John Donne: Life, Mind, and Art* (1980), makes the poetry and prose yet more fascinating. An "apostate," as Carey calls him, Donne converted sometime in the 1590s from his mother's deeply ingrained Catholicism, a religion barely tolerated in England during Elizabeth's reign. Catholics were barred from public office and university appointments; heavily taxed; liable to imprisonment, torture, and execution if found consorting with Jesuits; and under heavy suspicion in the formative period of

Copyright © 2009 Pearson Education, Inc. Publishing as Longman.

Donne's youth, the years leading up to the Armada of 1588. Members of Donne's own family, including his brother Henry, were imprisoned because of their Catholicism, and Henry died in the Tower before he could be tried. Carey argues that Donne could never quite shake the Catholicism he came to hate for its superstitions and intransigence vis-à-vis the English crown as exemplified by Donne's distant relative Thomas More. His writings accordingly go from virulent attacks on his former religion in his satires to poems that refer—longingly?—to pilgrimages, relics, and a generous, forgiving Church very different from the stern Protestantism he embraced probably to find preferment. For no matter how much they diverge in readings of Donne—as to whether his conversion sparked real repentance over a once-profligate life, or if the death of his beloved Anne drove him to new religious heights, changing the tenor of his poetry forever—all critics of Donne are in accord on one central point: he was ambitious. This marks his coterie poems, written to England's most powerful people in the hope of finding a patron (and on which see Arthur Marotti's John Donne: Coterie Poet, 1986); his treatises against Catholicism such as Pseudo-Martyr; and arguably his sermons where he was careful not to make kings feel too uncomfortable.

Donne's abandonment of his childhood religion led to his first major appointment, in Lord Egerton's household. Yet his love for Egerton's niece created another obstacle, and we might argue for an essential ingredient of self-destructiveness in Donne's personality, despite, perhaps because of, his over-weening egocentrism (is "Elegy 19: To His Mistress Going to Bed" about her, or him?). Self-doubt was another aspect of Donne's tortured verse, particularly evident in the Holy Sonnets. "Batter my heart, three-person'd God" is a masochistic and in many ways terrifying poem because Donne is so afraid that he can't do what it takes to receive God's grace. He is rather trapped in the kind of dilemma characteristic of a highly individualistic Protestantism. Or as Carey describes it: "To be saved, you must believe you are saved. But how can you believe you are saved, unless you are already saved? How can you assure yourself that you have taken the necessary psychological step, and attained faith? And if you need to assure yourself, must that not indicate that you have not yet taken it?" Protestantism, Carey concludes, was, at least for someone of Donne's sensitivities, "a recipe for anguish" (p. 57).

Students are likely to note the continuities in vocabulary and theme between the "love poems" often taught as "early Donne" and the "religious poems" often taught as "late" or at least "later Donne," but beware. Continuities there are indeed, in part because the spiritual and physical occupied shared terrain for Donne, in part because, as scholars are realizing, many of them were written at the same time. "Elegy 19" is, it is true, from 1593 to 1596, the first of Donne's fertile periods. But the Holy Sonnets probably date from 1607 to 1610, thereby possibly overlapping with "The Sun Rising," which was certainly not written before 1604, as Helen Gardner argues in her valuable introduction to John Donne: The Elegies, and The Songs and Sonnets (1965). (The fact that the poems were not published until after Donne's death only contributes to the fraught debates over dating.) There are, to

Copyright © 2009 Pearson Education, Inc. Publishing as Longman.

be sure, some erotic poems that are demonstrably early, some of them parodies of current vogues such as the sonnet sequence or pastoral poem. But Donne's mature poetry seems to have been largely the product of the early 1600s, the time of his marriage with Anne and ongoing struggles about a career, as well as with his attempt—never, in all honesty, too consuming—to fit himself into the tradition of English poetry. As students will easily ascertain, especially when comparing him to Shakespeare, he does not fit in comfortably, although Anne Ferry's penetrating study of "inwardness" in Donne sees his poems as nurturing the suspicion found elsewhere in the English sonnet tradition that the language of poetry could never be adequate to expressing the true self (The "Inward" Language: Sonnets of Wyatt, Sidney, Shakespeare, and Donne, 1983).

The career for which Donne is best known was one into which he would only fully settle in 1615, launching the period of his sermons and devotions. Prose was not a new medium to him, as attested by Pseudo-Martyr and Bia-thanatos, his treatise supporting suicide (another piece of evidence for his obsession with self-destruction). Students may instinctively want to shy away from the sermons—they're sermons, after all!—but in these very public orations the power of Donne's writing can be most keenly felt. We see here some of his most interesting stylistic nuances, and you will want to ask how they might have conveyed to their audience the speaker's desire to exert a powerful presence. The writings evince, among other things, a strong preference for alliteration, as in the Second Prebend Sermon ("irreparably, irrevocably, irrecoverably, irremediably," p. 689), repetition of phrases ("This is the fearful depth, this is spiritual misery," p. 689), arresting images (God as a sheltering bird), evocative contrasts ("Howling is the noise of hell, singing the voice of heaven," p. 690), and shifts between extremes: high/low, father/mother, as he turns his audience—a king—into a "Mother where the Holy Ghost would be a Father; conceive by him" (p. 690). He accentuates the visual in both poems and prose, and his detractors say that he uses this imagery in unhelpful ways, as in the service of dizzying and improbable contrasts and rapid, destabilizing movements from the small to the large. (The sun once shut out of the bedroom in "Elegy 19" becomes part of the room; in the Devotions his disease establishes an entire kingdom, "an empire" within him. For a good catalog see Winfried Schleiner's Imagery of Donne's Sermons, 1970.)

This last example might be forgiven because Donne was, after all, supposedly possessed of a fever while he wrote. But like the other moments, it illustrates Donne's uncertainties, powerfully articulated, regarding his essential solitude vis-à-vis God, his beloved, fellow Englishmen of the 1620s, the Anglican—and Catholic—faithful. If on the one hand, his Devotion "To whom the bell tolls" seems to speak to the interrelatedness of all things (and Carey has an interesting note here: What do we learn of the poor dead man himself for whom the bell is really tolling? Nothing!), on the other hand much of Donne's work is intent on crafting a "sphere" of only himself, or at best, himself and one other in a space that can be as claustrophobic as it can be liberating. In the Devotions he catalogs the numerous ways that God has of "knowing my sins" (p. 686), while Anthony Low has sug-

Copyright © 2009 Pearson Education, Inc. Publishing as Longman.

gested in *The Reinvention of Love* (1993) that Donne and Milton were the first to make of conjugal love a "little world of privacy and magical transcendence," separate from society, politics, and institutions of all kinds (p. 195).

The fact that Donne is not an easy writer to read, least of all in his poetry, suggests that he was not anxious to be a crowd-pleaser, considering himself in many ways a superior being apart, and not infrequently he sets himself up to create a new heroics of the individual personality: his own. There are shades of Milton here, although Milton had something outside himself—God and the Puritan Revolution—to which he felt unequivocally committed. Donne did not, as much as he tries to make that commitment a mistress, a wife, the Anglican Church. The desire to have a *useful* life, a career that would enable him to make a mark, necessarily compromised and rendered uncomfortable his aloofness. Or so one could tentatively argue, as does David Norbrook in "Monarchy of Wit and the Republic of Letters: Donne's Politics": "He constantly seeks to put his feet down on the ground, to become a part of a society from which he feels alienated. And yet he desires also to maintain a critical distance" (in *Soliciting Interpretation*, eds. Elizabeth Harvey and Katharine Eisaman Maus, 1990, p. 6). For all the forays made in the last several decades into this intriguing figure, there is still much of Dr. Donne that has yet to emerge.

Anne Bradstreet

Criticism of Bradstreet has come a long way since the late nineteenth century when one of the first scholars of American literature, Moses Coit Tyler, called Bradstreet a "painful poet; in which compliment every modern reader will cordially join." Or for that matter, since the 1640s when Bradstreet herself felt compelled to answer attacks on her writing with a poem on the late Queen Elizabeth:

> Now say, have women worth? or have they none?
> Or had they some, but with our Queen is't gone?
> Nay Masculines, you have thus tax'd us long,
> But she, though dead, will vindicate our wrong.
> Let such as say our sex is void of reason,
> Know 'tis a slander now, but once was treason.
> ("In Honour of that High and Mighty Princess
> Queen Elizabeth of Happy Memory," lines 100–105)

Clearly Bradstreet had a sharp and witty tongue that she didn't refrain from using; a pity that she couldn't have been around to respond to Tyler. Fortunately, others have answered him instead, taking part in a serious reevaluation of both her poetry and the Puritanism from whence it sprang. Ann Stanford argues that her writing is everywhere evocative of a rebellion against the strict religion that had led Bradstreet's family to flee England, pointing to the "clash of feeling and

Copyright © 2009 Pearson Education, Inc. Publishing as Longman.

submission" that informs her work and "keeps it fresh today" (*Anne Bradstreet: The Worldly Puritan*, 1975, p. 120). In *God's Altar* (1978), Robert Daly, far more sympathetic to Puritanism's poetic possibilities, argues instead that Bradstreet, like her fellow Puritans, "had to steer a middle course between two sinful extremes: loving the creatures too little was an affront to God, Who had created them and commanded man to love them; loving them too much, without subordinating that love to the love of their maker, was idolatry. Her poems were records of that middle course" (p. 127).

More recently, feminist readings of Bradstreet have suggested that she chafed at the limitations placed upon her in the relentlessly patriarchal culture of New England. The poems that she wrote early on—the ones that modern readers have found most hard-going—are long, allegorical pieces on the history of the world, reflecting a young, intelligent woman who read widely in history, English and French literature, the classics, and even physiology (Ann Stanford provides a list of her probable influences at the end of *The Worldly Puritan*). Not all these works are of a religious cast, and the poetry influenced by them seems at times to aspire to epic pretensions not unlike those found in Milton. Bradstreet's later poems, unpublished in her lifetime, tend to abandon these learned tomes for the personal themes and intimate voice that we find in the elegy to Queen Elizabeth: poems that do not in any way try to deny or transcend her position as a woman but rather insist on it and the domestic and familial concerns that preoccupied her. In "To My Dear and Loving Husband," she asks women to "compare with me . . . if you can" their conjugal loves (line 4); in "The Author to Her Book," she speaks of her text as fatherless, having only a mother whose poverty has caused her to "send thee out of door" (line 24). Her autobiography left to her children is a moving spiritual testament that curiously makes no mention of the two principal men in her life, her husband and her father, as Wendy Martin has noted in "Anne Bradstreet's Poetry: A Study of Subversive Poetry" (in *Shakespeare's Sisters*, eds. Sandra M. Gilbert and Susan Gubar, 1979).

Why Bradstreet shifted from her lengthy, learned poems imitating, among others, Spenser, Sidney, and the French Calvinist poet Du Bartas to the kinds of poetry included in the *Anthology* is not clear. Ann Stanford has suggested that the resistance Bradstreet encountered in the American settlement to her learned encyclopedic writing made her look elsewhere for inspiration. At the same time, it is the case that shortly before her death, Bradstreet was preparing the volume published in London for a new American edition, and her allegorical "Flesh and the Spirit" is relatively late, probably from the last decade of her life. Thus she may simply have divided her considerable poetic oeuvre into two parts: the public poems that address the theory of the humors, England's Civil War, and the monarchies of the world, and the more private poems that speak of marriage, the loss of her most treasured possessions in a fire, deceased grandchildren, and her spiritual welfare—poems, as such, that raise the questions and doubts that she assumed would be encountered by no one other than herself and her immediate family.

Copyright © 2009 Pearson Education, Inc. Publishing as Longman.

John Milton

Milton is challenging for a number of reasons, and students who may be initially loath to say much about the poem *per se* can at least be counted on to catalog their frustrations. This is not a bad way to start talking about *Paradise Lost* because it helps to establish differences between Milton's worldview and our own. Milton has had his share of detractors, particularly among women readers such as Virginia Woolf, who condemned him for being "the first of the masculinists" (even while she continues, "how smooth, strong and elaborate it all is! What poetry! I can conceive that even Shakespeare after this would seem a little troubled, personal, hot and imperfect"). Eighteenth-century readers such as Addison and Samuel Johnson condemned Milton's English, and the Romantics, who Harold Bloom has argued were terrorized by the powerful shadow Milton cast, largely got off on the poem by misreading it in fundamental ways. Hence William Blake's notorious statement in *Marriage of Heaven and Hell* that Milton "was a true Poet and of the Devils party without knowing it." For another thing, Milton was by the late 1650s an outcast, set against the vast majority of his peers. This included both the newly restored king and Anglican church, and Milton's fellow Puritans who, he believed, had failed in significant ways to bring about the revolution of God's chosen people. When he addresses his "fit audience," "though few" in the proem to Book 7, he seems to know of what he speaks: his was a limited, elite group of readers to whom he needs to make no concessions with respect either to his unrhymed, heavily Latinate, pentameter verses or his encyclopedic knowledge of biblical, pagan, and patristic lore. Almost unremittingly serious about his subject and himself—even *Macbeth* and Dante's *Inferno* have their comic moments, while the only chuckle *Paradise Lost* may provoke is when Adam asks Raphael in Book 8 whether angels have sex—Milton insists that we enter into his poem with serious intent as well.

Yet his seriousness is contagious. As students will hopefully discover, the poem's fascinations far outweigh its initial difficulties, and there are many ways into *Paradise Lost* that do justice to Milton's considerable achievement, no matter how hyperbolically that achievement may have been put by Milton himself. One is to talk about the life: to chart Milton's story of ardent revolutionary plans, defeat, and need to justify him*self*, not just God, throughout the poem. The Marxist historian Christopher Hill has given us in the last few decades a radical Milton who embraced increasingly extreme positions regarding divorce, freedom of conscience, and man's independence vis-à-vis a state apparatus. Satan in this view could be the wayward Oliver Cromwell and the cronies from which Milton came increasingly to disassociate himself, lured into virtual dictatorship and ultimate failure after an initially just battle against a repressive king. Or as David Quint has suggested in *Epic and Empire* (1993), Satan may be equivalent to the exiled king, Charles II, trying to regain a foothold in England after he and his father had already "fallen." Both views militate, importantly, against what have been sympathetic views of Satan in the past (like Blake's). We can see in Satan's powerful

Copyright © 2009 Pearson Education, Inc. Publishing as Longman.

soliloquies in Books 4 and 9 the expressions of a tragic victim, but Milton ends them with unequivocally loathsome sentiments regarding revenge and personal power. When he spots the vulnerable Eve, walking alone, Satan is first "abstracted" from his own wickedness by her beauty and only belatedly recalled to "thoughts of mischief" and hatred.

Another path to *Paradise Lost* is, of course, through earlier writings. The Bible is without doubt the most important one, and we might see in David's anguished Psalms a mirror for Miltonic lament, particularly in the moving exordia to Books 1 and 9 (which might be supplemented by the other two moments in which the narrator reveals most about himself, the openings of Books 3 and 7). The New Testament, of course, furnishes material for the accounts of Christ's redemption, found in both the Gospels and in the Apocalypse. The first few chapters of Genesis may provide the most interesting biblical connection, and you can ask students to compare the two very different accounts of creation in Genesis 1 and 2–3 and reflect on Milton's use of them when he gives us Eve's creation story in Book 4. (You may wish to read Christine Froula's essay, "When Eve Reads Milton: Undoing the Canonical Economy" for the argument that this wholly original account that draws on the story of Narcissus authorizes Eve's autonomy, in *John Milton*, ed. Annabel Patterson, 1992; Mary Nyquist, in "The Genesis of Gendered Subjectivity in the Divorce Tracts and in *Paradise Lost*," in a volume she coedited, *Re-membering* Milton, 1987, argues instead that Eve's very distance from scripture means that she has to be rewritten into more authoritative accounts told later in *Paradise Lost* by Adam, and her own lyrical story is marginalized as a result.) Genesis 1–3 gives us two stories of creation, products of very different periods: the second and third chapters, written first, emerged from the direct encounter of Hebraic nomadic culture with the agrarian societies of ancient Canaan and seeks to underplay woman's role; it gives us a distinctly local setting—and a local god who, like a potter, fashions Adam from clay. Genesis 1, probably written some four hundred years later during the Babylonian Captivity, attests to a far more powerful but also more distant god, one who does not distinguish between the sexes when he creates them both on the same day and in "his own image." While the excerpts from *Paradise Lost* in the *Anthology* do not cover material such as Adam's version of his own creation in Book 8, there is enough material to engage students in a thoughtful discussion of Milton's Genesis borrowings and how he has turned this kernel of a story into a full-fledged poem.

The epic tradition, of course, offers another way into the poem and is helpful to think about when ascertaining what Milton was *not* doing. To a large extent, he could be said to have put ancient epic to rest, particularly if we want to see Satan as a version of the wandering Odysseus or over-reaching Achilles. At the same time, it might be interesting to suggest that he is trying, like Dante, to redefine the epic project while using many of epic's tools. Most epics (Dante's included) have a journey at their center. Satan's, of course, which is compared in Book 9 to that of the overseas explorers who discover, among other things, innocent "Indians," is absolutely central, but the poem's *main* characters (assuming that's who Eve and

Copyright © 2009 Pearson Education, Inc. Publishing as Longman.

Adam are: this question could spark an interesting discussion) are supposed to be completely uninterested in going anywhere. They have started out where most epics end, in an ideal homeland, be it Ithaka, Latium, or Paradise. Too, epics tend to end in marriage, or at least in a reaffirmed coupling: Odysseus and Penelope reunited at last, Aeneas and the complaint Lavinia, Camões's Vasco da Gama and his men rewarded with lovely nymphs on a floating isle. But our first parents find themselves in Book 4 in the societal and sexual condition with which these poems end. Milton's poem, as it were, is oddly backwards. It ends where epic poetry usually begins, its subjects haunted by loss, exile, ruin, and separation, even if tempered by the promise of Christ's redemption.

The poem is written in the midst of this journey in which Milton and all his readers are involved, and you could argue that Milton had no choice but to avail himself of the "fallen" building blocks of epic poetry in order to write. (The invocation in Book 1, the most obvious way to get into the poem—note the complexity of syntax, all those puzzling "ors" and "ands," the double meaning of "fruit," the suspended presence of the "I" until line 12—gives us Milton's preoccupation with "firsts" and bold returns to origins; but after the commands and confident language that infiltrate the exordium, there is an immediate change of scene to, of all people, Satan, who has from a "height fallen." What is the effect of this jarring movement, and why does Milton move, like Dante, first to hell, rather than to heaven or paradise? Can the narrator ever separate himself from Satanic discourse and write an epic about innocence and pure beginnings? By the time he gets to Book 9, is the speaker necessarily more humbled, less sure of his relationship to his own poem?)

Close readings of epic devices like the exordia can enable you to point to the extent to which the formal and the "doctrinal" are everywhere linked in the poem; soliloquy, for example, seems to be used only by "fallen" characters (Satan and the narrator), while dialogue is clearly the preferred paradisal mode. Simile, so beloved by epic poets, is everywhere present in hell. It is useful to recall that it is the comparative vehicle *par excellence* and that Satan argues to his fellow fallen and to Eve that only through experience do we know God's power; we can only know who we are if we compare ourselves to other beings. This is what led to Satan's attack on God in the first place, when he compared himself to God and found himself wanting, and he later tempts Eve by telling her that she could become *like* God by tasting of the forbidden fruit. In what ways might Milton be trying both to marginalize simile and the comparatist dimension it opens up as "fiendish" (God speaks a far plainer language)? At the same time, does he perhaps try to reconstitute simile as a literary strategy through which his readers can learn how to read a deceptive universe? A good example to work with is one of the first extended similes in Book 1.299–313, which describes the fallen angels as the drying, dead "Autumnal Leaves" that are randomly carried by wind and water, and takes us on an abbreviated voyage through Etruria and Egypt, as well as through Homer, Virgil, and Dante, all of whom had compared humans to leaves. Yet the expanse of this simile is also carefully measured, for just earlier, Milton has said that Satan's "uneasy

Copyright © 2009 Pearson Education, Inc. Publishing as Longman.

steps" are "*not* like those steps / On Heaven's Azure" (1.295-297, emphasis added). Another example might be Milton's description of Eve in 4.713-719, where she is compared to Pandora: Are we meant to condemn the narrator for turning her proleptically into the Greek maiden whose box of gifts brought misfortune to the world? Or should we see *past* this moment and realize that Eve, like Pandora, will ultimately bring the gift of hope into a forlorn world?

If *Paradise Lost* is an inverted epic, then it should create a new space for formerly "forgotten" or marginal characters of epic poetry, such as women. Not surprisingly, critics have very different takes on Milton's placement of women characters. On the one hand, in the tradition of Woolf, Mary Nyquist sees Milton as the expression of a patriarchal authority that challenges and condemns Eve's desire for knowledge; especially offensive is line 299 in Book 4: "Hee for God only, shee for God in him." On the other hand, Joan Webber has suggested that *Satan*, not God, is the one who most fully exemplified patriarchy and that we are probably meant to chastise Adam for his own Satanically inspired desires for governance over his wife (*Milton and His Epic Tradition*, 1979). James Turner's portrait of a sensual Eden in *One Flesh: Paradisal Marriage and Sexual Relations in the Age of Milton* (1987) and Diane McColley's "Milton and the Sexes" from *The Cambridge Companion to Milton*, ed. Dennis Danielson (1999) may represent more balanced approaches. The latter article argues that Milton did as best he could in providing "poetic experience designed to expand the disciplined liberties of a regenerate people" in a period when women "did not hold official civil or ecclesiastical positions, attend universities, or engage in the major professions, though they did write and prophesy" (p. 177). The key question of the poem, broached after the initial exordium—"say first what cause / Mov'd our Grand Parents . . . to fall off / From thir Creator" (1.28-31)—is not answered by Milton, as so many others of his period (and before), with the single word "Eve." *Paradise Lost* offers a number of reasons for the "cause," beginning with "Th'infernal Serpent" and moving to two fully autonomous characters who are both empowered to make rational choices, particularly when they argue in Book 9 as to whether Eve should be able to go, alone, to the garden, and when each of them is confronted with whether or not to disobey God's command. Nor are they carbon copies of the other: Milton does his best to individualize Eden's denizens, to show how before the fall, "innocence" did not have a single set of attributes, and how after, they have widely differing responses to their painful situations. (Contrast Adam's words on suffering at the end of Book 12 with Eve's serene conviction in God's "great good" and her willingness to take upon herself the responsibility for the fall; note, too, that Eve has the last spoken words in the poem.)

Milton, that is, does not place the blame for the fall on a single set of shoulders. Nor does he make redemption the function of a single act, but rather the culmination of a long, often difficult, history of human and divine events, which it is Michael's job to relay to Adam (and God's to Eve, through a lively dream) in Books 11 and 12. Given the collaborative nature of the fall, it is subsequently difficult to pinpoint exactly at what moment the "sin" occurs: When Eve goes off alone?

Copyright © 2009 Pearson Education, Inc. Publishing as Longman.

When she is moved by Satan's rhetoric? When she tastes the apple? When she plots not to tell Adam that she ate the fruit? When Adam does eat? When they have their first, real, argument? When lust, not love, inspires their coupling? As regards the lines about Eve's living for "God in him," one must not forget this is a poem *about* cheerful service, and the highest calling can only be, as was Christ's, giving up one's life for another. In this potential anti-epic that tries to redefine what epic poetry can *do*, "the last," as McColley reminds us, "shall be first, in any case" (p. 189). Trying to determine pre-eminence in the kingdom of God only reiterates Satan's damning impulse, which he maliciously shared with Eve: to seek to "be as gods" because of a meaningless, if not false, sense of inferiority, and hence to seek to be different from what one is.

Copyright © 2009 Pearson Education, Inc. Publishing as Longman.

Mesoamerica: Before Columbus
and After Cortés

Teachable in a week's time, this section presents key texts from the greatest body of early modern indigenous literature that has survived from anywhere in the Americas, together with gripping accounts of the Conquest and its aftermath. The Mayan and Aztec cultures that are the focus of this section produced verbal and visual works of extraordinary power and beauty, which present a compelling blend of strangeness and immediacy. These cultures are close to us in a physical sense as well, as these profoundly distinctive non-Western cultures developed in the southern regions of our own continent—students should be reminded that North America includes Mexico as well as the United States and Canada. Though the works given in the *Anthology* are half a millennium old, they are not the products of vanished civilizations: to this day, some eight hundred thousand people in Mexico speak the Nahuatl language spoken by the Aztecs and their allies, often as their first and sometimes only language, while hundreds of thousands more in southern Mexico and Guatemala speak one of the many Mayan languages, of which Quiché is only the best known. Fences and border patrols notwithstanding, the long, porous border between the United States and Mexico has seen a steady back-and-forth flow of travel and migration, legal and otherwise, over the centuries, with far-reaching effects on both sides of the border.

To study the early literatures of this region, then, is to learn much about the early modern roots of the broader North and Central American culture, both as developed by indigenous peoples and as produced through the complex encounters of newly arrived Europeans with the people whose ancestors had been living in the "New" World for ten thousand years or more.

The texts in this section interact in many ways with the texts of the early modern "Old" World as well, first of all because the literature written during and following the Conquest was created in symbiosis with Spanish and European culture. Bernal Díaz del Castillo grew up reading the same knightly romances as did Cervantes a little later, and his account of the Conquest is filtered through this reading. More generally, the Spaniards' dealings with indigenous populations often adapted upper-class European modes of dealing with peasants at home, as shown in the conflicts between nobility and townspeople in Lope de Vega's *Fuenteovejuna* (Vol. C, p. 486), to give just one example. Further, the texts given

Copyright © 2009 Pearson Education, Inc. Publishing as Longman.

in this section were all recorded in the Roman alphabet, bringing Mayan and Nahuatl within the ambit of the "vernacular revolution".

The materials in "Perspectives: The Conquest and Its Aftermath" give a case study in early modern exploration, conflict, and adaptation, with haunting texts by native voices filling out the European-based perspectives seen in works like Camões's *Lusíads* (Vol. C, p. 290). The first three readings in the Mesoamerican section are works of largely pre-Conquest origin, though this is not a hard-and-fast distinction. The conquistadors destroyed most of the pre-Columbian books they found, and all the literature that survives was written down in the Roman alphabet during the decades after the Conquest; the major texts like the *Popol Vuh* and the collections of Aztec poetry bear many marks of the time of transcription, as their introductions discuss. Yet these works also give us a remarkable view into pre-Columbian modes of thought and expression, and so the section begins with them.

Popol Vuh

The extensive selections from the Mayan *Popol Vuh* can be thought of in three interwoven sections: the underworld adventures of the divine twins Hunahpu and Xbalanque, which limit the worldly influence of the underworld gods sufficiently for life to flourish on earth; the multiple creations that lead to humanity as we know it; and the migration of the Quiché ancestors, establishment of the modern social and political order, and the challenge posed by the coming of the Spanish.

A first point to note with students is how distinctive the text is both in narrative construction and in style. The authors of the *Popol Vuh* don't seem to care for neat divisions or progressions from one block of material to another: the twins' adventures interrupt the larger story of the creation of the world and of humanity, and as the introduction notes, in the full text their adventures are further interwoven, almost at random, with adventures of their father and uncle. Stylistically, too, the text blurs distinctions, notably between poetry and prose. Dennis Tedlock's eloquent translation won the 1986 PEN Translation Prize for poetry, not so much for the specific lyrics scattered through the text as for the whole work, which is really a kind of prose poem. At the same time, students can enjoy the lively realism with which these often fantastic events are presented, as when the hungry migrants smell the tips of their staffs "as if they were thinking of eating them" (p. 792).

The third block of material, the modern history that follows from the ancient events, isn't neatly set in chronological order at the end but frames the text as a whole, "amid the preaching of God, in Christendom now," as we're told at the very start (p. 776). A good way into this vivid but often enigmatic text is to begin by comparing the creation narratives with those of Genesis 1–11 (Vol. A): not only the Creation and the Eden story but also the Flood and Babel stories, which seem to be echoed here as well. It has sometimes been supposed (by scholars who want

Copyright © 2009 Pearson Education, Inc. Publishing as Longman.

to see this text as essentially archaic, a window into pre-Conquest life and beliefs) that parallels to the Genesis material are pure coincidence or that they express some Jungian archetypal collective unconscious or "primitive mind." Yet at several points the language seems to track the Bible's terms quite closely, as when the gods regret having made humans with too much knowledge, fearing that "they'll become as great as gods" (p. 789), echoing Adam and Eve's eating the fruit of the tree of knowledge that will cause them to "be like God, knowing good and evil" (Genesis 3:5). Most probably, the authors of this version of the *Popol Vuh* had begun to adapt their traditional stories in light of the preaching they had been receiving for some thirty years—as can be seen quite explicitly in a Mayan text contemporaneous with the *Popol Vuh*, the *Title of the Lords of Totonicapán*, which relates that the sea parted for the Maya to cross to their homeland when their ancestor Balam-Qitzé touched the water with his staff, "for thus the great God wished it to be done, because they were sons of Abraham and Jacob" (quoted in the introduction to Mesoamerica, p. 767).

By comparing the *Popol Vuh* to Genesis, students can think about the many parallels and divergences in the old myths, such as the preliminary creation of animals and then the divine search for a proper way to create humans in each text, or the pattern of destruction and new creation implied by the biblical Flood story and literalized in the *Popol Vuh*'s multiple creations. (In fact, on p. 781 it seems as though the Flood story has been superimposed on an older account in which the wooden people were killed by animals who ate them.) Both texts, moreover, can be seen in historical context as ancient accounts now being transmitted in a time of actual or threatened exile and dissolution—Genesis having been written during Israel's tenuous period of unity before the Babylonian exile (and likely reaching its final form during the exilic period itself), the *Popol Vuh* in the decades following the Spanish Conquest. The Bible's satiric presentation of Babylon as the impious Tower of Babel, cause of the division of languages, can be compared to the *Popol Vuh*'s regret at the division of languages that arises when the tribes emigrate from their ancient homeland: "Alas! We left our language behind. How did we do it? We're lost!" (p. 791). Surely this loss was felt with renewed concern under the impact of the Conquest and its threat of cultural as well as physical dispossession.

Over against this pattern of creation and destruction stands the indomitable resourcefulness of the trickster twins Hunahpu and Xbalanque, who could be compared in this respect with the biblical patriarchs of Genesis, such as Joseph (Vol. A, p. 159), gifted with foresight and the ability to outwit all opposition. The twins can also be compared with larger-than-life early modern characters like Rabelais's Gargantua and Pantagruel, or with fairytale heroes and heroines who often succeed through a special intimacy with birds, animals, and insects, central to the twins' deceptions of the underworld lords. At the same time, students can discuss the ways in which these folktale-like hijinks underwrite very serious matters such as the relations between the living and the dead. In particular, the institution of human sacrifice is represented first in the twins' climactic underworld

Copyright © 2009 Pearson Education, Inc. Publishing as Longman.

adventure (pp. 786–787) and then again in the later human history, when the god Tohil demands blood sacrifice in exchange for the gift of fire (pp. 790–791). (Note the irony, or the divine manipulation, by which Tohil demands human sacrifice to make fire after a first fire has been drowned out by rain—Tohil himself is the rain god.) These accounts serve in part to explain and justify the modern religious and political order, and the account of modern times at the text's end serves a political purpose as well, asserting that the dominant Quiché people had come to enjoy a natural leadership, a leadership welcomed by all their subordinate neighbors rather than won by force: the other tribes simply "arrived to give themselves up" (p. 794). This account naturalizes and overwrites what was in fact a long history of regional conflict and warfare, expressing but also seeking to limit ethnic and clan diversity and conflict.

Running through the entire *Popol Vuh* are patterns of doubling and quadrupling: we are given not a single hero but two pairs of twins, four gods, four ancestors, and four creations, rather than just one. Mayan society was built around complementary dualisms, such as the doublings of the divine Heart of Sky and Heart of Earth (names for Tohil), and doublings of male and female, human and divine, living and dead; even the ancestral homeland has a double name, "Seven Caves, Seven Canyons." Magic or sorcery enable gifted individuals to transcend these dualities, becoming "mother-fathers" like the four founding ancestors Jaguar Quitze, Jaguar Night, Mahucutah, and True Jaguar (p. 788). These doublings extend to the means of perception and understanding: vision and speech alternate throughout the text as powerful, dangerous skills, and students can trace the interweavings of both terms. They are highlighted in the deceptions of language and vision in the underworld scenes (the firefly imitating a cigar's glow, the squash disguised as a head, and the dueling dialogues of twins and underworld figures) and are then emphasized again in the modern period of migration and resettlement, focused on the retrieval of sacred writings. The supposedly "lost" hieroglyphic *Popol Vuh* itself would have been the most powerful synthesis of these dual forces, its pictures and hieroglyphs together giving access to the past and insight into the future, providing the foundation of cultural resistance and survival in the present.

Songs of the Aztec Nobility

As culturally distant from us as the pre-Conquest Aztec world was, its poetry has more in common with early modern European lyrics than do most indigenous American works. The Aztec empire had developed an exceptionally sophisticated court culture, supporting professional poets who composed these songs using elaborate metaphors with self-conscious artistry. Here, as in the European poetry of the time, students can see poets reworking old images and using them to witty or serious effect.

This kind of artistry can be shown to students with the first poem in this section, "Make your beginning, you who sing." The first stanza is a very traditional in-

Copyright © 2009 Pearson Education, Inc. Publishing as Longman.

vocation of the performer and his audience. "Eagles" and "jaguars" are two classes of warriors (see Vol. C, Color Plate 7, for a carving of an eagle helmet), and the stanza closes with an expression very common to the older Aztec poems, "Briefly are we here together," emphasizing the joys of fellowship in an ephemeral world.

The second stanza, however, radically changes the sense of this refrain. As can be seen in poems like "Burnishing them as sunshot jades" (p. 798), poems were often compared to jewels, given to the gods as precious offerings, a bond uniting heaven and earth. In this stanza, however, instead of desiring offerings as a way of sharing in the joys of life, the Giver of Life wants to destroy them, and the eagles and jaguars themselves—the poems' audience—share these precious offerings' fate by the stanza's end. "Briefly are we here together" takes on a tragic new meaning, signifying divine hostility rather than fellowship. The third stanza builds on this theme but then gives it an ironic further twist: the gods' very destructiveness assures that sorrow itself will have an end.

Traditionally, Aztec poems often celebrated poetry itself as the thing that could both embody and outlast the ephemeral beauties of the world and the joys of mortal fellowship, in ways comparable to Shakespeare's claim that "Not marble nor the gilded monuments / Of princes shall outlive this pow'rful rime" (Vol. C, p. 222). In the fourth stanza of "Make your beginning," however, the poem becomes a funereal shroud rather than a life-giving force, though in a further turn of the screw at the poem's end we regain an underworld connection with the dead warriors who have preceded us. The final stanzas develop this theme further, ending with the striking, stern irony of the poem's close: "*ayac ayac / mocauhtiaz in tlalticpac*"—"no one, no one / is left behind on earth."

This poem can be heard, in Nahuatl, on our companion Website, where students can also see the difference in effect when the translation is set in paragraph form rather than in the form of a Western lyric. Each way of presenting the poem has its merits, and attention to this difference can then lead into discussion of the rest of the poems, given here in John Bierhorst's excellent poetic prose version.

Students can fruitfully compare these poems with the lyrics of Donne (Vol. C, p. 676) and Bradstreet (p. 690) and the poems in "Perspectives: Lyric Sequences and Self-Definition" (p. 212). They can see how a common fund of imagery is deployed and varied across these poems, and they can compare the "I" of the singer with the self-definitions of the early modern lyric poets. In the Aztec poems, the "I" who speaks is rarely given any very specific identity, and yet these poems build up a kind of stylized or collective poetic identity. Students can be asked what they can discover in the poems about the (collective) figure of this poetic speaker: grief, longing, pride, fatalism and an embrace of conflict all figure prominently in these poems.

Whereas the first several poems in this selection all appear to be pre-Conquest compositions—though even they were still being sung in the decades after the Conquest, no doubt with new reference to the Conquest and its aftermath—the "Fish Song" and "Water-Pouring Song" give direct testimony to the impact of the Conquest itself. These poems can lead effectively into the Perspectives section that

Copyright © 2009 Pearson Education, Inc. Publishing as Longman.

follows, "The Conquest and Its Aftermath." The poet of the "Fish Song" has accepted the coming of Jesus Christ, and Bierhorst has suggested that the poem takes up the Gospel's imagery of the apostles whom Jesus calls to be "fishers of men" (Matthew 4:19). The poem humorously and poignantly addresses Mexico's newly installed bishop: All during Lent, you've eaten nothing but fish, but now Easter has come and you're still consuming us! As in "Make your beginning, you who sing," the poet finds a positive aspect in destruction itself; if they are sacrificed (presumably by overwork, illness, or starvation), then the fish will ascend to heaven, much as the Aztecs' own sacrificial victims had traditionally been expected to do.

The poet addresses past or present colonial-era native leaders, who have been given Christian names on baptism, such as Andrés de Tápia Motelchiuh, and invites the friar Frey Pedro to join along; this is likely to have been Frey Pedro de Gante, the singing master at the church of San Francisco in Mexico City, whose church bells peal in the final stanza.

A further development of water imagery is seen in the long, haunting poem "Water-Pouring Song," which builds on the fact that the Aztec capital of Tenochtitlán was built out in the waters of Lake Texcoco and was known in Nahuatl as *Atliyaitic*, "In the water's midst." This poem movingly recalls the battle over the city and its final fall, presenting the native survivors as pressed into menial service to carry water jars. As the poem develops, these carved and painted jars stand in for Aztec culture at large, and finally for the poem itself: "I weep, I sorrow, and I sing: I've broken these, my turquoise gems, my pearls, these water jars" (p. 804, stanza 3).

The poem goes on to describe a frightening ocean voyage to meet Pope Clement VII in Rome (pp. 806–808), where the poet sees the pope on his mat, blowing into the air with his turquoise blowgun and calling out for gold and the worship of God. Yet the poet hopes that God may still be sheltering the native warriors even after their defeat. The departed leaders are perhaps readying themselves to return and fight another day, and certainly they inspire their descendants to persevere and endure.

The final two poems in this selection (p. 808) show Jesus himself, Jesucristo, settled in Mexico, adapting himself to the local culture and especially its music and song, beginning to look almost more like a native prince than a foreigner. In the final poem, "God our father" (*Tiox*, an approximation of the Spanish *Dios*) is living in Moctezuma's palace, and through him the murdered ruler sings on.

PERSPECTIVES

The Conquest and Its Aftermath

This section provides a perfect case study of the conflicted encounter of worlds that is so much a part of early modern literature. No experience of contact and conquest anywhere in the world during this period left such a rich literary record from both

Copyright © 2009 Pearson Education, Inc. Publishing as Longman.

sides of the encounter, as the selections given in the *Anthology* amply show. Most of these texts are historiographic or apologetic in intent, rather than being composed as literature proper, but they provide context for the Mayan and Aztec literary works that precede them, and they furthermore give students an opportunity to see how fluid the line often was during this period between imaginative literature and historical writing, and indeed at times between poetry and prose.

╍╍ ☰◆☰ ╍╍

Christopher Columbus

Christopher Columbus's history would seem almost too well known to have to belabor in class. Yet this can make reading the man's words an unexpected pleasure, as students come to realize that they know less about him than they thought. The drama of his voyages is a gripping one, documented in a series of letters written over twelve years. In the face of mounting evidence to the contrary (some of it amassed by his fellow Italian Amerigo Vespucci), Columbus relentlessly insists that the New World was the Old World and that he and his family members deserved lasting rewards for his efforts. Samuel Eliot Morison's biography (1942) is still the best and most detailed life of the captain, while Margarita Zamora's *Reading Columbus* (1993) is a good account of the letters and their troubled contexts. You may also wish to have a look at Columbus's log, edited by Oliver Dunn and James E. Kelley as *The Diario of Christopher Columbus's First Voyage to America, 1492–93* (1989) and full of fascinating details. However, be forewarned: the log is as much the product of Bartolomé de las Casas as of Columbus, and scholars are still arguing about the extent of Las Casas's contributions. Finally, Zvi Dor-Ner's *Columbus and the Age of Discovery* (1991) is a masterful, highly entertaining account of the details of the voyages themselves, providing rich background on Columbus's unsavory crewmates, the flora and fauna of the late-fifteenth-century Caribbean, and the value of a Spanish *marivedi*.

The letter included in the *Anthology* is from the first and last of Columbus's four voyages. Columbus does not shy away from asking, boldly, for a payoff both for himself and his family. Along with the later Magellan, he was undoubtedly one of the most skillful navigators of modern times, and he knew it. He was also a visionary who drew for the source of his vision on the Bible, which (along with the Alexandrian cosmographer Ptolemy) was the origin of the view that all the habitable parts of the earth belonged to a single land mass, surrounded by a comparatively small amount of water. (Biblical commentators suggested that one-seventh of the world was water, perhaps in homage to the seven days of creation. They had theorized that if there was another vast land mass separated by oceans on two sides, there would be more water—and therefore perhaps more chaos— than the world could possibly sustain.) Thus the man whose voyage is (erroneously) said to have shattered the time-honored, biblically sanctioned conception of a flat world was a staunch believer in God's word, as well as in his status

Copyright © 2009 Pearson Education, Inc. Publishing as Longman.

as a chosen man—chosen, not unlike Moses, to deliver his people by reclaiming for the Christians the city of Jerusalem, center of the universe for him as it was for Dante. This he promised to do by contributing gold from the "Indies" to his Catholic monarchs, who had vastly increased their wealth in 1492 by exiling Jews from Spain's borders and gaining the Moorish kingdom of Granada, and then personally taking on the leadership of a new Crusade. The "Indies" and Jerusalem, New World and Old, were thus inextricably linked. (In his third letter, he waxes at length about the fact that he believes he has found the true Garden of Eden, in a spot that reminds him of a woman's nipple: this is how "Old" his New World was.) But the visionary and navigator did not translate into a skillful or even remotely competent governor of Caribbean islands. Granted, the sailors who accompanied Columbus on his voyages were a rowdy lot; many of them had been criminals. But Columbus's poor judgments in leadership provoked the impatience of even the most temperate subject, and the crew on Hispaniola mutinied against him. This is the necessary background for his letter of 1503, in which he says, "I never think of Española, and Paria, . . . without shedding tears" (p. 819). More charitably, the colonial enterprise in which he was engaged was new not only to him but to the Spaniards; unlike the Portuguese, they had no real practice at ruling territories overseas.

In the wake of the Columbus Quincentennial, much has been written criticizing the Columbus voyage and its aftermath as violently dismissive of the uniqueness of Amerindian cultures. We of course must differentiate between Columbus's discovery of the relatively underpopulated coastal regions of the Americas and the scattered islands of the Caribbean and Cortés's march some twenty-five years later into the Mexican interior, where he would ruthlessly destroy an advanced, highly sophisticated civilization similar to that of the Incas in Peru. This is not to say that Columbus protested what had been until 1492 the uniquely Portuguese practice of enslavement, nor to argue that he wasn't hopelessly Eurocentric. He was. His christening the islands in the king's name, his unfurling of Spanish flags and acts of possession that will be echoed, ridiculously, in the "actos possessivos" that Don Quixote is perpetually making and Sancho Panza's obsession with governing an island suggest how little Columbus could really see of the "others" already there. He set up a pattern for several centuries of native exploitation in the Americas, one perhaps based in part, as Roland Greene has suggested in *Unrequited Conquests: Love and Empire in the Colonial Americas* (1999), on a Petrarchan narrative that takes the "beloved" as an object to be tamed and rendered familiar rather than left "wild." Columbus can and certainly should be read profitably against a number of narratives revising the terms of the conquest in which he both knowingly and unwittingly participated, such as Césaire's *A Tempest* (Vol. C, p. 668) and Sor Juana Inés de la Cruz's "Loa" from *The Divine Narcissus* (p. 865).

But much as Columbus can be said to have opened the gateway to the annihilation of Indian populations that followed, he also needs to be read on his own terms. Thus you should have students return to the biblical texts that he echoes, especially Genesis. In an early letter, his acts of naming make him an

Copyright © 2009 Pearson Education, Inc. Publishing as Longman.

Adam who has landed in paradise and is given permission to name those he sees around him. But Columbus's optimistic declarations of "victory" would be severely mitigated over the next decade. The timid Arawaks did not fight the Spaniards, but other native populations would when Columbus, ever restless, moved on in his quest for spices and gold. Dangers at sea, unfriendly natives, rivers that were not, as he had first thought, "gold-bearing": the opposite of the Edenic myth confronts a Columbus whose biggest complaints seem to be that he is still unrewarded and even worse, that everyone, "down to the very tailors" begs to "be allowed to become a discoverer" (p. 820). His image of himself as an inimitable hero is threatened by his own success; and the real successes of which he had dreamt—finding the shortcut to Cathay and delivering Christendom from the heathens of Jerusalem—would forever elude him, as he sadly suspects during his final voyage. You thus might approach Columbus's first letter as the hopeful creation of an epic text and the last as his resigned acknowledgment of that epic's undoing.

━━ ☲◆☲ ━━

Bernal Díaz del Castillo

Bernal Díaz del Castillo was no more a professional writer than Columbus, and yet he is a master of colorful description and fast-paced narration. Students can look at the preface to his *True History* (Vol. C, p. 822) to see how Bernal Díaz slyly advertises his account, at once insisting that he is "no Latin scholar" and high-lighting "what a wonderful story it is" that he has to tell. His preface uses a strategy common among participants in the "vernacular revolution" described in Volume C: he may lack the polish and elegance of Latin scholarship and its fund of classi-cal references, but his account gains in immediacy and truth value, as he is "a fair eye witness," blind though he now is in old age.

Students should find his account compulsively readable, both for the drama of the events it describes and for the salty depictions of the brilliant but manipu-lative Cortés and the noble but doomed Montezuma. They can also look at the lit-erary and rhetorical means by which the authors construct their narratives and make sense of these unprecedented events. Bernal Díaz and his fellow soldiers think they're living in scenes out of the knightly romance of Amadis of Gaul (pp. 827–828), a prime role model for Cervantes's Don Quixote as well (Vol. C, p. 365–366). Bernal Díaz brings to life the wealth and splendor of the teeming Aztec capital and its mixture of beauty and horror, with its elaborate aviaries side by side with temple pyramids thick with the blood of sacrificial victims.

Even as he conveys the utter strangeness of this foreign culture, Bernal Díaz analyzes the Aztecs' personalities and actions shrewdly and with remarkable sym-pathy, showing respect and loyalty to Doña Maria and Montezuma in particular. He is actually more ambivalent toward his leader, Cortés, whose vanity and greed are recurrent themes in the account and whose insistence on confronting

Copyright © 2009 Pearson Education, Inc. Publishing as Longman.

Montezuma over his "idols" creates problems for the Spaniards from the very start. Students may note how, without directly criticizing Cortés for his rashness, Bernal Díaz shows their own chaplain, Bartolomé de Olmedo, counseling caution and re-straint—advice that Cortés promptly ignores (pp. 831–832). By contrast, Bernal Díaz's Montezuma is a cautious, crafty ruler who tries numerous expedients to keep his unwelcome visitors from reaching the capital but is then overwhelmed by events, with a mounting series of problems brought on by Cortés's seizing him after professing friendship, by the spread of smallpox, by the resentment of the Aztecs' own over-taxed allies, and then by Pedro de Alvarado's sudden massacre of many nobles as they danced at a festival (p. 835; compare this brief account with the much fuller native account on pp. 845–846).

Hernando Ruiz de Alarcón

Hernando Ruiz de Alarcón's *Treatise on the Superstitions of the Natives of this New Spain* shows some of the fruits of the Spanish missionaries' work, a century later. The natives have accepted the Christian faith, but they have blended in many elements of their traditional beliefs and practices. Appointed as an ecclesiastical judge to seek out and punish "heretical" mixtures of belief, Ruiz de Alarcón recorded many of the incantations used by native priests, healers, and common people in their daily lives. These incantations make an interesting contrast to the court poetry of the Aztec nobility; they are far simpler and more direct in address, and their themes are much more a matter of everyday life and concerns.

You can ask students to consider just how Ruiz de Alarcón's beliefs actually differ from those of his parishioners. He seems to accept that native sorcerers can really change themselves into animal form, for example, and their gods (or devils) do have the power to cause sickness and to heal. Indeed, he is particularly unsettled by the parallels he finds between native healing practices and the sacrament of baptism (p. 871). In all of this, the question arises: Are the natives hiding their pagan beliefs behind a veneer of Christianity, or are we seeing the beginnings of the mixed, syncretistic culture of modern Mexico?

RESONANCE

Julio Cortázar

Julio Cortázar's "Axolotl," the Resonance selection after Ruiz de Alarcón's text, uses a tale of human-animal transformation to suggest that ancient native cul-

Copyright © 2009 Pearson Education, Inc. Publishing as Longman.

ture persists in the midst of modernity. Even as the narrator resists falling into "mythology" (rejecting it as "easy, almost obvious," p. 858), he evokes Aztec transformations in a way that echoes the *Metamorphoses* of Ovid and of Kafka, finding "a mysterious humanity" despite the radical difference of the axolotl (pronounced "AH-sha-lot'l"). If one text struggles against another in *The Aztec-Spanish Dialogues of 1524*, here vision strives to overcome a rival power of sight and insight. The aquarium guard suggests that the narrator is trying to eat the axolotl alive with his eyes (p. 858), but then the axolotl's intense, lidless gaze consumes him instead. In the story's brilliant, metafictional conclusion, the narrator is now fully detached from his authorial self, which stays away from the aquarium, writing a story about axolotls that he only thinks he's making up.

Bartolomé de Las Casas

Las Casas's *Brief Relation of the Destruction of the Indies*, written only a few years after this former slaveholder gave up his estates in Cuba and became a Dominican friar, created such a stir that over a hundred years later it would provoke reactions such as the following by the Spanish crown:

> This book contains a narrative of [heinous deeds] committed, says the author, by Spanish soldiers, settlers in the Indies, and ministers of the Catholic King. It is advisable to seize these narratives as injurious to the Spanish nation, since *even if they were true* it would have sufficed to make a representation to His Catholic Majesty and not to publish them throughout the world, so giving the initiative to enemies of Spain and to heretics. [emphasis added]

"Even if they were true:" Las Casas was hell-bent on describing to the world the full-scale devastation of what had once been imagined as a promised land. Throughout his long lifetime, he experienced his country's hostility not only for having single-handedly created the "black legend" of the Spanish ("fierce, rapacious, cruel"; "without cause or pretext of plausible cause they did abominable and shameful things to a miserable people") but for having attempted to defend Indian rights by setting out, in three lengthy volumes, one of the first anthropological studies of the New World's indigenous populations. Converted, as he tells it, by a Dominican preacher who in 1511 berated the early colonists for their mistreatment of the natives—"Are you not men? Do they [the Indians] not have rational souls? Are you not obliged to love them as yourselves?"—Las Casas spent the rest of his long life answering these questions for his fellow Europeans.

Copyright © 2009 Pearson Education, Inc. Publishing as Longman.

His *Apologetic History*, excerpted in the *Anthology*, is far less polemical than the *Brief Description*. But it is no less revolutionary, as it argues that Indians have created complex social and political organizations very well on their own. It formed the basis for the great debate between the aging Las Casas and Luis de Sepúlveda in Vallolidad in 1550–1551, when Charles V suspended further conquests in the New World until his theologians had agreed on a just way of proceeding (the issue was never settled). For his defense of the Indians, Las Casas goes straight to the top: to Aristotle, the central authority of European political thought (as well, thanks to Aquinas, of medieval theology), who had said at the beginning of his *Politics* that those who did not live in the *polis* or city were either animals or gods. Rather than refute Aristotle, Las Casas argues for the existence of the *polis* among not only the Mexica and Incas but even the "primitive" Floridians. He thus denounces a skeptic such as Cortés who had wondered how the Mexica could have created a sophisticated culture, "considering that they are barbarians and so far from the knowledge of God and cut off from all civilized nations." The natives emerge not only as equal to Europeans but at times their betters; hence in the section excerpted in the *Anthology*, the Mexica are shown to be superior craftsmen. Their featherwork in particular evinces a closeness to nature that does not in any way limit or constrain their technical abilities; it only enhances them. (It is interesting to think about Las Casas's "natural" Indians in connection with a work such as Castiglione's *Courtier* [Vol. C, p. 242] and its dictum that the good courtier should dissimulate his art and make it appear purely "natural.") And it is amusing to see European craftsmen refusing to work in front of the experienced Mexica artisans for fear that the Mexica will improve on their products. At the same time, there is undeniable poignancy in the detail that the Indian who fashions so expertly a guitar is in chains.

As Anthony Pagden has shown in *The Fall of Natural Man* (1982), the *Apologetic History* is truly original insofar as the ancient historians "who attempted to chronicle remote or 'barbarian' societies—Herodotus, Xenophon" and the like, "had seen their work as primarily descriptive. Clearly none of them had had any desire to *prove*, as Las Casas had, that beneath the glaring cultural differences between the races of men there existed the same set of social and moral imperatives" (pp. 121–122). The Indians, however, lacked one thing: Las Casas fervently believes in the need to "uproot idolatry and the worship of demons, as well as other sins, by the word of God and the teaching of the Gospel," and he hardly approves of the human sacrifices practiced by the worshippers of Tenochtitlán (although he insists that the only victims to the gods were hardened criminals who deserved to die). But as he goes on to say in *Defense of the Indians*, such teachings can only be effected "with the example of a good life, not by war, since malice does not remove but spreads malice." If the Indians mistakenly refuse to receive the gospel, "they have only God as their judge"—not the Spaniards.

Copyright © 2009 Pearson Education, Inc. Publishing as Longman.

Sor Juana Inés de la Cruz

Like Virginia Woolf, Sor Juana wanted a room of her own, and by most calculations, she got one: although it was not infrequently invaded by the other sisters of the order of San Geronimo, or by members of the court of Mexico City paying her a visit, or, finally, by her own debilitating sense of her sinfulness before God. In a mysterious document written a year before her death, she forswore all of her intellectual work and agreed never to write again, repenting her actions of years past. After her death from plague in 1695, Mexico City's powerful Archbishop, who had opposed her while she lived, confiscated the books and manuscripts that remained in her cell (by today's standards, her Woolfian room was a fairly comfortable and spacious library) and fought to purge her name from memory. But it was too late. Her *Obras* had already been published in Madrid, and she has gone on to claim a place as one of Latin America's most distinguished writers. Thanks to the carefully annotated edition of her *Response* by Electra Arenal with Amanda Powell (*Sor Juana Inés de la Cruz: Respuesta and Selection of Poems*, 1994) and a detailed, engaging biography by Octavio Paz, available in translation (*Sor Juana: or, The Traps of Faith*, 1988), she has in recent years become much better known among English speakers as well.

But it was the very idea of *place* that haunted her throughout her lifetime: In what space among what she called her "*mudos libros*"—her silent books—could a *criolla* and a woman participate? "Much like Borges nearly three centuries later, [she] found originality in imitation," Ilan Stavans has said in the preface to Margaret Sayers Peden's translation of Sor Juana's writings (*Poems, Protest, and a Dream*, 1997). The *criollas* themselves, children of Spanish fathers and indigenous mothers, inherited two cultures instead of one. Even if in the eighteenth century they would attempt to define a uniquely Latin American culture independent of their colonizer (brilliantly described by Enrique Florescano in *Memory, Myth, and Time in Mexico*, 1994), they were always dependent on the language, religion, and political order of the Spaniards—a double legacy that has defined and problematized Latin America to this day. In her poems, Sor Juana both interrogates and dismisses the conventions of the Spanish baroque that had been practiced by Lope de Vega and Garcilaso de la Vega. Once those conventions are dismissed (as in her poem to her portrait), what, exactly, is left? Is it simply "nada" or is it something else, such as the poem itself that has dared to undo the conventions of a poetic practice that made the sonnet a vehicle for the commemoration of female beauty? Known for her beauty, Sor Juana becomes the Laura who speaks back, only to deflate the painter-poet who would have remembered her through the tired "imitations" of a European legacy that perhaps has no lasting truck in the New World.

Response to "Sor Filotea," to which you will surely want to refer from earlier in Volume C (p. 123), is one of the most eloquent defenses of women's learning ever

Copyright © 2009 Pearson Education, Inc. Publishing as Longman.

written, as it moves back and forth between what might be called Sor Juana's topos of humility—her protestations that she has no right to write—and her convictions in her vast, even unique, abilities. Students will want to discuss how sincere Sor Juana's protestations of self-deprecation really were, particularly when the person to whom she was responding—the Bishop of Puebla—chose to disguise himself as another nun (Filotea). She was treading on dangerous ground in late-seventeenth-century Mexico, when the Inquisition was still in full swing, and her work can be put into a category similar to that of contemporary figures such as More or Erasmus. Even though her *Response* is arguably more personal and immediate than their clever writings, its ironizing play destabilizes the reader's ability to know exactly how seriously to take the author.

Not all of the *Response* is represented in the *Anthology*, but it might be helpful to point out that it corresponds to a circular pattern: Sor Juana starts out protesting the necessity of her remaining silent, then she moves into an (ironic?) discussion of her unworthiness. From here, she talks about how, like Saint Teresa, she is compelled to write by her superiors. Then in one of the longest sections, she turns to the persecutions she has faced simply because she excels and because she has been granted the gift of "letters." We return to her compulsion to study, which is beyond her "*arbitrio*" or will to control, to a long section on her putative unworth, and then arrive at the close, which finds her protesting once more that she will remain silent and never write again. Throughout she is anxious to tie her extensive learning to sacred things, as though "*el deseo de saber*" (desire to know), as she so frequently calls it, always had as its true endpoint God alone. And it is God who has given her both her reason and "*la luz de entendimiento*." To deny that light of understanding and the use of her reason is to deny nothing less than God himself. Similarly, to deny women and poets their place is to deny a long biblical and patristic tradition clearly sanctioned by God and his representatives on earth, such as Jerome and Jesus, who had women as their trusted companions.

By stressing continuously her fight against her cursed "desire to know" and the suffering that she endures as a result of that useless struggle, Sor Juana engaged in an artful ploy; the exercise of her intellect is not the result of her own agency, but the product of God-given compulsions and gifts. At the same time, the mind that is the troubled beneficiary of those gifts is essentially nongendered: "is not my mind, such as it is, as free as Viera's [the preacher whose sermon she had criticized]: consider their common origin"—that is, in God. Using the Bible and Catholic tradition *against* her accuser, she shows how adroit she is at playing devil's advocate.

This adroitness is especially apparent in the "Loa," which like the sonnets questions conventions—the conventional beliefs, in this instance, that the mainland had about the "other" that was New Spain. By the late seventeenth century, the great efforts at conversion were over, and Sor Juana's "Loa," which prefaced her longer one-act play, *The Divine Narcissus*, was meant to be performed not in Mexico but in Spain, as though to rehearse for her Spanish counterparts the his-

Copyright © 2009 Pearson Education, Inc. Publishing as Longman.

torical moment of the conquest. Sor Juana's history is a revisionary one, in several ways. For one thing, while it clearly emphasizes the superiority of Christianity to the religion of the "Occident," it also points out the meaningful similarities between the two systems. Even though the bloody sacrifices referred to by Music at the beginning are no more, Christ's death is a sacrifice too, and arguably Sor Juana gives to the Aztec America in Scene 1 lines that could be true of the Christian dispensation: "We eat his body, drink his blood, / and by this sacred meal are freed / and cleansed from all that is profane" (1.65–67). This could argue for the universality of Christianity, suggesting that it was already present among the natives in some primitive form. But the fact that the play ends with a paean to the god of the seeds and that the formerly stern Zeal exits with the others, "*bailando y cantando*"—dancing and singing—shows how indigenous techniques of celebration and ritual are incorporated into the Christians' eucharistic celebration rather than completely "purged" (and in other works, Sor Juana wrote in the native language of Nahuatl).

It is worth noting that the "Loa" calls itself an allegory. The play it prefaced, *The Divine Narcissus*, is also allegorical, blending pagan with Christian symbolism: Narcissus, traditionally seen as foolishly absorbed with his own beauty, becomes a Christ in love with himself—a self equivalent to human nature. Like allegory, the "Loa" is syncretic rather than intent on obliterating a pagan system of belief. It reveals the incongruity between the desire to make two cultures one, and the bloodshed represented by Zelo that claimed so many lives. We see too a muted cry of rebellion against Spanish military practices such as the use of "centaurs" (probably horses) and "molten balls of burning lead," and America refers to the pompous Zeal as the true "*bárbaro*" or barbarian among the group. Finally, take careful note of the genders of the allegorical figures in the play: it is the female Religion who preaches the meaning of the "true word," effectively silencing Zeal, and Religion too who justifies bringing the play to Spain. In perhaps a curious allusion to Sor Juana herself, America steps forward at the play's end to beg forgiveness of Spain's poets for *her* "crude attempt" to describe the "mystery" of Christianity with her awkward lines (p. 873 in the *Anthology*)—yet another veiled reference to the Mexican nun's uneasy yet defiant relationship to the European traditions that shaped her.

Copyright © 2009 Pearson Education, Inc. Publishing as Longman.

Index*

---

* For authors who appear in Perspectives sections and who aren't listed individually here, see the Perspectives entry.